EMPLOYMENT DISPUTE RESOLUTION & STANDARD-SETTING IN IRELAND

Professor Paul Teague (QUB)

Dr. Damian Thomas (NCPP)

in association with

Labour Relations Commission

National Centre for
Partnership ∷ Performance

Published by
Oak Tree Press
19 Rutland Street, Cork, Ireland
www.oaktreepress.com

© 2008 Labour Relations Commission.

A catalogue record of this book is
available from the British Library.

ISBN 978-1-904887-22-5

Printed in Ireland by ColourBooks.

CONTENTS

FIGURES

TABLES

DEDICATIONS

Ann, Ellen & Eoin

Anne-marie, Caitlin & Darragh

FOREWORD

When the Labour Relations Commission (LRC) and the National Centre for Partnership & Performance (NCPP) commissioned this work, they set the authors, Professor Paul Teague and Dr. Damian Thomas, a considerable challenge. The authors were charged with providing a comprehensive account of the activities of Ireland's dispute resolution and employment rights bodies – what they do, how they have evolved since their establishment, and what their key priorities and targets are.

As part of this assignment, the capabilities and competencies of these agencies were assessed, the focus and relevance of their activities reviewed, and their accessibility and ability to deliver integrated services examined. Professor Teague and Dr. Thomas then compared, assessed and benchmarked the Irish system of dispute resolution and employment standard-setting against approaches adopted in the United Kingdom, Canada and Sweden. Rising admirably to the challenge, they have provided us with a comprehensive, focused and sharply analytical account that offers succinct, practical and thought-provoking findings.

As the State's main industrial dispute resolution body, the subject matter of this book goes to the very heart of the mission of the LRC. It also touches upon the core functions of the NCPP, in the context of its efforts to transform Irish workplaces through partnership-led change and innovation, and to oversee implementation of the Government's National Workplace Strategy.

The authors' findings suggest that changing labour markets oblige dispute resolution agencies to develop their repertoire of services continually, in order to keep pace with what is happening on the ground. Such change, they find, is best undertaken in an incremental, innovative and planned way. As such, there is little support among government, employer or trade union organisations for radical alteration to the Irish dispute resolution and employment standard-setting system. In fact, the comparative case studies reveal a widespread belief that too rapid a departure from core activities could affect detrimentally the identity and professional standing of bodies such as the LRC, the Labour Court and the Employment Appeals Tribunal. The authors cite instead a general preference among stakeholders in these organisations for incremental and developmental progress in dispute resolution delivery – in short, a desire for evolutionary, rather than revolutionary, change.

In terms of how our agencies compare with kindred organisations overseas, the study shows clearly that Ireland is broadly in line with international practice, both in relation to dispute resolution and employment standard-setting. On standard-setting in particular, the authors note that issues currently emerging in Ireland – such as access to enforcement bodies, the training of inspectors, the search for new compliance strategies, and dealing with migrant workers – are very similar to those emerging elsewhere.

They also find that the responses of Irish agencies to these issues are just as imaginative and innovative as anything being done in other jurisdictions. That said, an important observation in the study is that there is no universal solution for resolving disputes or for ensuring compliance with employment standards. As employment relations systems in the countries examined become more legalistic, the authors contend that there is an even greater need for developing complementary measures that can assist employment relations parties in building their capacity, both to resolve disputes and also to become more self-reliant in complying with labour standards.

Alongside such decentralised forms of regulatory enforcement, the study also advocates adopting more innovative problem-solving methods for dispute resolution. The authors note a growing emphasis on approaches such as mediation to resolve workplace disputes. Indeed, mediation is now an established part of the repertoire of mechanisms employed by both the LRC (Workplace Mediation Service) and the Equality Tribunal. There is also increased recognition of the need to develop more pro-active services for conflict management, and in this regard there is a growing recognition that the boundary between dispute resolution and dispute avoidance is becoming increasingly blurred.

Overall, the LRC case study identified a range of opportunities and challenges for the Commission as it faces the future. It is acknowledged to be an effective organisation, with an in-built capacity to evolve by adopting new programmes and implementing internal organisational change. The authors point to the recognition within the Commission of the need for more pro-active approaches to its work, where the services of the Commission range across different modes of conflict management and resolution. These issues are addressed at some length in the Commission's own *Statement of Strategy 2008-2010*. This Strategy, in turn, influences the internal business planning that responds to changing workplace needs, yet reassures clients of the continuing consistency and high standard of service to which they have become accustomed.

Finally, it is worth noting that this report is the result of an ongoing, mutually beneficial collaboration between the LRC and the

NCPP. As such, we are happy to commend this excellent study by Professor Teague and Dr. Thomas to a wide readership, and particularly to human resource practitioners and employee representatives in the workplace.

Kieran Mulvey   **Lucy Fallon-Byrne**
Chief Executive   **Director**
LRC   **NCPP**

CHAPTER 1

EMPLOYMENT DISPUTE RESOLUTION & STANDARD-SETTING IN A NEW INDUSTRIAL RELATIONS CLIMATE

1.1 INTRODUCTION

This is a study about the workings of the disputes resolution and employment standard-setting bodies in the Irish Republic. Three motivations lie behind this study:

- To develop, for the first time, a comprehensive account of what these bodies do, how they relate to one another and the problems they face in advancing their missions.

- To assess the extent to which a new agenda is emerging in relation to dispute resolution and employment standard-setting: Ireland has a fast-changing economy and society and it would be surprising if these transformations are not impacting on the character of Irish industrial relations.

- To assess whether disputes resolution and employment rights bodies, particularly the Labour Relations Commission, need to adopt new structures and capabilities, so that they can provide a range of services and programmes that are more in tune with the new industrial relations environment.

The purpose of this chapter is to set out the changes occurring to Irish industrial relations and to examine the implications for the various bodies. It is organised as follows:

- **Section 1.2** argues that adversarialism and voluntarism have been two of the key organising principles of Irish industrial relations, while **sections 1.3** and **1.4** suggest that important changes have been occurring to these principles in recent times.

- Then, in **section 1.5**, an assessment is made of changes that are occurring in the Irish labour market and the implications of these for employment disputes and standard-setting.

- **Section 1.6** argues that the growth in the volume and complexity of labour law has created a rights-based dimension to the industrial relations system, which, in turn, has generated new thinking about ways to secure organisational compliance with employment legislation.

- **Section 1.7** argues that the human resource management function is becoming more professional and strategic, which is leading to the emergence of new concepts and approaches to employment disputes and grievances and their resolution.

- The Conclusion brings together in **section 1.8** the arguments of the chapter and assesses the implications for the dispute resolution and employment standard-setting bodies.

1.2   THE ORIGINS OF IRISH INDUSTRIAL RELATIONS

Traditionally, the twin organising principles of the Irish system of employment relations have been voluntarism and adversarialism (Gunnigle *et al.*, 2002). On the one hand, the voluntary system of industrial relations is premised on freedom of contract and freedom of association and, in terms of the British/Irish tradition, is based on free collective bargaining on the one hand and relative legal abstention in industrial relations on the other. At the same time, the voluntary tradition never meant a total rejection of public intervention or labour law, but merely a preference for joint trade union and employer regulation of employment relations. On the other hand, adversarial employment relations is the situation where a strong 'them and us' mentality pervades the relationship between trade unions and employers. Each side sees itself as having divergent, if not competing, interests. Collective bargaining is used to obtain a compromise or accommodation between the divergent positions normally adopted by trade unions and management (Slicter *et al.*, 1960).

Two implications followed from voluntarism and adversarialism having a major influence on the conduct of employment relations. One was a reluctance on the part of both employers and trade unions to see the law playing a large part in shaping their relationships. Both regarded the law as potentially introducing too many contagions into the employment relations system. For their part, employers considered too much labour law as creating the danger of employees assuming that any slight reduction of an entitlement would cascade into an enormous loss, which could result in serious employment conflict. Trade unions regarded too much labour law as a potential straitjacket, as they were of the view that judges would almost always favour employers when hearing labour law disputes. They preferred taking their chances in interactions with employers in an employment regime that was not tightly framed by legislation.

The other implication was that collective bargaining was the fulcrum of the employment relations system, as it not only shaped the interactions between trade unions and employers but it also determined key labour market outcomes, such as pay levels and rate increases. Collective bargaining gave rise to a particular form of economic citizenship that worked from a (quasi-)collective contract towards the status of individuals: on the basis of a collective bargain between employees and workers, which balanced conflicting interests at the aggregate level, rights and obligations were ascribed to individual workers and enterprises, in a way that tended to exclude serious conflict at the microeconomic level or ensured that it was addressed through agreed collective procedures. It was this model of economic citizenship that energised the forward march of labour and gave special public status to trade unions as the guarantor of collective rights (Teague, 1999).

Although the industrial relations system was strongly voluntarist in character, the law nevertheless played an important role in the labour market – for example, in establishing boundaries to trade union and employer behaviour, particularly in the context of industrial disputes. The gradual expansion of labour law over time created a large plinth of employment rights in four interrelated areas:

- Basic labour standards – hours of work, overtime compensation, child labour restrictions, holiday entitlements, etc.
- Health and safety at work.
- Protection against workplace discrimination in hiring, promotion and dismissal and the equal treatment of employees according to sex, religion, ethnicity and disability.
- Mechanisms for employee representation and voice in the workplace.

Thus, in schematic terms, the employment relations system was centred on collective bargaining between employers and unions, with labour law having a subsidiary role. This system gave rise to a particular approach to workplace conflict and its resolution that was heavily collectivist in character.

1.3 THE CHANGING FACES OF ADVERSARIALISM

Although adversarialism and voluntarism have been core organising principles of Irish industrial relations, important changes have been occurring to both for some time now.

Consider first the matter of adversarialism. Trends suggest that the complexion of adversarialism is changing. In the past, strike and other forms of highly-visible industrial action were widely regarded as the weathervane for the intensity of adversarial relations between employers and trade unions. Like other countries, Ireland has experienced a marked decline in the number of big, prolonged confrontations between trade unions and employers. At the start of the 1980s, for instance, about 440,000 working days were lost due to strikes and other forms of industrial action. By 2005, this figure had dropped to approximately 26,670 working days lost. This decline, as shown in **Figure 1.1**, has not been continuous and smooth, as there has been some volatility in the employment relations scene. For example, in the 1990s, Ireland experienced about three years of falling industrial action, followed by a sudden increase in industrial unrest, which then quickly dropped away after a year. Surges in unrest are due mainly to a select number of public sector disputes involving a relatively high number of workers but, overall, the trend has been downwards and Ireland now has a low level of strike activity. In 2007, only 6 collective industrial disputes, which involved work stoppages, were recorded, the lowest number since the formation of the State, involving 6,038 workers.

FIGURE 1.1: DAYS LOST DUE TO INDUSTRIAL ACTION, 1985–2006

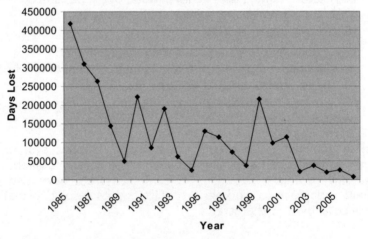

Source: Labour Relations Commission Annual Reports, various years.

Unsurprisingly, these trends have given rise to a widespread feeling that the country has secured a high level of industrial relations stability and may lead some to suggest that adversarialism is on the wane, but such a view would be misplaced. For, side-by-side with this decline of large scale industrial disputes, there remains a high number of small-scale disputes between employers and trade unions.

FIGURE 1.2: REFERRALS TO EMPLOYMENT DISPUTE AGENCIES, 1999-2006

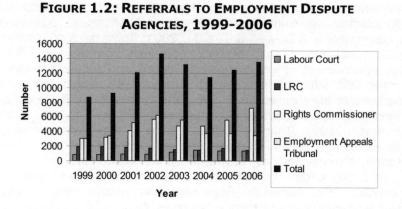

Figure 1.2 charts the number of cases dealt with by the public agencies involved in employment disputes resolution cases. It shows that all agencies have had a very high case load since the end of the 1990s. Many of these cases relate to employers and trade unions not being able to resolve disputes by themselves.

Consider the activities of the Labour Court. In the late 1990s/early 2000s, the biggest source of cases dealt with by the Court was referrals from the LRC but, in recent years, it has been direct referrals from trade unions and employers: about 90% of the Court's time is taken up with this activity. This suggests that the social partners are finding it difficult to resolve disputes internally within organisations.

It also suggests that adversarialism has not been squeezed out of the Irish system. Low-level, ongoing organisational disputes, alongside a decline in large-scale confrontational industrial conflicts, is probably the best way to characterise the present situation. This suggests that adversarial attitudes are still prevalent at organisational level, particularly in the public sector, despite nearly two decades of social partnership. On paper, social partnership promotes co-operative interactions between managers and employees, so that shared understandings and joint action can be fostered on business and workplace matters. Mutuality, and not adversarialism, is the by-word of social partnership (O'Donnell & Teague, 2001). However, it appears that the ideology of mutuality has not diffused as widely as many of the architects of national social partnership would have liked: 'them and us' attitudes are still alive. Thus, although the country is experiencing unprecedented levels of overall employment relations activity, low-level employment relations conflict remains a cause for concern and is a matter that needs to be addressed by the dispute resolution agencies (D'Art & Turner, 2002).

Clearly, there is considerable debate as to the extent to which the social partnership era has encouraged the diffusion of a more co-operative approach to employment relations at the workplace level (for example, see Gunnigle, 2000; McCartney & Teague, 2004; Roche & Geary, 2001; O'Donnell & Teague, 2001; Thomas, 2002). What is evident, however, is that the social partnership process has fostered the development of an increasingly dense and robust network of formal and informal institutional arrangements within the labour market that are focused on ensuring the development of flexible and effective approaches to conflict management (Mulvey, 2005, 2006; Thomas, 2002; Teague, 2005). Indeed, the aforementioned historically-low levels of overt industrial conflict, in part, are a testament to effectiveness of this network of institutions.

In 2000, under the Programme for Prosperity & Fairness, for example, the National Implementation Body (NIB), whose membership is comprised of the Secretary General of the Department of An Taoiseach, the Director General of IBEC and the General Secretary of the ICTU, was established. In practice, this body's role is to 'police the social partnership' and to intervene in particular high-profile disputes that have the capacity not only to generate economic and social problems but also potentially to undermine or unravel the relevant national agreement. In one respect, the setting up of the NIB represented a formal institutionalisation of the informal 'settlement masters' role that leading figures from both ICTU and IBEC have periodically undertaken in intervening to resolve high-profile industrial disputes (Teague, 2005). Since 2000, the NIB has played a key role in a number of major industrial disputes. The NIB's role, in particular, is to steer the parties to a dispute back into the formal arena of dispute resolution. Additionally, as will be discussed in **Chapters 2 and 3**, in the last two national agreements, the social partners also have negotiated agreed sets of sequential procedures, designed to settle disputes in relation to the pay terms of the agreement. Both of these developments are indicative of the emphasis that the social partnership has placed on securing labour market stability. However, it is important to note that, while there is clearly a strong emphasis on dispute prevention, it is evident that agencies such as the LRC and the Labour Court also recognise the importance of dispute avoidance and, in this context, both bodies have functioned as strong advocates of the need to develop a more co-operative and partnership-style employment relations culture at the level of the workplace (see **Chapters 2** and **3**).

1.4   THE WEAKENING OF VOLUNTARISM

The other mainstay of Irish industrial relations has been voluntarism (Roche, 1997). Over the years, strong trade unions were an indispensable feature of voluntarism, as it meant that employers faced a genuine countervailing power in the system of free collective bargaining. However, in recent decades, the trade union movement has experienced mixed fortunes. On the one hand, as shown in **Figure 1.3**, the absolute numbers of those belonging to a trade union have increased over the past few decades.

FIGURE 1.3: UNION & EMPLOYMENT GROWTH COMPARED, 1987–2003

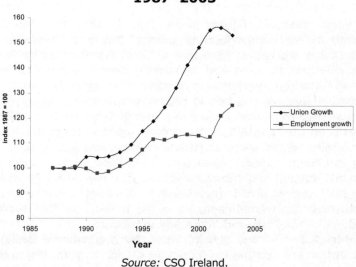

Source: CSO Ireland.

Yet, when we turn to trade union density levels (the share of the labour force in trade unions) in **Figure 1.4**, the trend is less comforting for organised labour. Since the mid-1980s, Irish trade union density levels have been declining, from a high of nearly 48% in 1983 to just over 35% in 2004. Specifically, during the period of social partnership, trade union density has fallen from 43.8% to 35%, while trade union density in the private sector is down to 20%.

FIGURE 1.4: UNION DENSITY, 1982–2004

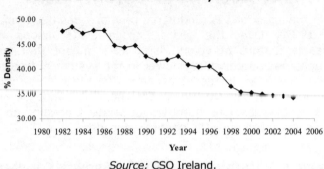

Source: CSO Ireland.

The latest available figures show that significant changes have occurred in the composition of unions. **Table 1.1** compares the percentage of workers in particular sectors declaring themselves to be union members in 1994 and 2004 and, clearly, virtually all sectors have experienced membership decline. The only exception is the agriculture, forestry and fishing sector, where membership remained more or less the same; however, membership in this sector has always been low. **Table 1.1** also shows that the rate of decline varies dramatically across sectors. Heavy membership losses occurred in three sectors: other production industries; construction; and transport, storage and communications. However, the rate of decline in public sector union membership has not been as severe. Nonetheless, the trends captured in the table show that more than two-thirds of the Irish work force are non-union.

Table 1.2 sets out density rates by occupational grouping in 2004. In every occupational category, apart from the associate professional and technical group, union members are outnumbered by non-members, in some cases by a factor of 2:1. Some of the figures are not particularly surprising: most managers are not likely union members. However, other figures are revealing: one would have expected a greater rate of trade union membership in craft and related jobs, particularly as the number of craft jobs has increased by 10% in the past 15 years. Overall, these figures must be depressing for unions, as most private sector employees are not union members.

TABLE 1.1: SECTORAL COMPOSITION OF UNIONS, 1994–2004

Sector Group	1994 Member %	1994 Non-member %	1994 Undeclared %	2004 Member %	2004 Non-member %	2004 Undeclared %
Agriculture, Forestry & Fishing	10.9	86.0	3.2	15.0	74.5	10.5
Other Production Industries	52.8	46.0	1.1	37.2	58.0	4.7
Construction	46.8	52.3	1.0	27.1	67.4	5.5
Wholesale & Retail Trade	22.8	71.9	5.3	19.6	75.4	5.0
Hotels & Restaurants	21.0	67.4	11.4	9.9	86.3	3.8
Transport, Storage & Communications	65.9	32.6	1.5	46.9	47.5	5.6
Financial & Other Business Services	34.3	63.9	1.8	22.5	72.2	5.2
Public Administration & Defence	76.4	21.2	2.3	74.7	21.0	4.5
Education	67.9	29.7	2.3	59.1	35.9	5.0
Health	57.9	38.6	3.6	51.4	44.3	4.3
Other Services	20.8	71.7	7.5	18	76.4	5.6

Source: Quarterly Household Survey, Central Statistics Office.

These trends have been fuelled mainly by the emergence of non-union forms of employment relations. The increasing number of multinational enterprises moving into the country, which have been reluctant in recent times to cede recognition to trade unions, is an important factor behind this trend. The growth of small enterprises, those enterprises with 50 or fewer employees, which have traditionally been a poor recruiting ground for organised labour, have also played a role. Although Ireland is some distance away from 'employment relations without trade unions', falling trade union density rates have important implications for conflict resolution in the workplace. In particular, they raise the question whether organised labour can operate as effectively as in the past as the guarantors of economic citizenship. In the heyday of collective bargaining, by virtue of having high density rates, trade unions were an important institution for establishing and upholding employee rights and responsibilities in the workplace. This role, a positive by-product of voluntarism, is now under pressure because of declining density rates.

TABLE 1.2: OCCUPATIONAL GROUPINGS OF UNION MEMBERS, 2004

Broad Occupational Group	Union Member %	Non-union %	Undeclared %
Managers & Administrators	28.7	65.9	5.4
Professional	37.2	58	4.7
Associate Professional & Technical	49.4	45.4	5.3
Clerical & Secretarial	35.7	59.1	5.2
Craft & Related	33.5	61.4	5.2
Personal & Protective Service	30.2	65.6	4.2
Sales	18.6	76.5	4.8
Plant & Machine Operatives	41.4	53.6	5.0
Other	28.7	66.3	5.1

Source: Quarterly Household Survey, Central Statistics Office.

This is not to say that either voluntarism or trade unions is no longer important. Trade unions remain a powerful force in the Irish economy and play a leading role, not only in setting the industrial relations agenda, but also in upholding the employment rights of many working people. No doubt, traditional forms of industrial relations conflict will occur in the future and it is important that the LRC and other bodies have the capabilities to address these situations. Nonetheless, the fact remains that the majority of working people now work in non-union firms. In this situation, it would be remiss of the employment rights and dispute resolution bodies not to develop strategies that ensure that these people enjoy the rights to which they are entitled and have the ability to vindicate these rights should they feel that these have been infringed. Moreover, it is only responsible that the dispute resolution authorities strive to ensure that the procedures used to address workplace disputes in all organisations operate in a fair and efficient manner. In other words, the challenge for the dispute resolution and employment rights bodies is to retain some of the old competences that served them well in the past when dealing with industrial disputes but, at the same time, to develop new policies for the new industrial relations environment in which they are now operating.

1.5   LABOUR MARKET CHANGE & INDUSTRIAL RELATIONS

The important changes that have been occurring to the labour market in Ireland are having an impact on industrial relations. Perhaps the biggest change has been the rise in female employment (Fitzgerald, 2005). In the early 1980s, the number of females participating in the Irish labour market was quite low in comparison with international standards. However, this picture has been transformed, due to the relentless rise in the numbers of women in work during the past 20 years. Nowadays, Ireland has the highest female participation in the EU for those under 30. This change in the gender complexion of the labour market is giving rise to a new people management agenda inside organisations. Family-friendly policies, for example, are diffusing rapidly, both in the private and public sectors, as many women seek to balance work and family life (Dex & Smith, 2002). To protect women properly, new conflict resolution policies may be required. Old-style grievances procedures that relied mostly on advocacy and representation might not be suitable to address fully disputes such as sexual harassment. New procedures that emphasise more evidence-gathering and investigation may be required to ensure that these grievances are treated in a sensitive, yet vigorous, manner (Dobbin & Sutton, 1998).

A second change of more recent origin is the growing internationalisation of the Irish labour market (Lane & Ruane, 2006). In 2002, 40,321 work permits were held by non-EEA nationals, a significant increase on the 18,006 permits held in 2000. In 2002, the number of new permits issued was 25,936, which is very significant, given that the overall increase in the labour force for the year was 29,400. Those holding permits work predominantly in the service and catering sectors; about 61% of permit-holders work in these two sectors. In the late 1990s, immigrants with work permits were largely highly-skilled. However, since 2000, there has been a dramatic rise in the number of permits being granted to unskilled immigrants. This growth in the international profile of the Irish labour market has important implications for conflict management systems. To avoid potential clashes between 'home' and 'foreign' employees at the workplace, organisations need to intensify dispute prevention activity by developing diversity programmes and related initiatives. In addition, dispute resolution agencies will have to introduce special initiatives to ensure that migrant workers can access their services. For example, measures will have to be taken to ensure that proper interpreter facilities are provided at any formal hearings of employment conflict resolution procedures.

The internationalisation of the Irish labour market is likely to increase the impact of new identity politics on employment relations, including conflict resolution (Piore & Safford, 2005). A feature of most advanced societies in the past 20 years has been an increasing tendency for people to view their status on the basis of religion, gender, sexual preference and ethnicity rather than on the basis of class. Thus, many social groups have come to see their problems at work as related to their social identities and not to their identities as employees. There are two knock-on effects from this development. Most identity groups are more likely to use legislative and judicial routes to solve employment problems rather than participate in trade unions and pursue 'collectivist' solutions (Kelly & Dobbin, 1999). Identity groups learn from each other. If one group is even moderately successful in obtaining a change in an employment practice that is in its favour, then it is likely that other identity groups will begin to campaign on a similar theme. Already, identity groups based on ethnicity are having an impact on the resolution of workplace conflict. An interesting study conducted by Hyland (2005) showed that, whereas 2% of the total cases addressed by the Rights Commissioner Service in 2002 involved migrant workers, the same figure for 2004 had increased to 8%. This trend is likely only to increase in forthcoming years.

A feature of the Irish labour market that it shares with other advanced economies is the simultaneous growth in demand for highly-skilled, knowledge-based workers and for low-skilled, menial workers: jobs are disproportionately being created at the top and bottom ends of the labour market. This development is triggering quite different dynamics in relation to dispute resolution and employment standard-setting. On the one hand, much of the growth of low-paid jobs has manifested itself in urban labour markets. In many towns, small firms and other new forms of business organisations in a variety of industries, ranging from construction to supermarkets and restaurants, are creating jobs that are very difficult to regulate. Certainly, the work of the employment inspectors is likely to be tested by the significant increase in jobs in the low-paid sector. Pressure is likely to grow for new and more sophisticated enforcement strategies to ensure compliance with employment legislation. Standard spot inspection visits are unlikely to prove sufficient to ensure that those working in precarious employment enjoy the rights to which they are entitled. It may well be that the rise in economic vulnerability requires a dedicated response from government. Certainly, other countries have found it necessary to launch such a strategy.

The growth of employment at the upper end of the labour market is likely to trigger a different type of dynamic. These workers usually make a differential contribution to organisational performance. As a result, organisations are eager to retain their services. To reduce the possibilities of skilled workers leaving, organisations frequently develop what is known as 'relational psychological contracts' with these employers (Rousseau, 2004). Relational psychological contracts involve developing a battery of human resource management policies and a range of promises and obligations designed to forge loyalty and trust between designated workers and organisations. New forms of dispute resolution that seek to address grievances and problems quickly, and on an individual basis, are part of this portfolio of activities. Thus, the growth in knowledge workers is generating an indirect demand for new-style dispute resolution systems. Public dispute resolution authorities will need to keep abreast of this development, as it might change what is understood as best practice in this area.

All in all, the Irish labour market is changing rapidly, and in different ways. These developments are likely to create new challenges for public agencies that are charged with enforcing employment standards. New compliance and enforcement strategies are likely to be required to address the multitude of issues that are emerging in modern, complex labour markets. In addition, the character of disputes is likely to change to some degree, as a result of the different composition of the labour market and the emergence of new forms of work. Changes are also likely in the procedures and practices used to resolve disputes. Keeping abreast of these changes and, at the same time, influencing their shape is likely to be a top agenda item for the public dispute resolution agencies. The message is clear: if the dispute resolution and employment standard-setting bodies do not keep pace with unfolding labour market developments, their ability to act in a decisive and efficient manner will be reduced. The big question is whether the dispute resolution agencies in Ireland have remained connected to ground-level developments in relation to workplace disputes.

1.6 THE SPREAD OF LABOUR MARKET REGULATION

The significant growth in the volume and complexity of employment legislation over the past 15 years has also had a big impact on Irish industrial relations (Teague, 2005).

TABLE 1.3: LABOUR LAWS ADOPTED SINCE 1990

Act	Purpose
Industrial Relations Act 1990	Updates and amends previous industrial relations legislation.
Payment of Wages Act 1991	Covers methods of payment, allowable deductions and employee information, in relation to wages by means of a payslip.
Unfair Dismissals Act 1993	Updates and amends previous legislation dating from 1977.
Maternity Protection Act 1994	Replaced previous legislation and covers matters such as maternity leave, the right to return to work after such leave, and health/safety during, and immediately after, the pregnancy.
Terms of Employment (Information) Act 1994	Updated previous legislation relating to the provision by employers to employees of information on matters such as job description, rate of pay and hours of work.
Adoptive Leave Act 1995	Provides for leave from employment, principally by the adoptive mother, and for her right to return to work following such leave.
Protection of Young Persons (Employment) Act 1996	Replaced previous legislation dating from 1977, and regulates the employment and working conditions of children and young persons.
Organisation of Working Time Act 1997	Regulates a variety of employment conditions, including maximum working hours, night work, annual and public holiday leave.
Employment Equality Act 1998	Prohibits discrimination in a range of employment-related areas on the grounds of gender, marital status, family status, age, race, religious belief, disability, sexual orientation and membership of the Traveller community; also prohibits sexual, and other, harassment.
Parental Leave Act 1998	Provides for a period of unpaid leave for parents to care for their children, and for a limited right to paid leave, in circumstances of serious family illness.
National Minimum Wage Act 2000	Introduces an enforceable national minimum wage.
Carer's Leave Act 2001	Provides for an entitlement for employees to avail of temporary, unpaid carer's leave, to enable them to care personally for persons who require full-time care and attention.
Organisation of Working Time (Records) (Prescribed Form & Exemptions) Regulations 2001	Obliges employers to keep a record of the number of hours worked by employees on a daily and weekly basis, to keep records of leave granted to employees in each week as annual leave or as public holidays, and details of the payments in respect of this leave; employers must also keep weekly records of starting, and finishing, times of employees.

Act	Purpose
Protection of Employees (Part-Time Work) Act 2001	Replaces the Worker Protection (Regular Part-Time Employees) Act, 1991; provides for the removal of discrimination against part-time workers, where such exists; aims to improve the quality of part-time work, to facilitate the development of part-time work on a voluntary basis, and to contribute to the flexible organisation of working time, in a manner that takes account of the needs of employers and workers; guarantees that part-time workers may not be treated less favourably than full-time workers.
Industrial Relations Act 2001 and **Industrial Relations Act (Miscellaneous Provisions) 2004**	Establishes (2001 Act) a series of procedures that trade unions can use to progress 'a right to bargain' claim for employees in non-unionised companies; revises and simplifies these procedures (2004 Act).
Employees (Provision of Information & Consultation) Act 2006	Provides for the establishment of a general framework, setting out minimum requirements for the right to information and consultation of employees in undertakings with at least 50 employees; gives employers the option of concluding agreements before a date to be prescribed, following enactment of the Bill; also places the onus on employees to trigger a request that an employer sets up an information and consultation procedure.

Table 1.3 sets out the main pieces of legislation that have been adopted. As a result of these new laws, the employment relationship is now more heavily regulated than ever before. Moreover, the increased recourse to labour market legislation shows little sign of easing. In forthcoming years, the Government is committed to refashioning existing EU-inspired employment regulation, as part of the EU drive to update and modernise European labour market legislation. Thus, although the Government is committed to delivering a leaner regulatory environment, it is difficult to see how this can be done in the employment area, without seriously reducing the established body of employment rights.

A number of developments have arisen from this increase in employment legislation. First, it has led to a considerable extension of individual employment rights, thereby enlarging the legal arena in which employees can seek redress for alleged employment grievances. As a result, it should come as no surprise that there has been a significant rise in the number of individuals seeking vindication of their employment rights. One useful proxy measure, shown in **Figure 1.5**, is the significant rise in the number of cases handled by the Rights Commissioners, a service dedicated to addressing cases of individual and small group employment rights violations.

FIGURE 1.5: REFERRALS TO THE RIGHTS COMMISSIONERS, 1998-2007

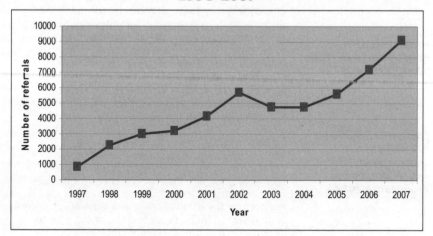

Source: Labour Relations Commission Annual Reports, various years.

The significant growth in the volume and complexity of labour law, alongside the declining density of trade unions, has given rise to a rights-based dimension to industrial relations activity. Rights-based industrial relations activity has five important consequences:

- Employment law has a greater influence on labour market behaviour.
- An increasing range of employment relations activity, in some way, is regulated by the law.
- More aspects of employment relations activity are being solved by, or with, reference to employment law.
- The legal profession is increasingly involved in the processing and settling of employment relations grievances.
- A process has been created that involves people interacting with employment relations issues as legal subjects and not as members of a collective institution such as a trade union.

Rights-based industrial relations activity throws into sharp focus the manner in which public agencies enforce labour standards. The growth in the volume and complexity of labour law, for example, runs the danger of creating a mass of rules that may be difficult to enforce through conventional regulatory procedures (Supiot, 1999). Traditional top-down enforcement approaches usually involve inspections of worksites to investigate whether firms are complying with legislation. If violations are found, then the organisation is likely to face some form of sanction. Whether this approach is fully effective in a rights-based industrial relations regime is open to question. First, even though there has been a growth of labour law, regulatory resources are severely limited, which means that only a tiny proportion of organisations can be inspected properly (Estlund, 2005). In other words, the probability that an organisation will receive a site visit is fairly low, which may encourage firms to be complacent about complying with the law.

Over-regulation is another problem. A combination of extensive employment rules and an increase in the number of surprise visits may result in too much emphasis being placed on deterrence, which focuses regulatory effort on detecting violations, establishing guilt and penalising wrongdoers (Lobel, 2006). However, too much reliance on deterrence runs the danger of triggering a culture of regulatory resistance among organisations, which may introduce an excessively adversarial ethos into the enforcement process. In this situation, employers may become less willing to enter into a dialogue with employment rights bodies to design innovative procedures that ensure compliance with regulations without impairing productivity and competitiveness. Faced with the problem of over-regulation, enforcement agencies should not retreat into the counter situation of passive regulation – in which employment laws are under-enforced. This is an equally unattractive situation, as it could well result in the regulatory regime lacking credibility (Ayres & Braithwaite, 1992).

Thus, a rights-based employment relations regime makes it even more imperative for public agencies to navigate between the twin dangers of over-regulation and under-enforcement. This imperative has given rise to a new governance agenda for the regulation of employment relationships; at its centre is the notion of effective compliance with employment rules rather than adversarial enforcement. Effective compliance has a number of dimensions: one is that enforcement activities are targeted on those firms and sectors that evidence suggests are at a high risk of violating labour standards and regulations; the other is that a system of responsive regulation, which involves using both 'carrot and stick' measures, is used to encourage compliance. Ayres & Braithwaite (1992) use the idea of an 'enforcement pyramid' to capture the meaning of responsive regulation: at the bottom of the pyramid are firms that comply with regulations voluntarily; in the middle of the pyramid are various support and assistance schemes to help firms comply with regulations; at the top of the pyramid are traditional deterrence-oriented strategies that involve sanctions and penalties to obtain compliance.

By putting the emphasis on compliance rather than enforcement, the new governance approach is seeking to change the dynamics of the regulatory regime for employment standards. Greater importance is placed on prevention rather than punishment, on obtaining the goals of employment legislation rather than penalising regulatory violations. Less energy is channelled into developing legal cases, and more on developing sustainable compliance strategies inside organisations. More effort is made to build up relationships with firms and industries to help them construct corporate strategies that will guarantee compliance with the law in the course of improving competitiveness.

Thus, the new governance agenda is about public agencies moving away from enforcing overly-prescriptive regulations and rules in a bureaucratic, top-down manner to a more open-textured and consensus-orientated approach that uses new techniques, such as benchmarking and rolling standards of best practice, to obtain compliance with employment legislation (Teague, 2005). In concrete terms, these new approaches to achieve compliance with employment standards involve a number of activities:

- Awareness, which includes actively informing employers and employees of their rights, responsibilities and obligations.
- Responding to inquiries and advising people and organisations of processes to either vindicate rights or ensure compliance with regulations and standards.
- Identifying and auditing enterprises and sectors at high risk of not complying with standards.
- Resolving instances of non-compliance through support and learning programmes.
- When necessary, enforcing appropriate penalties, in certain cases of employment standards violations.
- Evaluating on a regular basis the effectiveness of established programmes.

It will be interesting to find out the extent to which this new governance agenda is having an influence on the activities of the employment rights bodies.

1.7   PEOPLE MANAGEMENT & NEW APPROACHES TO WORKPLACE DISPUTE RESOLUTION

Managing people at work has become far more professional and strategic. In the past, people management was a 'Cinderella' function within the organisation, with worker welfare being the almost exclusive focus of human resource managers. Today, people management is closer than ever before to the formulation and implementation of corporate strategy. A new set of beliefs and assumptions about the nature of the employment relationship underpins the work of human resource managers. On the one hand, they are heavily orientated towards market-based measurement strategies that seek to establish targets for employees and then appraise how successful they have been in meeting them: human resource managers are the praetorian guard of the new performance management movement. On the other hand, they are sophisticated enough to realise that it will be difficult to obtain the necessary levels of effective commitment to high quality work through performance management tactics alone.

Thus, many organisations do not simply adopt market-driven people management policies; a whole range of counter-balancing policies are also pursued. In an effort to appeal to the extrinsic motivation of employees, for example, many companies are implementing new forms of share ownership arrangements that seek to encourage loyalty and commitment to the company by tying an aspect of employee compensation to the overall performance of the company (Kruse, 2002). They also develop a battery of 'soft' policies, so that employees will identify more with the organisation. Many organisations are putting in place family-friendly policies, so that employees can attend to children and other family needs (Hooker *et al.*, 2007). Well-being programmes are being introduced to encourage employees to adopt healthier lifestyles and to provide a quick, easily accessible service to employees feeling stressed, and so on.

Thus, modern human resource management seeks to implement both 'hard' and 'soft' policies. The relative strength of each strand varies from organisation to organisation. However, there is considerable emphasis within the profession on introducing people management policies that raise the capabilities and performance of employees. All aspects of the employment relationship appear to be the subject of reform proposals, whether it is recruitment and selection, rewards systems, employee involvement or whatever. Dispute resolution is not an exception to this general trend. Human resource managers are being encouraged to introduce innovations into the way workplace grievances and disputes are handled, whether they are collective or individual in character (Kochan & Lipsky, 2003). Consider the matter of collective employment disputes: A considerable body of literature is emerging, encouraging employers to pursue interest-based bargaining techniques – as opposed to adversarial bargaining techniques – when dealing with trade unions and employees (Barrett & O'Dowd, 2006).

TABLE 1.4: ADVERSARIAL BARGAINING V INTEREST-BASED BARGAINING BEHAVIOUR

Adversarial Bargaining	Interest-based bargaining
Establish targets in advance.	Assess all stakeholder interests in advance.
Overstate opening positions.	Convert positional demands from constituents into interests.
Mobilise support amongst constituents.	Frame issues based on interests.
Appoint the key spokespeople.	Avoid positional statements.
Divide and conquer the other side.	Use sub-committees and taskforces for joint data collection and analysis.
Give as little as possible for what you get.	Generate as many options as possible on each issue.
Always keep the other side off-balance.	Take on the constraints of your counterparts.
Never 'bargain against yourself'.	Ensure constituents are educated and knowledgeable on the issues.
Use coercive forms of power, where appropriate.	Troubleshoot agreement.
An agreement reluctantly accepted is a sign of success.	An agreement fully supported by all sides is a sign of success.

Adapted from Cutcher-Gershenfeld (2003).

Table 1.4 sets out the main differences between adversarial and interest-based bargaining behaviour. Adversarial bargaining is about 'hard', sometimes confrontational, interactions between employers and employees: the assumption is that the interests of employers and employees are in competition, which encourages a head-to-head tussle in a nakedly-instrumental bargaining contest. Integrative bargaining, on the other hand, encourages a more co-operative approach to the settling of employment relations matters. It is about following a set of techniques and processes that leads to settlements incorporating the interests of all parties (Walton *et al.*, 1994). The assumption is that, while management and workers may not always see things eye-to-eye, they have more in common than is often assumed and can work out their differences through dialogue and mutual adjustment. Collaboration and joint action are the bywords of integrative, or interest-based, bargaining (Walton, 1987), which normally involves a five-stage process:

- **Phase one** is the preparation stage, at which negotiators obtain a mandate from their respective constituencies and collect evidence in support of their positions.

- **Phase two** is when the negotiations start proper: the negotiations agenda is formally framed and discussions on particular topics open.
- **Phase three** is the exploration stage, at which a variety of options are considered to settle the particular items on the negotiation agenda.
- **Phase four** is when the negotiators focus on particular settlement options and discuss ways of tying these together into a settlement package. It is at this stage that the outline emerges of an overall agreement.
- **Phase five** is the end stage, at which a formal agreement is concluded. Sometimes, this phase is difficult, as translating the broad principles of an agreement that emerges at phase four into detailed text is by no means straightforward or easy.

Using integrative bargaining techniques is more likely to allow organisations to manage workplace conflict comprehensively and in a manner that does not leave a legacy of embittered relations.

In addition to the new emphasis on interest-based bargaining, human resource management is being encouraged to adopt a more pro-active approach to the resolution of individual grievances and disputes. Much of this approach involves the mainstays of dispute resolution – conciliation, mediation and arbitration – being repackaged and given the title of alternative dispute resolution (ADR) systems. **Table 1.5** outlines the various practices and procedures associated with ADR.

TABLE 1.5: DISPUTE RESOLUTION PROCEDURES

Procedure	Description
Preventive ADR	Averting conflict at work by creating procedures that promote co-operative management-employee interactions. Preventive ADR may not actually stop disputes, but it provides a mechanism for channelling disputes into problem-solving processes.
Negotiated rule-making	Where the substance as well as the procedures of any law, rule or regulation are negotiated over before they become final. Often called 'reg-neg'.
Joint problem-solving	Parties, who usually represent opposing interests on an issue, use interest-based problem-solving procedures to reach a settlement.
Negotiated ADR	Where disputants reach their own (without a neutral) resolution to a dispute or matter through interest-based principles of problem-solving (coming to a solution that satisfies all disputants' interests and concerns).

Procedure	Description
Interest-based problem-solving	Resolving problems by identifying interests (needs, desires, concerns, fears) and coming up with options that address all the interests of those involved in solving the problem.
Negotiate	To discuss, bargain and confer with another (or with multiple parties) to arrive at a settlement of some matter.
Facilitated ADR	Where a neutral assists disputants in reaching a satisfactory resolution to the matter at issue. The neutral has no authority to impose a solution.
Mediation	A voluntary process where a neutral, acceptable to the disputants, assists the parties in resolving a mutual problem, exploring options for resolution that focuses on the future relationship of the parties. The neutral is neither a decision-maker nor an expert adviser.
Conciliation	To reconcile or appease in an act of good will with the assistance of a neutral.
Ombudsperson	A neutral, who reviews a complaint and assists in reaching a fair settlement. Sometimes, this neutral will be used as a clearing-house for the various types of ADR procedures suitable for the matter at issue.
Fact-finding ADR	Where a neutral, often but not always a technical or subject matter expert, examines or appraises the facts of a particular matter and makes a finding or conclusion. This procedure may be binding or non-binding, depending upon the parties.
Early neutral evaluation	Where a neutral reviews aspects of a dispute and renders an advisory opinion as to the likely outcome.
Expert fact-finding	Where a neutral with appropriate expertise in the matter reviews aspects of a dispute and renders either a recommendation or decision.
Advisory ADR	Where a neutral reviews the defined aspects of a dispute and gives an opinion as to the likely outcome.
Mini-trials	In this instance, the neutral may predict the likely outcome of a formal adjudication. The process is voluntary, quick and non-judicial.
Non-binding arbitration	A decision rendered, which is essentially a recommendation. The neutral may advise on a possible settlement.
Imposed ADR	Where a neutral makes a binding decision regarding the merits of a dispute. Disputes are usually over a possible breach of contract or agreement. The neutral party may be an individual or panel. This type of ADR is closest to traditional dispute resolution.
Binding arbitration	A third party (individual or panel) renders a decision with which the disputants must comply. There are limited appeal rights to a higher authority.

This classification shows the catch-all character of ADR. It also shows the wide variety of techniques that are available to organisations interested in developing state-of-the-art conflict management systems. Clearly, in designing a conflict management system, an organisation is highly unlikely to incorporate all the procedures outlined above. The table is best regarded as an *a la carte* menu of practices, from which organisations can pick and choose, so that the resulting dispute resolution system fits with the culture and characteristics of the organisation. However, in adopting a modern, comprehensive approach to dispute resolution, an organisation is seeking to address problems as soon as they arise and to put in place policies that prevent them emerging in the first place. It is an approach that is part of the wider effort to make the human resource management function more professional and strategic.

Thus, new thinking and approaches are emerging to address collective and individual disputes at the workplace. As a result, innovative dispute resolution systems can be found in both unionised and non-union companies. Unionised firms can introduce new approaches to collective and individual dispute resolution approaches, while non-union firms are more likely to focus on the individual dimension. Although both unionised and non-unionised firms can be innovative in relation to dispute resolution, it is important to realise that the professionalisation of human resource management has led to competing 'old' industrial relations and 'new' human resource management assumptions, and even values, about workplace disputes.

From an industrial relations perspective, the employment relationship is an unequal power relationship in which employers possess considerable resource advantages over employees (Edwards, 1992). As a result of this power imbalance, employees are unlikely to raise complaints and grievances against an employer on whom they are dependent for their living. Formal procedures that place unions at the centre of the dispute resolution system are thus considered the only realistic way of addressing this power imbalance. Power rarely enters the human resource management vocabulary (Folger & Cropanzino, 1998). Instead, employer-employee interactions are seen as displaying a high level of interdependency. As a result, notions of trust and unity of interest are regarded as underpinning relations between employees and employers. Thus, from a human resource management perspective, there is no compelling case why collectivism should be the operating assumption of a dispute resolution system (Lewin, 1987). From this point of view, unions are not the only guarantors of procedural justice in the workplace. Other arrangements that operate in the absence of trade unions are considered as effective in ensuring that employees are treated fairly and with respect, when a grievance is being investigated or a disciplinary action taken. Professional integrity on the part of human resource management, and the employer's need for a relationship of reciprocity with employees, ensure that procedural justice prevails in non-union firms (Peterson, 1992).

Industrial relations and human resource management approaches also treat workplace conflict differently (Lewin, 2001). From the industrial relations viewpoint, workplace conflict is virtually inevitable, given the power imbalance between employers and employees and the competing interests held by both. Not only that, workplace conflict can actually be beneficial, as it can clean the air and rejuvenate employer-employee interactions. In contrast, the human resource management perspective is that employment grievances and disputes are symptoms of managerial failure. Thus, workplace conflict is not seen as either desirable or inevitable, but something that needs to be managed effectively and kept to a minimum. Yet a further difference is that human resource managers are most reluctant to allow external public agencies to play a role in their dispute resolution procedures. They also make strenuous efforts to avoid an employment grievance or dispute ending up in front of an Employment Tribunal or any other public dispute resolution agency. The focus is very much on building up *internal* dispute resolution systems to address workplace conflict (Fernie & Metcalf, 2004). The traditional industrial relations approach does not have such qualms about using public dispute resolution agencies. Occasional external input from these bodies is considered extremely useful, as it can unlock an impasse by using creative approaches not considered hitherto by either management or unions. Dispute resolution bodies are also seen as playing the important role of codifying and helping to diffuse best practice dispute resolution practices.

These contrasting industrial relations and human resource management approaches are important, as they project different visions of a fair and efficient dispute resolution system (Budd & Colvin, 2005). As a result, public dispute resolution agencies find themselves operating in an industrial relations system in which the understanding of procedural and substantive justice at the workplace varies significantly across organisations. In this context, it becomes difficult for agencies to develop coherent and integrated services that appeal across the economy. However, the problem does not end here. A consequence of the professionalisation of human resource management is that there is a sizable group of firms determined not to have any links with public dispute resolution agencies, and which actively pursue policies towards that end. Thus, the public dispute resolution agencies are operating in an industrial relations environment which is less friendly to their activities than ever before.

1.8   CONCLUSION

The central thesis of this introductory chapter is that a variety of economic and social changes has resulted in important changes to Irish industrial relations, whose impact has been two-fold:

- They have contributed to the fragmentation of industrial relations in Ireland, in that interactions between employers and employees are no longer housed within a coherent industrial relations framework, and different pockets of the economy are organised according to different employment relations rules.

- The changes have had a strong impact on the character of the employment standard-setting process and the dynamics of workplace disputes and their resolution.

Some aspects of the new environment are examined in this introduction and the conclusion is that public dispute resolution and employment standard-setting bodies face a series of challenges to remain efficient at completing the tasks they were set up to do.

In the remainder of this book, we assess the work of the various agencies involved in dispute resolution and employment standard-setting to assess how they have met these challenges. We also assess the dispute resolution process in three countries to compare how Ireland is faring in addressing workplace disputes, relative to other countries.

2

THE LABOUR RELATIONS
COMMISSION

2.1 INTRODUCTION

The purpose of this chapter is to describe and examine the range of dispute resolution and prevention activities undertaken by the primary public dispute resolution agency in Ireland, the Labour Relations Commission.

The chapter is organised as follows:

- Following an initial overview of the organisation in **section 2.2**, the next sections examine the three divisions that are responsible for delivering the LRC's range of services and programmes: the Conciliation Service Division (**section 2.3**); the Advisory Services Division (**section 2.4**); and the Rights Commissioner Service (**section 2.5**).

- The Labour Relations Commission is very much a product of the Irish social partnership and **section 2.6** explores aspects of its relationship with this process.

- One of the features of the LRC has been its commitment to developing new conflict management initiatives and **section 2.7** is concerned with its most recent initiative in this area: the Workplace Mediation Service.

- Finally, **section 2.8** explores some of the advocacy and awareness-raising initiatives undertaken by the LRC, in seeking to promote improvements in employment practices and procedures.

2.2   THE LABOUR RELATIONS COMMISSION: AN OVERVIEW

2.2.1   An encompassing mandate

The Labour Relations Commission (LRC) was established under the Industrial Relations Act 1990 and has, *inter alia*, statutory responsibility for "promoting the improvement of industrial relations".

The Commission has a chief executive, approximately 45 staff and a board with employer, trade union and independent representation. In addition to this, there are currently 14 Rights Commissioners.[1]

In seeking to fulfil its statutory role, the LRC considers its mission to be:

"To promote the development and improvement of Irish industrial relations policies and practices through the provision of appropriate, timely and effective services to employers, trade unions and employees." (LRC, 2005a)

This encompassing mandate has ensured that, although the resolution of collective disputes has always been a core activity, the work of the LRC is not confined solely to the provision of this key service. Indeed, since its establishment, the Commission has gradually, and successfully, evolved into a key public institution for the resolution of employment disputes and the promotion of co-operative, stable management-union/employee interactions within the Irish labour market.

2.2.2   Key functions and services

In addition to a Corporate Services Division, the Commission has three main service divisions: namely, the Conciliation Service Division; the Advisory & Research Service Division; and the Rights Commissioner's Service Division. As will be discussed later in this chapter, these three divisions have been responsible for the development and delivery of a broad range of flexible and innovative services, initiatives and programmes that the LRC has put in place, in seeking to fulfil its statutory mandate. Critically, as a result of an ongoing emphasis on improving, reviewing and enhancing its range of services, the Commission has developed an integrated and flexible conflict prevention and dispute management system. As highlighted in its most recent strategy document (LRC, 2005a), this flexible conflict prevention and dispute management system is underpinned by a number of key principles (see **Table 2.1**).

---

[1]   As indicated in **Section 4**, the number of Rights Commissioners eventually will be increased to 13 in line with commitments contained in the Social Partnership Agreement *Towards 2016*.

TABLE 2.1: THE KEY PRINCIPLES OF THE LRC'S CONFLICT PREVENTION & DISPUTE MANAGEMENT SYSTEM

The provision of a full suite of dispute resolution procedures.	An emphasis on resolving disputes close to the point of origin.
Affording employees appropriate access to public bodies that handle complaints regarding infringements to employment rights.	A pro-active approach to dispute prevention and/or resolution.
The promotion of joint action and collaborative problem-solving by managers, employees and trade unions.	An emphasis on upgrading employment relations practices and procedures in organisations with poor employment dispute records.
The development, promotion and review, in consultation with the social partners, of Codes of Good Practice.	The development of procedures that provide an option for agreed arbitration and adjudication on issues incorporating both disputes of interest and employment rights.

Source: Adapted from LRC (2005a).

2.2.3 An evolving strategic framework

In 2005, the Commission, drawing upon its own experiences and successes, and its analysis of the changing nature of the economy, workplace relations and the employment legislative environment, formulated its new strategic framework for 2005-2007 (LRC, 2005a). In particular, this new strategic framework was designed to respond to two key trends within the Irish labour market:

- The increased fragmentation of employment relations practices.
- The gradual evolution of a more robust and complex regulatory environment for the governance of management-employee interactions.

Building on its previous strategy statements, this new framework established three strategic goals for the organisation over the period 2005-2007 (see **Table 2.2**).

In seeking to achieve these goals, the Commission highlighted the importance of continuing to assess and diversify its own practices, services and procedures and to augment its problem-solving functions, services and strategies. More specifically, their implementation was viewed as being dependent on the Commission reconfiguring its core service divisions to develop a more diversified Conciliation Service Division; an expanded Advisory Service Division; and an enhanced Rights Commissioner Service. The next three sections of this chapter are concerned with examining each of these three core service divisions.

TABLE 2.2: THE LRC'S STRATEGIC OBJECTIVES, 2005-2007

Strategic Objective 1	Providing dispute resolution services for all parts of the employment relations system, which places a premium on the early identification of disputes and on augmenting our capacity to solve them expeditiously.
Strategic Objective 2	Develop stronger innovative and flexible prevention activities to assist sectors and enterprises.
Strategic Objective 3	Continuous improvement and professional excellence to ensure the delivery of high quality and timely services to employers, employees and trade unions.

Source: LRC (2005a).

2.3   THE CONCILIATION SERVICE DIVISION

2.3.1   Conciliation: A flexible and tailored dispute resolution service

The Conciliation Service Division provides an impartial, fast, effective and high-quality conciliation service to employers, employees and unions in both the public and private sectors. The provision of this dispute resolution service has been the cornerstone of the LRC's work since its establishment and, arguably, for many constituencies – the social partners, politicians, individual employers and trade unions – it defines the identity of the organisation.

Conciliation can be characterised as a 'facilitated search for agreement'. Within this process, an industrial relations officer (IRO) from the Commission, acting as an independent and impartial chairperson, seeks to frame negotiations and discussions between the representatives of employers and employees in a way that facilitates the parties to reach a mutually-acceptable agreement.

A Conciliation Conference involves an initial joint meeting, and then separate individual meetings, all chaired by an IRO. The process is free, non-legalistic and informal. Critically, it is also wholly voluntary, as it can only begin with the consent of both parties to a dispute, and there is no binding or compulsory element, as a settlement must be based on mutual consent. In effect, there are only two possible outcomes to a Conciliation Conference: the settlement of a dispute[2] or continuing disagreement. In the latter event, the parties can refer the dispute to the Labour Court for recommendation.

---

[2]   A settlement is where the parties reach a mutually acceptable agreement in conciliation or where they accept a proposal put to them by the IRO.

Although there is a long-standing tradition within the Irish dispute resolution machinery of providing a conciliation service to resolve collective disputes, in practice, the professional conciliators within the Commission are not bound by any definitive or delineated set of mechanisms as to what constitutes conciliation or the type of behaviours and skills they should bring to the process. Indeed, while the IROs are fully aware of the different dispute resolution methods, and the various techniques and skills associated with them, they also recognise the overlap between them and the fact that, in practice, many of the 'theoretical' distinctions become blurred (see **Figure 2.1**).

FIGURE 2.1: THE CONTINUUM OF DISPUTE RESOLUTION PROCESSES

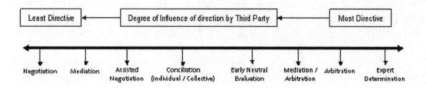

Adapted from Trevelyan (2006, p.7).

Instead, the philosophy of the Commission has been to develop a flexible and tailored service, capable of drawing on and adapting a range of approaches from across the continuum of dispute resolution processes in seeking to assist the parties in reaching a mutually-acceptable agreement (see **Figure 2.1**). For example, depending on the context, an IRO may adopt a very structured and interventionist stance in seeking to encourage the parties to reach agreement. Equally, in other situations, the style adopted may be more akin to mediation, or as one official characterised it as 'mediation with an interventionist edge'.[3] Interestingly, although in many ways the tone, setting, language and mechanics of the conciliation process convey a traditional, even adversarial, industrial relations bargaining context, equally, it is imbued with a flexible problem-solving ethos, which recognises that due process and meaningful dialogue are the main route to effective dispute resolution.

---

[3] Within the mediation discipline, particularly in the area of family mediation, there is a strong tradition of the mediator adopting a very neutral, non-interventionist role in the actual process. This characterisation of the IRO engaging in 'mediation with an interventionist edge', in a sense, was capturing the manner in which skilled officials draw on and customise a range of dispute resolution techniques in seeking to reach a mutually-acceptable solution.

2.3.2   Organisational structure

The Conciliation Service Division is structured into four geographical regions outside Dublin, together with a National Public Sector Unit that was set up in 2004. There is a strong emphasis on team-working within the Division, with monthly meetings to review recent activities, share experiences and monitor trends and developments within the labour market. This team ethos also underpins the delivery of services: while the Public Sector Unit co-ordinates activity in this area, officials from across the Division deliver the actual services to public sector organisations. In seeking to contribute to the provision of an integrated conflict management service, there has been an increased emphasis on cross-divisional collaboration and activity. For example, officials from the Advisory Service participate in the Conciliation Service's Working Together Projects, while officers from the Conciliation Service are involved in training and development activities co-ordinated by the Advisory Division. Moreover, this interaction has been institutionalised formally with the establishment of the Workplace Mediation Service (see **section 2.7**).

The Conciliation Service also has sought to exploit the potential of information and communication technology, both to improve the quality of service delivery and to make accessing the service more user-friendly. In this regard, an important innovation was the development, in 2005, of an online referral system, whereby customers can apply online for the assistance of the service.

2.3.3   Key trends in conciliation activity

Since the mid-1980s, there has been a dramatic decline in industrial action in Ireland and, although this correlates with general international trends, the scale of this decline is still fairly remarkable (see **Figures 2.2** and **2.3**).

Despite the emergence of relative industrial peace, there remains a high level of demand for the services of the Conciliation division from across a fairly broad range of sectors. In 2006, a total of 1,504 disputes were referred to the Conciliation Service, compared to 1,692 disputes referred in 2005. The Division chaired 1,959 conciliation conferences over the course of 2006, compared to 1,924 in the previous year. Indeed, despite the dramatic fall in overt industrial conflict, the workload of the Division, in terms of formal meetings convened, has remained fairly consistent over the period 2001 to 2006 (see **Figure 2.4**).[4]

---

[4]   The figure for meetings includes both formal conciliation conferences and also additional formal meetings, such as the chairing of Joint Labour Committees, Joint Industrial Councils, Conciliation Councils, etc. For example, in 2006, the total of 2,095 meetings consisted of 1,959 conciliation meetings and 136 other formal meetings.

FIGURE 2.2: STRIKE STATISTICS & TRENDS, 1984-2005

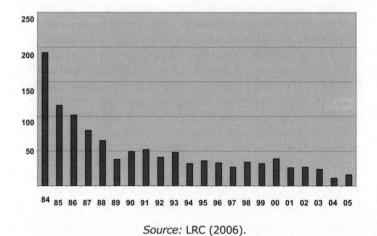

Source: LRC (2006).

FIGURE 2.3: ANNUAL DAYS LOST DUE TO INDUSTRIAL ACTION, 1970s-2005

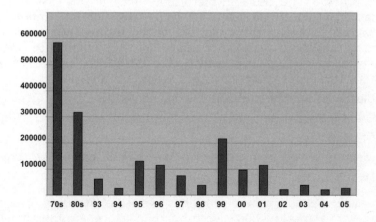

FIGURE 2.4: THE CONCILIATION SERVICE'S ACTIVITY, 2001-2006

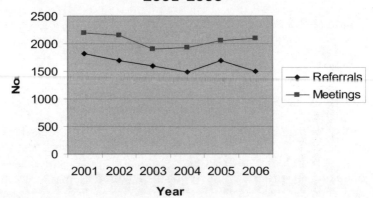

At one level, a combination of intensified competition, increased internationalisation, deregulation and the relentless pace of technological change suggests that a certain underlying pattern of potential disputes is inevitable. Notwithstanding the actual level of referrals, there is also clear evidence of insufficient local engagement by the parties on the issues in the dispute and, for this reason, the LRC has highlighted the need to focus attention on improving organisations' in-house capacity for preventing and resolving disputes as close as possible to the point of origin. Finally, in terms of the most typical types of dispute dealt with by the Conciliation Service, they remain the traditional staples of collectivist industrial relations:

- Claims for improvements in pay and conditions.
- Disciplinary cases.
- Grading issues.
- Disputes arising from changes in how work is done or company restructuring.

A discernible trend in recent years has been the increased level of demand from across the public sector and, indeed, the establishment of the National Public Sector Unit was a response to this development. In 2006, for example, the public sector accounted for 41% of all dispute referrals and 35% of all Conciliation Conferences convened. An interesting feature of this growing demand has been the evidence of increased engagement by parties who previously, due to a reliance on in-house conciliation and arbitration schemes, had not normally availed of third-party intervention. Consequently, it is now evident that the Conciliation Service is providing for a wider range of public sector workers and agencies than was originally envisaged under the Industrial Relations Act 1990. These trends reflect the challenges faced by employers and trade unions across the whole public sector in dealing with the agenda of change and modernisation. Although benchmarking and the associated verification mechanisms have contributed to a more stable process of public service pay determination, they do not necessarily resolve outstanding issues such as extensive work practice change, restructuring, reorganisation and outsourcing. Indeed, over the 2003 to 2006 life span of *Sustaining Progress* (2003), the public sector was the source of most structural change disputes dealt with by the Conciliation Service. The complexity of the issues being addressed, in conjunction with the multiplicity of work practices, multiple locations and the potential for establishing precedents across a sector or sub-sector, ensured that resolving these types of dispute necessitated the LRC engaging in intensive and protracted negotiations, a factor that imposed considerable burdens on the resources of the organisation. Given the extensive commitments to public service change and modernisation contained within *Towards 2016* (2006), the LRC anticipates a continued high level of demand from the public service. This envisaged trend, therefore, re-affirms clearly the importance of developing and enhancing initiatives that can assist the parties in this sector to build their capacity to address change and modernisation in a more pro-active, co-operative and progressive manner (see **section 2.4**).

2.3.4   Public service negotiating bodies

A key area of the service's work is the chairing of various national level negotiation bodies in health, local government, education and the prison service. This activity is considered to have fostered a greater degree of stability and co-ordination within the collective bargaining process in these areas. For example, the Health Service National Joint Council (NJC) is recognised as contributing to the emergence of a more stable and co-operative industrial relations environment in this key sector. The role of this body has been re-affirmed in *Towards 2016* and it is perceived as having the potential to foster a more partnership-based approach to the practice of industrial relations, including the resolution of disputes. In particular, with varying degrees of success, these formal national level arrangements have served to facilitate pro-active engagement and effective dialogue on critical change issues, which, if not addressed appropriately, had the potential to become adversarial disputes.

2.3.5   Working Together projects

Building on this foundation of peak-level engagement, and influenced by the work that Acas (UK) has undertaken in the National Health Service and with local government in particular, the Conciliation

Service now is actively seeking to develop *Working Together* projects in the public service. The objective of these projects is to develop pro-active conflict management activities, which will enhance the quality and effectiveness of manager-employee interactions in this sector. The focus of these initiatives will be preventative and, in particular, will involve the use of innovative approaches that can assist the parties in managing and anticipating change and in establishing mechanisms and procedures that will enhance their problem-solving capacity in relation to workplace issues. If successful, these projects will introduce state-of-the-art conflict management into the public service, in a manner that will reinforce a partnership-style culture within their employment relations system. As the emphasis of these projects is on both preventative action and improving the quality of relations, they will involve officers from both the Conciliation and Advisory Sections, thus ensuring that the relevant in-house experience is used fully.

In planning this innovative initiative, the Conciliation Service has targeted a number of specific sectors and engaged in intensive dialogue with senior employers and trade unionists, in order both to secure commitment from them and to ensure that the Division can provide a customised and appropriate response to their particular needs. There is clearly an experimental dimension to this initiative and, for this reason, the Service is concentrating on rolling out a small number of projects initially. The focused manner in which this initiative has been planned, allied to the awareness that there is an appetite amongst practitioners for an alternative to protracted adversarial style bargaining in dealing with public service modernisation, suggests that there will be a strong demand for this form of preventative and pro-active intervention.

2.3.6   Joint Labour Committees and Joint Industrial Councils

Industrial Relations Officers from the Conciliation Service also act as the chairpersons to a number of Joint Labour Committees (JLCs) and Joint Industrial Councils (JICs), which operate under the aegis of the Labour Court.[5] Although the influence of these institutional mechanisms has declined considerably in recent decades, potentially they still can make an important contribution to orderly industrial relations in certain sectors. In response to the increasing frequency of industrial action in its sector, the Construction Industry National Joint Council established the Construction Industry Disputes Tribunal as an effective 'fast-track'

---

[5]   The function of Joint Labour Committees is to provide an agreed minimum standard of pay and conditions within a designated economic sector/occupation, while the Joint Industrial Councils have a more specific focus on promoting harmonious industrial relations and on dispute resolution.

procedure for dealing with local and national issues. This body presently is chaired by an officer from the Conciliation Service and, interestingly, a recent examination of a particular sub-sector of the industry, commissioned by the National Implementation Body, included in its recommendations a proposal to institutionalise formally this convention of the Commission providing the chair to this Tribunal. Chairing such bodies, moreover, provides another channel of engagement for conciliation officers and, as such, serves to reinforce their relationships with, and standing amongst, key labour market actors. Additionally, under *Sustaining Progress,* the Conciliation Service had a designated role in an agreed set of mechanisms for resolving specific disputes relating to the terms of the national agreement and this activity, re-affirmed in *Towards 2016,* is described in **section 2.6**.

2.3.7   Preventative mediation

Although the core function of the Conciliation Service has always been, and will remain, the resolution of collective disputes, it now clearly plays a more active role in preventative mediation and/or dispute avoidance activity. As indicated above, the LRC has a broad remit, focused on the promotion of good industrial relations and on encouraging the parties to develop their own mechanisms for strengthening in-house relationships, procedures and structures. Consequently, in circumstances where it was evident that organisations in dispute had specific internal employment relations problems, it was always the approach of the relevant conciliators to encourage them to engage with the Advisory Service with a view to improving these industrial relations issues. This complementary relationship was formalised, moreover, with the development of the Frequent User Initiative (see **sub-section 2.4.4**). Significantly, however, through initiatives such as the Working Together projects, the Conciliation Service has now developed a more active involvement in the area of preventative mediation. Moreover, as described below, the future strategic direction of the Service is premised on incorporating a stronger dispute prevention ethos into its core conciliation activities.

2.3.8   Evaluation

Since the early 1990s, the LRC has provided a highly effective conciliation service, with approximately 81% of disputes referred to it being resolved amicably. Moreover, this very high level of dispute resolution has been consistently achieved over a number of years (see **Figure 2.5**).

**FIGURE 2.5: THE CONCILIATION SERVICE'S SETTLEMENT
RATE, 2001 – 2007**

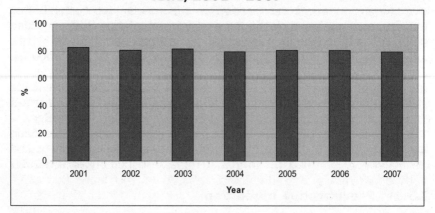

Although a number of interrelated factors have contributed to the historically-low levels of industrial conflict in Ireland, the capacity of the LRC to resolve disputes clearly has been critical and, clearly, has contributed to the considerable standing and credibility that the Conciliation Service enjoys amongst the social partners, employers, trade unions, employees and politicians. Indeed, the continuing high-level commitment on the part of the labour market parties to the resolution of disputes through voluntary engagement with a third party is testament to the reputation that the Conciliation Service enjoys. This high standing was re-affirmed in the LRC User Satisfaction Survey 2005, where 89% of respondents stated that they were either 'very satisfied' or 'satisfied' with the Conciliation Service (McGill, 2005). However, the same survey revealed some concerns regarding time delays in processing referrals and the limitations on the level of follow-up support available.

2.3.9   The skill and experience of staff

The Commission's continued capacity to provide such a high-quality Conciliation Service is heavily dependent on the skills, competencies and experience of its staff. Indeed, the Director of this Division has characterised conciliation as a 'people-based activity'. All of the conciliators have a high level of expertise in a range of conciliation and mediation techniques, combined with a deep knowledge of the industrial relations landscape – that is, the parties, the issues, and the processes. They have also built up over time strong, highly-personalised relationships with the principal actors in the labour market, based on their capacity to resolve disputes effectively and their activities in related areas. From the outset, the Conciliation

Service certainly benefited from the fact that its initial complement of staff came from the then Department of Labour and, as such, the staff were very much 'embedded' in the milieu of collective-based industrial relations. Interestingly, a considerable *cadre* of the original staff remains with the organisation, which has certainly been important in terms of retaining key skills and expertise. The establishment of the LRC itself undoubtedly gave a certain energy to the process of conciliation, which has been re-inforced by the social partnership's emphasis on intensive dialogue and problem-solving in dealing with industrial relations issues at all levels (O'Donnell & Thomas, 1998; Thomas, 2002). The quality of the staff also reflects the Commission's continued investment in training and career development. Significantly, in the LRC User Satisfaction Survey 2005, both employers and trade unions alluded to the facilitation skills, flexibility, reputation, knowledge and commitment of the staff as being among the key strengths of the Conciliation Service (McGill, 2005; LRC Annual Report 2006).

2.3.10 A long-term solutions focus

Finally, the Commission is now committed to developing within its conciliation framework a longer-term, solutions-orientated focus, which will encourage organisations to adopt policies and practices that will upgrade their in-house conflict management procedures. Aside from contributing to the strategic objective of encouraging parties to resolve disputes close to the point of origin, this approach also has the potential to transform organisational practices, improve employment relations and reduce reliance on third-party intervention. In promoting this innovative approach, the Service is aware that conciliation provides it with a unique and privileged form of engagement, in which there is an opportunity to drive forward longer-term strategic solutions rather than merely seeking to respond to parties on an *ad hoc* basis as disputes arise. Indeed, as noted above, one of the concerns raised by clients regarding the Conciliation Service was the limits on the degree of follow-up support available and this approach seeks, in part, to alleviate this issue.

This initiative is still in its embryonic stage and the Conciliation Service is currently planning intensive in-house deliberations involving the Advisory Service team around the challenges and opportunities associated with developing a longer-term, solutions-orientated focus. For example, the Division is aware that this approach could create situations in which parties are exposed to approaches and proposals for which they are not yet ready and that this could damage their perception of the Conciliation Service. Mediating this balance between resolving disputes and encouraging long-term solutions will be critical and, consequently, internal debate focused on generating innovative approaches is essential. Equally, the potential benefits in terms of the impact on the quality of industrial relations within client organisations is such that it is important that this initiative is progressed, while recognising that protecting the integrity of conciliation activity must remain the paramount consideration.

As indicated at the start of this section, the Conciliation Service provides a flexible, effective and high-quality conciliation service to employers, employees and unions in both the public and private sectors. While it is essential that the capacity to deliver such a service is retained, it is also evident that the Conciliation Service increasingly is engaged in activities that go beyond reactive dispute resolution *per se*. Consequently, although dispute resolution will remain a core feature of the Division's future work, it appears that, increasingly, in seeking to provide an effective and relevant service, it will be undertaken as part of a more diversified and integrated set of activities linked to the statutory mandate of the Commission.

2.4   THE ADVISORY SERVICE DIVISION

2.4.1   Promoting good practice – Forging a new role and identity

The Advisory Service Division (ASD) works with employers, employees and trade unions in non-dispute situations, to assist them in developing effective employment relations practices, procedures and structures, capable of fostering sustainable, co-operative and mutually-beneficial relationships. Since its establishment in 1992, the ASD has gradually evolved from providing one core service – industrial relations diagnostic audits – to the delivery of a range of activities that are designed to promote, develop and implement best industrial relations policies, practices and procedures.

In this regard, it is important to emphasise the experimental dimension to the ASD's establishment, as hitherto public policy had been premised primarily on supporting the orderly conduct of voluntary collective bargaining, as opposed to pro-actively encouraging a shift from adversarial industrial relations towards a more co-operative, consensus-based approach. Consequently, in the early years, there was a degree of uncertainty as to the precise role and identity of the ASD within the broader public dispute resolution architecture and, in fact, during this initial period, it generally replicated the Acas (UK) model, in terms of undertaking diagnostic reviews of organisations' employment relations environment.

Although the ASD staff were able to draw on the skills and experience they had honed in undertaking previous facilitation and conciliation activity, it was also evident that they had to develop new competencies related to their more pro-active mandate of improving industrial relations practices and procedures. In effect, the ASD built its capacity in this area through a combination of in-house training, exposure to international best practice and a strong element of learning by monitoring and reviewing its practices in action. It was also apparent that the ASD had to overcome a degree of reticence from client organisations, who were not convinced that a statutory public dispute resolution agency should be undertaking this type of activity.

Gradually, the ASD has forged a strong identity for itself, premised on an integrated and high-quality range of services, which are focused on building and maintaining positive partnership-style working relationships and enhancing problem-solving capacity, so as to enhance the well-being of the enterprise and to assist in employment creation and retention. The scale of this activity is shown in the 145 projects undertaken by the ASD during 2005, in areas such as preventative mediation/facilitation, joint working parties, advice and workshops, research, voluntary dispute resolution and training. Following a brief description of the organisational structure, the remainder of this section seeks to examine the various strands of this work.

2.4.2   Organisational structure

The ASD consists of three units:

- **Advisory:** Responsible for the development and promulgation of Codes of Practice and the delivery of enterprise-level projects, such as IR audits.
- **Research & Information/ICT:** Responsible for the LRC's research and information activities and manages all internal and external ICT-related initiatives.
- **Strategy & Standards:** Responsible for assessing the effectiveness of the Commission's services, surveying customer satisfaction levels and promoting best industrial relations practice.

2.4.3   Industrial relations: Reviews and audits

In the first few years of the LRC's existence, the ASD's primary role was to undertake diagnostic industrial relations reviews in a small number of private sector companies experiencing crisis. This process, which involves a thorough audit of existing industrial relations practices and procedures, together with a survey of the views of all the relevant stakeholders in an enterprise, was designed to examine the range of problems that exist within an organisation and/or the dynamics underpinning working relations. Following an audit, a confidential report, containing conclusions and recommendations, is issued and, in some instances where it is more appropriate to focus on the change agenda, a series of recommended improvements to industrial relations procedures and practices is presented. As a new entity, this process of undertaking diagnostic reviews was an important initiative for the ASD, as it underpinned the building of strong relationships with both individual companies and the social partners and it contributed to the development of the ASD's credibility and identity within the public policy domain.

Despite its importance, however, there was a growing internal recognition that this process was primarily a reactive service, focused on providing an in-depth analysis of problems and issuing a relatively limited menu of recommendations. Consequently, in 1996, it was decided to enhance the potential impact of this process on an organisation's industrial relations environment by offering post-report monitoring and, where necessary, assistance in the implementation of required changes and improvements, in the form of a joint working party. The latter involves the ASD in providing assistance in establishing and chairing a joint working party comprised of company management/representatives and employees and/or employee representatives. The objective of these joint groupings is to agree and implement recommendations or decisions to improve industrial relations practices and culture within an organisation. The facility is designed to give the parties direct involvement in developing agreed solutions to workplace difficulties and, thereby, potentially avoiding further problems with these issues.[6] The development of joint working parties clearly brought a strong element of preventative mediation/facilitation into the process of seeking to improve an organisation's industrial relations culture and associated practices and procedures and, as such, correlated with the emphasis on preventative mediation/intervention that was gradually becoming an integral feature of the ASD's work.

In accordance with the Commission's commitment to upgrade its service continually, the ASD began, in 2005, to use *Re-Solve* – a computer-based toolkit for the speedy gathering and analysis of information from groups of people – as a standard part of the diagnostic review process. Aside from speed, the primary advantage of *Re-Solve* is that it promotes collaboration, where time, distance, cost and personal and group dynamics can prevent people getting together. Additionally, it also assists in the monitoring of progress within an organisation and the Commission is beginning to use this technology to support other activities such as interest-based bargaining and dispute resolution. The experience of one company where *Re-Solve* was used as part of an industrial relations review was

---

[6]   In addition to IR audits encouraging this activity, in some instances, Labour Court recommendations can also include proposals that the parties to a dispute establish, with the support of the Advisory Service Division, a joint working party to devise procedures for the implementation of various elements of the Court's recommendation.

that the process facilitated the parties moving quickly to the stage where they were working on an agreed joint agenda focused on improving working relations.

In 2004, the LRC commissioned a study of the 115 company reviews that it had undertaken to date (Cronin, 2004). The objective of this research was to use the considerable reservoir of knowledge that had been garnered over 12 years, as a means both of generating insights for practitioners and of assisting in improving the quality of service. Interestingly, the most common problem reported – evident in 80% of organisations reviewed – was poor and/or non-existent communications structures and insufficient consultation on issues affecting employees. The recommendations proposed as a result of these reviews generally fell into three broad categories:

- Developing more structured communications and consultation systems.
- Encouraging greater clarity in procedures and roles.
- Fostering a greater recognition of the rights and responsibilities of those involved in the IR process.

This research also sought to evaluate the impact of the diagnostic reviews, through a small representative survey. Importantly, this survey indicated that 54% of respondents perceived that the review process had resulted in some improvements in industrial relations, while 45.4% suggested that significant improvements had occurred (Cronin, 2004). In particular, it was considered that the diagnostic audit and, where appropriate, the follow-up support, had resulted in:

- Enhanced co-operation.
- Increased acceptance of change.
- Improvements in internal communications.
- Greater levels of trust.
- Enhanced problem-solving capacity.
- Better industrial relations procedures.

Significantly, it was highlighted that that these improvements were not due solely to the implementation of the various recommendations, as respondents also stressed the importance of the process being impartial, confidential and non-confrontational. These procedural dynamics were particularly important in fostering greater openness and trust between the parties.

Ultimately, this research concluded that the company review process has functioned as an effective mechanism both in opening up communications and dialogue within organisations experiencing IR difficulties and in creating a greater willingness to engage in joint problem-solving. The research, moreover, highlights the importance –

both in terms of avoiding disputes and also of improving working relations – of having in place effective practices and procedures for communicating and consulting with staff and, as such, it re-affirms the potential of the Employees (Provision of Information & Consultation) Act 2006.

2.4.4   Frequent Users Initiative: Preventative mediation

The first attempt at actually putting in place formalised preventative mediation activity was the launch of the Frequent Users Initiative in 1995. Through co-operation with the Conciliation Service, major organisations that were 'heavy users' of the Labour Court, Conciliation Service and Rights Commissioners were identified. This over-reliance on third-party intervention was clearly indicative that internal employment relations practices and procedures were not functioning properly and, as such, were constraining the capacity of organisations to improve performance and provide a quality working environment. As indicated earlier, the statutory remit of the Commission is to promote good industrial relations and so the existence of 'frequent or heavy users' indicated that engagement with the Conciliation Service in a dispute context was not in itself generating improvements in relationships, processes and structures within these organisations, many of whom were significant employers. Therefore, there was a clear need for some form of pro-active preventative intervention in a non-adversarial context (no live dispute) and so the Frequent Users Initiative (FUI) was developed to fill this gap. Aside from representing the first foray into the area of preventative mediation, the FUI demonstrated formally the complementary and symbiotic relationship between the Advisory and Conciliation Services. Additionally, there was strong political support for this type of pro-active initiative, as it accorded with the consensual problem-solving approach to industrial relations advocated by the national-level social partnership process.

The focus of the FUI was to work pro-actively with identified organisations, with a view to improving their internal capacity for conflict management. In particular, this engagement focused on identifying weaknesses in current practice and encouraging the adoption of more progressive measures with the potential to improve current industrial relations practices. Significantly, the Advisory Service has used engagement under the auspices of the FUI to promote an integrated approach to conflict management that emphasises the need to improve internal communication, consultation and employee involvement. Thus, from the mid 1990s, there was a strong partnership ethos inherent in the Commission's approach to preventative mediation and, indeed, in some instances, participating organisations have rebranded the practices and structures they subsequently adopted as workplace partnerships.

2.4.5   Advice and assistance: Preventative mediation

Gradually, in part due to the perceived success of the FUI, the ASD began to undertake preventative mediation work with organisations that were not necessarily heavy users of the Commission, but which, in anticipation of potential problems ahead, were seeking to enhance their capacity for dealing with industrial relations issues. Thus, unlike FUI, where the LRC targeted potential clients, organisations actually came to the Advisory Service for advice on, and assistance with, developing disputes and grievances procedures, adopting new work practices and addressing structural change.

The provision of detailed quality advice, on request to both employers and trade unions (together or separately) or employers alone (where there is no union recognised in the workplace) on good practice in putting in place negotiating agreements, grievance/ disciplinary procedures and other industrial frameworks, is now an integral element of the ASD's work. Depending on the issue involved, this advice may focus on encouraging organisations to adopt relevant Codes of Practice. In some instances, this initial engagement can lead to more direct assistance, whereby the ASD works with employers and trade unions and encourages them to experiment with mechanisms such as interest-based bargaining and/or joint problem-solving.

The ASD does not seek to provide off-the-shelf solutions to organisational needs but, instead, works with the relevant stakeholders to design customised approaches that will enhance organisational performance, improve the employment relations culture, generate mutual gains and assist in employment creation and retention. There is clearly a strong partnership ethos to this type of work and, as such, this advocacy role has been assisted both by the social partners' formal endorsement of voluntary workplace partnership in *Partnership 2000* (1996) and by the establishment of other public agencies, such as the National Centre for Partnership & Performance (in 2001), whose remit clearly complements the work of the ASD. In recognition of this, in recent years, there has been increased formal and informal co-operation between both these organisations. The ASD's recent work in targeting SMEs is also, in essence, a form of preventative mediation, which seeks to promote good practice employment relations.

2.4.6   Codes of Practice

Another important strand of the ASD's work is the development and promulgation of statutory Codes of Practice, in accordance with Section 42 of the Industrial Relations Act 1990. The objective of these statutory instruments is to set out recommended good/best practice in relation to a particular employment/workplace issue or legislative provision and, in essence, these codes have functioned as another form of preventative mediation. Under the relevant legislation, it is possible for either the Minister[7] or the LRC to propose the development of a particular Code; however, in practice, the latter situation has never arisen. Although the first such code, *Code of Practice on Dispute Procedures, including Procedures in Essential Services* (LRC, 1992), was prepared in the aftermath of a specific dispute in a major public utility, subsequently two main factors have driven their development. First, the decision to prepare codes on particular issues has become closely associated with the dynamics of national-level social partnership arrangements, with four specific codes, including the *Enhanced Code of Practice on Voluntary Dispute Resolution* (LRC, 2004b), being developed specifically in response to commitments made within the social partnership process. A secondary factor has been codes that have emerged directly from requirements in specific employment legislation, as in the case of the *Code of Practice on Sunday Working in the Retail Trade* (LRC, 1998).

The preparation of a Code involves officials from the Commission working closely with the social partners and, where required, other affected stakeholders, to prepare a consensus-based draft Code, which is then forwarded to the Minister for Enterprise, Trade & Employment, who designates it as a statutory Code of Practice. The drafting of Codes can be a challenging and problematic process for the Commission, especially when this form of soft regulation attempts to progress issues on which either the legislative process or peak-level social partnership negotiations have failed to generate sufficient consensus. In some instances, this context can result in the development of an essentially compromise position, which can limit the potential effectiveness of the regulatory instrument. Equally, this process generally has worked relatively well and, as outlined below, there are now 10 statutory codes of practice *in situ*:

- *Code of Practice detailing Procedures for Addressing Bullying in the Workplace* (LRC, 2002a).
- *Code of Practice for Protecting Persons Working in Other People's Homes* (LRC, 2007).
- *Code of Practice on Access to Part-Time Work* (LRC, 2006).
- *Code of Practice on Compensatory Rest Periods* (LRC, 1998b).
- *Code of Practice on Dispute Procedures, including Procedures in Essential Services* (LRC, 1992).
- *Code of Practice on Duties & Responsibilities of Employee Representatives & the Protection and Facilities to be Afforded Them by their Employer* (LRC, 1993).

---

[7]   Responsibility at present lies with the Minister for Enterprise, Trade & Employment.

- *Code of Practice on Grievance & Disciplinary Procedures* (LRC, 2000).
- *Code of Practice on Sunday Working in the Retail Trade* (LRC, 1998a).
- *Code of Practice on Victimisation* (LRC, 2004a).
- *Code of Practice on Voluntary Dispute Resolution* (LRC, 2002b).
- *Enhanced Code of Practice on Voluntary Dispute Resolution* (LRC, 2004b).

These Codes are effectively 'soft' regulatory instruments, as they attempt to stimulate improvements in current practice by providing guidance on both recommended good practice and/or appropriate procedures in respect of potentially-contentious workplace issues. Where a Code is directly linked to specific employment legislation, the emphasis on adopting good practice is complemented by a focus on encouraging compliance with certain provisions of the relevant legislation. For example, the *Code of Practice on Sunday Working in the Retail Trade* (LRC, 1998a) seeks to assist employers, employees and employee representatives in observing the provisions of the Organisation of Working Time Act, 1997. This twin emphasis on putting in place practices or procedures that encourage legislative compliance – thereby avoiding referral to a public agency on the matter – and improving organisational capacity for addressing potentially-problematic workplace issues, ensures that the Codes, in effect, are a form of preventative mediation or facilitation. In practice, the Codes provide an agreed platform for encouraging better working relations and the ASD's experience suggests that, where organisations have agreed to adopt such Codes, it facilitates the process of improving internal employment relations practices, structures and procedures. Additionally, although the Codes do not have the force of law, they can be taken into account in the course of proceedings before the Labour Court, the Employment Appeals Tribunal and the Equality Tribunal, where these touch on relevant issues.

Although the Codes of Practice, in terms of the scope of issues they have addressed, have evolved in a somewhat *ad hoc* and re-active manner, they are indicative of the growing reach of statutory instruments in relation to workplace issues, albeit in the form of a type of soft regulation. It is evident, moreover, that the usage of such instruments probably will continue to expand in the medium term, at least. For example, the Commission is currently in the process of preparing a draft Code in relation to the Employees (Provision of Information & Consultation) Act 2006. The Act is an important legislative development in Irish employment relations, given that it confers on employees a statutory-based right to be informed and consulted in the workplace. The Act introduces a general legislative framework and, consequently, the proposed Code has the potential to augment the legislation by outlining the types of practices and procedures that can assist organisations to improve their current practice in relation to informing and consulting employees. Given the divergence of opinion between the social partners on the Act, engineering an effective consensus will be highly challenging for the Commission.

Additionally, in recognition of the need for special measures to support the employment rights of those people employed in the homes of others, the parties to the Social Partnership agreement, *Towards 2016* (Taoiseach, 2006), mandated the LRC to develop an appropriate Code of Practice. The *Code of Practice for Protecting Persons Employed in Other People's Homes* (LRC, 2007) provides a comprehensive framework for an agreed understanding of rights and responsibilities for the protection of those who, potentially, can be very vulnerable workers. In particular, this new framework seeks to improve the quality of the working environment in this growing sub-sector of the economy by encouraging increased compliance with existing employment regulation and labour standards.

It could be suggested that the use of Codes to address certain issues represents a *de facto* fall-back for the failure by the social partners to reach a workable consensus in other arenas. Conversely, it could be argued that the emergence at the European level of less prescriptive framework-type Directives and the potential that there will be an increased reliance on social dialogue agreements to promulgate social policy, combined with the recognition of the difficulties of trying to craft national legislation capable of covering all potential employment scenarios, especially in a dynamic and changing labour market, suggests that this form of soft regulation could be a potentially-important mechanism for giving practical effect to future developments aimed at regulating the employment relationship. Realising the potential of this form of soft regulation, however, appears to require the development of a more structured, dynamic and symbiotic relationship between the processes and actors involved in framing legislation and/or negotiating national agreements and those involved in preparing associated Codes of Practice.

In terms of the effectiveness of these various Codes, a 2004 LRC survey of industrial relations practitioners – employers and trade unionists who have used the Commission's services – revealed that they are highly-regarded and widely-used (LRC, 2004). The vast majority of practitioners surveyed (94%) were aware of the various Codes and, significantly, 86% of respondents indicated that they made use of them. In this context, the most widely-used Codes were those relating to grievance and discipline; bullying and harassment; duties and responsibilities of employee representatives; and dispute resolution and procedures in essential services. There was also a strong consensus amongst respondents (80%) that these statutory instruments are the most effective mechanism for promoting the adoption of good practice in the management of industrial relations at the national level. Interestingly, this survey also revealed a demand amongst practitioners for the preparation of new Codes of Practice on issues such as cultural diversity, family-friendly work arrangements and transfer of undertakings. As noted above under the appropriate legislation, the LRC can propose new issues for consideration, although to date this facility has not been used. Despite the high level of awareness of the Codes amongst practitioners, survey respondents also suggested that they could be promoted more effectively. The LRC has acted upon this finding by developing a Code of Practice service guide, including material on the LRC website[8], and actively using the guides in seminars and workshops designed to encourage the adoption of good practice employment relations. Finally, under *Sustaining Progress* (2003), the ASD has been heavily involved in processing cases referred under the *Enhanced Code of Practice on Voluntary Dispute Resolution* (S.I. 76 of 2004).

2.4.7   Training and development

In response to the findings of its User Satisfaction Survey, in 2005, the LRC developed for the first time a limited Training & Development Service, which incorporates specialised training programmes in the following areas:

- Conflict prevention/resolution and employee relations challenges for employee representatives and employees.
- Conflict prevention/resolution and employee relations challenges for managers.
- Skills development and general information for employee representatives elected for the purposes of the Employees (Provision of Information & Consultation) Act 2006.
- General information for managers and employee representatives on the Employees (Provision of Information & Consultation) Act 2006.
- Implementing and maintaining effective communication strategies.

The ASD is responsible for coordinating this service, although the actual training is delivered by experienced cross-functional teams. There is a strong emphasis on providing customised and tailored training – for example, the West/Mid-West Conciliation Team

---

[8]   http://www.lrc.ie.

developed a programme in conflict management training for Directors of Nursing, at the request of the Irish Nurses Organisation.

This dedicated training initiative is indicative of the Commission's commitment to developing continuously its range of services to meet client needs, and it builds on and complements the type of developmental work that the ASD has undertaken with employers, employees and unions. Given the potential resource implications associated with developing and delivering training and development initiatives, the emphasis to date has been on providing a limited, but focused, high-quality training programme. In particular, there has been a strong emphasis on programmes that can enhance certain core competencies and contribute to the Commission's strategic objective of supporting enterprises to develop stronger innovative and flexible in-house conflict management systems.

2.4.8   Building research capacity

In response to a commitment within the LRC's *Strategy Statement 2005-2007* (LRC 2005a), the Research & Information/ICT Unit has sought to develop a more comprehensive research strategy. An integral part of this research strategy has been an increased emphasis on identifying priority areas for collaboration in undertaking projects with both other relevant public agencies and third-level institutions, the output from which includes:

- A survey of HRM practices in multinational companies.
- The publication of a research report, *Migrant Workers & Access to the Statutory Dispute Resolution Agencies* (LRC, 2005b).
- The undertaking of a Review of the Joint Labour Committee System.
- The initiation of a project concerned with 'Building Capacity in Dispute Resolution & Avoidance'.
- Research seminars and conferences.

There is also an important internal dimension to this research strategy that recognises the need to build on existing LRC/Labour Court/ODEI/EAT data to support evidence-based policy decision-making. This data, combined with the extensive practical experience of staff, potentially provides a deep reservoir of knowledge that could be used to support the ongoing evaluation of existing policy services and initiatives. An indication of the potential of this largely untapped resource was the in-house study of 12 years of the Labour Relations Commission Advisory Service Division's work (Cronin, 2004). The full implementation of a comprehensive IT-based case management system, which hosts approximately 50,000 records, further enhances this potential, although there are clear resource implications associated with increasing this type of research activity. The LRC has also sought to put in place a more systematic basis for collecting the views of clients and the Research Unit undertook a User Satisfaction Survey (McGill, 2005).

The main objective of this emphasis on building the LRC's research capacity is to improve the quality and effectiveness of the organisation's range of policy services and initiatives. The insights and learning from this activity can be fed directly into existing services and disseminated widely, adding to the knowledge of all industrial relations and HR practitioners. Additionally, in seeking to remain relevant, the LRC is aware of the need to ensure that its services and initiatives reflect the ongoing dynamics of workplace change and labour force development. With the increased pace of change in recent years, the importance of supporting leading-edge research in priority areas related to the core work of the Commission, arguably, has increased.

As indicated above, this research should seek to improve the quality and effectiveness of services – for example, in response to the research finding that unfamiliarity with both the English language and the nuances of procedures, processes and time requirements presents obstacles for migrant workers in accessing the services of the statutory dispute resolution agencies, the Commission decided to publish its information literature in several languages, including Mandarin-Chinese, Polish, Portuguese and Russian. Similarly, the Commission has used the User Satisfaction Survey not to only identify client needs but also to initiate action designed to address deficiencies in service provision (McGill, 2005).

2.4.9 Evaluation and summary

Given the developmental nature of its work, the ASD does not have the overt type of performance indicators that are available to the Conciliation Service, for example. The Division is aware of the need, however, to build more effective monitoring processes into its various activities so that it can track the impact of its intervention on an organisation's employment relations practices and procedures. As indicated above, however, a survey of clients who had availed of IR audits revealed a very positive evaluation of the process, in terms of its impact on the industrial relations environment within their respective organisations. The User Satisfaction Survey also confirmed a positive rating for the Advisory Service, with 81% of respondents either 'very satisfied' or 'satisfied' with the ASD (McGill, 2005). In terms of the perceived strengths of the service, respondents highlighted:

- A quality and professional service.
- The skills and experience of the staff.

- The capacity to address entrenched positions, build trust and assist the parties in reaching a resolution.

The same survey, however, also pointed to several weaknesses in the ASD – in particular, the lack of sufficient information on the services provided and a degree of ritual engagement by employers on certain issues, thus preventing closure.

From fairly uncertain beginnings, and an initial focus on just one main service, the Advisory Service Division has evolved to provide a comprehensive set of activities, programmes and services aimed at promoting improvements in employment relations practices and procedures. In particular, it has developed a strong focus on preventative mediation, as part of its overall developmental focus. Despite progress on this issue and support from other institutional developments, the scale of referrals to the statutory dispute resolution agencies is indicative of the need for a continued focus on improving and enhancing the quality of employment relations. Additionally, it is arguable that developing the scale and quality of the ASD's engagement with sectors and organisations operating within the non-unionised environment could be an increasingly important aspect of the division's future workload.

2.5   THE RIGHTS COMMISSIONER SERVICE

2.5.1   The Rights Commissioner Service: An expanding role and remit

The Rights Commissioner Service investigates disputes, grievances and claims that individuals or small groups of workers make under relevant industrial relations and employment rights legislation (see **Table 2.3**). The Rights Commissioners operate as part of the Labour Relations Commission; however, they are wholly independent in the performance of their duties.

The Rights Commissioner Service was established by the Industrial Relations Act 1969 to provide a non-legalistic and fast third-party procedure for resolving employment grievances and disputes (other than pay and pensions), involving individual and/or small groups of employees, in the context of industrial relations legislation and structures. From a number of perspectives, the establishment of the Rights Commissioner Service in 1969 was an innovative and, indeed far-sighted, initiative, given that there was minimal statutory employment legislation in Ireland at the time. First, it introduced a first instance dimension to dispute resolution within a predominantly voluntarist system. Second, it demonstrated that Ireland recognised the importance of having in place an extra-firm procedure for upholding employment rights through essentially non-legalistic activity. Third, from its inception, the service has been premised on the adoption of a non-adversarial problem-solving approach to dispute resolution, which highlights that some of the key characteristics of what is often termed 'alternative dispute resolution' in fact have a long tradition within the Irish public dispute resolution machinery.

TABLE 2.3: LEGISLATION AFFORDING A STATUTORY ROLE TO THE RIGHTS COMMISSIONERS

ACTS	Year
Industrial Relations Acts	1969 - 1990
Unfair Dismissals Acts	1977 - 2005
Payment of Wages Act	1991
Maternity Protection Acts	1994 - 2004
Terms of Employment (Information) Act	1994
Adoptive Leave Acts	1995 - 2005
Protection of Young Persons (Employment) Act	1996
Organisation of Working Time Act	1997
Parental Leave Act	1998
Protection for Persons Reporting Child Abuse Act	1998
National Minimum Wage Act	2000
Carer's Leave Act	2001
Protection of Employees (Part-Time Work) Act	2001
Competition Acts	2002 - 2006
Protection of Employees (Fixed-Term Work) Act	2003
Industrial Relations (Miscellaneous Provisions) Act	2004
Safety, Health & Welfare at Work Act	2005
Employees (Provision of Information & Consultation) Act	2006
Employment Permits Act	2006
STATUTORY INSTRUMENTS	**Year**
European Communities (Protection of Employment) Regulations	2000
European Communities (Protection of Employees on Transfer of Undertakings) Regulations	2003
European Communities (European PLC) (Employee Involvement) Regulations	2006

In the period since its establishment, however, the role, function and, indeed, importance of the Rights Commissioner Service within the public dispute resolution architecture has changed dramatically. Although Rights Commissioners have retained their function within the industrial disputes arena, they have also acquired gradually a more encompassing quasi-judicial role in respect of employment rights. While the resolution of industrial relations disputes remains a core role of the Service, referrals under this legislation now account for only 16% of the total received (see **Table 2.4**).

TABLE 2.4: REFERRALS TO THE RIGHTS COMMISSIONERS, BY ACT, 2006

Act	Percentage of Total
Payment of Wages Act 1991	33%
Industrial Relations Acts 1969-2004	16%
Organisation of Working Time Act 1997	15%
Unfair Dismissals Acts 1977-1993	12%
Terms of Employment Information Act 1994-2001	10%
Other Acts	8%
Protection of Employees (Fixed Term Work) Act 2003	6%

Source: Labour Relations Annual Report, 2006.

The primary catalyst for changes in the function and role of the Rights Commissioner Service has been the considerable expansion of employment legislation, under which the Rights Commissioners have been afforded a statutory role (see **Table 2.3**).[9] Although this shift into the employment rights-based arena began in 1977, with the passage of the Unfair Dismissals Act, up until the early 1990s, the Rights Commissioners still operated primarily within the industrial dispute arena. Since the early 1990s, however, the proliferation of employment legislation – primarily focused on developing individual rights – has underpinned a sea-change in the nature and scope of the functions provided by the Service. As a result of this legislative activity, Rights Commissioners now deal with claims and complaints in relation to issues such as pay, holidays, working conditions, contracts and pensions, in an enhanced role beyond that envisaged by the establishing legislation. The impact on the Service of this discernible shift towards a rights-based system has been re-inforced by other key labour market trends – in particular, the continued decline in trade union density, the increased diversity of the workforce, the growth of the SME sector and the dramatic expansion of the labour force.

---

[9]   Indeed, there are only two pieces of employment rights legislation under which the Rights Commissioners have no role: statutory redundancy and employment equality.

2.5.2   Referrals: The nature, scale and scope of activities

The gradual, but perceptible, change in the function and role of the Rights Commissioner Service within the public dispute resolution infrastructure has clearly impacted on the nature, scale and scope of the activities undertaken by the Service. The first significant trend has been the increase in the number of referrals to the office, with referrals rising by 139% between 1999 and 2006 (see **Table 2.5**). Between 2005 and 2006 alone, referrals rose by 28%, thus exerting further pressure on an already-stretched service. The pressures emanating from the increased workload have been augmented by the widening of the scope of jurisdiction afforded to the Rights Commissioner Service. With the introduction of the Safety, Health & Welfare Act, the Rights Commissioners now have a statutory role in relation to a broad range of industrial relations and employment rights legislation, covering issues such as pay, holidays, working conditions, contracts and pensions (see **Table 2.3**). In contrast up until 1995, its jurisdiction was determined by just three pieces of legislation.

TABLE 2.5: REFERRALS TO THE RIGHTS COMMISSIONERS, 1999-2007

Year	1999	2000	2001	2002	2003	2004	2005	2006	2007
Referrals	2,996	3,206	4,156	5,692	4,737	4,749	5,598	7,179	9,077

Source: LRC Annual Report, 2006.

In addition to being afforded jurisdiction over a broader array of employment statutes, the Rights Commissioners also operate within an increasingly complex legislative environment, due to the fact that more recent employment laws contain within them complex issues and provisions relating to workplace practice, rights and entitlements. Referrals under the Fixed Term Working Act, for example, have proven to be quite complex cases, characterised by substantial and detailed submissions, often requiring more than one hearing, thus exerting considerable demands on the Service. Significantly, referrals under this Act have continued to increase, rising from 119 to 276 between 2004 and 2007 (see **Table 2.6**). Submissions under this legislation and the Part Time Working Act have been dominated by the public service, which is interesting, given that the Service was originally established with a strong private sector focus in mind.[10]

---

[10]   Under the Fixed Term, Part-Time and Organisation of Working Time Acts, trade unions can lodge separate claims on behalf of individuals within the same workplace. In such

TABLE 2.6: REFERRALS BY LEGISLATION, 2001-2007

	2001	2002	2003	2004	2005	2006	2007
Adoptive Leave Act 1995	1	0	0	0	1	1	2
Carers Leave Act 2001	1	0	2	0	0	1	1
Competition Act 2002	0	0	0	0	0	0	0
European Communities (Protection of Employment) Regulations 2000	2	1	2	4	2	6	09
European Communities (Protection of Employees on Transfer of Undertakings) Regulations 2003	13	11	96	66	116	128	151
Industrial Relations Acts 1969-1990	1,363	1,334	1,464	1,171	1,236	1,172	1,182
Industrial Relations (Misc. Provisions) Act 2004	0	0	0	7	84	62	32
Maternity Protection Act 1994	9	21	24	8	26	23	26
National Minimum Wage Act 2000	59	48	68	63	72	107	114
Organisation of Working Time Act 1997	740	967	631	611	665	1,087	1,591
Parental Leave Act 1998	43	23	26	24	20	15	17
Payment of Wages Act 1991	1,125	1,177	1,285	1,538	1,875	2,275	2,961
Protection of Employees (Fixed-Term Work) Act 2003	0	0	10	119	296	443	204
Protection of Employees (Part-Time Work) Act 2001	27	1092	99	85	75	133	62
Protection of Young Persons (Employment Act) 1996	1	0	1	0	3	7	3
Protection for Persons Reporting Child Abuse Act 1998	0	0	0	0	1	0	1
Safety, Health & Welfare at Work Act 2005	0	0	0	0	2	119	408
Terms of Employment (Information) Acts 1994-2001	141	150	183	245	301	711	1,295
Unfair Dismissals Acts 1997-2001	632	868	846	808	823	889	1,038
Total Referrals	**4,156**	**5,692**	**4,737**	**4,749**	**5,598**	**7,179**	**9,077**

Source: LRC Annual Reports.

circumstances, where the cases have potential group or wider workforce implications, a Rights Commissioner, by agreement, can hear all of the cases at one hearing.

The recommendations in relation to the Fixed-Term Work Act potentially will have a significant impact on employment practices and status across the public service. Currently, following hearings, the Labour Court is processing a number of appeals on key issues, the outcome of which will set precedents for interpretation of the legislation that could further increase the number of referrals to the Rights Commissioner Service under this particular statute.

As is evident from **Table 2.4**, four pieces of legislation – the Payment of Wages Act; the Industrial Relations Acts; the Unfair Dismissals Acts; and the Organisation of Working Time Act – accounted for 82% of total referrals in 2005. Although the jurisdiction of the Rights Commissioners has widened, it is also evident that core aspects of the employment relations process – pay systems, working hours and dismissal – remain the main source of workplace grievances and disputes that the Commissioners address. Conversely, while the resolution of individual industrial relations disputes continues to be a core function of the Service, referrals under the Industrial Relations Acts 1969-1990 now account for only 22% of the total received, despite the fact that this was the catalyst for the Service being established initially (see **Table 2.6**).

As indicated in **Table 2.6**, the Payment of Wages Act generates the highest number of referrals to the Service. A key contribution to this trend has been the increased usage by migrant workers seeking redress, particularly in relation to the issues of working hours in excess of statutory limits or underpayment in reference to the minimum rates of pay in industries covered by Employment Regulation Orders or Registered Employment Agreements. A high proportion of the claims under this Act are made against indigenous SMEs and relate to basic entitlements such as wages or holidays.

Another trend in relation to the nature of referrals to the Service has been the significant increase in workload associated with relatively new employment rights legislation. As is evident from **Table 2.6**, the number of cases being generated by relatively new enactments – such as the Protection of Employees on Transfer of Undertakings Regulations; the Protection of Employees (Fixed Term Work) Act; and the Industrial Relations (Miscellaneous Provisions) Act – has increased steadily, thus exerting further pressure on the Rights Commissioner Service.

2.5.3 The Rights Commissioners: Experienced practitioners

The Rights Commissioners are appointed by the Minister for Enterprise, Trade & Employment, having been nominated by either the ICTU or IBEC and approved by the Board of the LRC, on the basis of their extensive experience and expertise in the employment/industrial relations arena. Although the individual Rights

Commissioners operate within the ambit of the Labour Relations Commission, they are not employees of the organisation and, in essence, are formally independent of the Commission. While the individual Commissioners are drawn from either a trade union or employer background, once appointed they act in an independent manner in undertaking their statutory duties. The fact that each Rights Commissioner must possess an extensive knowledge of process and procedures in an increasingly complex legislative environment and, at the same time, display a range of dispute resolution competencies – investigation, negotiation, facilitation and mediation – appears to validate the established tradition of appointing experienced industrial relations experts. This approach has ensured that, while the function and role of the Service has changed, with a corresponding increase in the scale and complexity of the workload, the quality of the service delivered to date has been maintained.[11]

Although the individual Rights Commissioners continue to operate in a relatively independent manner, gradually they have begun to work as a more cohesive group. They now meet as a group with the LRC management on a quarterly basis to discuss issues that are arising in cases, different approaches to hearings, their experience of certain pieces of legislation, points of rulings, issues of legislative jurisdiction and recent legal advice clarification. Although this process is somewhat informal and *ad hoc*, it is encouraging a more open and constructive debate between the Commissioners and, importantly, it has facilitated the exchange of shared learning and the emulation of good practice. Despite the value of this regular engagement, it is arguable that continuing to enhance the quality of service now necessitates a more institutionalised and formal support structure both for capturing the knowledge that arises from the Rights Commissioners' activities and for ensuring that it informs their work in dealing with similar issues and/or pieces of legislation.

Briefing sessions on new legislation are also held with officials from the Department of Enterprise, Trade & Employment and the Commissioners use these exchanges also to highlight issues or problems arising in the application of certain pieces of legislation.

2.5.4   How the process works: Pragmatic problem-solving

A Rights Commissioner becomes involved in an employment dispute when a claimant requests their intervention under a particular piece of legislation. On notification of the claim to the employer by the Rights Commissioner Service, the parties will be encouraged to settle

---

[11]   In Canada, both provincial and federal dispute resolution agencies recruit their mediators and conciliators from among experienced industrial relations practitioners.

their dispute, which is indicative of the strong problem-solving ethos that has characterised the Service since its establishment. If a settlement is not possible at this stage, it is the responsibility of the Rights Commissioner to conduct an investigation, gather as much information as possible and to hold a hearing.

The hearings are formal, but non-adversarial. At the hearing, each party is given the opportunity to present their case, often with the support of a written submission. This, however, is not a court of law and, as such, evidence is not taken under oath and there is no cross-examination process. Despite the fact that they are increasingly dealing with claims pertaining to employment rights, the Rights Commissioners continue to adopt a pragmatic, problem-solving approach.

Following the hearing, the Rights Commissioners issue either a decision or a recommendation, depending on the legislation under which the case is referred. All recommendations are binding on the parties and are legally enforceable, unless made under the Industrial Relations Acts 1969-2001. The whole process from lodging a claim to the issuing of a decision or recommendation takes, on average, about six or seven months.

Significantly, under the original terms of the 1969 establishing legislation, the Rights Commissioners have the option of determining whether a case is suitable for mediation. This is an important option, and approximately one-third of the cases are settled with the assistance of the Rights Commissioner, by having a discussion with the parties in the course of the formal hearing. The decision of whether to try and mediate a settlement on the day is left to the judgement of the individual Rights Commissioner. This re-affirms the importance of having in place very experienced practitioners, as this type of intuitive competency is honed through extensive practical experience. Although some Rights Commissioners are more likely to mediate than others, there is a general acceptance within the Service that this remains an important dispute resolution option, even in the context of the more legalistic environment in which the Commissioners now operate. In part, this reflects the fact that, even in rights-based cases, it is very rare that one party is completely 100% either in the right or in the wrong. Consequently, even when legislation has been contravened, there is still scope to mediate a settlement that vindicates an individual's rights, is mutually acceptable and, importantly, does not in any way weaken employment rights. Mediating cases that are referred to the Service requires a considerable degree of skill and experience. In practice, the Rights Commissioner must perform a delicate balancing act between actively assisting the parties to reach a mediated settlement and, at the same time, retaining their neutral status and being capable of resorting to issuing a recommendation or decision, if the mediation process fails and formal proceedings are instigated.

Recourse to mediation in settling disputes or claims is considered particularly appropriate in instances where there is still an employment relationship and, as such, it is beneficial to assist the parties in restoring normal working relations. In the majority of cases, the employment relationship, however, has already ended. It is also recognised that engaging in mediation is generally more time-consuming, which is an important consideration for the Service, given the pressure that it currently operates under and, in particular, the continuing backlog of cases.

2.5.5   Dispute prevention and compliance

Significant outcomes of the Rights Commissioners' hearings are that, in approximately 85% of the cases, they find in favour of the claimant and that, in many instances, there are multiple infringements of employment legislation by the employer concerned. This infers that there are a small, but significant, number of enterprises, in particular indigenous SMEs, that are failing to comply with basic employment standards. In part, this may reflect a 'hard core' of businesses prepared to flout employment law until they are brought before the relevant State agency.

The relatively high level of claimant success suggests there is considerable potential both in increasing the level of current sanctions and in engaging in more innovative preventative activity. In relation to the current level of penalties, the fact that some of the legislation has no provision for awarding compensation over and above, for example, actual wages owed or lost, ensures that it can be viewed as relatively 'cheap' to refuse to comply with employment law. In this regard, it is important to note that an integral part of the new system of compliance and enforcement agreed within _Towards 2016_ (2006) is a commitment to introduce new legislation that will strengthen the penalties regime and scope for redress across all employment legislation.

The level of claimant success also suggests that there is potential for increased dispute prevention activity and, in particular, for the relevant public agencies to improve how they connect with, and inform, employers about both their obligations and also basic good practice to avoid infringing the law. The Rights Commissioner Service has participated in the SME workshops that the LRC organised to inform employers about their statutory responsibilities and to highlight examples of good practice that would ensure compliance and enhance their HR practices and procedures. The relatively low attendance at these workshops, however, demonstrates that it is difficult for public dispute agencies to penetrate those sectors of the economy in which compliance with legislation is already problematic. Many of the organisations that fail to comply with legislation tend to be outside the sphere of influence of employer representative bodies and, therefore, it is difficult to engage with them. User-friendly information on the Rights Commissioner service has also been produced and disseminated widely, as part of the LRC's overall commitment to raising awareness of the services it provides to employers and employees. Despite the increase in advocacy-related activities, there is still not a good level of awareness among employees of their employment rights. Indeed, many employees only obtain knowledge of their rights after a problem has arisen and/or the employment relationship has ended. Similarly, it is still apparent that too many employers are ignorant of their obligations under employment legislation until they find themselves before a body like the Rights Commissioner Service. In this context, the commitment contained within *Towards 2016* (2006) in relation to developing a comprehensive campaign, involving the social partners, to promote employment rights, obligations and entitlements to employers, employees and to workers from overseas in particular, indicates an awareness of the need to develop more innovative and targeted dispute prevention activities, as a means of both improving employment standards and also reducing the growth of referrals to the public dispute resolution agencies.

2.5.6 Migrant workers

A key challenge for the Rights Commissioner Service is to adapt its services and procedures to changes in the labour market and, in particular, to the increasing diversity within the workforce. Already, this latter trend is impacting on the work of the service, as it is estimated that the number of cases involving migrant workers has risen from approximately 2% to 8% of all cases between 2002 and 2004.[12] The main issues brought to the Rights Commissioner Service by migrant workers relate to working excess hours and underpayment in reference to legally-established industry norms (LRC, 2005b). A disturbing trend, moreover, was that, in almost all the cases, the employee listed multiple complaints of legislative infringement, which suggests the extent to which certain employers are transgressing employees' rights (LRC, 2005b). There is a general recognition within the Service of the need both to improve employees' knowledge and understanding of the process and procedures and to make the service more user-friendly and less bureaucratic. In the case of migrant workers, the general difficulties faced by all employees in accessing the services of public dispute resolution agencies are compounded by problems relating to language; perceptions of State institutions; fear regarding their employment status; the lack of engagement with formal institutional supports and

---

[12] This figure refers to the first eight months of 2004 only.

the delays in processing claims. This combination of factors appears to contribute to the relatively high percentage of migrant workers' cases that are either withdrawn or in which the claimant does not appear at the hearing. The high success rate in favour of claimants, when cases are actually heard, however, demonstrates that the system does have the capacity to vindicate those whose rights have been transgressed. This is particularly evident in instances in which the worker in question has the capacity, with support from trade unions or advocacy groups, to see the claim through the full process. This suggests that improving non-nationals' experience of the Service will require an integrated range of approaches that both raises awareness and also encourages closer linkages with trade unions and/or other advocacy bodies such as the Migrant Rights Information Centre and the Citizen Information Centres.

2.5.7   Support structures and advice

Although the Rights Commissioner Service remains formally independent of the LRC, administrative and managerial support is provided by Commission staff and, while there have been discernible improvements in the quality of support provided, it is recognised that it still operates at a relatively basic level. The continued expansion in the scale and scope of the Service's activities suggests the need to develop a more appropriate and enhanced support structure that can assist in the delivery of the service and provide added value.

As outlined earlier, there is a strong recognition within the Commission of the need to provide better information and to raise both employers' and employees' awareness of employment legislation and associated employment rights. Rights Commissioners, however, do not provide any advice on rights or entitlements under different pieces of employment legislation, as this could give rise to potential claims of interest. Similarly, the secretariat to the Rights Commissioner Service does not provide advice to parties on particular courses of action, such as under which Act they should pursue a particular claim. Therefore, if a claim is made under the wrong legislation, the Rights Commissioner may have to rule it out on this ground and there is no process within the Service for providing the claimant with the appropriate information. Instead, individuals seeking such advice are directed to the Employment Rights Information Unit (Department of Enterprise, Trade & Employment), which can provide information on the legislation and advice on how to fill the appropriate form as part of its overall service. Organisations such as Citizens Information Centres and Migrant Rights Centres have also become increasingly important sources of information and advice on employment rights and the processes and procedures associated with pursuing grievances and/or claims. Despite this, however, there has been some internal debate about the potential benefits for clients of providing an in-house advice service related to the Rights Commissioner Service, though at present this issue has not moved beyond the deliberation phase.

2.5.8 Evaluation and future issues

From the social partners' perspective, there is generally a good level of satisfaction with how the Rights Commissioner Service currently operates. The commitment in *Towards 2016* (2006) to increase the number of Rights Commissioners to 14 is both a formal acknowledgement of the expansion of their workload and recognition of the effective service they provide. The LRC's User Satisfaction Survey also revealed a positive assessment of the Service with 68% of respondents either 'very satisfied' or 'satisfied' with the Service. The same survey also revealed that both employers and trade unions felt that more resources should be afforded to the Service to address delays in processing cases.

Despite the fundamental changes in its operating environment and the considerable extension to the scale and scope of its activities, the Rights Commissioner Service continues to provide an effective, non-legalistic and relatively quick third-party procedure for resolving employment grievances and disputes involving individual and/or small groups of employees. In particular, the Rights Commissioner Service has retained its capacity to 'bring issues to an end' and it remains an important forum for employee voice in terms of individuals having the right to be heard. The considerable experience and skill of the individual Rights Commissioners, combined with an emphasis on adopting a pragmatic and flexible problem-solving approach, has contributed to the continued effectiveness of this service. Interestingly, despite the proliferation of employment rights-based disputes, the option to mediate remains an important resource for the Service in settling cases.

It is also apparent, however, that there are pressures on the system that will need to be addressed. The workload of individual Rights Commissioners clearly is becoming increasingly burdensome. At one level, this reflects the sheer number of cases being brought before the Rights Commissioners. The increasingly-complex legislative environment in which the Service now operates reinforces the burden of the workload. There is certainly a view that, at present, there are too many individual pieces of legislation. Additionally, resolving cases under a number of the more recent statutory instruments has proven to be a relatively-protracted process, especially where the decision or recommendation has the potential to establish important employment-related precedents. There also appears to be a need for more systematic consultation between the Service and those responsible for framing related legislation, in order to bring a greater degree of consistency to issues such as point of referral, sanction and appeal mechanisms.

Addressing these challenges will require an increase in resources and the development of a more appropriate administrative support structure. In this context, the plan to increase the number of Rights Commissioners to 14 is a positive development. Although this chapter has highlighted the importance of having in place highly-experienced and skilled practitioners, the changing nature of the Service may require that the process of recruiting highly-experienced HR/IR practitioners nominated by the social partners is reconfigured to expand the pool of potential Rights Commissioners and, in particular, to ensure that the Service retains the capacity to deal with the scale and scope of referrals to it. Finally, with the advent of more resources, there may also be scope for developing tighter time-frames around the hearings process and the issuing of decisions and recommendations.

2.6   SOCIAL PARTNERSHIP & THE LABOUR RELATIONS COMMISSION

2.6.1   A supportive relationship

The Labour Relations Commission is a product of national-level social partnership and, importantly, it has developed a strong supportive and complementary relationship with this national-level process. The social partnership's articulation of the benefits of consensual, co-operative industrial relations clearly provides a supportive institutional environment for the work of the LRC. The social partnership continues to address key parts of the industrial relations agenda that otherwise could lead to increased conflict within the labour market. Additionally, as noted earlier, the social partnership's emphasis on intensive dialogue and problem-solving in dealing with industrial relations issues adds momentum and support to the work of the Conciliation Service. It is suggested that the social partners' 'intensive propensity to communicate' has contributed to a more stable industrial relations environment, where people are able to understand each other, and that this creates a context more conducive to resolving disputes that continue to arise:

> "They (the social partners) may not agree with each other but they are capable of communicating more effectively. This fosters the development of trust – not just at the level of the enterprise, but at every other level you can think of." (Foley, 2005)

The Conciliation Service operates on the basis that process and dialogue are the main routes to dispute resolution and part of the impact of the social partnership has been to reinforce and endorse this insight.

The social partnership's articulation of the benefits of consensual, co-operative industrial relations also provides support to the developmental work that the Advisory Service undertakes with public and private sector organisations. Although some commentators have suggested that the social partners have failed to build sufficiently on their formal endorsement of workplace partnership in terms of becoming pro-active champions of this form of employment relations (see Gunnigle, 2000; Roche & Geary, 2001), they still provide varying levels of institutional support to activities designed to encourage more progressive industrial relations (O'Donnell & Teague, 2001).

However, this is very much a complementary and symbiotic relationship. A feature of the social partnership agreements is that they have all included a generalised voluntary commitment to industrial peace. A more recent development has been the establishment of an agreed set of mechanisms and institutional frameworks for the orderly processing of industrial disputes and grievances in relation to matters covered by the national agreement.[13] Securing the peace dividend that is associated with the social partnership, however, has been heavily dependent on the activities of the LRC, the Labour Court, the NIB and various informal and *ad hoc* arrangements that collectively form a robust and flexible network of interconnecting institutions focused on conflict management (Mulvey, 2005; Thomas, 2002; Teague, 2005). The LRC's continued capacity to resolve disputes, and to contain the overt manifestation of industrial conflict, has secured its position as one of the pivotal institutional supports for the social partnership process. At one level, this support is evident in the role played by the LRC in resolving a number of high-profile disputes that have had the potential to unravel support for the national-level partnership. More specifically, as the primary public dispute resolution agency, it has contributed directly to the securing of labour market stability, which is considered to be one of the key benefits of the social partnership and, as such, serves to legitimise its continuation. Moreover, the overlapping and supportive relationship between the LRC and the national-level social partnership was re-inforced during the course of *Sustaining Progress* (2003), due to the Commission's direct involvement in two key areas of activity directly linked to the social partnership process:

- The orderly resolution of disputes.
- Voluntary dispute resolution.

---

[13]   These frameworks include the Health Service National Joint Council and the Local Government Joint Council, discussed earlier in relation to public sector negotiating bodies.

2.6.2   *Sustaining Progress* – The orderly resolution of disputes

As the primary dispute resolution agency, the LRC has always had an indirect role in terms of securing compliance with the successive national agreements and, in particular, it has been careful to uphold the legitimacy of these national programmes in seeking to reach acceptable solutions to various disputes. Significantly, this role was institutionalised more formally in *Sustaining Progress* (2003), which afforded the Conciliation Service a designated role in an agreed set of detailed mechanisms for the orderly resolution of disputes in instances of:

- The employer pleading inability to pay the terms of the agreement (clause 1.10(ii)).[14]
- The employer seeking cost-offsetting measures to implement a pay award (clause 1.10(iii)).
- Disagreement around the issue of 'normal' ongoing change (clause 1.10(v)).
- Alleged breaches of the agreement (clause 19.9).
- Change in the Civil and Public Service (clause 22.2).

In relation to pay-related disputes (clauses 1.10(ii) and (iii)), an integrated set of consecutive mechanisms for resolving grievances was established, which included:

- Attempts at local resolution.
- Referral, if necessary, to the LRC for conciliation.
- The engagement by the Commission of an independent assessor to report on the economic, commercial and employment circumstances of the enterprise.[15]
- Further engagement with the Conciliation Service.
- Finally, if necessary, referral to the Labour Court.

In cases of referrals to the Court under clause 1.10(ii), the decision of the Court is binding. In contrast, the Court's recommendations on referrals under clause 1.10 (iii) are non-binding. However, under the terms of the National Agreement, in the event of the rejection of a recommendation, the parties must observe a three week 'cooling off' period before industrial action is proposed. In practice, up until the

---

[14]   These clauses refer to the relevant sections of *Sustaining Progress* which dealt with these matters.

[15]   The independent assessor was selected by the Commission from a panel of experts, nominated by the social partners.

end of June 2005, the Court's recommendation had been accepted in all but one case.

As indicated above, *Sustaining Progress* (2003) also established procedures for the resolution of disputes relating to 'normal ongoing change', alleged breaches of the agreement and disagreement over matters covered by the agreement. Finally, the Conciliation Service also was requested to facilitate in situations within the Civil and Public Service, where disputes arose in relation to verification of the change. Under these various clauses, by the end of 2005, the Commission had dealt with 87 pay-related cases, 23 cases relating either to ongoing change or to alleged breach of the agreement and five cases concerned with verification of change in the Civil and Public Service.

When first negotiated, some commentators suggested that these provisions potentially could be problematic, in part because they represented a further weakening of the voluntarist regime. This assessment, however, has proven to be misplaced and, indeed, it is important to note that the labour market parties *voluntarily* agreed to these mechanisms, including the provisions for binding determinations. From the Commission's perspective, these mechanisms have proven to be fairly effective, as evidenced by:

"... the low level of references to the assessor on the one hand and the low level of reliance on binding decisions of the Labour Court for resolution of disputes on the other." (LRC, 2005c)

In practice, the majority of cases are resolved at the conciliation level within the LRC or between the parties, following submission of the assessor report. To date, only nine cases have been referred to the Labour Court. Similarly, the labour market parties have displayed a clear willingness to use these agreed mechanisms to address issues in a pragmatic matter and the fact that *Towards 2016* (2006) re-affirms these dispute resolution procedures is testament to their perceived effectiveness.

There are a number of factors that appear to explain the relative success of these new procedures and it is worth briefly highlighting them as, arguably, they provide insights into how new mechanisms and/or procedures for dispute resolution potentially can be integrated into an established institutional context. The factors include:

- The considerable skill, flexibility and depth of experience that the Conciliation Service's own staff brought to the process.
- The professionalism and independence of the assessors.
- The LRC, NIB and the Labour Court all have adopted a robust and effective approach to implementing this agreed set of dispute resolution mechanisms.
- The labour market parties are fully aware of the robust and integrated nature of the mechanisms that are in place for

processing a dispute in instances where they fail to reach a satisfactory agreement. Arguably, this has served to constrain the actors towards reaching pragmatic solutions to disputes, as opposed to having solutions potentially imposed on them by a third party. The effectiveness of the conciliation phase of this process has been enhanced by the fact that failure to agree at this stage can lead to the appointment of an assessor with investigative powers. Equally, in relation to 'inability to pay' cases, the prospect of a binding decision being issued has empowered both the conciliation process and the standing of the assessor.

- Finally, it is important to stress that, while the detailed set of mechanisms agreed under *Sustaining Progress* (2003) were a new departure, they did not represent a sea-change in how disputes were resolved; instead, they were a further evolution in the industrial relations system and, indeed, the culture of dispute resolution that has emerged gradually in the period since the early 1990s. In this regard, a combination of pre-existing good working relationships and the labour market parties' understanding of, and familiarity with, the public dispute resolution system, allied to a general willingness to make the agreed process work ensured that 'the new mechanisms' were up and running relatively quickly and smoothly.

2.6.3   Voluntary dispute resolution

A second key strand of activity related to the social partnership process has been the Advisory Service Division's heavy involvement, during the lifespan of *Sustaining Progress* (2003), in processing cases under the Enhanced Code of Practice on Voluntary Dispute Resolution (S.I. No.76 of 2004). This Code provides a recognised framework for the processing of disputes in situations in which negotiating arrangements are not in place and where collective bargaining fails to take place. This Code represented a further development and enhancement of the pre-existing Code (S.I. No.145 of 2000), through the definition of a specific time-frame for the processing of claims under the Code and the 2001 and 2004 Acts (26 weeks, with a provision of up to 34 weeks) to the point of issuance of a determination, except when the parties agree to an extension. Under this process, the time afforded to the ASD for facilitating the resolution of issues in dispute was set at six weeks. Although the origins of the initial code on this issue (S.I. No.145 of 2000) were the deliberations of the High Level Group on Trade Union Recognition, established under *Partnership 2000* (1996), it is important to stress that this process is not about trade union recognition but about the resolution of issues in dispute other than trade union recognition.

Table 2.7 provides a summary of the S.I. No.76 cases referred to the ASD from mid-2004 up until the end of 2005. Over this period, the number of referrals has grown relatively quickly and, even though approximately half are not actually processed, the associated workload has grown considerably both in terms of the number of cases and also due to the dynamics involved in resolving the issues.

TABLE 2.7: ANALYSIS OF S.I. NO.76 REFERRALS

	Cases	Issues	Comment
S.I. referrals by end of 2005	**149**	**777**	18 cases (12%) with 10 or more issues.
Company did not engage	28	130	19% of all referrals.
Referrals withdrawn by union	17	75	11% of all referrals.
Cases ongoing	29	168	
Cases completed	**75**	**405**	This figure includes cases where all the issues were resolved at the LRC, where issues were referred to the Labour Court or where collective bargaining was negotiated.
Collective bargaining negotiated	6	33	8% of all cases completed.
All issues resolved at LRC	25	121	33% of all cases completed.
Issues referred to Labour Court	60	203	80% of all cases completed. Of these 60 cases referred to the Labour Court, there were 26 cases where 76 issues were resolved by the LRC.

Source: LRC Annual Report 2005.

The decision to give the ASD responsibility for processing referrals under this Code was due, in part, to its experience in dealing with non-unionised companies. Given the sensitivity surrounding this issue, there was also a perception that the Division's association with union-based collective bargaining was less overt than that of the Conciliation Service. In practice, however, staff from the ASD are essentially engaging in conciliation activity as they are involved in negotiating a resolution of disputes relating to core industrial relations issues such as pay, sick pay, overtime, grievance and disciplinary procedures.

While the skills and competencies are similar to those deployed in 'traditional conciliation' activity, there is a different institutional context associated with referrals under this Code, which invariably changes the dynamics of the process. First, unlike conciliation, which is premised on two parties voluntarily engaging in the process, referrals under S.I. No.76 involve a union bringing to the Commission a somewhat reluctant employer, whose preference is not to engage in collective bargaining. Second, the nature of the employment relations environment in such companies ensures that there has been little or no engagement on the issues at the local level and, therefore, the relevant IRO has no real foundation on which to build a sustainable negotiated settlement. The relatively tight time-frame of six weeks further compounds this situation and, in general, reaching viable agreements has proven to be a highly-pressurised process for the staff involved. Interestingly, this has resulted in an increased reliance on 'shuttle diplomacy' in seeking to reach a negotiated settlement. Consequently, aside from the growing number of cases, the pressure and difficulties associated with S.I. No.76 cases has ensured that the workload for the division is increasingly burdensome.

By the end of 2005, 75 cases, involving 403 issues, had been fully processed through the initial stage of S.I. No.76 and, of these, 202 issues were resolved at the LRC stage with the remainder (203 issues) referred to the Labour Court. Given the time delays associated with the initial Voluntary Dispute Resolution Code (S.I. No.145 of 2000), the introduction of specific time frames under S.I. No.76 was a welcome development, which has certainly improved how the process is managed. It has also served to allay one of the key criticisms that unions, in particular, had raised regarding this process. In retrospect, however, the designated time-frame may have been too tight, particularly as the ASD's own data suggests that, were the parties to agree to extend the time-frame, the resolution rate would be 12 to 15% higher.

An internal review by the LRC of the outcomes associated with S.I. No.76 referrals indicates that reaching a successful agreement at the LRC stage is dependent on a high level of co-operation from both employers and unions. In instances where both parties displayed a genuine effort to engage with the process, 66% of the issues were resolved at the LRC stage. This contrasts with a resolution rate of 14% when only the employers genuinely engaged, and a resolution rate of 27% when only the union fully participated.

From the Commission's perspective, this process has been moderately successful, as it is currently constituted. There is a degree of concern regarding the relatively high number of issues being referred to the Labour Court, although given the difficult institutional context in which these issues are being processed, the resolution rate achieved at the LRC is commendable. Aside from the growing number of cases and associated issues, the difficulties associated with this area of activity means an increasingly burdensome workload for the ASD. In this regard, the Commission has articulated the need for more time to be afforded to the ASD to resolve/engage on issues at the local level before entering formal conciliation, as this would assist both in improving the resolution rate at the LRC stage and in relieving some of the pressure associated with the process.

2.7   THE WORKPLACE MEDIATION SERVICE

2.7.1   The Workplace Mediation Service

In late 2005, on a pilot basis, the Labour Relations Commission launched its Workplace Mediation Service, aimed at providing an effective and tailored response to particular types of issues and disputes emerging within workplaces in Ireland. The LRC characterised this new service as:

> "... a voluntary, confidential process that allows two or more disputing parties to resolve their conflict in a mutually agreeable way with the help of a neutral third party, a mediator."

This new service is viewed as being suitable for addressing disputes involving individual or small groups of workers and, in particular, targets complex disputes that require sensitive and dedicated assistance in seeking a resolution, including:

- Interpersonal differences, conflicts, and difficulties in working together.
- A breakdown in working relationships.
- Issues arising from grievance and disciplinary procedures (particularly, before it becomes a formal matter).
- Industrial relations issues that have not been the subject of referral to the Rights Commissioner Service, Conciliation Service or another statutory dispute resolution agency.

2.7.2   The development and design of the Workplace Mediation Service

The key driving force for the development of the Workplace Mediation Service (WMS) was the perception amongst experienced staff that the growing individualisation of disputes, combined with the increased incidence of issues in the workplace that were highly personal in nature, potentially created a context in which there was real demand for a dispute resolution service with the capacity to resolve such disputes. Its development is indicative of an attempt to operationalise internal conceptual thinking regarding the need to design dispute resolution services that reflect broader workplace, societal and regulatory changes. The fact that the assigned project management team had pre-existing expertise of this discipline re-inforced the momentum for exploring the practicalities and potential of developing a workplace-focused mediation service. The decision to adopt a pro-active approach on this matter was further encouraged by the ongoing work of the Expert Review Group on Bullying & Harassment, which suggested that addressing highly-interpersonal disputes, often with a high level of emotional investment, would be a growing area of activity for the public dispute resolution system. Consequently, from a strategic perspective, it was considered important that the LRC was in a position to respond pro-actively to any potential recommendations from this policy grouping.

The presence of a small number of staff with a specialised interest in the area of mediation provided a platform for a relatively extensive process of intra-organisational consultation and debate, from which emerged a detailed proposal for the establishment of a dedicated Workplace Mediation Service. At the board level, there was an initial hesitancy in relation to this proposal, due to concerns regarding its potential impact on the delivery of other 'core services'. The eventual ratification of this initiative, however, on one level, was indicative of the Board's confidence in the expertise of the staff, as from start to finish this was very much an internally-driven experiment, albeit in response to external labour market dynamics. More specifically, its implementation re-affirmed the strategic objective of developing a dispute resolution system for all parts of the employment system. Although the WMS is somewhat experimental and challenging, it also accords with the philosophy of the Commission, which since its inception has displayed a willingness to develop an increasingly broad suite of programmes and services in response to changes in the workplace and the labour market.

A number of key elements collectively contributed to the design of the WMS. First, the fact that the individuals who made up the management team had both academic and professional experience of the mediation discipline ensured that they drew upon many of the accepted principles of good practice in relation to programme design;[16] this was re-inforced by the engagement with outside agencies during the formalised training phase. Second, it was decided from the outset that it was important to differentiate this new initiative formally from the existing Conciliation Service, due in part to the perception that outsiders might have of the latter. More

---

[16]   All three had a postgraduate qualification in this discipline and were also involved in the Mediation Institute of Ireland, the professional body for mediators operating in a broad range of fields: workplace, equality-based, family and commercial mediation.

fundamentally, it reflected the fact that, in terms of focus, types of disputes, approach, competencies and even the atmosphere/manner of interaction, this was to be clearly different from the existing collectivist-based conciliation and/or facilitation activities that the LRC engaged in. Equally, the architects of this service also were deeply wedded to the belief that it is not possible, nor necessarily advantageous, particularly in practice, to differentiate starkly between different dispute resolution approaches. Although, as already noted, the WMS was both experimental and new, according to one of its principal proponents:

> "It did not represent a dramatic sea-change for us, as in practice we view it as another approach along the spectrum of dispute resolution techniques from which we in the Commission draw upon in resolving disputes, albeit one that is evidently less directive, softer and requires additional skills to those honed in the area of conciliation." (Senior Official LRC, Authors' Interview, 2006)

Consequently, the WMS was envisaged as evolving out of, and being influenced by, pre-existing conciliation and advisory activity and, in practice, it was intended to be complementary to the existing activities of the Commission.

Fourth, it was decided that the development, management and implementation of the WMS would take place on an inter-divisional basis, drawing on the skills and experience of practitioners from both the Conciliation and Advisory Services. As the LRC's own strategy had highlighted, such co-operation has the potential to contribute to improving the calibre, quality and scope of the organisation's services. Although informal co-operation has been a feature of the LRC's work, it was considered important that this new service was established formally on a 'cross-divisional basis' and, indeed, both the three-person management team and the broader group of mediators are drawn from both divisions.

Finally, the deliberation about the design and focus of the WMS was shaped by the breadth of internal experience and skills within the organisation. This internal dimension was important, as the objective of this initiative was to design a customised and effective response to emerging workplace issues. It was essential, therefore, that this new initiative accorded with the strategic objectives of the organisation. These various elements all shaped the process eventually put in place – **Table 2.8** outlines the key design principles that underpin it.

TABLE 2.8: DESIGN PRINCIPLES FOR THE WORKPLACE MEDIATION SERVICE

Voluntary	Mediation can only take place if both sides agree, and any party is free to withdraw at any stage
Confidential	The process is private and confidential, unless the parties agree otherwise.
Solutions-focused	The purpose of the process is to reach a workable and mutually-agreeable solution to a conflict or issue of difference.
Impartial	The mediator is impartial and does not take sides.
Informal and user-friendly	The service is designed to foster trust and rapport with all parties.
Fast	It takes place as soon as schedules permit.

Source: Adapted from LRC Workplace Mediation Service Information Booklet (2005).

2.7.3 Building organisational capacity

In seeking to implement a new dispute resolution service, it was critical that the organisation had sufficient numbers of staff with the appropriate skills and competencies to deliver a high-quality, effective and expeditious workplace mediation programme. Consequently, the management team has focused heavily on building organisational capacity, by putting in place a customised, and comprehensive, training programme for the eight officers who volunteered for the mediation team.

Acas (see **Chapter 9**) was selected to deliver this programme, which was devised to reflect that the participants had a wealth of conciliation and facilitation experience and already had many of the skills that were relevant to mediation. The training focused on enhancing or refocusing these skills to the dynamics of workplace mediation.[17] In mediation, there is clearly a greater reliance on soft skills, such as empathy, listening, constructive summarising, rephrasing and normalising. As one of the designers noted:

> "... these types of soft skills or techniques can be used intuitively in a conciliation setting; however, there is a stronger reliance or emphasis on them within mediation." (Senior LRC Official, Authors' Interview, 2006)

---

[17] The design of this training programme was an iterative process between Acas and the WMS management team. Indeed, one of the latter became involved in the actual delivery of the programme.

The training also reflected the fact that the atmosphere of interaction with the parties is different from traditional conciliation, as is the language and tone of sessions. Similarly, while building relationships is a feature of conciliation activity, the personalised nature of mediation ensures that building trust and rapport with the parties is pivotal to its operation.

The strong focus on training and learning continued into the pilot roll-out phase, as the management team hosted regular meetings with the team to share experiences, highlight problems and identify good practice. Although time-consuming, this was seen as providing an opportunity to shape and improve the quality of the service. Finally, given the importance of building on practical experience, once they have undertaken a sufficient number of real cases, all of the mediation team will participate in a professionally-accredited advanced mediation training programme.

2.7.4   Implementing the Workplace Mediation Service

Although the WMS was launched in late 2005, the experimental nature of this initiative meant that it is operated initially in a pilot mode, in which there is a strong emphasis on closely monitoring and reviewing the process. Consequently, although it was advertised in the LRC's literature and on its website, deliberately there was no high-profile launch or active marketing campaign, due to a degree of uncertainty as to the volume and nature of referrals the service would receive. Certainly, the feeling of the management team was that, if the WMS delivered a credible and quality service, the volume of cases could grow very quickly.

The management team, who are also active as mediators, is responsible for case assignment and careful consideration is given to this process in order to maximise staff exposure to different types of situations. During the pilot phase, a system of co-mediation was put in place, with a view to encouraging reflection and learning between the officers concerned, something that is not available in conciliation, for example.[18] The emphasis on ensuring a user-friendly and informal service also informs the overall approach to case management. Unlike conciliation, in which the administration team is responsible for the scheduling of hearings, etc., as soon as a case is referred to the WMS, the assigned officer assumes responsibility for contacting the parties and scheduling meetings. This approach reflects the importance of personalising the service and building an early rapport with the parties, especially on issues in which there is often a high level of personal emotional investment. This less bureaucratic

---

[18]   Co-mediation also ensures that staff achieve more readily the threshold of cases necessary for embarking on the advanced training programme.

approach is also important, given that the majority of parties will never have interacted before with a public dispute resolution agency. Finally, as part of the emphasis on close monitoring and review, the management team meets on a weekly basis, in addition to monthly team-based review sessions. Although this close monitoring and review of the process in the pilot phase is seen as contributing to improvements in the quality and effectiveness of the service, it is also demanding in terms of time invested by already busy staff.

2.7.5   The labour market parties' perspective

The ratification by the board of this initiative indicates that the leadership of both ICTU and IBEC are supportive of this new dispute resolution service. In relation to individual trade unions, it was the LRC's perception that it would not face any principled or ideologically-based opposition to what many would consider a form of 'alternative dispute resolution'. Instead, the main challenge for the LRC was to overcome a degree of reticence from trade union officials regarding engaging with approaches about which they may know little. Incentivising engagement by officials, therefore, means demonstrating that mediation is particularly appropriate to the growing number of individual, sensitive and highly-personalised disputes for which neither traditional collectivist grievance procedures nor more formalised procedural arbitration appear particularly suitable. Certainly, the growing number of bullying and harassment cases that trade union officials are dealing with appear to fall into these categories, especially if the aim is to restore normal working relationships between the parties concerned. As was the case with the Equality Tribunal's mediation service, legitimacy, and consequently demand from trade unions, ultimately will depend on the effectiveness, quality and relevance of the service. Similarly, although employers tend to be more willing to engage with 'new forms' of dispute resolution, the same litmus test will apply. The fact that, even in the low-key pilot phase, the WMS generated a sufficient body of work suggests that the in-house assessment of the demand within the labour market for such a programme is correct.

2.7.6   Trends and benefits

Over its first full year of activity (2006), the Workplace Mediation Service was engaged actively in 24 cases, although the number of contacts and enquiries far exceeds this number. Of this figure, 14 cases were from the public sector, while the remaining 10 were from the private sector. Generally, the types of workplace dispute requiring mediation involve interpersonal workplace relationships, often between managers/supervisors and subordinates, and have tended to revolve around issues such as behaviour role and status within the workplace. Issues around disciplinary and grievance procedures have also arisen, together with workplace bullying. The majority of cases relate to individuals, although three cases concerned group issues, generally centred on group dynamics, relationships and reporting relationships. The fact that in its first full year of operation, albeit on a low key footing, this service was involved in 24 live cases and received even higher numbers of enquiries is indicative of the potential demand for mediation and appears tentatively, at least, to re-affirm the decision to put such resources and effort into developing it.

TABLE 2.9: POTENTIAL BENEFITS OF THE WORKPLACE MEDIATION SERVICE

It provides an opportunity for those involved to address the issues, explore options and reach a workable outcome through a mutually-agreeable course of action.

It creates a safe place for people to have their say and be heard, which is important in disputes that are not only personal, but in which there is often a high level of emotional investment.

The service is informal, user-friendly and non-adversarial, which is particularly advantageous when the parties have little or no experience of dispute resolution agencies.

The service is quick, as with immediate assignment, the mediator can speak to the parties and have a meeting within two weeks. This is extremely fast compared to other dispute resolution processes as, for example, it takes on average four months for the Rights Commissioners to hear a case.

There is potential for a high success rate in terms of the resolution of workplace disputes.

This service can generate both innovative and customised solutions to workplace disputes.

There is a strong focus on re-establishing normal working relationships, which research suggests is an outcome that the majority of parties want in seeking to resolve such disputes.

This process does not duplicate other dispute resolution services and, as a one-stop-shop for these issues, there is no scope for the parties to shop around the various public agencies.

Finally, even if the mediation process is unsuccessful, there is the opportunity for the mediator to assist the parties in agreeing a joint way forward in relation to the issues in question.

Because this service is still relatively new, strong evidence-based assessment of the benefits is not possible. However, experience of other similar mediation initiatives, in conjunction with the type of mediation service that the LRC has put in place, suggests that it has the potential to generate a number of benefits for individual employers, employees and employee representatives (see **Table 2.9**).

2.7.7 The future development of the Workplace Mediation Service

The development and implementation of the WMS is an important and innovative initiative for the LRC. In particular, this service brings the Commission into new terrain that is firmly focused on resolving disputes involving individuals or small groups. Although a new and innovative service, it did evolve out of the staff's existing skills and knowledge base and, from the outset, was internally-driven. In particular, it reflects the perception amongst experienced practitioners that changes in the labour market and workplace are generating a demand for this type of service. Additionally, while the WMS could be characterised as a form of 'alternative dispute resolution service', it does seek to build on and complement the existing range of services provided by the Commission.

However, it is important to recognise the level of investment in terms of staff time that went into planning and preparing this service – indeed, this continued in the pilot implementation phase due to the ongoing emphasis on monitoring progress and sharing good practice. Consequently, during 2007, the management team responsible for the Workplace Mediation Service undertook an internal evaluation as part of the wider intra-organisational discussions regarding the development of a new strategy for the LRC. Significantly, it was concluded that the Workplace Mediation Service was a successful development and that it should be fully integrated into the core suite of dispute resolution services offered by the Commission. Aside from the positive assessment of the initiative itself, this decision also reflects a consideration of the impact of the LRC being afforded a role in relation to mediation and investigation of bullying and harassment cases, as the skills and experience being developed in relation to mediation would feed directly into this process. It is recognised, however, that achieving this objective of integrating workplace mediation fully will require not only further internal reflection but also consultation with the key stakeholders and users of the Commission's services. At one level, this consultation will assist in the further refining of the service to ensure that it is relevant to the demands of users. Equally, it will have to consider how best to achieve this integration, particularly if the workload associated with this area increases substantially, and there is clearly potential for this. Such an occurrence would pose serious questions for the LRC in relation to the allocation of staff resources as, for example, all of the mediators at present are also either conciliators and/or advisors/facilitators. For this reason, the manner in which the WMS is developed further, integrated and, indeed, promoted will be an important exercise for the Commission.

2.8 ADVOCACY & AWARENESS-RAISING – REACHING OUT TO NEW CONSTITUENCIES

2.8.1 SME regional seminars and workshops

As was highlighted in **section 2.4**, preventative mediation is a core part of the work that the ASD undertakes with companies, in seeking to promote improvements in current employment practices and procedures. The ASD now is seeking to expand its preventative mediation focus into the SME sector. The primary catalyst for this new focus is the heavy and increasing usage of the Rights Commissioner Service by the SME sector, particularly indigenous companies. The fact that the vast majority of complaints are upheld highlights the limited HR capacity that exists within this sector. Indeed, in-house evidence suggests that the majority of SMEs that engage with the Rights Commissioner Service, not only are failing in relation to basic compliance with employment regulations, but have also failed to put in place accepted, and relatively standard, good practice in areas such as dispute and grievance procedures.

Since the User Satisfaction Survey suggested that there was a lack of awareness of the Commission's services, the ASD sought to promote good practice and to encourage compliance by hosting a series of regional workshops, aimed specifically at small and medium-sized employers. [19] These seminars provided information both on the LRC's services and on current good practice in a range of employment areas – for example, highlighting agreed Codes of Practice on various issues. By providing such information, and by encouraging SMEs to upgrade their current employment relations, the LRC aimed to ensure a greater level of compliance with existing regulations, thereby preventing disputes from emerging. These fora also facilitated employers in raising issues of interest to them and in seeking assistance on these matters from highly-qualified staff. Despite the fact that these seminars, like all of the LRC's services, were free, the attendance at them was somewhat disappointing. This highlights the difficulty that the LRC faces in seeking to penetrate sectors that traditionally do not engage with statutory third parties, unless it is in the context of a 'case' being brought to one of them. As part of this process, the LRC has sought, with limited success, to build stronger

---

[19]   The LRC and the Employment Rights Information Unit of the Department of Enterprise, Trade & Employment provided all the relevant information material at these workshops.

relationships with organisations such as the Small Firms Association and ISME (Irish Small & Medium Enterprises Association), athough, as noted earlier, many of the SMEs that decide to disregard their obligations under employment legislation tend to be outside of the remit of employer representative bodies.

2.8.2   Awareness-raising and information provision

One of the key areas of concern that was highlighted by the LRC's most recent User Satisfaction Survey was the lack of adequate information on, and insufficient promotion of, the range of services provided by the Commission. In seeking to address this concern, the Commission has undertaken a number of specific awareness-raising initiatives as part of a broader Information & Communications Strategy, co-ordinated by the Research & Information/ICT Unit (Advisory Service Division).

These activities have included:

- **LRC Service Guides:** A new suite of information literature in the form of information packs and seven stand-alone information leaflets has been developed.[20]

- **Corporate DVD and CD-ROM:** A film on DVD was commissioned and produced, with the aim of describing the organisation, promoting awareness of what it can achieve for existing and potential customers, and highlighting its contribution to the Irish economy.

- **LRC Wall-chart:** A wall-chart, detailing the various codes of practice and other general employment rights information, was developed and widely disseminated.

- **Workshops and Conferences:** As outlined earlier, the LRC hosted a series of regional seminars for SMEs that were designed to promote the services that the Commission has to offer companies in this sector. The LRC has also hosted a series of research seminars and conferences in recent years.

- **Website:** As part of the implementation of the Commission's ICT Strategy & Plan, considerable improvements were made to the content, navigation and image of the LRC's website. All of the Commission's publications are available on the website and, since 2005, it is possible to apply online for the assistance of the Conciliation Service.

---

[20]   Information leaflets have been developed on the following: Role & Functions of the LRC; Conciliation Service; Advisory Service; Rights Commissioner Service; Workplace Mediation Service; Codes of Practice; and Customer Service Charter.

As part of the overall awareness-raising strategy, the Commission also has sought to disseminate its material widely and, in particular, to reach beyond its traditional client base – for example, material has been distributed to the Citizen Information Centres. Similarly, in response to the emergence of a more diverse workforce and, in particular, the increased numbers of migrant workers accessing the Rights Commissioner Service, the LRC has sought to build stronger linkages with bodies such as the Migrant Rights Information Centre and has made its material available in a number of different languages, including Polish, Portuguese, Mandarin and Russian. Significantly, in 2006, more foreign-language information guides were downloaded than the English-language equivalents. Additionally, the LRC has distributed its multi-media pack to all second and third-level schools and colleges. Collectively, these initiatives represent a considerable improvement in the LRC's advocacy and awareness-raising activity and, as a consequence, there has been an unprecedented level of activity associated with the website.[21]

Although the Commission still finds it difficult to connect with companies in the indigenous SME sector of the economy, the continued growth of the indigenous SME sector, and the clear evidence that it is a major source of referrals to the Rights Commissioner Service, indicates that, given its national mandate, the LRC will have to continue to work to improve its linkages within this sector. This will involve continuing to explore and develop opportunities for opening up dialogue, addressing misconceptions and raising awareness of the skills and services on offer. Additionally, it is apparent that the LRC will have to continue to be innovative and forward-thinking in seeking to inform and engage with an increasingly diverse, multi-cultural and fragmented labour force.

2.9 CONCLUSION

This chapter has sought to highlight and examine the broad range of activities, services and programmes that the LRC oversees in providing an effective, flexible and integrated conflict management system. The willingness and, indeed, capacity of the LRC to provide this system, which continues to enjoy a high level of support and credibility amongst its key stakeholders, the government and the social partners, is attributable to a number of interrelated factors and characteristics.

---

[21] In 2006, there were 280,000 individual visits to the LRC's website, with the Rights Commissioners section recording the highest level of traffic. Overall, the number of visits to the website increased by 50% between 2005 and 2006 (LRC Annual Report 2006).

The LRC's encompassing statutory mandate has afforded the organisation the institutional scope gradually to increase its focus on dispute prevention and improving the quality of employment relations, whilst continuing to deliver a high-quality and effective dispute resolution service. Although the latter remains a core activity, it is now undertaken as part of a more diversified and integrated set of initiatives, services and programmes that seek to promote the development and improvement of Irish industrial relations, policies and practices. Additionally, this national mandate has been the catalyst for the LRC's recent attempts both to extend its reach into those sectors of the economy not covered by the scope of collective bargaining and also to address individual/small group disputes.

An integral feature of the LRC's evolution as a public agency concerned with conflict management has been the increased emphasis on the symbiotic and complementary relationship between the dispute prevention and dispute resolution activities. Although both the Conciliation and the Advisory Services will continue to focus on their core activities and have specific skills and competencies, it is recognised that increased inter-divisional and cross-functional cooperation has the capacity to enhance the calibre and range of services provided by the LRC. Although there has always been a degree of informal interaction between these two divisions, it has become a more prevalent and formalised feature of the work of the Commission. As highlighted in this chapter, the ASD co-ordinates training activities that involve staff from the Conciliation Service and even undertakes dispute resolution in respect of a specific code of practice. Similarly, in planning Working Together projects, the Conciliation Service worked closely with the ASD, and will continue to do so as these projects are rolled out. Interestingly, the Conciliation Service is committed to building a stronger preventative mediation element – a central part of the ASD's work – into its core dispute resolution activity. Finally, the Workplace Mediation Service is a formally-institutionalised expression of inter-divisional cooperation that highlights the potential of such collaboration to generate innovative new services.

The co-evolution of national-level social partnership has provided a strong, supportive institutional environment both for the LRC's dispute resolution activity and also for the development of initiatives designed to support more collaborative problem-solving by managers, employers and unions. However, this is a complementary relationship, as the Commission is an integral part of a robust and flexible network of interconnecting institutions focused on conflict management. In this context, the LRC's continued capacity to resolve disputes effectively ensures that it provides an important institutional support to the social partnership process.

The Commission's capacity to deliver what is an increasingly-broad range of quality services is heavily dependent on the high levels of skill, experience and commitment demonstrated by its staff. In particular, the LRC staff displays a high level of competency in a range of dispute resolution/prevention techniques and approaches, which is combined with a deep-seated knowledge of the industrial relations landscape and extensive contacts with the principal actors in the labour market.

Although evidently aware of the differences between various dispute resolution approaches (conciliation, facilitation, arbitration, mediation, etc. – see **Figure 2.1**), in practice, the LRC's officers do not operate within any strictly delineated definition of the skills and behaviours associated with a particular approach. Rather, these approaches are seen as occupying different positions along a dispute resolution continuum, where, in practice, there can be overlap between them. This continuum is viewed as providing a range of tools and techniques that officers can draw upon and adapt in seeking to generate an appropriate solution to a particular issue. This pragmatic problem-solving philosophy has enhanced the capacity of the Commission to provide a flexible, innovative and effective service to clients.

The evolution of the LRC also has been characterised by an important degree of innovation and experimentation. As indicated above, the establishment of the ASD had an experimental dimension to it from the outset and, indeed, its early years were characterised by a degree of uncertainty as to its precise role and identity. This element of innovation and experimentation has continued and is exemplified by the development of the Working Together projects and the Workplace Mediation Service.

Finally, the Commission is strongly of the view that the key to its success in delivering effectively on its statutory functions is that its services remain relevant to the modern Irish economy and, in particular, that these services are capable of responding to the speed and dynamics of change within the labour market and the workplace. Therefore, the LRC is committed to ongoing reviews of its services, working practice and organisational capacity, with a view to adaptation, experimentation and development, in order to meet the changing needs of employers, employees and their representatives. As this chapter has sought to highlight, the Commission undertakes a whole range of activities to ensure that it remains both effective and relevant, including:

- Undertaking User Satisfaction Surveys to identify client needs and concerns.
- Collaborating with other public agencies and third-level institutions to build research capacity.

- An emphasis on shared learning and exposure to international best practice.
- An ongoing review of its services, working practice and organisational capacity.
- Encouraging staff to experiment and develop new initiatives.
- Ongoing investment in staff training and career development.

2.9.1   The issues facing the LRC

Although this chapter has sought to highlight the effectiveness of the LRC in providing an integrated suite of dispute resolution and prevention activities, there are a number of issues that the organisation will have to address if it is to retain its capacity to deliver a high-quality service. As indicated above, the LRC is highly dependent on the skills and experience of its staff. Given the more complex and legalistic environment in which it now operates, and the emergence of an increasing number of disputes concerning protracted and highly-specialised issues like pensions, there is a concern that a continued reliance on recruitment from the parent department (Department of Enterprise, Trade & Employment), combined with ongoing investment in staff training and development, will be insufficient to equip the service with the range of skills it requires going forward. Therefore, there appears to be merit in re-examining this issue, particularly in light of the fact that, in other jurisdictions, similar agencies 'recruit' from the open market individuals with specialist skills and/or considerable experience in industrial relations/HR.[22]

Despite the dramatic decline in strike-related activity, the workload of the LRC – as indicated by referrals to the Conciliation Service and the Rights Commissioners, for example – continues to grow. Aside from the actual number of cases, there is clear evidence of an increasingly-burdensome and pressurised workload, due in part to the more complex regulatory environment, but also reflecting the characteristics of certain types of work, such as processing cases under the Voluntary Dispute Resolution Code or negotiating change within the public sector. As the number of cases is likely to continue to rise in the short to medium term, this re-affirms the importance of assisting organisations to improve their own in-house capacity for resolving/preventing disputes. Although this is one of the Commission's strategic objectives, it can be difficult to focus attention and resources on this issue when there is pressure on to resolve 'live' disputes in an expeditious manner. This appears to re-affirm the importance of the Commission's strategic interest in building into its

---

[22]   See, for example, the Canadian case study (**Chapter 8**).

conciliation framework a longer-term solutions-orientated focus, aimed at encouraging organisations to adopt policies and practices that will upgrade their in-house conflict management procedures. Although the development of such an approach is only at an embryonic stage within the Commission, and notwithstanding the associated sensitivities, there appears to be merit in the LRC exploring in consultation with the social partners the feasibility of fast-tracking a pilot project that aimed to achieve this longer-term outcome.

Given its status and role in relation to collectivist industrial relations, the LRC will continue to face considerable hurdles in seeking to extend its reach into sectors or companies that operate outside this environment. Although the ASD has built up linkages with non-unionised companies – providing them with advice and training, for example – the limited success of its SME regional workshops re-affirms the difficulties it faces in seeking to extend beyond its natural terrain. The continued decline in trade union density and collective bargaining, however, confirms that, if it wants to remain relevant, the LRC will have to develop ways of engaging with more elements of what is an increasingly-fragmented employment relations landscape.

In seeking to develop a more extensive range of services and programmes, it is important that the LRC retains its capacity to deliver its core services. To an extent, this has not yet been an issue for the Commission, as the newer types of dispute resolution/prevention initiatives have built upon, and complemented, the existing services provided. Indeed, there is no sense yet of such 'alternative' dispute resolution procedures in anyway replacing or undermining existing service provision.

It is important, however, to recognise the considerable resources that were invested in planning and formulating a new initiative, such as the Workplace Mediation Service. Additionally, if there is a proliferation of referrals to this service, or indeed a high level of demand for an initiative like Working Together projects in the public service, the consequence will be serious issues relating to allocation of resources. For example, a number of the mediators under the WMS are also conciliators and, as such, if the WMS becomes a more demanding service in terms of mediators' time, will it take priority over conciliation in terms of an individual's allocated workload?

Another matter that needs some consideration is the greater use of evidence-based management. In making policy, the LRC has sought to make judicious use of facts when deciding about the development of dispute resolution programmes. As noted above, it has made a conscious effort to collaborate with other public agencies and third-level institutions to build its research capacity with regard to employment relations issues. At the same time, however, the organisation has a substantial, and rich, internal body of information and data that perhaps could be marshalled in a more systematic and formalised manner to guide strategic decision-making. Given the importance of evidence-based policy development, the LRC should seek to strengthen its capacity to survey, collate and analyse external and internal sources of information, in order to develop better-informed profiles of both disputes and conflict management systems in industries and organisations. Such activity would facilitate the LRC in identifying those 'dispute' problems that need priority attention. Additionally, it would facilitate the Commission in selecting the most appropriate repertoire of policies for addressing such disputes in a more focused manner.

There also appears to be scope for exploiting more fully the LRC's considerable reservoir of knowledge and experience of workplace relations, particularly in relation to the ongoing development of employment regulation and legislation. Certainly, the degree of early consultation and interaction with the Commission on employment rights regulation, for example, is highly variable and often can be dependent on the section or individuals who have responsibility for progressing a particular piece of legislation. This often can lead to situations where the LRC finds itself adopting a re-active posture to recommendations contained in legislation prepared by its parent department. A more structured and regularised system of consultation between the LRC and those involved in drafting relevant legislation would have the potential, at the very minimum, to improve the consistency of employment rights legislation, in relation to issues such as first point of referral, sanctions and appellate mechanisms. Additionally, drawing on the knowledge of the LRC in this more formalised manner also could serve to engender a more pro-active developmental approach to the process of employment regulation.

The manner in which the LRC seeks to address these challenges in part will shape its future role and identity within the public dispute resolution framework. At present, the LRC is the primary agency for dispute resolution and prevention within the State and it is unlikely that this status will change in the near future. Equally, however, the LRC is seeking to reconfigure this identity in order to ensure that its services are relevant to the changing labour market. As such, it is seeking to develop a client base that includes unionised and non-unionised workplaces, SMEs and larger companies and groups of employees and individuals. To an extent, this represents the LRC's major challenge, particularly as its success to date means that there is very little external pressure for any major change in how it operates. Conversely, however, there is an equally strong argument that, in order to preserve its own particular identity in the long term, the LRC will have to undertake a degree of institutional change and, consequently, the current strategic framework of the LRC is premised on facilitating and encouraging such change.

3

THE LABOUR COURT & IRISH INDUSTRIAL RELATIONS

3.1   INTRODUCTION

Virtually all industrial relations systems have some form of semi-judicial body to address employment law and employment relations disputes. However, the functions of these bodies vary from country to country and their activities are usually deeply rooted in the industrial relations system to which they belong. The Labour Court is the oldest employment dispute body in Ireland and handles both industrial relations disputes and cases involving the vindication of employment rights. This chapter examines the role of the Court in Irish industrial relations, by examining the range of functions it carries out. It argues that the role of the Court has evolved considerably over the years and that it now acts, not only as a problem-solver of difficult industrial relations disputes, but also as a judicial enforcer of a tranche of employment rights. Through this activity, the Court establishes important conventions with regard to acceptable and unacceptable behaviour in the labour market, which contributes positively to industrial relations stability in the country.

The chapter is organised as follows:

- The first two sections (**sections 3.2** and **3.3**) assess the role of the Labour Court in industrial relations, its competencies and organisational structure, as well as its method of working.

- Then the role of the Court in supporting the regime of social partnership is examined (**section 3.4**).

- After this examination, the contribution made by the Court to the governance of industrial relations is explained (**section 3.5**).

- **Section 3.6** assesses the difficult issue of the role of the Court under the Industrial Relations Acts 2001 and 2004.

- **Section 3.7** evaluates the role of the Court in contemporary Irish industrial relations.

- The Conclusion brings together in **section 3.8** the arguments of the chapter.

3.2   THE ROLE OF THE LABOUR COURT

The Labour Court was established by the Industrial Relations Act 1946 to provide conciliation and adjudication services in trade disputes and to set up Joint Labour Committees, a Register of Employment Agreements and Joint Industrial Councils, institutions aimed either to promote orderly collective bargaining or to establish minimum pay rates and working conditions in vulnerable economic sectors. However, this early remit has been reshaped and enlarged, mainly due to continuous changes to employment legislation.[23] The Court has the competence to act in the following disputes: industrial relations, employment equality, organisation of working time, national minimum wage and fixed and part-time work. Most of the employment laws give the Court an appellate and enforcement function. The Court was also given the competence to hear appeals of decisions reached by other employment rights bodies, such as the Rights Commissioners. In addition, it was given the authority to make legally-binding orders, when the decisions of other employment rights bodies were not being implemented. Thus, for example, the Organisation of Working Time Act 1997 gave the Labour Court the role of hearing appeals from either employees or employers relating to decisions made by the Rights Commissioners and the ability to enforce legally the Rights Commissioners' decisions if these were not being implemented.

Perhaps the biggest change to the Labour Court was brought about by the Industrial Relations Act 1990, which led to the Conciliation Service it had operated for decades being transferred to the newly-formed Labour Relations Commission (LRC). Another important change to the Court concerned its involvement in employment equality matters: the Anti-Discrimination (Pay) Act 1974 gave the Court the responsibility to handle equal pay cases; however, in 1999, this function was transferred to the Equality Tribunal. Thus, the role of the Court has evolved over time.

The current mission of the Court is:

"... to find a basis for real and substantial agreement through the provision of a fast, fair, informal and inexpensive arrangement for the adjudication and resolution of industrial disputes".

---

[23]   The Labour Court's structure and functions have been changed by a series of amendments to the original Industrial Relations Act in 1969, 1976, 1990, 2001 and 2004. In addition, its areas of responsibilities have been increased, by the following legislation: Anti-Discrimination Pay Act 1974; Employment Equality Act 1977; Pensions Act 1990; Organisation of Working Time Act 1997; Employment Equality Act 1998; National Minimum Wage Act 2000; Protection of Employees (Part-Time Work) Act 2001; and Protection of Employees (Fixed-Term) Act 2003.

The Labour Court is not a court of law and operates more like an industrial tribunal. Its function is to provide a variety of services, free of charge, for the fast resolution of disputes. The Court seeks to act as a 'court of last resort', by which is meant that, whenever possible, an employment dispute should be settled by an organisation using in-house procedures. If the dispute cannot be settled internally, then public dispute resolution agencies, such as the Rights Commissioners and the LRC, should be used in an effort to reach a settlement; and only after these agencies have failed to obtain an agreement should the Court get involved in the case. In addition to being a 'court of last resort', the Labour Court also has the authority to investigate employment disputes if it is considered appropriate.

Formally, there are numerous ways a case can end up in the Court:

- **LRC referrals:** Sometimes the LRC's Conciliation Service is unable to find a mutually-acceptable settlement to a dispute and, at the request of the parties involved, the matter is referred to the Labour Court.

- **LRC waivers:** On occasions, the LRC will waive its conciliation function and pass the matter straight to the Labour Court.

- **Labour Court intervention:** The Court, in the context of a major industrial dispute, can take the initiative and invite the parties to use its services.

- **Ministerial intervention:** The Minister for Enterprise, Trade & Employment may refer a dispute to the Court.

- **Direct referral:** If an employer refuses to use the services of the Rights Commissioners to settle an industrial dispute, the employee or group of employees involved (or their representatives) can make a direct referral to the Labour Court, provided they agree in advance to accept the recommendation of the Court.

- **Appeals:** Either party to a dispute that has been heard by the Rights Commissioner, or investigated by the Office of Equality Investigations, can appeal the recommendation or decision. In the case of a Rights Commissioner, one of the parties can appeal to have the recommendation enforced.

3.3 THE ORGANISATION OF THE LABOUR COURT

The Court consists of nine full-time members, of whom three are nominated by IBEC, three by ICTU and three by government. Government-sponsored members fill the positions of Chairman and Deputy Chairmen of the Court. Only in exceptional cases do all nine members sit at the one hearing. The usual practice is for a hearing to consist of three members drawn from the respective constituencies. A team of civil servants, divided into five administrative sections that specialise in particular tasks, assists the Court. Hearings are held in Dublin and other parts of the country.

The Court can make 'recommendations' or 'determinations'. Recommendations set out the Court's assessment of a dispute and the terms on which it should be settled. These are not binding on the parties of a dispute but carry a high level of informal authority, as the parties to disputes are expected to give them due consideration. They are 'soft regulation' instruments. Determinations, which are binding, are made by the Court in cases that are appeals of decisions made by the Rights Commissioners and the Director of the Equality Tribunal. They are also made when the Court is dealing with cases involving breaches of registered employment agreements or infringements to legally-binding labour legislation.

Most of the cases dealt with by the Court are referred to it by another part of the public employment dispute resolution machinery – the LRC or the Rights Commissioners, for example. In referral cases from the LRC, the normal practice is to receive a written report from the Conciliation officer involved in the case, explaining why no agreement was reached at the conciliation stage. In cases relating to appeals of the Rights Commissioners' decisions, the Court not only receives all the relevant paperwork but also requests written statements from the various parties involved in the case. All written submissions must set out the factual background to the case and elaborate on the propositions of fact and law on which they are based. Written submissions are reviewed by the secretariat of the Court and, if they are considered deficient in any regard, the matter is raised with the relevant parties. Usually, the Court holds pre-hearing meetings to inform the parties of the nature of the upcoming proceedings, to discuss the legal issues involved in the case and to explore the possibility of reaching an agreement. Cases are dealt with expeditiously by the Court: the target is for a hearing to take place within 12 weeks of the date of the referral. Parties have six weeks to make formal submissions and to provide a full list of witnesses to be called.

Requiring the disputing parties to make formal written submissions and holding pre-hearing meetings is an important practice. Written submissions allow parties to gain a greater appreciation of the strengths and weaknesses of their case. Moreover, written submissions, along with pre-hearing meetings, allow the main interests in the disputes to be more clearly defined. Often, employment relations disputes, whether individual or collective, are fuelled by factors not directly relevant to the case – for example, personal animosities. Bringing the key issues of the dispute into focus makes the reaching of a settlement easier (Susskind *et al.*, 1999). Written information ensures that there is more information and greater transparency about the case, which should allow the parties to act in a more reasonable manner and allow the Court officials hearing the case to assess the merits of the competing arguments. These practices oblige the parties to justify their actions, focus on the interests in the case and think about possible avenues to the resolution of the dispute, and thus assist the Court in reaching settlements to disputes in a non-adversarial manner.

3.4   THE LABOUR COURT & SOCIAL PARTNERSHIP

The workload of the Labour Court has increased substantially in recent years. **Figure 3.1** shows that, between 1998 and 2005, the number of cases received by the Court has virtually doubled from 701 to 1,392. The number of cases completed by the Court has also been on an upward curve: in 2005, it completed a record 812 cases. However, even with increases in efficiency, the gap between the cases received by the Court and the cases it completes has widened. With its present resource-base, the Court has not been able to deal with the scale of demand on its services.

FIGURE 3.1: CASES COMPLETED & RECEIVED, 1998-2006

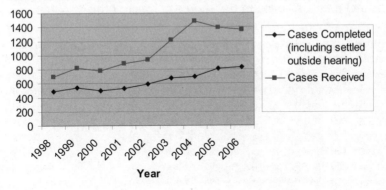

Figure 3.2 details the sources of the cases received by the Court. In the late 1990s/early 2000s, the largest source of cases were referrals from the LRC but, in recent years, direct referrals from trade unions and employers have been the major source of cases, which suggests that the social partners are finding it difficult to resolve disputes about the nature and interpretation of collective agreements in-house.

FIGURE 3.2: SOURCES OF CASES RECEIVED, 1998-2006

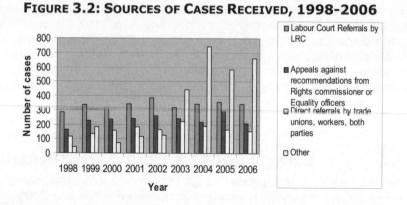

Year

Figure 3.3 shows that the Court deals mostly with industrial relations cases - about 90% of the Court's time is taken up with this activity. Each year, it deals with a relatively small number of cases in the areas of working time, national minimum wage and part-time and temporary work, even though legislation gives it a role in maintaining standards in these areas. **Appendix 1** sets out in greater detail the types of industrial relations cases that are dealt with by the Court. It shows that the broad area of pay, compensation (including allowances and bonuses) and pensions are the source of most of the disputes.

FIGURE 3.3: TYPES OF CASES COMPLETED, 1998-2006

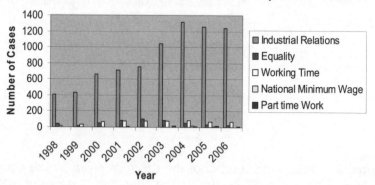

Year

The Court has to deal with a high number of disputes relating to the operation of National Social Agreements. These disputes relate to disagreements between the social partners about the procedures used to negotiate the local pay increase permitted by the National Agreement. The Court can also hear cases that relate to the payment of the rate increases set down by the National Agreement. About 90 such cases have arisen and all have been solved by the LRC: the Court has not got involved.

The continuing high number of industrial relations cases reinforces the point made in **Chapter 1** that small-scale industrial relations disputes persist inside many organisations. One possible explanation for this trend is the peculiar dynamics of the Irish system of social partnership. Certainly, this system has made a positive contribution to the historically-low levels of strikes and other forms of industrial action, and bodies overseeing social partnership, such as the National Implementation Body, have played an important role in preventing particular employment disputes. Moreover, although National Social Agreements are only concluded following an intense period of hard negotiations, a strong sense of interdependence and mutuality appears to have been forged between the representatives of employers and trade unions at national level: it is as if both have been captured by the social partnership system, as neither wishes to be the first to walk away from it. However, because the National Agreements have not operated in a highly rigid or centralised manner, the ties that tend to bind the social partners together at the national level have not been transferred to the organisational level (Teague & Donaghey, 2004). Thus, a fair amount of adversarialism remains between employers and employees inside some organisations.

In this situation, the Labour Court has operated as an important institutional support for the social partnership arrangement. By dealing effectively with the increasing number of small-scale employment relations disputes, the Court has prevented a fault-line emerging in the social partnership arrangement: unresolved ground-level disputes could have created an unfavourable employment relations environment for the operation of the National Social Agreements. However, the flip-side of this positive role is that some organisations may become too dependent on the Court when sorting out their human resource management problems: the danger is that the Court may be functioning as a 'court of first instance', which goes against its *raison d'être*. It is a weakness of the social partnership arrangement that it has not picked up on this growing trend of low-level disputes and done more to ensure that the same rules of the game that govern employer-employee interactions at the national level also apply at organisational level.

3.5   THE LABOUR COURT & THE GOVERNANCE OF INDUSTRIAL RELATIONS

Other important institutional mechanisms and procedures to govern particular industrial relations matters fall under the auspices of the Labour Court. One aspect to the work of the Court is to hear appeals against decisions made by the Rights Commissioners and the Director of the Equality Tribunal. In 2005, the Court dealt with 96 appeals relating to Rights Commissioners' recommendations, a number which is more or less the norm. The Court upheld the initial recommendation in 59 cases, revised the initial recommendation in 30 cases and overturned the initial recommendation in nine cases (the remaining case was deemed to be outside the competence of the Court). The number of equality appeals heard by the Court has been gradually declining, due to legislative changes. This is why it dealt with only 31 such appeals in 2005 (the figure for 2004 was 55). The Court upheld the initial recommendation/decision in 18 cases, revised one recommendation/decision and overturned the initial recommendation/decision in eight cases. These figures suggest that the Court does not operate simply as a rubber-stamping body for decisions made by other parts of the public machinery for the resolution of employment disputes, but it endeavours to act impartially in all cases, which no doubt adds to its credibility.

The Court has the responsibility to establish Joint Labour Committees (JLCs). These are statutory bodies that establish statutory minimum standards of pay and working conditions in particular sectors. At the moment, there are 19 JLCs in operation. The Labour Court provides a secretariat to support the activities of these bodies. The membership of a JLC consists of employee and employer representatives in the relevant sector and an independent chairperson. The task of the JLC is to agree terms and conditions of employment for particular employment grades or categories of workers. These agreements are published and submissions are invited, if employees consider their employment conditions to be inferior to those set out in the agreement. The JLC assesses each submission and, if it is considered to have merit, then the JLC can make a proposal to the Labour Court for the issuing of an Employment Regulation Order (ERO), which makes the wages and terms of conditions set out in the JLC's agreement legally-enforceable. If the agreement is breached, then the Labour Inspectorate can investigate the matter and a prosecution can follow. In 2005, the JLCs held 28 meetings and the Court made 17 EROs on request from particular committees.

Potentially, an ERO is a useful instrument to establish minimum labour standards in a particular industry. However, there are question marks about the effectiveness of EROs as regulatory instruments. One concern is that the contents of an ERO may not be disseminated sufficiently widely in the relevant economic sector. As a result, employers may not be aware of any changes made to pay and working conditions that have been made by the ERO, which potentially leaves them in violation of a statutory instrument and their employees without their correct entitlements. Thus, there appears to be a case for a more high-profile publicity arrangement to alert employers and employees of terms and conditions established by EROs.

Another problem is that the implementation of EROs is made difficult by certain of their clauses being difficult to understand or interpret precisely. Employers regularly complain that EROs are badly-written and lack clarity, thus making it uncertain which employees are covered by the instrument and which are not. Labour inspectors complain that EROs are difficult to enforce, because they have become outdated or sit badly with other pieces of employment legislation that regulate minimum wages and part-time work. Moreover, there is a worry that a JLC may not have the competence to provide clarification on the provisions of the EROs, particularly as to how these relate to other employment legislation. Thus, there appears to be considerable difficulties in actually operating EROs, which inevitably blunts their effectiveness as a regulatory instrument. A case appears to exist for a series of reforms to standardise the format of an ERO so that it is easier for employers and employees to understand and implement its terms and conditions.

The Court can also register, and thus give its *imprimatur*, to Joint Industrial Councils (JICs), voluntary bodies, consisting of employers and employees from a particular industry, which negotiate terms and conditions for the sector, provided they fulfil the conditions established by relevant industrial relations legislation. Currently, the Joint Industrial Council for the Construction Industry is the only operating JIC registered with the Court. Two other Councils exist – for State Industrial Employees and the Electrical Contracting Industry – but these are not registered. However, the Court provides secretarial support for these bodies, as well as for the JIC for Construction. The relatively small number of these essentially sector-level, collective bargaining arrangements reflects, in part, the lack of a tradition of employer/trade union interactions at this institutional level: the near 20-year regime of social partnership has reduced even further the incentive for employers and trade unions to engage in sector-level employment relations activities.

Notwithstanding this observation, the JIC for the construction industry is an important arrangement, being the body for the setting and enforcement of labour standards in the sector. The JIC oversees the pension arrangements for the industry, the sickness scheme, including levels of benefits, as well as rates of pay and conditions for particular occupations and crafts. It has also established the

Construction Industry Disputes Tribunal, which seeks to settle alleged violations of collective agreements within the industry. The Tribunal consists of three members: an independent Chairperson and employer and employee representatives. Agreed procedures are laid down for the handling of disputes, and appeals are permitted to the appropriate public dispute resolution body. Thus, the JIC establishes its own private form of industrial relations governance but, at the same time, it is also connected with the public agencies. Recently, the ability of the JIC to ensure compliance with labour standards in the industry has received considerable attention. The 'race-to-the-bottom' debate, which suggests that migrant workers are placing downward pressure on wages and working conditions, as well as displacing Irish workers, has stirred this interest. The construction industry is seen as one of the main sectors for these 'social dumping' activities. Thus, the JIC and its internal machinery are under some pressure to ensure that standard-setting violations are detected and put right quickly. Certainly, trade unions are closely monitoring the building industry and are likely to identify cases that will test the capacity of the JIC to address employment disputes on a collective basis. If the JIC is unable to settle such disputes, then the Labour Court is likely to get involved in these cases, which are usually high-profile. Thus, even though there are only a few Joint Industrial Councils, these arrangements have the potential to embroil the Court in highly controversial and emotive industrial relations disputes.

The Registered Employment Agreement (REA) is a further instrument that the Court can use to influence industrial relations behaviour and outcomes. REAs were an invention of the Industrial Relations Act 1946 and recently received a modern legal endorsement in the Industrial Relations Act 2004. An REA is an agreement on pay and working conditions, negotiated by employers and trade unions (or representatives of employees), which is registered with the Labour Court. Before an agreement can be registered, the Court has to be satisfied that it does not contravene any industrial relations legislation. The effect of registration is to make the agreement legally-enforceable in respect to every category of worker designated as being covered by the agreement, even if such a worker is not party to the agreement. A registered agreement can be altered, if the parties make an application to the Court; if the Court is satisfied with the application, then it makes an Order for the alteration.

Most of the collective agreements concluded by the JICs are registered with the Labour Court. Collective agreements reached at organisation level, both in the private and semi-State sector, can also be registered. Either party to an agreement can file a complaint with the Labour Court, if it considers that a breach has occurred to a registered agreement. If the Court upholds the complaint, then it may make an Order setting out what needs to be done to restore full compliance with the agreement. Any party that fails to comply with the Order is liable for prosecution. In essence, REAs are a way of giving voluntary collective agreements legal backbone. **Appendix 1** shows that the number of disputes relating to Registered Employment Agreements dealt with by the Court increased substantially in 2005, which reinforces the point made earlier that employers and trade unions are finding it difficult to keep within the terms of negotiated collective agreements.

These activities give the Court a number of overlapping functions in its effort to ensure that the governance of employment relations works smoothly and fairly. One function is that of appellate court – it provides a mechanism for people to challenge decisions made by other employment rights bodies. Another is that of arbitrator – it settles disputes about the operation of registered agreements in a manner that tie the various parties to what they had agreed to do. Yet a further function is that of standard-setter – it has the authority to establish minimum conditions relating to certain sectors and to take legally-enforceable action if these are violated. All these functions give the Court an important role in the smooth functioning of the employment relations system.

3.6   THE LABOUR COURT & THE INDUSTRIAL RELATIONS ACTS 2001 & 2004

Over the past few years, the Court has been busy with cases arising from the Industrial Relations (Amendment) Act 2001 and the Industrial Relations (Miscellaneous Provisions) Act 2004. These statutes make provision for the referral of disputes to the Labour Court, where it is the practice of the employer not to engage in collective bargaining. This is a hugely-contentious matter, as it deals with the sensitive matter of trade union recognition. Thus, it is important to deal with this matter fully. The best starting position is to point out that employees enjoy a constitutional right to union membership, but employers have also a constitutional right of free association: in effect, they have a right either to accept or to reject a request for union recognition. A persistent argument of trade unions is that they experience considerable difficulties organising workplaces, due to the absence of strong trade union recognition laws. D'Art & Turner (2005) suggest that this organising problem may be getting worse, as employer resistance to union recruitment campaigns is intensifying and becoming more sophisticated: new workplaces, in particular, appear to go to considerable lengths to avoid unionisation. New legislation to facilitate union recognition from employers has been a consistent demand of unions for more than a decade and is a major issue in national social agreement negotiations.

Gunnigle (2000) argues that the established public policy regime for handling union recognition disputes favours employers. Traditionally, the system worked as follows: the Labour Court dealt with union recognition cases by issuing a non-binding recommendation on how to resolve the dispute. Over the years, the Court typically made recommendations that supported employee demands for union recognition. Gunnigle *et al.* (2001) argue that a sizeable number of employers did not comply with these recommendations, because they faced no effective legal or public sanctions for adopting this approach. The main reason why no effective sanction could be introduced was that employers have a constitutional right of free association not to deal with a trade union. As a result, the enforcement regime to address trade union recognition problems was considered weak and ineffectual.

This matter produced heated exchanges in the negotiations preceding the signing of several national social partnership agreements. In 2000, the High Level Group on Trade Union Recognition, which was set up to devise a solution to the problem, proposed a new procedure to address employer and union concerns about union recognition in a two-part report.

The first part recommended that the Labour Relations Commission establish a Code of Practice on Voluntary Dispute Resolution. The LRC supported this recommendation and introduced such a code in October 2000. The code created a new procedure for resolving union recognition disputes, which starts when a union makes a claim on the company that relates not to recognition, but to an employment relations matter, for example, improved pay and conditions. If the company refuses to recognise the claim and collective bargaining does not occur, the claim can be referred to the LRC. The LRC first brings together the disputing parties in an effort to reach a voluntary settlement. If no resolution results, the LRC can make its own proposals. However, if these fail to produce a settlement, the parties are asked to enter a mutually-agreed 'cooling-off period', which normally lasts for about six months. During the cooling-off period, the LRC may engage expert assistance, including the involvement of ICTU and IBEC, to help solve the dispute. If the cooling-off period ends without the dispute being resolved, the LRC disengages from the process.

The second part of the High Level Group's Report set out the procedures to be followed in this deadlock situation. It is also the procedure invoked when an employer or union refuses to use the voluntary dispute resolution code. These procedures formed the basis of the Industrial Relations (Amendment) Act 2001. When the parties refuse to participate in the LRC's voluntary code, the Act allows the case to be heard by the Labour Court. Normally, the Court issues a non-binding recommendation on the substantive matters of the dispute: recommendations of the Labour Court cannot mandate collective bargaining between a union and employer. If this recommendation does not lead to a settlement, either party can ask the Labour Court for a determination, which more or less repeats the contents of the recommendation but also opens up two other possible resolution procedures. Under the first option, either party (but, in nearly all cases, the union) waits for 12 months for the determination to be implemented. If this does not happen, the party can go to the Circuit Court to have the determination enforced legally. Under the alternative option, known as the fast-track procedure, either party to the dispute can seek a review of the determination after three months. Provided that the circumstances of the case have not changed radically, the review simply re-affirms the initial determination. If the decision of the review has not been implemented within six weeks, the case can be brought before the Circuit Court for a legally-binding 'enforcement order'.

Some unions were unhappy with the 2001 Act, as it did not introduce any new regulation on trade union recognition disputes, and also because the procedures created were much too cumbersome. The focus was more or less on procedural matters, with the Act introducing a 'right to bargain' rather than a proper recognition procedure. This dissatisfaction caused the matter to figure once again in the negotiations leading to the 2003 social partnership agreement, *Sustaining Progress*. The procedures established by the Industrial Relations Act 2001 were revised by the agreement. Under the new deal, the government committed itself to providing the LRC and the Labour Court with the necessary resources to ensure that union recognition dispute cases are settled within a maximum time frame of 34 weeks, instead of the two-year period that was the norm under the 2001 Act. Under the new arrangements, the voluntary stage at which the LRC seeks to obtain a voluntary agreement lasts only six weeks. If no agreement is reached, then the case goes automatically to the Labour Court, which is obliged to issue a recommendation within three weeks. A trade union then has four weeks to seek a binding determination, which ultimately can be enforceable legally. Another part of the new package was a new victimisation code that clarified the meaning of the term. The new code is used by the LRC and the Labour Court when addressing cases involving allegations of victimisation against individuals involved in union-organising activity. These changes were made law in the Industrial Relations (Miscellaneous) Act 2004.

One of the unintended consequences of the Industrial Relations Acts 2001 & 2004 has been the creation of a 'shadow' form of collective bargaining in non-union firms. It must be remembered that the procedure set up by the Industrial Relations Acts 2001 & 2004 did not directly relate to trade union recognition, but enabled a trade union to raise an employment relations grievance, such as a claim for improved pay and conditions, at the Labour Court on behalf of employees in a non-union organisation. The thinking behind this procedure is that, if unions have the ability to pursue indirectly an industrial relations issue on behalf of non-unionised employees, then employers might be persuaded to recognise a trade union and establish a conventional collective bargaining relationship. Between 2002 and 2005, 52 cases were brought under this arrangement, but activity on the matter has gathered pace since the 2004 Act streamlined the procedure. Major unions, particularly SIPTU, have stepped up their activities on the matter. Most of the cases have involved small non-unionised firms that employ less than 50 people. In the majority of cases, the Court has backed the union case and the firms involved have been obliged to increase pay levels to identified going industry rates; in some cases, the percentage increase has been significant. In other cases relating to pay, the Court has instructed organisations to comply with the terms of existing national social agreements. However, the cases have not only related to pay. In one case, for example, the Court decided that the company should introduce a 39-hour week, which is commonplace in most unionised settings.

Only a few cases have involved large firms and multinationals. In some of these cases, the Court has sided with the employer against the union claim: the prevailing pay and working conditions were not deemed to be out-of-line with the unionised sector. There have been a few cases involving large firms in which the Court has sided with the union and these have caused a stir. In three cases, *Quinn Cement v SIPTU, Goode Cement v SIPTU/AGEMOU* and *Ashford Castle v SIPTU*, the Court has been obliged to issue legally-binding determinations, as the companies refused to comply with the initial recommendations. However, even after the Court issued these determinations, the three companies declared that under no circumstances would they cede trade union recognition.

The biggest *cause celebre* of the procedure has been the Ryanair dispute. Ever since 1998, there has been a trade union recognition dispute between the airline and its pilots. A number of high-level initiatives were made to resolve the dispute, without much success. In 2004, a dispute arose within Ryanair, as a result of the company's decision to convert its Dublin fleet. Part of the conversion involved retraining pilots, who were told that they could either pay the €15,000 cost of training or sign a bond abandoning their entitlement to raise matters with the Labour Court. Some of the pilots wanted this proposal to be negotiated by Impact, a trade union to which they belonged, but Ryanair refused to negotiate with the union. The matter ended up at the Labour Court at the end of 2005 and, at a preliminary hearing, it ruled that a trade dispute existed between Ryanair and Impact, which opened the door for the Court to use the provisions of the Industrial Relations Acts 2001 & 2004. Almost immediately, the airline referred the matter to the High Court, which, however, ruled that the Labour Court had the jurisdiction to address the case. The company reacted to this decision by referring the matter to the Supreme Court, which overruled the High Court judgment and found in favour of Ryanair. Without going into the details of the ruling, this judgment is likely to make Labour Court proceedings related to cases brought under the Industrial Relations Acts 2001 & 2004 more formal and legalistic. This is likely to increase the time and costs involved in taking such cases and could also make it more difficult to pursue such cases successfully.

Overall, the experience so far suggests that the 'right to bargain' procedures set out in the Industrial Relations Acts 2001 & 2004 have had an impact on the pay and working conditions of some small firms and, at the same time, generated considerable controversy, involving a select number of large firms. Interviews with employer organisations suggest that none of the organisations that have been brought to the Labour Court under the legislation have conceded union recognition: they remain non-union companies.

One suggestion is that the procedures have led to a shadow form of collective bargaining, whereby the Labour Court effectively transposes pay and conditions from the unionised sector to the non-unionised sector. Too much weight should not be put on this view. For a start, it must be remembered that the Court has dealt with only about 52 cases under 'the right to bargain' procedures, which is minuscule relative to the number of non-union firms that exist in the country. Moreover, the Supreme Court ruling in the Ryanair case is likely to confine the standard-setting role of the Labour Court under the two Acts to relatively low wage sectors: its ability to 'shadow bargain' for employees in non-union companies in high wage sectors may well have been emasculated by the ruling.

3.7   THE ROLE OF THE LABOUR COURT IN A NEW INDUSTRIAL RELATIONS ENVIRONMENT

The Labour Court is a key aspect of the Irish public machinery for the resolution of employment disputes. When it was first established in 1946, it was seen initially as acting as an industrial relations tribunal to resolve disputes between employers and unions. The rationale for creating the Court was to provide an expert panel to help settle difficult industrial relations disputes in an inexpensive and informal manner. Since its formation, the remit of the Court has expanded significantly. Perhaps the most important new area of competence is employment rights. Jurisdiction in this area started when Ireland joined the EU in 1972 and the Court was given responsibility for employment equality rights under European law. This involvement in the adjudication of employment rights cases has expanded ever since, in line with the growth of employment rights legislation.

Thus the Court has now a multi-purpose role but, in each of its activities, it seeks to advance socially-responsible employment relations practices. It tries to do this by remaining true to its core mission of providing fast and inexpensive arrangements for the adjudication and resolution of industrial disputes. Sometimes, this is solely a matter of assessing whether an infringement has occurred to legally-established employment rights or existing collective bargaining agreements. However, often it has to go beyond this role and construct the meaning of reasonable employment practices and behaviour in a particular industrial relations situation or in relation to a particular piece of legislation. It is obliged to perform this interpretative role for two reasons:

- Collective agreements between employers and trade unions sometimes are not drafted precisely, which opens up the possibility of conflict about whether a particular policy or practice is in line with the spirit and intent of the agreement.

- A piece of employment legislation may be insufficiently prescriptive on a particular matter, thus requiring the Court to establish the type of practices that are consistent with the initial intentions of the legislation.

Thus, because labour legislation and collective agreements can be incomplete, the Labour Court not only must adjudicate employment disputes but must also help to establish order and predictability in the labour market by framing what is acceptable and unacceptable employment relations behaviour. Thus, the Labour Court plays an important problem-solving role in the employment relations system. It reduces a lot of the indeterminacy and ambiguity associated with the employment law, social partnership and collective bargaining systems. As a result, it makes a positive contribution to the maintenance of employment relations stability.

Customer care surveys suggest that it carries out its various functions in an efficient manner. The Court is considered to be accessible and fair, delivering an objective and timely service. All the evidence suggests that the Court enjoys a high level of legitimacy, as it is widely seen as an integral part of the employment relations system in Ireland.

At the same time, the Court faces a number of challenges when carrying out its work. When the Court was first established, it was envisaged as operating in an informal and non-legalistic manner but, over the years, this objective has more or less faded away, as the operation of the Court has become increasingly legalistic. The officials of the Court continually lament this development but, in truth, it was almost inevitable, due to the expansion of employment legislation. People increasingly think of themselves as legal subjects and, as a result, almost automatically turn to lawyers when they become involved in an employment dispute. This situation is unlikely to change in the foreseeable future; legalism is here to stay. As a result, the Court has to adopt its structures to this new environment. The legal support given to Court officials may have to increase and the legal training they receive may have to be intensified.

Another challenge is the increased number of small-scale employment relations disputes handled by the Court. A number of factors are likely to be behind this development. One is that, as pressure intensifies on organisations to improve performance, so the push for workplace change also increases. Workplace restructuring invariably means disrupting established ways of doing things; the potential for workplace conflict increases considerably in these situations. The danger for the Court is that it becomes involved in these cases too early, due to a trade union or employer attempting to use it as an institutional lever to advance their respective case against the other. As a result of this tactic, the Court may become a 'court of first instance' rather than a 'court of last resort'. Getting drawn into disputes too quickly, not only overloads the case work of the Court, but it can also damage the integrity and status of the Court: its identity as an authoritative semi-judicial body may be undermined, if it gets drawn into the bargaining games of employers and unions. It is difficult to see how the Court on its own can address this issue. Instead, it needs to work more closely with the LRC and Rights Commissioners to devise effective strategies to make these institutions more effective buffers between workplace disputes and the Court.

Perhaps the biggest challenge to the Labour Court is the sizeable growth in the non-union sector. This challenge comes in two parts. The cases arising from the Industrial Relations Acts 2001 & 2004 touch on one aspect of this challenge. Some of these cases that relate to large non-union firms are proving quite controversial, as the organisations have displayed considerable reluctance to comply with the rulings of the Court. In other cases, it is suggested that the Court may be attempting to push out the boundaries of the legislation so that it acquires competence to act in a wider range of employment relations matters in the non-union sector. The Supreme Court ruling in the Ryanair case effectively has put the brakes on this strategy, to the extent that it was being pursued. Stepping back from the specifics of particular cases, a struggle is ongoing over the role of the Labour Court in the non-union sector. On the one hand, non-union organisations, in the main, want to see the Labour Court with a minimal role in determining whether organisational employment practices are consistent either with a particular piece of employment legislation or with the national social agreement; on the other hand, the Court wants to enlarge its role in the non-union sector, in order to maintain its relevance in the Irish business environment. It is too early to predict the outcome of this tussle.

The other dimension of the non-union challenge for the Labour Court relates to the workings of the Joint Labour Committees. These bodies were first set up to establish a floor for pay and working conditions, mainly in economic sectors where there was a high level of precarious employment and low pay. Although these bodies continue to operate, they do not appear to have the same relevance as they had in the past. This is an unfortunate situation, as there has been a significant growth in employment in low-wage, vulnerable sectors. Thus, just at a time when more standard-setting is required, there appears to be a fall-off in the activities of the agencies designed to establish these standards. This is not the direct responsibility of the Labour Court, as it is up to the social partners to ensure that JLCs operate properly. At the same time, JLCs come under the aegis of the Court, so it has an indirect responsibility to revive the activities of bodies that could play a very important role in creating a safety net for the least well-off employees in Irish society.

3.8 CONCLUSION

Economies and societies are evolving all the time. As a result, there is an onus on public institutions that promote order and stability to keep abreast of these changes. Failure to do so may result in them losing functionality – they are no longer able to carry out the tasks they were put in place to do. A loss of functionality can very quickly turn into a loss of legitimacy and then lead to obsolescence. Adapting to change requires public institutions to undergo internal reform to acquire new competencies and tasks – sometimes, it even requires internal mutation. We can see that the Labour Court has been very successful in adapting to change. Sometimes new roles were imposed upon it by legislation and, other times, it was the result of autonomous internal action. The upshot is that, while the key motivations for establishing the Court – providing a quick, accessible and impartial service to resolve disputes – may have stayed the same, its competencies have expanded considerably. The Court has successfully absorbed these new activities and retained its status as a body that seeks to carry out its duties fairly and with integrity. Adapting to change invariably generates controversies and causes difficulties for the Court: mapping out its role under the Industrial Relations Acts 2001 & 2004 is one example of such a controversy.

Developing stronger working relationships is the chief lesson that the LRC should take from this chapter. Over the years, the LRC and the Labour Court have enjoyed close informal links, not least because they share the same premises. However, there have been few formal connections that have involved the two agencies launching joint initiatives. Yet the scope for such initiatives appears to exist. Joint legal training for Rights Commissioners and Labour Court members might be productive, as it might result in the two bodies interpreting employment legislation in a similar way. The recent problem of small-scale collective employment disputes relating to the interpretation of collective agreements might be addressed more successfully if the two bodies worked closely together on the matter. Similarly, the desire on the part of the Court to restore its role as a court of last resort may be realised more easily through joint work with the LRC. The rationale for greater joint working is simple: doing things together may allow the LRC and Labour Court to address matters that might remain beyond the reach of each agency if they acted separately.

APPENDIX: CASES TO THE LABOUR COURT, BY CATEGORY OF DISPUTE

Category of dispute	1998	1999	2000	2001	2002	2003	2004	2005
Allowances, bonuses, premiums	25	39	48	34	35	56	61	54
Contracting out	2	1	1	4	1	2	2	5
Demarcation	1	3	0	1	1	0	0	1
Discipline	23	20	6	13	16	14	19	13
Dismissal	65	44	61	39	56	48	30	42
Equal pay	9	10	27	7	3	5	0	9
Equal treatment	31	21	25	31	57	40	12	8
Hours of work, Working time	10	39	45	48	47	63	8	12
SLC/ERO	1	0	0	1	0	1	0	0
Lay off	9	3	9	9	8	1	0	0
Leave	6	4	10	5	14	8	11	15
Local agreement procedures	18	17	33	24	41	32	55	75
Other disputes	2	0	0	0	0	0	2	0
Overtime - shift pay	15	8	8	6	12	11	13	17
Pay claim (other)	90	99	91	130	138	121	84	106
Pay claim under National Agreement	9	18	4	22	23	34	28	38
Pension/Insurance	18	18	19	16	21	28	30	47
Productivity	2	14	1	6	26	4	5	4
Promotion/Demotion	23	28	25	23	13	33	46	36
Promotion	1	0	0	0	0	0	0	0
Recruitment	8	4	1	3	5	2	5	4
Redundancy	16	30	20	29	26	40	37	46
Registered Employment Agreements	7	15	43	16	11	25	52	76
Relocation	5	14	6	6	10	10	10	18
Reorganisation/Rationalisation	19	16	20	18	14	12	11	7
Shift work	4	4	2	5	2	4	3	6
Sick pay	9	5	2	4	5	6	12	10
Temporary employment	2	3	1	0	1	2	4	3
Union Recognition/Negotiating rights	7	10	7	8	4	17	10	16
Uncategorised	29	0	0	0	0	0	0	0
Training	0	0	0	0	0	1	0	0

4
DEVELOPING AN ALTERNATIVE DISPUTE RESOLUTION CAPACITY – THE EQUALITY TRIBUNAL'S EQUALITY MEDIATION SERVICE

4.1 INTRODUCTION

This chapter of the report explores the development and evolution of the Equality Tribunal's Mediation Service, which was introduced in 2001 as an innovative and alternative form of dispute resolution for claims of alleged discrimination. In particular, this chapter explores:

- The development and design of the new Mediation Service (**sections 4.2** and **4.3**).
- How the process works (**section 4.4**).
- The operational outcomes (**section 4.5**) and benefits (**section 4.6**) associated with mediation.
- The perception of the service from a users' perspective (**section 4.7**).

Going forward, the chapter then:

- Considers an issue that has emerged in other jurisdictions as to the appropriateness, from a public interest perspective, of using mediation in a human rights-based context (**section 4.8**).
- Assesses the key lessons for the Labour Relations Commission from this example of a public agency actively mainstreaming a new and innovative form of dispute resolution (**section 4.9**).
- Assesses the future challenges to the Equality Mediation Service in the Conclusion (**section 4.10**).

4.2   THE EQUALITY TRIBUNAL: STATUTORY ROLE & REMIT

Established in 1999, the Equality Tribunal[24] is an independent quasi-judicial statutory body, whose core function is to mediate and/or investigate complaints of unlawful discrimination under the following legislation:

- Employment Equality Acts 1998-2004.[25]
- Equal Status Acts 2000-2004.[26]
- Pensions Acts 1990-2004.

Although established initially to address complaints of employment-related discrimination, the evolution of a more comprehensive legislative framework has resulted in the Equality Tribunal's statutory remit being extended to cover complaints of unlawful discrimination on the nine protected grounds (gender; marital status; disability; race; age; membership of the travelling community; family status; sexual orientation; and religion) in relation to employment, occupational benefits (for example, pensions), the provision of services and accommodation, the disposal of goods and property and in certain aspects of education.

TABLE 4.1: REFERRALS TO THE EQUALITY TRIBUNAL, 2000-2006 (GROUPED)

Referrals	2000	2001	2002	2003	2004	2005	2006
Employment equality	102	182	254	244	296	399	448
Collective agreements	0	0	0	3	1	2	0
Equal status	7	*854	597	366	185	223	166
Pensions Act	0	0	0	0	1	7	14
Overall Referrals	**109**	**n/a**	**851**	**613**	**483**	**631**	**628**

Source: Equality Tribunal Annual Reports, 2000-2006.

*   This figure refers to individual claims referred under the Equal Status Act, as no figure for grouped cases was provided for this year.

---

24   Until 2002, the Equality Tribunal was known as the Office of Director of Equality Investigations (ODEI). On the establishment of the ODEI in 1999, the Equality Service of the Labour Relations Commission was transferred to this new body.

25   Cases on the ground of gender may be brought to the Circuit Court.

26   Since mid-2005, cases relating to licensed premises must be brought to the District Court.

As is evident from **Table 4.1**, this expansion in the jurisdiction of the Tribunal has generated a substantial rise in the number of cases (grouped)[27] of unlawful discrimination being referred to the office since 2000. It is envisaged that the level of referrals will remain relatively high as a result of both a rise in the generality of cases under the Employment Equality and Equal Status Acts and the immediate impact of recent legislative changes. For example, under the Equality Act 2004, the Tribunal took over first instance jurisdiction for discriminatory dismissal and victimisatory dismissal from the Labour Court and, between 2005 and 2006, there was a rise of 12% in the number of cases relating to discrimination in work dealt with by the Tribunal. Indeed, since 2004, the number of employment cases has risen by 50%, including a dramatic rise in the number of claims on the grounds of race and a very high number of claims alleging dismissal for discriminatory reasons. The Tribunal also is operating now in a more complex legislative environment. Notwithstanding the very low starting base, the number of cases alleging discrimination in relation to pensions doubled between 2005 and 2006. Additionally, these cases have proven to be both time-consuming and complex for the Equality Officers involved. Conversely, there was 25% fall in the number of equal status cases between 2005 and 2006 and this decline was particularly marked for cases brought on the grounds of age.

Overall, as legislation has bedded down, the Tribunal has noted that a significant number of cases pose increasingly complex legal issues that require intensive research and close scrutiny of the governing legislation. While many cases continue to turn on questions of fact, equally during the course of 2006 the Tribunal issued decisions on a range of areas that clarified the law. This combination of a relatively high number of cases and the growing complexity in the issues raised and the precedent case law is exerting considerable pressure on the Office and its staff, both in terms of an increasingly burdensome workload and a considerable backlog of cases awaiting redress.

4.2.1   Investigation

As indicated above, the Equality Tribunal can deal with referrals of alleged discrimination *via* two different, though not mutually exclusive, routes: investigation and mediation.

The traditional, and longer-established, method for processing complaints of discrimination is through an Equality Officer conducting a quasi-judicial investigation into a referral. In such cases, Equality Officers have extensive powers to enter premises, including workplaces, and to obtain information to enable them to conduct their

---

[27]   The Tribunal's statistical information is given as grouped cases rather than individual claims. Each case can have more than one complainant and, overall, in 2006, for example, more than 7,000 individuals made complaints to the Tribunal.

investigation. A key part of the investigation is a request for written submissions from both the claimant and the respondent in a case. The Equality Officer then will arrange a formal joint hearing(s) of the case, at which each party has an opportunity:

- To present their case.
- To call witnesses.
- To respond to points raised by the other party.
- To answer questions from the investigating Equality Officer.

These quasi-judicial proceedings provide invaluable information on the case. On completion of the investigation, the Equality Officer issues a written decision, setting out the reasons for deciding in favour of either the claimant or the respondent. These decisions are legally binding, and are also published by the Tribunal both in written format and on its website. In effect, the investigation process is like an Equality Court and, indeed, has been described as a 'court of first instance' (Teague, 2005).

Significantly, in the context of this chapter, since 2000, the Equality Tribunal has provided a Mediation Service as an alternative dispute resolution process to that of investigation, in respect of claims for equal pay in employment and complaints of discrimination, harassment, sexual harassment and victimisation under the Employment Equality Acts 1998-2000, the Equal Status Acts 2000-2004 and the Pensions Acts 1990-2004. The remainder of this chapter, therefore, involves an analysis of this particular alternative dispute resolution process.

4.3   ESTABLISHING & DEVELOPING THE EQUALITY TRIBUNAL'S MEDIATION SERVICE

The Equality Tribunal's Mediation Service was launched formally in March 2001, with the stated aim of providing an innovative and alternative avenue of redress to the quasi-judicial investigation process in respect of claims of unlawful discrimination arising under the respective Irish equality legislation.

From the Tribunal's perspective, mediation is characterised as:

"... a process whereby a neutral and impartial third party (equality officer) facilitates the parties in a dispute to explore their area(s) of dispute and, where possible, to assist them in reaching a mutually acceptable settlement. The mediator, who has no power to impose a resolution, empowers the parties to negotiate their own agreement on a clear and informed basis, should each party wish to do so." (Equality Tribunal, 2002)[28]

Significantly, the basis for the establishment of this Mediation Service was a formal commitment in the original establishing legislation, the Employment Equality Act 1998 (Section 78), to provide such a service and, indeed, similar commitments were also enshrined in subsequent equality legislation.[29] Although it was possible under the pre-existing equality legislation to bring discriminatory claims to the Labour Court for conciliation/mediation, in practice, this option was rarely exercised. Establishing mediation as a statutory option within the new and expanded equality legislation therefore, was an attempt by the legislators to encourage the wider usage of alternative dispute resolution procedures in addressing claims of unlawful discrimination by making it a statutory-based option. In particular, the legislation provides that:

"If at any time after a case has been referred to the Director ... it appears to the Director that the case is one which could be resolved by mediation, the Director shall refer the case for mediation to an Equality Mediation Officer".

Although the legislation establishes mediation as a statutory-based option, on a par with investigation, it remains a voluntary process and, indeed, the Acts clearly stipulate that mediation cannot proceed if either party objects. The option for parties to engage in mediation remains open until the day of a formal investigatory hearing and the investigating Equality Officer can adjourn a hearing to give the parties the chance to revolve the case by mediation.

As is evident from **Table 4.2,** the number of referrals to the Mediation Service, and the number of cases completed, has grown considerably since 2001. In relation to referrals, there has been a three-fold increase in the number of cases, while the number of completed cases more than doubled between 2002 and 2006.

Significantly, in 2004, the Director of the Tribunal chose to exercise the statutory power to assign all cases to mediation where neither party objected, thus establishing mediation as the default option in relation to claims of unlawful discrimination under the relevant legislation. The process remains voluntary, but the onus is now on the parties to object to engaging in mediation. Additionally,

---

[28]   This description is adapted from the Equality Tribunal (2003 & 2006). This working definition was clearly influenced by the work of the US academics Bush & Folger (1994), who described mediation as: *'Mediation is generally understood as an informal process in which a neutral third party with no power to impose a resolution helps the disputing parties to reach a mutually acceptable settlement'.*

[29]   See Equal Status Act 2000 (section 24) and the Pensions Act 2004.

this change in policy does not constrain in any way an individual's right to have their case investigated, as it remains the case that, where either party objects or withdraws from mediation, or if the process does not result in a mutual agreement, the complainant may seek an investigation and the issuing of a decision by another Equality Officer from the Tribunal.[30]

TABLE 4.2: MEDIATION REFERRALS & OUTCOMES, 2001-2006

Year	Referrals to Mediation	Completed Mediation Cases (Resolved & Non-Resolved)
2001	56	19
2002	105	64
2003	109	105
2004	253	95
2005	249	124
2006	223	150

Source: Adapted from Equality Tribunal Mediation Reviews, (2002 – 2006).

This change in strategy was stimulated primarily by the growing backlog of cases being generated by the increased number of referrals to the Tribunal (see **Table 4.1**); the capacity of mediation to progress cases more speedily than the investigative route was seen as the optimum way of reducing the backlog.[31] The immediate impact of this policy shift is highlighted by the dramatic increase of 132% in the number of referrals to mediation during 2004 and, while the number has fallen subsequently, it remains relatively high (see **Table 4.2**). Although more effective case management was the primary catalyst for this policy shift, it is also indicative of the increased capacity of the Mediation Service, and the growing confidence in this alternative dispute resolution process as a viable and appropriate avenue of redress for claims of unlawful discrimination. Interestingly, some of the mediators have indicated that this shift also has increased the number of cases coming to mediation where one and/or both of the parties are not prepared for, or willing to, engage in

---

[30] In such cases, in accordance with the Tribunal's commitment to confidentiality, the relevant Equality Mediation Officer may not pass on any information that was revealed during a mediation session to the appointed Investigator.

[31] Similar reasoning has also been evident in other jurisdictions, where mediation-style initiatives have been introduced and/or expanded to address a backlog of human rights/equality cases. See, for example, Kochan *et al.* (2000) and Zweibel & MacFarlane (2001).

mediation.[32] In part, this may account for the 36% increase in the number of non-resolution agreements that were issued in 2005, though importantly, the overall resolution rate remained approximately the same as the previous year. It may be that this initial upturn will drop, once clients and their representatives become more aware of the fact that mediation is now the default option unless an objection is raised. Despite the fact that mediation is a much quicker process, the substantial increases in the number of referrals to mediation now is creating a consequential backlog in this area as well, to the extent that the Equality Tribunal is actively exploring the possibility of outsourcing some of its burgeoning caseload to an external panel of accredited mediators.

4.3.1 Building capacity and designing mediation principles

In seeking to fulfil the statutory mediation mandate afforded to it, the Tribunal faced two immediate challenges:

- Building its internal capacity to deliver a Mediation Service.
- Developing and designing the guidelines, practices and approaches that would shape how mediation was conducted.

Given the interrelationship between these challenges, it was important that the Tribunal addressed them in tandem.

In relation to the challenge of building internal organisational capacity, in 2000, the Tribunal provided mediation training for an initial group of five Equality Officers. This training was sourced from the Mediation Institute of Ireland (MII) and was based primarily on the style and practice used in family mediation, at the time the predominant influence within the MII. In practice, this proved to be an interactive process, with participants bringing their knowledge and experience as Equality Investigators to bear on the training, to ensure that it was adapted to their particular needs. This initial training phase continued as the Mediation Service was implemented, as the mediators had to participate in a number of actual mediations in order to secure Part 1 Accreditation with the MII.[33] This initial foundation was augmented subsequently by additional training, though this later training was delivered by mediators with expertise in intra-organisational conflict resolution and thus was even more customised to the ongoing work of the Mediation Service.

---

[32] Experience to date suggests that parties to a dispute rarely respond to correspondence that informs them that they must object to a case going to mediation; instead, they tend to raise their objections in person, once the process has started.

[33] No Equality Officer is permitted to take mediations on their own, without having first attained MII Part 1 accreditation.

Since 2000, nine members of staff have undergone mediation training and have been professionally accredited by the MII. The Tribunal remains committed to ongoing professional learning and training as part of its strategic objective to expand the service it currently provides.[34]

The Mediation Service also initiated formalised peer group sessions that provided the mediators with an opportunity to discuss relevant issues, share experiences, highlight problems and identify good practice. In recent years, in part due to the pressure of work, this initiative has become moribund and, interestingly, a number of officials highlighted the potential value of re-establishing these structured learning sessions. As is evident from the number of referrals and mediated outcomes (see **Table 4.2**), from a virtual standing start, the Tribunal has built a considerable capacity to deliver an effective and high-quality mediation service. The quality and level of training and professional development provided has been a vital element in this development, as was the fact that the participants in the training were already highly-experienced equality practitioners.

As they underwent training, the Equality Officers also were developing the principles and guidelines that would underscore the operations of the Mediation Service. Interestingly, the legislation was fairly non-descriptive in this regard, merely outlining a number of basic protocols for the new service (see **Table 4.3**).

TABLE 4.3: STATUTORY-BASED PROTOCOLS FOR THE MEDIATION SERVICE[35]

Once a case has been referred, the Director has the authority to refer the case for mediation to a Mediation Officer. Mediation cannot take place if either party objects.
Mediation shall be conducted in private.
If the case is resolved, the Equality Mediation Officer shall record the terms of the settlement in writing.
The written record shall be signed by the complainant and the respondent.
The written record, when signed, shall be legally-binding and enforceable (subject to the limits on redress set out in the Acts).
A copy of the written record is retained by the Tribunal.

---

[34] As of mid-2006, one Equality Office had attained Part 2 Accreditation, while a number of the team were currently undertaking training towards this professional level. In addition, one of the Mediation Team successfully completed a Masters Degree in Mediation & Conflict Resolution in 2005.

[35] See Employment Equality Act 1988 (s.78) and Equal Status Act 2000 (s.24).

TABLE 4.4: THE PRINCIPLES OF MEDIATION AT THE EQUALITY TRIBUNAL

Consent	If the Director of the Tribunal considers a case could be resolved by mediation, it will be referred to an Equality Mediation Officer. If either party objects to the case being dealt with by mediation, the case will not be referred. Both parties will be asked whether they object to a mediation referral.
Impartiality	The Mediation Service guarantees impartiality and does not take sides with either party.
Voluntary process	Mediation is a voluntary process and mediation cannot proceed if either party objects. Likewise, each side may withdraw their consent at any stage of the process and mediation will be terminated immediately. The complainant may request the resumption of the investigation, as laid down in the Act.
Accessibility	The Mediation Service is committed to ensuring accessibility for all persons. Special arrangements, as appropriate, will be put in place for any person with special needs who wishes to use the service.
Participation	It is essential that everyone necessary to reach a settlement participates in the mediation process.
Power-balancing	The Equality Mediation Officer has a duty to ensure balanced negotiation and to prevent manipulative, or intimidating, negotiation techniques.
Third parties	Third parties (advisors or representatives) are welcome at mediation. The Equality Mediation Officer will facilitate all parties involved in reaching an agreement and will discuss, at the outset of the mediation, how best third parties can contribute to the mediation process.
Advice	The Equality Mediation Officer will give information only in those areas where s/he is qualified to do so by training and experience. Where the mediation may affect other rights and obligations, the Officer will advise the parties to seek independent advice.
Issues for discussion	It is the responsibility of the parties to identify, if necessary with the help of the mediator, the issues on which they wish to negotiate. The parties are responsible for the terms of any settlement they reach.
Confidentiality	Mediation is conducted in private and none of its activities or proceedings, including the terms of any settlement reached, are published.[36]
Joint sessions	Mediation is normally conducted in the presence of all participants; however, in some instances, with the consent of both parties, it may be beneficial to hold bilateral negotiations.[37]
Disclosure	The mediation process is premised on the full disclosure to both parties of all the relevant information to a dispute.

---

[36] The Service further guarantees that any information disclosed to an Equality Mediation Officer remains confidential to the Mediation Service and will not be released to an investigating Equality Officer, if the dispute is not resolved at mediation and the investigation is resumed.

[37] In such instances, the conditions and procedures for bilateral discussions will be clarified and agreed with the parties beforehand.

Settlement	Once each party has signed up to a settlement, the agreement becomes legally-binding and may be enforced on application to the Circuit Court.
No settlement	If agreement cannot be reached, and it appears to the Equality Mediation Officer that the case cannot be resolved by mediation, then a notice to that effect will be issued to both parties. At this stage, the complainant has 28 days to lodge a referral and seek an investigation of the case.

Source: Equality Tribunal Mediation Review 2005, pp.20-21.

Although, on the one hand, this presented the Tribunal with a considerable challenge, equally, it afforded considerable latitude to customise and tailor a dispute resolution process that accorded with the needs and mandate of the organisation. As is evident from **Table 4.4**, in developing this alternative avenue of redress, the Tribunal incorporated the basic legislative protocols into a much more robust and comprehensive set of principles that have served to shape and underscore the operation of the Mediation Service.

4.3.2   A flexible and customised mediation model

Critically, in operationalising these principles, the Tribunal has developed its own flexible and customised model of mediation that draws from a range of mediation orientations such as the Milan, Narrative, Future-focused and Transformative Models (see **Table 4.5**) and also incorporates elements of labour relations negotiation and conciliation:

> "We have evolved a service of our own. We would have considerable experience at this stage. Employment and equal status mediation consists of a little bit of industrial relations, of commercial mediation and of family mediation." (Gerry Hickey, Head of the Tribunal's Mediation Service, *Industrial Relations News*, No.36, 2005)

The evolution of this flexible and customised mediation model reflects the impact of a combination of factors, including exposure to international best practice; the professional training that was provided; the knowledge and experience of the Equality Officers, the comprehensive set of mediation principles above and the relatively expansive statutory remit of the tribunal.

The initial family mediation-style training was certainly influential, both in terms of some of the key principles that were adopted originally and also in relation to some of the core skills and instruments that are used in conducting equality mediation. Significantly, however, the Mediation team, drawing on their own professional experience, gradually expanded beyond the relatively-limited focus of the Milan-type model,[38] to develop and implement a process and associated set of principles more appropriate to the types of issues, problems, concerns and challenges generated by the diverse range of discrimination cases now referred to the Tribunal as result of its expansive statutory remit. The type of approach adopted is heavily dependent on the nature of the case being processed, although different mediators also have their own style and preferences. For example, where the relationship between the parties has ended, or where it was a once-off interaction, a version of the Milan-type orientation might be the most appropriate. In circumstances where there is an ongoing relationship, and where repairing and/or improving this personal association would be beneficial, the Transformative or Future-focused model is more suitable. In other instances, where it is clear that both parties are focused on the financial compensation element of an eventual agreement, the process can resemble industrial relations-type bargaining.

TABLE 4.5: MEDIATION ORIENTATIONS

Milan (family mediation model)	The emphasis in this approach is on providing a mutually-agreed settlement around a number of core issues, in situations in which a relationship has broken down.
Transformative model	In this approach, the focus is on understanding the parties' perceptions, feelings, interests and concerns, so as to assist them in transforming their attitudes or thinking. This model is considered particularly appropriate where there is an ongoing relationship between the parties (working relationship or service provider).
Future-focused	Although similar to the transformative model, in that there is an emphasis on building understanding, within this orientation, there is a stronger focus on influencing, for the better, how the parties will act (behaviour/practices) in the future.
Narrative-style	In this approach, the parties give their version of the events and the role of the mediator is to draw out the main issues, merge the versions, remove the personalised emotional content, moderate the language and get agreement on what happened, so that the parties can move on and identify what needs to be done to prevent this occurring again. In essence, this approach represents a more focused, and intensive, version of the opening dialogue that is an integral part of all mediation sessions.

There is a strong degree of overlap between the different orientations outlined in **Table 4.5** and, in practice, the Equality Mediation Officers will draw on and combine elements from different approaches in

---

[38] Given its roots in family mediation, the Milan model tends to be associated with situations in which the relationship has broken down, and in which there is a focus on a number of limited issues – in the family context, this tends to be the issues of finance, children and property.

seeking to facilitate the parties in reaching an agreed settlement. The capacity and willingness of the Tribunal to provide a flexible and customised dispute resolution process reflects both its growing confidence in this discipline and also the considerable skill and experience of the organisation's staff, as ultimately the effectiveness of the service is dependent on the quality of the in-house team of mediators.

4.4   THE STRUCTURE OF MEDIATION: HOW THE PROCESS WORKS

Although the preceding section highlighted the flexible and customised nature of the Tribunal's Mediation model, there is also a well-established structure to the conduct of mediation sessions, premised on four inter-related stages, as outlined below:

- **Introduction:** After an explanation of the guidelines and principles underlying the mediation process, the session begins with both sides being offered an opportunity to tell their side of the story. This dialogue is a critical element of the mediation process and, in many instances, it is often the first time that the two parties have spoken to each other since the alleged incident(s) of discrimination.

- **Identification of the issues**: The Equality Mediation Officer assists the parties, based on the opening dialogue, to identify the gap between them and the key issues that need to be addressed. Unlike an investigation, the Mediation Officer makes no findings in fact or law and cannot take a position on the case in question. The parties are asked how they might see the dispute being resolved and, if they wish to negotiate on particular aspects of the framework, the Mediation Officer assists them.[39]

- **Agreement:** If the basis of an agreement is reached, the Equality Mediation Officer will prepare a written record of the settlement, which is forwarded to each party. There is then a 'cooling off' period, to allow the parties to make an informed decision, including if necessary taking advice from a third party, as to whether they want to consent to the draft agreement. If they accept the agreement, it is signed by each party and, once this occurs, it becomes a legally-binding document that may be enforced.

---

[39] In some cases, these latter discussions on the finer details of a possible settlement will take place with each side separately at a side-conference (caucus).

- **Non-resolution:** If agreement cannot be reached, and it appears to the Equality Mediation Officer that the case cannot be resolved through mediation, a Non-Resolution Notice is issued to that effect. Once this is issued, the complainant has 28 days to make an application for resumption of the investigation of the case. If this is not properly made within this time period, the Tribunal ceases to have jurisdiction in the case. In a number of cases, Non-Resolution Notices are not required, even though no resolution has been reached within the mediation process. This occurs in cases, where, after engaging in mediation, the parties either have settled the dispute between themselves or the complainant has decided they do not want to pursue the matter further, and as such the case is considered closed.

4.4.1   The mediator: Role and core competencies/skills

As indicated in the definition of mediation provided earlier (see **section 4.3**) the primary role of the Equality Mediation Office is to facilitate dialogue between the parties and to assist them, where possible, in reaching a mutually acceptable settlement. In this regard, it is essential that the mediator is capable of building a rapport with the parties and of creating an atmosphere in which they are prepared to discuss openly issues in which there is often a high level of personal emotional content.

Within the mediation process, it is important that the Equality Mediation Officer remains impartial and independent. As experienced investigators, all of the Tribunal's mediators are experts in equality legislation; however, unlike an investigation, they are not there to interpret the law or to decide on the facts and they cannot take a position on the relative merits or validity of the case in question. Additionally, it is important that the mediator does not allow their views on how the same issue would be dealt with in an investigation to colour how it is processed in mediation. In seeking to embed this principle of 'neutrality', the Equality Mediation Officer does not consult the case files prior to a mediation session – in essence, the first time s/he hears the case is in the opening narratives from the participants. At times, this practice can be problematic, especially in cases in which there is a considerable history with which the other participants are *au fait*; however, in balance, it is still considered by the Tribunal to be the optimum approach.[40]

---

[40]   The only concession to this protocol is in cases where there is a degree of commercial complexity and, in such instances, it is considered appropriate for the Officer in question to familiarise themselves with the context of the case in question.

It is also apparent that participants often expect the Equality Mediation Officer to take a more directive and interventionist role in the mediation process. For example, they often ask for the Officer's opinion of the validity of their case or seek answers to specific issues. In accordance with the Tribunal's mediation principles, an Officer cannot give advice to either side but can point to sources of information (for example, Equality Officer Decisions) or advice (for example, trade unions or Citizen Information Centres). Similarly, the Officer cannot give an opinion on how a party should proceed in the course of mediation, as again this would be an infringement of the principle of neutrality.

Within a structured session, the mediator's role is to assist the two parties to reach an acceptable agreement. The mediator has no power to impose a settlement and it is essential that neither party feels pressurised to reach an agreement. Indeed, it is considered inappropriate for a mediator to assume, or suggest, from the outset that the parties should compromise on what they regard as their principles and statutory rights. This clearly contrasts with industrial relations-type conciliation where, in essence, the assumption that a compromise will be reached is the underlying dynamic of the process; more specifically, the role of the conciliator in this context is to guide or direct pro-actively the parties towards what the conciliator perceives as an acceptable solution.

Following the opening narratives from the participants, the mediator uses a range of techniques – reframing, constructive summarising, normalising, etc. – to facilitate the parties in identifying both the actual problems, which are often hidden, and the core issues, relevant to the act, that need to be addressed in seeking to reach a resolution. While the mediator will frame the basis of a proposed settlement, the parameters of such agreement must originate from suggestions made by the parties. For example, if it became apparent that it was important that a particular practice did not occur again, the mediator might suggest that the respondent develop a relevant code of practice or policy statement. The impetus for such an initiative, however, must stem from the parties; it cannot be suggested, merely because the mediator thinks that it is standard good practice in such cases. This necessitates a degree of balancing by the mediator, for while s/he will assist the parties actively in teasing out solutions they have in mind, the mediator must not recommend or suggest their own preferred solutions, even though participants often have an expectation that this is part of the mediator's role. In contrast, in an industrial relations context, a conciliator will frequently draw on their own expertise to suggest solutions or ways out of an impasse and thus both will craft the terms of a potential agreement and will encourage acceptance of it. In writing up a proposed mediation settlement, the mediator clearly has a pivotal role in ensuring that its tone, language and content reflects the mediation proceedings and is the basis for a possible resolution. Ultimately, however, ownership of the agreement lies with the parties and, although it may be requested by one or both participants, the mediator cannot make any value judgement as to whether they consider it to be a 'good agreement or not'.

As already indicated, the capacity of the Tribunal to deliver a customised and flexible Mediation Service that is fair, effective and expeditious is dependent on the quality of its staff and **Table 4.6** outlines the range of skills and competencies that Equality Meditation Officers themselves identified as being necessary to undertake equality mediation. Although this is a composite list, in that not every skill/competency was highlighted by each interviewee, it does give an indication of the range of skills, techniques and instruments that an experienced mediator will draw upon within equality mediation.

TABLE 4.6: EQUALITY MEDIATION CORE SKILLS & COMPETENCIES

Legislative knowledge	Reframing
Managing the dynamics of the process	Rephrasing
Listening	Empathy
Patience	Constructive summarising
Power-balancing	Normalising

Source: Authors' Interviews with Equality Mediation Officers.

Within a mediation session, the mediator is responsible for managing the dynamics of the process and for ensuring that both parties are comfortable with engaging in this form of dispute resolution. Given the highly-personalised and emotional nature of many of the cases, there is a strong reliance on skills or techniques such as reframing, constructive summarising and normalising in seeking to stimulate a dialogue that can assist the parties constructively in reaching a possible resolution. Reframing involves the mediator translating for one party what the other is 'exactly saying' and it is particularly useful where there are considerable differences in the participants' educational and/or economic status and/or their access to third party representation. Such situations may also necessitate the mediator engaging in 'power-balancing', whereby they 'intervene' within the process to ensure that both parties are being given a fair hearing within the mediation session and that no party is disadvantaged because of their relative economic and/or educational status. In using this technique, the mediator must strike a balance between intervening, power-balancing and retaining the overall context of impartiality.

"It is a delicate exercise ... having established your neutrality and independence at the start of the process, once the session starts you (the mediator) may sway back and forward and delicately intervene to ensure there is a power balance, that is the process is fair to both sides ... while, at the same time, ensuring that at the end of the process, both parties' confidence in your impartiality and independence has been retained". (Authors' Interview with Equality Mediation Officer).

The mediator is also responsible for managing the inputs and interactions of any third-party representatives and, again, if not handled appropriately, this can dilute the effectiveness of the mediation process.

The capacity of the Tribunal to provide a highly customised service, capable of adapting and combining a range of approaches to suit these different contexts, reinforces further the importance of having in-house a highly experienced team of professional mediators. This was re-affirmed by the Tribunal's User Survey, which revealed that both complainants and respondents (92% of survey respondents) expressed high levels of satisfaction with the role played by individual mediators. In this regard, the Tribunal has clearly benefited from the fact that, to date, it has managed to retain a core complement of highly-experienced Equality Mediators.

4.5   OPERATIONAL OUTCOMES

As noted above, the ongoing evolution of the Equality Mediation Service and, in particular, the decision to establish 'default mediation' has resulted in a substantial expansion in the number of case referrals (grouped and individual) to mediation under the relevant equality legislation. This section of the chapter is concerned with outlining the key operational outcomes from this process, including a brief examination of the terms of the mediated settlements. **Table 4.7** describes the main elements of mediation outcomes in the period 2002 to 2006, in terms of both resolved and non-resolved cases under both the Employment Equality and Equal Status legislation.

As is evident from **Table 4.7**, the number of resolved cases – that is, mediations reaching agreement – increased by 12% between 2005 and 2006 and, indeed, the total of 84 cases for the latter year is the highest figure ever recorded by the Equality Mediation Service. In addition, **Figure 4.1** shows that the number of cases resolved through this avenue of redress has increased substantially since the launch of the initial Mediation Service in 2001. This increase is an indication both of the considerable expansion of the Mediation Service and also its emergence as a credible mechanism for resolving equality related disputes. Interestingly, however, the number of non-resolved cases – that is, cases in which the Mediation Officer issues a 'non-resolution notice' – also has increased significantly since 2001. As already suggested, this rise might be a reflection of the impact of the shift to default mediation (see **Figure 4.2**).

TABLE 4.7: MEDIATION OUTCOMES (COMPLETED MEDIATIONS), 2003-2006

Mediation Outcomes	2003		2004		2005		2006	
	Resolved	Non-resolved	Resolved	Non-resolved	Resolved	Non-resolved	Resolved	Non-resolved
Employment Equality Acts 1998 - 2004								
Single	30	23	24	15	42	32	62	50
Group	0	1	0	3	1	2	3	6
Subtotal	30	24	24	18	43	34	65	56
Equal Status Acts 2000 - 2004								
Single	25	8	28	11	29	14	16	9
Group	9	9	7	7	2	1	3	1
Subtotal	34	17	35	18	31	15	19	10
All Equality Legislation								
Single	55	31	52	26	71	46	78	59
Group	9	10	7	10	4	3	6	7
Total	64	41	59	36	75	49	84	66
Resolution Rate	61%		62%		61%		56%	

It is important to note that this policy shift does not appear to have exerted a major impact on the resolution rate, though the rate did drop from 61% to 56% between 2003 and 2005 (see **Figure 4.3).** More importantly, the resolution rate enjoyed by the Mediation Service has increased from the first two years of the service's operation and, since 2003, it has enjoyed a resolution rate of between 56% and 62%, which is considered by the Tribunal to be a very satisfactory level of achievement.

FIGURE 4.1: CASES RESOLVED BY EQUALITY MEDIATION, 2001-2006

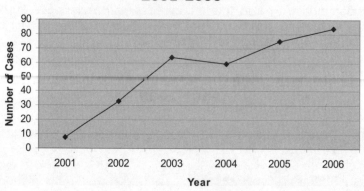

FIGURE 4.2: NON-RESOLVED CASES, 2001-2006

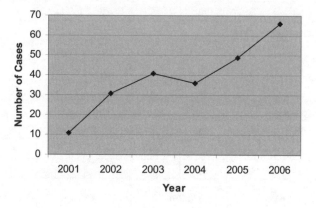

FIGURE 4.3: MEDIATION RESOLUTION RATE, 2001-2006

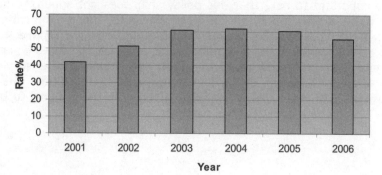

It is also necessary to indicate that, in 2005, the Tribunal began to take into account, in considering the impact of mediation, the number of mediation cases where the complaint was not pursued, following engagement in a structured mediation session. These are cases where non-resolution notices are not required to be issued, despite the fact that the mediation process has not resolved the issue in terms of a formal agreed settlement – for example, cases where, after engaging with the mediator at mediation, parties either settled their dispute informally between themselves or the complainant decided that they did not wish to pursue the matter further. In either instance, from the Tribunal's perspective, this results in a closed *case* and, in 2006, there were 35 such cases. Taking this category into consideration, 185 mediations were conducted in 2006, an increase of 28% on 2005. Additionally, when the closed cases figure is added to the figure for resolved cases, approximately 64% (119 in total) of the actual complaints dealt with by the Mediation Service in 2006 were disposed of formally through this process.

4.5.1   Mediation Agreements

As already indicated, a successful resolution of a mediation case will result in an agreed, and legally-binding, written agreement that is mutually acceptable to both parties. The remainder of this section outlines some of the main characteristics of these agreements.

Although there is a general perception that agreed settlements in cases of alleged discrimination invariably include some aspect of monetary compensation, it is interesting to note that a significant percentage of agreements involved no monetary payment. This characteristic is particularly evident in relation to Equal Status agreements, where, in 2004 and 2005, 43% of all mediated agreements involved no cash payments.

TABLE 4.8: PERCENTAGE OF AGREEMENTS WITH NO MONETARY COMPENSATION, 2004-2005

	2004	2005
Employment Equality Legislation	33%	28%
Equal Status Agreements	43%	43%

In relation to Employment Equality Agreements, where payments were made to complainants, the range of compensation awarded in the majority of cases was relatively modest – for example, in 2004, the amount awarded ranged from a minimum of €400, to a maximum of more than €21,000. This range was even more substantial in 2005, with a minimum award of €250, up to a maximum of over €100,000.

In 2004, 94% of all cash awards were for sums less than €10,000, while in 2005 the equivalent figure was 71%.[41]

With regards to Equal Status agreements, a similar pattern in terms of the scope of compensation awards is also evident – for example, individual payments in 2005 ranged from a minimum of €100, up to €40,000. The majority of compensation awards, however, were quite modest, with an average payment figure of €1,850 for 2005.[42]

As will be suggested in the next section, one of the potential benefits of mediated agreements is the capacity for the parties to craft innovative and creative features, which not only resolve the dispute but also accord more directly with the needs of the complainant. This imaginative dimension has emerged as a particular characteristic of equal status agreements and **Table 4.9** gives a flavour of the innovative elements that have featured in mediated settlements.

TABLE 4.9: IMAGINATIVE ELEMENTS WITHIN MEDIATED EQUAL STATUS AGREEMENTS

Payment of airline tickets	Payment of tickets to an event
Undertaking to welcome people to the respondent's premises and provision of complimentary meal/drinks.	Improving disabled access to premises and/or facilities, including the installation of specialised equipment.
New system to assist the deaf community to deal with parking issues.	The provision of speech and language training and access to other training courses.
Payments to charities and/or sporting organisations.	Provision of shopping/entertainment vouchers.

Source: Adapted from Equality Mediation Reviews, 2004 and 2005.

As was described previously, mediation sessions are structured and conducted in a manner that clearly affords voice to the claimant in terms of providing them with the opportunity to articulate their perceived grievance. There is, however, a strong focus on enabling dialogue and on improving the parties' attitudes and perceptions of each other, and the issue(s) under consideration, with a view to improving future attitudes and practices. In this regard, it is significant to note that apologies for a particular practice or treatment

---

[41] The individual circumstances of each employment equality case made it inappropriate, from the Tribunal's perspective, to identify particular criteria linked to a payment or to calculate an average monetary award.

[42] Similar figures in terms of the average payment and the minimum/maximum awarded were recorded for 2004.

and/or its effects were a feature of 34% and 29% of all mediated agreements in 2004 and 2005 respectively. Significantly, all of the Equality Mediators interviewed stressed that one should not underestimate the importance of an apology to the claimant, in terms of not only vindicating their principles, but also in relation to facilitating an improvement or repairing of relationships between the parties. As one Officer noted:

> "It is surprising just how important and, indeed, powerful a tool an apology can be. It can change the whole dynamic between parties in a mediation context … in contrast, you may actually win a case under an investigation decision but you may never receive an apology and this can, in some instances, be a source of ongoing grievance." (Authors' Interview with Equality Mediation Officer)

4.6   THE POTENTIAL BENEFITS OF MEDIATION

Since its establishment in 2001, the Tribunal has promoted the mediation alternative actively and, in so doing, it has proclaimed that this mode of alternative dispute resolution has the capacity to provide a range of potential benefits to the parties involved in a case, including:

- **Speed and informality**: Compared to investigation, mediation represents a quick and informal route to resolving a dispute. On average, from the point of referral to the resolution of a case, takes eight months through mediation compared to 24 months for investigation. A relatively speedy resolution can also prevent problems from festering and becoming more intractable. Additionally, processing a case *via* mediation is less stressful for the participants, compared to a formalised quasi-judicial Equality investigation. This benefit of speed is also beneficial from a case management point of view, as it helps prevent a backlog of cases building up and improves service delivery. Currently, some 40% of Tribunal cases are now going to mediation. However, while the overall backlog of referrals to the Tribunal has reduced, there is now an increasing backlog building up in the mediation area.

- **Win–Win:** A successful resolution to mediation is dependent on reaching an agreement that is mutually acceptable to both parties and, thus, mediation has the potential to create a win-win situation, in contrast to an Equality investigation, which, by its nature, will result in a winner and loser. Additionally, it is not always evident that the 'winner' in an investigation necessarily will be pleased with the content of the issued decision.

- **Empowerment:** The mediation process provides the parties to a dispute with the power to reach an agreement that is mutually acceptable to them, rather than having a decision imposed on them by an Equality Investigation Officer.

- **Creativity and sustainability:** Given that a mediator strives to facilitate the parties to clarify their relevant concerns and perspectives, agreements reached at mediation often correlate more directly with the actual needs of the parties than a decision imposed by a third party. In particular, there is greater scope for the parties within the mediation context to develop creative and practical solutions to problems that have arisen. Additionally, due to a sense of ownership and/or creativity, agreements reached at mediation are more likely to be comprehensive and sustainable and they appear to operate more successfully than imposed decisions. This is a particularly important benefit in situations where there is an ongoing relationship between the parties.

- **Restoring and improving relationships:** Within mediation, there is potential to restore and/or improve relationships, particularly important in contexts where it is envisaged that there will be an ongoing relationship between the parties (a work context or in relation to the provision of a service). Indeed, the fact that the monetary terms of most settlements are fairly modest suggests that, very often, it is the dynamics of the process – the opportunity to be heard, to receive an explanation and/or apology and the restoration of normal relations, etc. – that can be the real intrinsic value for a claimant. The formal and quasi-judicial character of an investigation, allied to the fact that the outcome will have a winner and loser, ensures that this 'restorative' dimension is less apparent.

- **Costs:** The voluntary nature of the mediation process ensures that the costs associated with it are virtually zero. Importantly, engaging in mediations does not negate in any way an individual's right to have their claim investigated, as they can walk away from the process at any stage and ask for an investigation to be initiated.

4.7   REPRESENTATION & USERS' PERSPECTIVES

In accordance with the Tribunal's guidelines, third-party advisors and representatives can be present at mediation sessions and the Tribunal endeavours to ensure that everyone necessary for the effective processing of a case is present. Representation, however, is not obligatory; 54% of cases involve no representation. Since 2001, both respondents and claimants have availed of representation from an increasingly broad range of bodies and organisations, including trade unions, employer representative bodies, lawyers, citizen advice centres, civic bodies and rights-based advocacy groups. There has been a slight increase in the level of legal representation; however, this has not led to the process becoming overly-legalistic, which often is a charge levelled at the Employment Appeals Tribunal. To date, the Tribunal has encountered no problems resulting from the involvement of the legal community in the mediation process; however, it continues to monitor this trend.

In developing a Mediation Service, the Tribunal recognised that there was a degree of uncertainty amongst users about its appropriateness in a rights-based context and, certainly, many user groups were more comfortable with the well-established investigative route. In this regard, the Equality Tribunal has actively promoted the new service and, as part of that promotion, it established a Users Forum, whereby staff from the service meet with employer bodies, trade unions, the legal community and civic and representative groups associated with the 'protected grounds' (Traveller groups or disability organisations – see **Table 4.10**). The aim of these quarterly meetings is to foster a greater understanding about mediation, how it works and the potential benefits of the process. Many of the representatives attending such sessions are also involved in investigations and, thus, it is important that they are fully aware of the different character of the mediation process. The Tribunal views this interaction, moreover, as a two-way educative process, as it also provides an opportunity for users to raise and discuss issues and to make suggestions as to how to improve the workings of the service.

TABLE 4.10: MEMBERSHIP OF USERS FORUM, 2005

Bar Council	Equality Authority
Health Service Employers Agency	Irish Business & Employers Confederation
Irish Congress of Trade Unions	Irish Insurance Federation
Irish Traveller Movement	Law Society
National Gay & Lesbian Federation	National Women's Council of Ireland
People with Disabilities in Ireland Ltd	National Consultative Committee on Racism & Interculturalism

Interestingly, at the outset, trade unions were somewhat reticent about engaging in equality mediation, due to a degree of uncertainty about this new form of dispute resolution. The capacity of mediation to deliver sustainable and innovative settlements, however, has served to alter this perspective, and trade unions are now supportive of this process. Trade unions, in particular, recognise that the future-focused character of mediation has the potential, in certain circumstances, to deliver tangible improvements in current practice, which benefits not only the claimant but also the wider membership within an organisation. In this regard, trade unions have developed a key role in monitoring the implementation of mediation settlements.

In general, the employer representative bodies were more comfortable from the outset with mediation and, while they display a greater propensity to use legal representation, they are generally happy with the process. As noted already, there has been a slight increase in the level of legal representation and, in general, the lawyers' focus within the process is on getting the best deal for the client rather than necessarily resolving the issue(s) *per se*. In part, there is an element of 'justifying their presence', which can create a certain dynamic that has to be managed carefully. As with both the employers and trade unions, however, the legal community are generally supportive and positive about the service provided.

As part of the process of engaging with users, the Tribunal also undertook a survey of users of the Mediation Service, including respondents and claimants and their representatives. Significantly, the results showed that the majority of users (84%) considered the Mediation Service provided by the Tribunal to be of a high quality. Additional analysis of this data, moreover, revealed that the satisfaction ratings enjoyed by the Mediation Service compared favourably with those of longer-established mediation programmes in other countries (O'Byrne, 2005).[43] This Users Survey also revealed very high satisfaction ratings in relation to the terms of agreements, the conduct of mediation sessions and the role of the mediator. In a comparatively short space of time, the Tribunal has succeeded in introducing an alternative form of dispute resolution into a relatively complex environment that has gained the confidence and support of claimants, respondents and representative groups. There is clearly an element of 'output legitimisation', in that the quality of the service and its capacity to deliver for all the relevant stakeholders has justified its continued development and expansion.

4.8   EQUALITY: THE PUBLIC INTEREST ROLE

In the USA and Canada, where there is a longer-established tradition of using ADR for addressing claims of human rights/equality discrimination, some concern has been raised as to whether such

---

[43]   This research also showed that, only in programmes dedicated to a particular field – for example, schools – did other surveys record a noticeably higher satisfaction level that the 84% expressed by users of the Tribunal's Mediation Service.

instruments amount to the emergence of a private justice system that does not serve to protect the public interest – in terms of procedural fairness and the disclosure of how disputes are solved. In part, it is suggested that mediated settlements may fail to bring to light the depth of a problem, including broader systemic discrimination. Finally, critics have raised the concern that individuals or groups from marginalised communities may feel pressurised to compromise their principles and statutory rights (Kochan *et al.*, 2000). It is important to note that there is strong evidence to allay these criticisms (Kochan *et al.*, 2000) – for example, the case study of the Canadian Human Rights Commission in this book (**Chapter 8**) shows clearly the complementary relationship between a strong public interest role in relation to human rights and the use of a range of 'alternative dispute resolution' initiatives (see also Kochan, 2005; Zweibel & MacFarlane, 2001). In the context of this chapter, however, it is pertinent to explore briefly some of the issues surrounding this debate.

At one level, 'academic' concerns over the potential impact of ADR on the public interest role of a body like the Equality Tribunal are somewhat dissipated by the fact that, in the Irish context, it is the Equality Authority that has been afforded an advocacy and developmental role in relation to equality issues. In undertaking this mandate, the Equality Authority works pro-actively to achieve a positive change in the situation and experience of 'protected groups and individuals', by stimulating and supporting a societal commitment to equality. In particular, the Authority works to support planned and systematic approaches to equality in the workplace and in the provision of goods and services.[44] It is also worth stressing that, through its published decisions, the Equality Tribunal continues to provide a high standard of protection against discrimination and makes a robust contribution to a balanced and sustainable body of case law. Additionally, these decisions foster awareness of what does and does not constitute discrimination and, in this regard, they have an indirect role in contributing to the prevention of discrimination.

More specifically, it is important to re-iterate the voluntarist nature of Equality Mediation, which ensures that engaging in this process does not entail any abdication of the right to refer a case for investigation. Second, as discussed earlier, it is evident that the conduct of equality mediation is not premised on an assumption of compromise and the Equality Mediators are adamant that it is not their role to 'push the parties' towards such a conclusion. Finally, as

---

[44] This activity includes the development of codes of practice, provision of support for equality reviews and action plans, research and a range of joint initiatives with social partner bodies, service providers and organisations from within the nine grounds. In cases of strategic importance, at its discretion, the Equality Authority can provide legal advice and/or representation for those making claims of discrimination under the equality legislation.

already indicated, the mediator has a pivotal role to play in ensuring a sense of fairness, in terms of the individual parties' experience of the mediation process. These key characteristics of mediation appear to address some of the concerns that have been raised in other jurisdictions, regarding a potential weakening of statutory rights or principles and the positive evaluation by users of both the overall service and the mediator's role seem to re-affirm this perspective.

However, it is worth noting that, although mediation settlements are legal documents that are enforceable, the Tribunal itself has no role in monitoring whether the terms of an agreement have been implemented.[45] Instead, this is the responsibility of the claimant and it is evident, for example, that trade unions see this as an increasingly important part of their role in cases in which they are involved as representatives. Under the existing legislation, the Equality Tribunal ceases to have any jurisdiction once a mediated settlement is signed by both parties and there appears to be limited enthusiasm within the organisation for such a monitoring/ enforcement role.

4.9   DEVELOPING NEW FORMS OF DISPUTE RESOLUTION: KEY LESSONS FOR THE LRC

In the period since 2001, the Equality Tribunal has succeeded in establishing equality mediation as a credible, non-confrontational and informal mode of dispute resolution, which is flexible and future-orientated and has the capacity to deliver creative and sustainable settlements. The Tribunal's experience of developing and expanding such an alternative form of dispute resolution, moreover, potentially holds a number of lessons for the Labour Relations Commission and other public dispute resolution agencies.

The Tribunal's experience demonstrates that mediation is an appropriate and effective mechanism for dealing with disputes within an increasingly complex rights-based regulatory environment. This reflects the fact that, in rights-based cases, it is very rare that one party is 100% in the right or in the wrong. More specifically, it highlights the potential of a mediated settlement both to vindicate an individual's principles and their right to be heard, while, at the same time, producing a settlement that is mutually acceptable to both the claimant and the respondent.

Importantly, the introduction of a new statutory option to mediate claims of discrimination did not serve to undermine or weaken the

---

[45] This contrasts with the experience of the Canadian Human Rights Commission (see **Chapter 8**).

more established and traditional investigative route but, instead, operated in tandem with the latter to enhance the overall capacity of the Tribunal to function as a public forum of redress. The maintenance of the principle of voluntarism, even in the context of the shift towards default mediation, and the fact that mediation does not entail an abdication of the right to ask for an investigation were particularly important in this regard. This confirms the importance for the LRC of ensuring that any new or 'alternative' forms of dispute resolution and/or avoidance complement existing service provision and add to the organisation's overall capacity to provide a flexible and integrated conflict management system.

Although the catalyst for the development of the equality mediation option was the establishing legislation, it is evident that the pro-active manner in which the Tribunal has assumed this remit has served to underpin the establishment and expansion of this innovative service. In particular, the strategic policy shift towards 'default mediation' provided a strong institutional push towards 'encouraging' individuals and representative groupings to engage in this process, while maintaining the overall principle of voluntarism. Additionally, the Tribunal also has used User Forum meetings to foster a greater shared understanding about the nature and benefits of the process. Although, there was/is a growing societal interest in this form of mediation, it is arguable that the Equality Tribunal has not merely tapped into this but, to an extent, has sought to generate a demand for this form of dispute resolution

While it is critical that new initiatives in dispute resolution and/or avoidance accord with broader economic and social changes, the relevant public agency has to engage in a degree of policy deliberation and experimentation in seeking to make the connection between new initiatives and what may in fact be somewhat diverse or even weak socio-economic signals. This chapter re-affirms the approach of the LRC in relation to the establishment of the Workplace Mediation Service, which is very much an internally-driven, bottom-up initiative, based on what experienced staff perceived as an appropriate and necessary response to emerging patterns of workplace disputes. This chapter highlights that, in introducing any new initiative, a strong advocacy role has to be undertaken, particularly in terms of engaging with influential representative groups. Equally, it suggests to the LRC that, in seeking to build its dispute resolution and avoidance capacity, there may be a need to take specific policy decisions designed to hardwire, or embed, innovative approaches within the routine of its conflict management service.

The Equality Tribunal's growing confidence in its mediation service also highlights the importance of affording dispute resolution agencies the scope to customise and tailor any new initiatives, in accordance with their organisational needs. In particular, it is important that the design of such initiatives reflects not only best practice and, where appropriate, professional training, but that they are also shaped by the experience and knowledge of the staff who will be responsible for delivering the service. The flexible and customised nature of the Equality Tribunal's Mediation Service re-affirms the importance of the LRC's prevailing operational philosophy, which is premised on providing a service that is capable of drawing on, and adapting, a range of approaches from across the continuum of dispute resolution processes, in seeking to assist the parties in reaching a mutually acceptable agreement. It is critical, therefore, that the development of any new initiatives accords with, and supports, this overarching flexible framework.

The institutional capacity to provide such a flexible and dynamic dispute resolution service is heavily dependent on sufficient numbers of highly-experienced and skilled staff and, as noted earlier, the increasingly burdensome caseload facing the Equality Mediation Service has resulted in the Tribunal exploring actively the possibility of outsourcing cases to an external pool of accredited mediators. Although this scenario is due, in part, to the decision to make mediation a default option, it does reveal both the potential resource implications associated with seeking to provide new and innovative services and a particular policy response to this challenge. Similarly, if the decision was taken to shift the LRC's Workplace Mediation Service from its present status as a relatively low-key pilot initiative to a core part of the Commission's work, clearly there could be associated resource pressures. In such a context, would the LRC seek to meet this challenge through a combination of outsourcing and training-up existing staff, or would it engineer a policy change and seek to 'buy in' the appropriate level of expertise and skill through the open recruitment of professional mediators, as is the norm in many other jurisdictions?

Although the process of regular formalised meetings to discuss issues and exchange experiences no longer takes place, the fact that Equality Mediators stressed the value of such meetings, and indicated that they should be re-established, demonstrates the potential benefits of having in place internal processes for capturing such practical knowledge. The LRC's IT-based case management system to an extent harbours the potential to provide a more structured and formalised means of capturing, collating and analysing the considerable in-house knowledge of 'disputes' – types of case, emerging trends, experience of what works in resolving them, etc. – that resides within the Commission. In essence, this already occurs within the LRC, though often in an informal way and, as such, it would be a case of enhancing and formalising this process of tapping into the 'knowledge' of employees. Although this would necessitate allocating sufficient internal resources to this area of work, developing such a richer and accessible pool of data/evidence clearly would benefit both policy formation and service delivery.

In establishing and, indeed, in expanding the Equality Mediation Service, the Tribunal had to overcome both a degree of inertia – in terms of the need for such a service, given that there was a well-established investigative process *in situ* – and also a level of uncertainty as to its appropriateness. Since 2001, these concerns have largely dissipated, as evidenced by the positive evaluation of the service provided. Central to this positive evaluation has been the Tribunal's capacity to deliver an effective and quality service that provides benefits for all users – claimants, respondents and their representatives. In this regard, there is clearly a strong element of 'output' legitimisation and, as such, ultimately, the key to the success of any new dispute resolution service is that it is both relevant and capable of delivering tangible benefits for the organisation's clients.

The future-focused dimension of mediation, whereby it seeks to improve current practices and procedures is clearly important for the LRC, given both its existing range of preventative mediation activities and its strategic commitment to enhancing individual organisations' in-house capacity for resolving or avoiding disputes. As noted earlier, the Conciliation Division currently is exploring the practicalities of building a longer-term focus into its conciliation activity. This may result in the recognition of the need to make greater use of certain techniques and instruments associated with 'future-focused' or 'transformative' mediation within the conciliation context. Equally, such deliberations could yield a more fundamental policy shift, whereby, in appropriate circumstances, future-focused/transformative mediation is an integral part of an agreed set of sequential mechanisms through which a collective dispute potentially can travel in seeking a resolution.

4.10 CONCLUSION: FUTURE CHALLENGES FOR THE EQUALITY MEDIATION SERVICE

This chapter has demonstrated how the Equality Tribunal has successfully developed and implemented a Mediation Service as an alternative and innovative form of dispute resolution to the traditional quasi-judicial process of an Equality Investigation. In particular, from fairly uncertain beginnings, in that this was a completely new departure, the Tribunal has established equality mediation as a credible, non-confrontational and informal mode of dispute resolution, which is flexible and future-orientated and has the capacity to deliver creative and sustainable settlements. The high approval ratings for the service across all user groups – respondents, claimants and their representatives – confirms that it is now perceived as a credible and legitimate avenue of redress for dealing with alleged claims of discrimination under equality legislation.

Critically, the Mediation Service has served to enhance the overall capacity of the Tribunal to function as a forum of redress, with 40% of cases referred to the Office now processed through mediation. In particular, this has assisted in reducing the backlog of cases and in improving service delivery. More specifically, as highlighted in **section 4.6**, it has delivered a range of tangible benefits for the users of this service. For the Equality Tribunal, the main strategic objective in relation to the Equality Mediation Service is to continue to develop and expand this service. Achieving this objective, however, will require additional resources, in terms of access to more professional and experienced mediators, as the existing team of in-house mediators are struggling already to cope with the rise in the number of referrals, the diversity of challenges and the increasing complexity of the legal environment. As already indicated, the Tribunal currently is putting in place a short-term plan to outsource cases to an external pool of accredited mediators. A potentially more problematic issue, however, is the fact that the Tribunal is to be relocated under the Government's decentralisation strategy. Critically, to date, practically all of the Equality Mediators have indicated that they will not be relocating and, thus, under the existing arrangements they will have to be replaced. Clearly, losing this number of experienced and skilled staff would impose considerable constraints on the capacity of the Tribunal to offer a high quality Mediation Service, as the quality of the staff is the key to the success of this process. The Tribunal also recognises that it needs to develop an even more pro-active process of engagement with user groups, in order to foster a greater level of understanding as to the benefits of mediation. In particular, while bodies such as IBEC and ICTU have been supportive of the Mediation Service, they have not functioned yet as active champions of it and so there is a need to work more closely with these bodies on this issue. Equally, given the growing interest in mediation and ADR in general across the public service, there is clearly scope for building stronger linkages with other practitioners in order to exchange experience and knowledge and, in effect, to create a community of practice within the public policy sphere.

5

THE EMPLOYMENT APPEALS TRIBUNAL

5.1 INTRODUCTION

This chapter is concerned with the workings of the Employment Appeals Tribunal (EAT), which is arguably the most legalistic and formal of all the public dispute resolution agencies in Ireland. In particular, this chapter focuses on:

- The statutory remit of the EAT (**section 5.2**).
- The nature of its proceedings (**sections 5.3** and **5.4**) and its caseload (**section 5.5**) and, in so doing, considers the position and identity of the organisation within the broader public dispute resolution architecture (**section 5.6**).

Then, in evaluating the service provided by the Tribunal (**section 5.7**), this chapter explores the potential for incorporating some form of alternative dispute resolution mechanism into the workings of the organisation in order to support the EAT in continuing to provide an effective and fair service in what is an increasingly complex operating environment (**section 5.8**).

Finally, the Conclusion (**section 5.9**) brings together the arguments of the chapter.

5.2 THE EAT'S ORIGINS & STATUTORY REMIT

The EAT is an independent, quasi-judicial, statutory body, whose sole function is to adjudicate on disputes relating to individual employment rights. In this regard, the EAT is committed to providing an accessible, speedy, fair and informal forum for individuals to seek remedies for alleged infringement of their statutory employment rights. Established by the Redundancy Payments Act 1967, the mandate of the original Tribunal was to adjudicate in disputes about redundancy between employers and employees and, until 1977, it was known as the Redundancy Appeals Tribunal. In 1973, the Minimum Notice & Terms of Employment Act extended the Tribunal's functions to adjudicating on claims for statutory minimum notice. In 1977, under section 18 of the Unfair Dismissals Act 1977, it was renamed as the Employment Appeals Tribunal.

Since its inception, the Tribunal's remit has expanded continuously, as a result of the substantial increase in employment legislation under which it has been afforded a statutory role. Although, as noted above, this process began in the 1970s, it is the proliferation of employment legislation – primarily focused on developing individual rights – introduced in the period since 1990 that has expanded substantially the legislative responsibility afforded to the EAT. Consequently, it now has jurisdiction under 15 Acts of the Oireachtas and two statutory instruments to deal with individual employment rights disputes that arise either during the course of, or on the termination of, an employment relationship. The EAT is also an appellate body, adjudicating on appeals from the recommendations or decisions of the Rights Commissioners under 12 pieces of employment rights legislation. Unusually, claims for unfair dismissal can be made, in the first instance, either to the EAT or to a Rights Commissioner. In the latter case, an appeal lies from the recommendation of the Rights Commissioner to the EAT. As of 2006, the Tribunal therefore deals with disputes under the following legislation:

- Adoptive Leave Act 1995.
- Carer's Leave Act 2001.
- Competition Act 2002.
- European Communities (Protection of Employees on Transfer of Undertakings) Regulations 2003.
- European Communities (Protection of Employment) Regulations 2000.
- Maternity Protection Act 1994.
- Minimum Notice & Terms of Employment Acts 1973-2001.
- Organisation of Working Time Act 1997.
- Parental Leave Act 1998.
- Payment of Wages Act 1991.
- Protection for Persons Reporting Child Abuse Act 1998.
- Protection of Employees (Employers Insolvency) Acts 1984-2001.
- Protection of Young Persons (Employment) Act 1996.
- Redundancy Payments Acts 1967-2003.
- Terms of Employment (Information) Acts 1994 and 2001.
- Unfair Dismissals Acts 1977-2001.

5.3 THE EAT'S ORGANISATIONAL STRUCTURE

The EAT consists of a full-time chairperson, and 31 vice-chairs. In addition, there is a panel of 72 other members, 36 nominated by ICTU and IBEC respectively and appointed by the Minister for Enterprise, Trade & Employment, usually for a three-year term. Under the Redundancy Payments Act 1979, there is also provision for the appointment of additional vice-chairs and members whenever the Minister for Enterprise, Trade & Employment is of the opinion that such appointments are necessary for the speedy dispatch of the business of the Tribunal. Under statute, the chairperson must be a barrister of at least seven years' standing and, although not a requirement, the vice-chairs invariably tend to be legal practitioners or, at the very least, have a strong legal background.

EAT hearings normally consist of either the chair or a vice-chair and two members, drawn from both the employer and trade union panels.[46] The EAT operates on a regional basis – enabling it to host divisional sittings in towns and cities throughout Ireland, which is clearly beneficial in terms of improving access for the parties to a dispute. In 2006, there were 1,062 sittings at 36 locations throughout the country; of these, 517 took place in Dublin, with 545 sittings being held in provincial areas.

Twenty-four civil servants, assigned by the Department of Enterprise, Trade & Employment, staff the EAT secretariat, which is responsible for the administration of claims referred under the various pieces of employment rights legislation. Its role is to provide administrative support to the EAT in its adjudication on disputes between employees and employers. Officers of the secretariat process applications from the date of receipt and act as secretaries at hearings. They also draft determinations, following Tribunal deliberations, for consideration by the Tribunal and notify the parties concerned of the decisions or determinations of the Tribunal.

5.4 THE EAT'S LEGALISTIC CHARACTER

When it was established, the objective of the EAT was to provide a speedy, inexpensive and informal avenue of redress for the settlement of disputes involving an alleged infringement of statutory employment rights. Although clearly cognisant of the more expansive and complex legislative environment that it now operates in, the EAT remains committed to an overall policy goal of providing an accessible, inexpensive, quick, fair and informal forum for the

---

[46] A Vice-Chairman of the Employment Appeals Tribunal, when acting as Chairman (at the request of the Minister or the Chairman) has all the powers of the chair.

resolution of employment rights disputes. In practice, however, the operations of the EAT have become increasingly legalistic and formal, especially in comparison to the activities of the other agencies that comprise the Irish public dispute resolutions system. A number of factors, arguably, have contributed to this development. The requirement for the chair of the Tribunal to have a legal background, in conjunction with the gradual adoption of the rules of evidence and other legal conventions and procedures, has undoubtedly fuelled this particular development. To an extent, the Tribunal maintains that this more legalistic focus was a necessary and appropriate response to the gradual emergence of a more complex and expansive rights-based regulatory environment.

The requirement for the Tribunal to act judicially certainly adds to the formality of its proceedings, and this is further re-inforced by the nature of the cases that it has to address. For example, experience shows that unfair dismissal cases – given that they involve a dispute over a person losing their employment – have the potential to have considerable and long-lasting impact on both the individual and employer involved in the case. In this context, the Tribunal has placed considerable emphasis on ensuring a high level of professionalism, fairness and due process in accordance with the legislation in the conduct of its proceedings.

The widespread usage of professional legal teams also has resulted gradually in a greater level of formalism in the proceedings of the tribunals. Under the legislation, a party to an application may appear and be heard in person, or be represented by counsel or solicitor, or by a representative of a trade union, or by an employers' association or, with the leave of the Tribunal, by any other person. Any party to a case may have one or more representative(s) acting on their behalf. In 2006, the number of cases heard by the Tribunal under the various Acts or combination of Acts, where the parties had representation, was 1,012:

- 1,050 employee parties were represented (273 by trade unions, 641 by legal representation and 136 by other persons).
- 826 employer parties were represented (55 by employer associations, 574 legal representation and 197 by other persons).

These figures indicate that the predominant means of representation is by legal teams, as they accounted for 61% and 69% of the representation for employee and employer parties respectively. The recourse to representation, particularly, legal representation, is also high in relation to unfair dismissal cases. In 2006, for example, the total number of cases heard by the Tribunal under the Unfair Dismissal Acts 1977 to 2001, where the parties had representation, was 687:

- 736 employee parties were represented (137 by trade unions, 524 by legal representation and 75 by other persons).
- 650 employer parties were represented (48 by employer associations, 460 by legal representation and 142 by other persons).

Once again, it is evident that representation in such cases is dominated by professional legal teams, as they accounted for 71% of the employee and employer parties' representation in such hearings during 2006.

Although different chairs may display a different emphasis in how they do their business, the legal and formalistic character of the EAT ensures there is a strong degree of unanimity in the operation of hearings, in that that every witness is sworn in and there is an opportunity for cross-examination. Importantly, the Tribunal emphasises the need to ensure that there is no disadvantage as a result of lack of representation. Although, ultimately, this is left to the discretion of the chair, most will be careful to allow people to tell their story and will assist them with helpful questioning, if so needed. Additionally, they will endeavour to ensure that participants fully understand the process and assist them in coming to terms with what can be an intimidating atmosphere.

It is important to note, however, that the Tribunal's hearings are not a 'court of law' in the strictest sense. For example, while it has the authority to take evidence under oath, this is rarely used and the 'strict rules of evidence' associated with, say, civil courts proceedings are not always enforced. Indeed, from the perspective of the legal community, the approach to direct and cross-examination, rules of evidence, etc. adopted in Tribunal hearings is considered much more informal and flexible than in a formal court of law. Conversely, however, from the perspective of employment relations practitioners, trade unionists and employer representatives, the Tribunal still is considered to be the most legalistic and formal of all the public dispute resolution agencies.

5.5   THE EAT'S CASELOAD

In terms of the number of cases referred to the EAT, as either claims or appeals, there has been a quite a variable trend between different periods, due in the main to the combined impact of the broader economic context and changing legislative environment in which the organisation operates. For example, there was a major growth in cases during the 1980s, associated with an expansion in employment legislation and the large-scale redundancies that characterized this period (Wallace *et al.*, 2004). In the 1990s, however, the number of cases referred was considerably lower, as this was a period of unprecedented employment growth in Ireland. Then, as is evident from **Figure 5.1**, the EAT experienced a considerable increase in total referrals between 1999 and 2002, followed by a marked decline and levelling-off in the number of cases over the past three years, 2004 to 2006. Wallace *et al.* (2004) suggest that the upturn in cases in the earlier period (1999-2002) was caused primarily by the growth in cases under both Minimum Notice & Terms of Employment and Redundancy legislation, in the context of slowdown in the economy. The subsequent fall in the number of cases from 2003 onwards is the direct result of legislative changes introduced in 2003 that allow for claims under the Minimum Notice legislation, in circumstances where the employer has been declared insolvent, to be paid from the Social Insurance Fund without an order from the Tribunal. This has resulted in the number of claims referred to the EAT under this legislation falling by approximately 69% between 2003 and 2006 (see **Table 5.1**). Though significant in terms of the numbers, this reduction has not benefited the Tribunal significantly, in terms of reduced operational time, as these claims are generally listed in conjunction with other cases and are dealt with extremely promptly at divisional hearings – literally, in a number of minutes.

FIGURE 5.1: REFERRALS (CLAIMS & APPEALS) TO THE EAT, 1999-2006

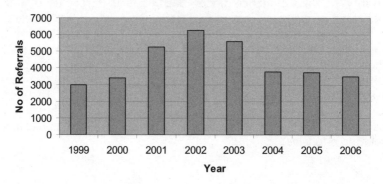

In this context, the 'number' of cases is not an accurate barometer of the workload pressures that impinge on the EAT. Overall, however, the number of cases referred to the Tribunal in 2006 was 3,480, which represents a fall of just 6% from the previous year (see **Table 5.1**). This levelling-off also is evident in the core business of the Tribunal – cases referred under the Unfair Dismissals legislation. As is evident from **Table 5.2**, the Tribunal 'allows' a much larger number of cases than it dismisses. Of the 3,113 claims referred directly to it in

2006, the Tribunal was able to 'dispose of' 2,908 (93%), the same rate as achieved the previous year. As such, at one level, in terms of actually removing or disposing of individual referrals from the overall organisational caseload, the EAT is very efficient, though, as will be discussed in more detail later, this is partly explained by a high level of withdrawals.

TABLE 5.1: CLAIMS & APPEALS REFERRED TO THE EAT, 2002-2006

Legislation	2001	2002	2003	2004	2005	2006
Minimum Notice & Terms of Employment Acts	3,216	3,966	2,799	1,061	1,035	858
Unfair Dismissals Acts 1977-2001: Direct referrals	894	1,247	1,365	1,249	1,280	1,167
Unfair Dismissals: Appeals against Rights Commissioners Decisions/Recommendations; Appeals for implementation	63	64	151	125	134	124
Redundancy Payment Acts	612	485	731	738	621	680
Protection of Employees (Employers Insolvency) Acts	6	7	20	3	9	5
Payment of Wages Act: Appeals against Rights Commissioners' Decisions	75	85	80	103	110	101
Maternity Protection Acts	1	3	1	2	2	0
Terms of Employment (Information Act): Appeals against Rights Commissioners' Recommendations/ Appeals for implementation	56	6	24	20	28	42
Adoptive Leave Acts: Appeals against Rights Commissioners Decisions	0	0	0	0	0	0
Protection of Young Persons (Employment) Act: Appeals against Rights Commissioners' Recommendations	0	0	0	0	0	0
Organisation of Working Time Act	264	327	415	396	486	403
Parental Leave Act: Appeals against Rights Commissioners' Decisions	5	2	3	2	1	4
Protection for Persons Reporting Child Abuse Act: Appeals against Rights Commissioners' Decisions	0	0	0	0	0	0

Legislation	2001	2002	2003	2004	2005	2006
European Communities (Protection of Employees on Transfer of Undertakings) Regulations 2003: Appeals against Rights Commissioners' Decisions	0	2	1	9	21	95
European Communities (Protection of Employment) Regulations 2000: Appeals against Rights Commissioners' Decisions	0	65	0	1	0	1
Carers Leave Act: Appeals against Rights Commissioners' Decisions	0	0	0	0	0	0
Competition Act 2002	0	0	0	0	0	0
Worker Protection (Regular Part-Time Employees) Act 1991[47]	65	0	0	0	0	0
Total Referrals	**5,257**	**6,529**	**5,590**	**3,754**	**3,727**	**3,480**
Total Disposed Of	**3,994**	**4,602**	**5,857**	**3,615**[48]	**3,467**	**3,169**

Source: Employment Appeals Tribunal Annual Reports, 2002 to 2005.

Although the jurisdiction of the Tribunal has been expanded considerably by the growth in associated employment legislation, as is evident from **Table 5.1**, in 2006, seven areas accounted for 98% of the total referrals. This pattern is replicated in terms of claims referred directly to the Tribunal (excluding appeals against the recommendations of Rights Commissioners), as four pieces of legislation – redundancy, minimum notice, unfair dismissal and organisation of working time – accounted for all but five of the 3,113 claims referred directly in 2006 (see **Table 5.2**).

Significantly, unfair dismissal cases accounted for 38% of the claims directly referred to the Tribunal in 2006, and 37% of the total number of direct claims disposed off in the same period. Unlike some of the other claims referred to the Tribunal, by their very nature, unfair dismissal cases are time-consuming, stressful and demanding for all the parties concerned. Although the EAT provides an important forum within which individuals and organisations have the opportunity either to redress a perceived infringement of their rights or to clear their name, experience both in Ireland and in other jurisdictions shows that it can also be an extremely stressful and unhappy

---

[47] The Act was repealed in 2001 by the Protection of Employees (Part-Time Work) Act, which brought in a number of improvements for part-time workers. The EAT has no role under this new legislation, as the initial complaint/referral is to the Rights Commissioners, while the Labour Court was afforded the appellate function.

[48] This is an approximate figure for the 2003 total.

experience that can often extract a heavy toll in personal terms. Indeed, the EAT estimates that unfair dismissal cases now account for approximately 95% of its total workload in terms of actual 'time spent on cases' at hearings. Consequently, although the legislative authority of the EAT has expanded gradually, its core work is focused on processing unfair dismissal cases.

TABLE 5.2: SUMMARY OF CLAIMS REFERRED TO THE EAT & THE OUTCOME OF THE CLAIMS DISPOSED OF IN 2006[49]

Act	No/ of Claims referred*	Allowed	Dismissed	Withdrawn during hearing	Withdrawn prior to hearing	Total number of claims disposed**
Redundancy Payments	680	205	81	106	193	585
Minimum Notice & Terms of Employment	858	206	164	242	221	833
Unfair Dismissal: Direct Claims	1,167	170	206	379	311	1,066
Protection of Employees (Employers' Insolvency)	5	1	3	0	0	4
Organisation of Working Time	403	92	83	146	99	420
Part-Time Workers	0	0	0	0	0	0
Total	**3,113**	**674**	**537**	**873**	**824**	**2,908**

* Some claims referred in 2005 are not yet disposed of.
** Some claims disposed of in 2005 were referred in 2004.

As noted above, the EAT enjoys a particularly high disposal rate in terms of clearing cases referred to it, either directly or as appeals. Examining **Table 5.2**, however, it is apparent that an 'uncomfortably high' number of cases are withdrawn, either just before the beginning

---

[49] This table excludes appeals to the Employment Appeals Tribunal against Rights Commissioners' recommendations. In 2005, there were 296 such appeals.

of Tribunal hearing or sometimes during the proceedings (Teague, 2005). In 2006, 58% of all of the direct referral cases that were disposed of by the Tribunal were accounted for by withdrawals, either during or prior to a hearing. Unfair dismissal cases are now the core work of the Tribunal in terms of actual time spent on cases, although **Table 5.2** indicates a high withdrawal rate (65%) for such referrals. Although a case can be withdrawn at any time, practical experience reveals that there is a recurring tendency for the parties to withdraw the case just before the hearing begins – an approach commonly referred to as 'settling on the steps'. Interestingly, this patterns accords with the experience of similar tribunals in other jurisdictions.[50] Additionally, approximately 36% of all unfair dismissal cases are disposed of as a result of withdrawals during the actual hearing of a case at a formal sitting of the Tribunal. Interviews with members of the Tribunal suggested that, in such instances, the cases tend to be withdrawn very early on in the actual hearing process. There are plausible and acceptable reasons for the relatively high rate of withdrawals, related to the types of issues that are involved in cases and strongly legalistic character of the Tribunal process. Certainly, cases withdrawn before the start of formal proceedings are explained by a number of factors, including the parties becoming aware of the weight of the evidence, people not wanting to go through the ordeal of a hearing, a realisation of the potential costs of a binding ruling compared to a negotiated settlement, or because the parties realise that they have reached the final round of a 'hard bargaining game' and are now willing to settle rather than go through the ordeal of a Tribunal sitting.

In terms of containing costs and reducing operational delays, it is worth noting that, in instances, where a case is withdrawn on the day of a hearing, or early on during an actual sitting, although the case is considered to have been settled or disposed of, in addition to administrative costs, the tribunal members' time will have been allocated and expenses occurred. Unlike the civil courts, there is not a panel of cases waiting to be heard by that division, if a scheduled hearing of a case does not take place and/or if it finishes quickly. In this context, it is interesting to note that, in Canada, the trend of parties 'settling on the steps' just before the formal beginning of an adjudication hearing for unfair dismissal cases was a catalyst for the federal-level Labour Standards Inspectorate exploring the potential of implementing an ADR option, in part, with the aim of reducing the administrative and legal costs associated with such occurrences (see **Chapter 8**).

---

[50] See example of the Labour Standards & Workplace Equity Directorate in Canada (**Chapter 8**).

Finally, it is worth considering the scope for redress available to the Tribunal in relation to unfair dismissal cases. In effect, under the legislation, where an employee has been found to have been unfairly dismissed, under the Acts (1977-2005), s/he can be awarded:

i. Re-instatement in his/her old job, thereby entitling the employee to the benefit from any improvement in terms and conditions of employment which may occur between the date of dismissal and the date of re-instatement.

ii. Re-engagement in his/her old job, or in a suitable alternative job, on conditions which the adjudicating bodies consider reasonable.

iii. (a) Where financial loss has been sustained by the employee, financial compensation in respect of such loss, subject to a maximum of two years' remuneration. The precise amount of compensation can depend on such matters as where the responsibility for the dismissal lay, the measure taken to reduce financial loss, or the extent to which negotiated dismissal procedures were followed, if these existed, or

(b) Where no financial loss has been sustained by the employee, financial compensation may be awarded subject to a maximum award of four weeks' remuneration.

In relation to financial compensation, there is a popular misconception that parties who have had their cases for unfair dismissal upheld by the Tribunal receive high levels of compensation.

TABLE 5.3: COMPENSATION AWARDS BY THE EAT IN DETERMINATIONS OF UNFAIR DISMISSAL, 2006

Compensation Award €	Number	Compensation Awarded €	Number
0	4	5,001 – 6,000	5
1 – 250	3	6,001 – 7,000	11
251 - 500	16	7,001 – 8,000	10
501 - 750	6	8,001 – 9,000	6
751 – 1,000	11	9,001 – 10,000	10
1,001 – 2,000	25	10,001 – 15,000	25
2,001 – 3,000	20	15,001 – 20,000	5
3,001 – 4,000	13	20,001 – 25,000	3
4,001 – 5,000	12	> 25,001	36
Total Awarded: €2,627,003: Total number of determinations of unfair dismissal: 221 Average Award: € 11,887			

Source: EAT Annual Report 2005, p.32.

Table 5.3 sets out the distribution of compensation awarded by the Tribunal in 2006 in relation to determinations of unfair dismissal. It shows that, out of a total of 221 determinations, only 36 (16%) involved awards in excess of €25,000. Similarly, there were 69 (31%) instances of awards of over €10,000, while the corresponding figure for awards of less than €5,000 was 110, which represented approximately 50% of the total number of determinations of unfair dismissal by the Tribunal. Overall, the total amount awarded by the Tribunal in 2006 was €2,627,003, with the average award totalling €11,886. The clear message emerging from these official figures is that winning a case at the Employment Appeals Tribunal does not usually lead to high levels of monetary compensation. In this regard, it is important to note that the level of compensation that can be awarded by the Tribunal in individual cases is statutorily constrained by the provisions of the Acts (see above) and directly related both to the period of loss and to the level of earnings in the job at the time.

In relation to determinations of unfair dismissal in 2006, it is important to note that the Tribunal ordered re-instatement in two cases and re-engagement in another five. Consequently, the restoration of the employment relationship was the outcome in only 3.2% of all the unfair dismissal determinations in 2005. Although this is a very low figure, comparative results from similar Tribunals in other jurisdictions confirms similarly low levels of re-employment or re-engagement in unfair dismissal cases. Although some commentators have been critical of the very limited instances in which individuals return to their original employment (D'Arcy & Garavan, 2006), members of the Tribunal – including trade union members – maintain that the relative buoyancy of the labour market, in conjunction with the fact that the relationship between the employee and the former employer in most instances has deteriorated, to the extent that they are both prepared to endure the stress and pressure associated with a Tribunal hearing, ensures that, in practice, very few individuals actually want to return to their former employment.

5.6 THE EAT'S ROLE & IDENTITY

As noted in **Chapter 1**, a relatively robust and effective public dispute resolution architecture has evolved in Ireland over the last two decades. With regards to the positioning of the EAT within the public dispute resolution system, it is significant that, of the overall figure of 3,480 cases referred to the organisation in 2006, 2,820 (81%) involved disputes concerned with the actual termination of the employment relationship. Additionally, if one includes claims in respect of holiday pay entitlements at the time of the termination, then 3,324 cases _per annum_, or 96% of all referrals to the Tribunal, are associated with the ending of a particular employment relationship. Indeed, the proportion of the cases disposed of by the Tribunal in the same period that were also concerned with disputes relating to the termination of an employment relationship is even higher. As such, within the public policy sphere, the EAT is essentially a forum for adjudication of disputes where the employment relationship has ended. This particular role has shaped an organisational identity focused on high standards of fairness and professionalism and ensuring due process in accordance with the appropriate legislation. While, clearly, this has delivered tangible benefits, arguably it also has fostered a 'legalistic' organisational culture, which, to date, has been less open to exploring the potential advantages of incorporating alternative dispute resolution mechanisms or approaches to dispute resolution. Indeed, there is a strong feeling within the Tribunal that adopting ADR innovations such as a mediation option, not only would serve to undermine the right of individuals to have their 'day in court' but also would dilute the legal robustness of the EAT's work. As such, the prevailing wisdom within the Tribunal is that such 'innovations' are potentially too risky, as they would interfere with the effectiveness of the integrated set of conventions and approaches that the Tribunal has adopted gradually during its 40-year life.

5.7   EVALUATION

In general, there is a broad consensus that the Employment Appeals Tribunal provides an effective, and highly professional, service, especially given the growing demands on the resources of the organisation and the increasingly-complex legal environment in which it now operates. This positive assessment is confirmed by the Tribunal's customer satisfaction surveys, which show a high level of satisfaction with the service provided. The success of the Tribunal in achieving such ratings is attributable largely to the fact that both the civil servants and the senior people responsible for the operation of the Tribunal are highly motivated and professional individuals, who are committed to the settling of disputes in a manner that is fair to all (Teague, 2005). Interestingly, although the EAT proceedings undoubtedly have become more legalistic, in an interview with the authors, the Chair of the EAT stressed the important contribution that the panel members nominated by ICTU and IBEC make to the process. In particular, their deep knowledge and experience of workplace issues and employment-related disputes is considered invaluable in processing cases in a fair and equitable manner.

From the perspective of one highly-experienced trade union member of the Tribunal, the EAT's systems and processes work well for both claimants and respondents, in that it hears the cases in a fair and equitable manner (Authors' Interview). This same individual, moreover, indicated that, although there are tangible deficiencies, particularly in relation to delays and intervals in hearing cases, these are not insurmountable problems and that, while there is clearly scope for enhancing the service provided, overall the Tribunal can be considered to be a relatively successful organisation, in terms of fulfilling its operational mandate.

In its submission to the Employment Rights Review Group, IBEC generally concurred with this assessment of the workings of the EAT. The main concerns raised by IBEC related to the need to improve the operational structure of the Tribunal, either by having a small number of full-time divisions or slightly more part-time divisions (DETE, 2004a). Implementing these types of structural changes, IBEC maintained, would contribute to improvements in consistency, predictability, efficiency and the turnover of cases.

In contrast, ICTU was more strident in its critique of the EAT, asserting that the gradual legalisation of the EAT had undermined the original objective of what the body was set up to do (DETE, 2004b). Although recognising that, following the enactment of the original Unfair Dismissals Act 1977, the operation of the EAT necessarily became more formal, from Congress's perspective, the gradual legalisation of the process has served to mitigate against the objective of providing easy and clear access for employees to redress alleged infringements of employment rights. Indeed, ICTU goes so far as to contend that, for many union members and officials, the EAT can be a 'cold place for workers' and that, despite the best efforts of some divisions, the EAT is considered to be an intimidating place (DETE, 2004b). One of the consequences of the increased legal formality within the Tribunal, according to Congress, is that many claimants and respondents feel the need to incur legal expenses, none of which can be recovered (DETE, 2004b).

EAT members would certainly refute some of this criticism. As already noted, there is a strong emphasis on the chair ensuring fairness in the operations of the Tribunal, particularly in instances where an individual does not have access to representation. Interestingly, however, in its response to submissions from various parties, while defending its quasi-legalistic approach, the EAT agreed that the dispute resolution system had become more complex and confusing for those whom it was intended to service and that this was frustrating the desired objective of enabling an aggrieved employee to pursue a claim without legal or trade union representation (DETE, 2004b).

Significantly, despite the EAT's emphasis on providing a quick and efficient service, there is clearly a growing problem of lengthening delays in the processing of cases to conclusion, particularly in relation to unfair dismissal cases. As is evident from **Table 5.4**, the average waiting time between the date of receipt and the date of hearing for an unfair dismissal case has increased considerably between 1999 and 2006: in the Dublin region, it now stands at 27 weeks and, although this is not the highest figure reached in this period, it still represents a doubling of the 2001 figure; despite a new regional divisional structure, the waiting time in the provinces also continued to rise, more than doubling from 19 to 44 weeks between 2001 and 2006. Given the potential impact that such cases have on the parties concerned, and the stress associated with being involved in such a formal and legalistic process, it is clearly a concern for the Tribunal and its clients that waiting times have remained stubbornly high. In part, the complex and time-consuming nature of unfair dismissal cases has contributed to the delays and the EAT itself strongly maintains that it does not have sufficient numbers of secretaries to meet its burgeoning workload.

TABLE 5.4: AVERAGE WAITING PERIOD BETWEEN DATE OF RECEIPT & DATE OF HEARING FOR UNFAIR DISMISSAL CASES, 2006

Average Waiting Period for Dublin								
	1999	2000	2001	2002	2003	2004	2005	2006
Weeks	9	8	13	23	29	26	28	27
Average Waiting Period for Provincial Areas								
	1999	2000	2001	2002	2003	2004	2005	2006
Weeks	10	12	19	19	28	39	41	44

Source: EAT Annual Reports, 2002 -2006.

Aside from the issue of administrative resources, however, other factors also appear to be contributing to the increasing delays in processing cases to their conclusion. For example, ICTU maintains that the practice of 'settling on the steps', just before a hearing is due to commence, is a factor in increasing waiting times, as this ties up a full division of the Tribunal for a period that could have gone to examining other cases. Second, the convention of (re)appointing all of the members of the Tribunal at the same time every three years is problematic, as it ensures that cases cannot be scheduled as the end of a three-year term approaches in case there is a run-over, since if one member leaves a division, the case must start again. As a result, there is a somewhat low occupancy rate in the last three to five months of a member's term, thus contributing to delays in the scheduling of hearings. Third, some practitioners have highlighted that, while the part-time nature of the membership is cost-effective from the Government's perspective, it is not conducive to efficiency as it can contribute to a propensity to postpone hearings, due to other commitments.

While accepting that the 'setting-down' system, which is designed primarily for the convenience of parties, renders some applications for postponements inevitable, the Tribunal itself has striven to reduce the number of postponements requested by the parties involved. At present, if a postponement is sought immediately, or within five working days of receiving the notice of hearing, and the consent of the other party to the case has been obtained, it may be granted; if, however, a postponement is sought later, and/or without the consent of the other party, generally it is refused. The implementation of the setting-down system has reduced the number of sitting days lost due to postponements, down from 200 to 66.5 between 2002 and 2006.

Finally, the legalistic and formal character of the overall process is also considered to be a factor in causing delays in the processing of cases.

5.8   ENHANCING THE SERVICE PROVIDED

Although the EAT can be considered to provide a relatively fair and effective service, the deficiencies evident in relation to delays, and the concerns expressed by some client groups (in particular, trade unions) in relation to the overly-legalistic nature of its proceedings, suggest that there is scope for adopting initiatives that would enhance the quality of the service provided.

In 2006, the Tribunal set up an Internal Working Group to address the issues identified in the submissions made to the Review Group on the Functions of the Employment Rights Bodies (DETE, 2004a). This working group undertook an in-depth review on the service it provides to the parties who use the Tribunal and, in particular, there was a focus on the procedures for hearing cases. The working group's recommendations are now being considered actively by the Tribunal. Notwithstanding the outcomes of this process, there are a number of suggested measures that could assist the Tribunal in its endeavours to improve further the service it offers.

First, as is the case with many of the other dispute resolution agencies, there appears to be considerable merit in the EAT developing more formal and structured arrangements for gathering and analysing information and data on important matters such as 'withdrawals', as this would provide rich information about the motives and behaviours of people and organisations involved in dispute resolution. A more formalised and focused approach to information-gathering on such issues would facilitate a more informed assessment of the quality of the service being provided. Additionally, it would provide a rich source of data that could be used to inform innovations in policy development and service delivery.

As highlighted earlier, there is a strong degree of reticence within the Tribunal as to the appropriateness of alternative dispute resolution mechanisms, such as mediation, to the resolution of unfair dismissal cases. In this regard, gathering detailed information on withdrawals would be useful in assessing whether innovations, such as pre-session hearings to promote quick settlements of dispute, would be appropriate.

Experience from other public dispute resolution agencies in both Ireland and abroad strongly suggests that there is considerable merit in the EAT exploring the potential of mediation or similar processes. In particular, both the Equality Tribunal and the Labour Standards Directorate (Canada) have introduced a default mediation option, which has assisted both organisations in reducing their backlog of cases and, in the case of the latter, has contributed to reductions in administrative costs. In both instances, the use of mediation also has generated a range of benefits for both claimants and respondents and improved the quality of the dispute resolution service provided. Critically, in both cases, the introduction of a mediation option has served neither to weaken in any way specific statutory rights nor to constrain the right of an individual to seek redress for an alleged infringement of their rights. As already noted, the EAT has articulated the view that such ADR mechanisms would dilute the legal robustness of its approach to unfair dismissal cases. In this context, it is important to reiterate that the Labour Standards Directorate (Canada) has adopted mediation as one of its range of approaches for dealing specifically with unfair dismissals and, from its perspective, sees no contradiction between a commitment to upholding an individual's statutory-based employment rights and the use of ADR techniques, as they are considered to be complementary processes.

The fact that mediation in both examples (the Equality Tribunal and the Labour Standards Directorate (Canada)) is voluntary is particularly important, as is the fact that agreeing to participate in it does not preclude in any way an individual from asking for a formal investigation. The adoption of protocols regarding the disclosure of information provided during a mediation session, and the importance of confidentiality, also have re-inforced the legitimacy of these ADR mechanisms. Finally, in both the Equality Tribunal and the Labour Standards Directorate (Canada), mediation has been adopted in a manner that has ensured it is integrated into the overall approach to dispute resolution, so as to expand the range of mechanisms on offer and, importantly, to enhance the quality and effectiveness of the service provided.

There are also a number of administrative measures that could be adopted that would address some of the problems that the Tribunal currently faces. There is certainly a strong case for moving to a cyclical system of nominating members, so that not all the members are up for (re)nomination at the same time.

Finally, as is the case with other public dispute resolution agencies, there is ongoing scope for improving external communication processes in a manner that raises public awareness of the EAT's role in relation to the resolution of employment-related disputes.

5.9   CONCLUSION

This chapter sought to provide an overview of the operations of the Employment Appeals Tribunal. It demonstrated that the EAT provides a fair and effective service and is an integral part of the State's dispute resolution machinery. In the course of its 40-year existence, the Tribunal has developed gradually an overtly-legalistic, and formal, identity and mode of working. Although there are good reasons for this, not least the highly-complex legislative environment in which the EAT now operates, it is suggested that this particular identity has served to mitigate against the exploration of the potential of ADR-type techniques to assist the organisation in addressing certain deficiencies, such as the delays in processing cases and the perception that hearings are a somewhat intimidating environment for certain groups of employees. Critically, the research undertaken for this report highlights that alternative dispute resolution approaches and principles can make an important contribution to redressing alleged infringements of individual's statutory rights without weakening in any way the overarching legal framework. In this context, it is considered important that the EAT embrace learnings from other good practice examples in both Ireland and abroad and seek actively to incorporate more informal and problem-solving mechanisms into its current approach to dispute resolution. Although this will require a reconfiguring of its organisational and operational identity, it is argued that this can be achieved, in part, by embracing the attributes and characteristics that were envisaged as shaping the work of the original Tribunal, when it was established some 40 years ago.

6

THE LABOUR INSPECTORATE & THE NEW DYNAMICS OF EMPLOYMENT STANDARD-SETTING

6.1 INTRODUCTION

Labour inspection is a long-established principle in the governance of the employment relationship. Most countries have some form of labour inspection system to ensure that organisations comply with relevant employment legislation. The responsibilities of labour inspectors vary from country to country but, usually, they consist of a mix of providing information and advice, monitoring and enforcing legislation and performing educational and advisory activities. These systems of enforcement and compliance ensure that labour market regulations, devised by governments so that employees enjoy decent conditions at the workplace, have credibility. In the absence of effective enforcement mechanisms, employers may not be motivated to ensure that all employees have, at least, minimum standards of work. As a result, not only may employees be deprived of their rights, but pressure may also mount on law-abiding firms to end compliance with work standards. Thus, labour inspection is important to maintaining labour market order and stability.

Recently, the effectiveness of the system of labour inspection has been in the spotlight in many advanced economies. One concern is whether existing, long-standing employment laws and regulations have kept pace with the way employers have structured the work relationship (Supiot, 1999). This raises the problem of the law not providing adequate protection for employees, particularly those working in vulnerable economic sectors. Another worry is whether traditional labour standard compliance strategies are adequate to provide protection to workers in labour markets buffeted by globalisation, structural economic change and the rapid diffusion of new technologies. Thus, the issue of modernising labour inspectorates and the labour standard-setting process more broadly has emerged as an important employment policy matter in some countries (Saunders & Dutil, 2005). Ireland is one of these countries, although the spotlight on the labour inspectorate did not arise out of any deep-seated concern about how it was operating, but rather as a result of a growing realisation that it may have to play an even more pivotal role in maintaining labour market order in the future.

In this chapter, we chart the evolution of labour inspection in Ireland and assess the meaning of recent developments that have led to its expansion. The chapter is organised as follows:

- **Section 6.2** outlines two contrasting models – one Anglo-Saxon and the other Latin – of labour inspection.

- **Section 6.3** explains how Ireland developed an Anglo-Saxon approach to labour inspection.

- Then the workings of the labour inspectorate are set out in **section 6.4**.

- **Section 6.5** assesses some of the shortcomings of the current system, as well as some of the initiatives that have been made to revise the labour inspectorate, along with other employment rights bodies.

- **Section 6.6** sets out the main recommendations of the new national social agreement, *Towards 2016*, in relation to labour inspection and employment standard-setting.

- **Section 6.7** assesses whether these changes will impact on the functioning of the LRC to any significant degree.

- The Conclusion brings together in **section 6.8** the arguments of the chapter.

6.2   MODELS OF LABOUR INSPECTION

In Ireland, the proper enforcement of labour standards can be traced to the British-inspired Industrial Code of 1802. This code was revised on several occasions and mutated into the Shops Act 1912, which made local authorities responsible for labour inspection. Around the same time, Trade Boards were established to set legally-enforceable, minimum rates of pay in some low-paid sectors. Thus, by the early 20th century, labour standard-setting was a well-established principle of employment law, although the Industrial Relations Act 1946 represented the first thorough attempt to establish a comprehensive national system of labour inspection.

Developments at the international level consolidated these domestic moves towards an effective labour inspection regime. In 1923, just four years after being established, the International Labour Organisation (ILO) adopted a Labour Inspection Recommendation, a non-binding decision on how member governments should organise labour inspection systems. In 1947, the ILO went further and adopted Labour Inspection Convention No.81, a binding decision on those governments that ratify it, which set out the broad principles, duties and activities that should underpin national labour inspection regimes. This Convention, which is one of the most ratified of the ILO conventions, was re-inforced by the adoption of Protocols in 1969 and 1995. The political effect of this Convention was to signal to national governments that comprehensive and effective regimes of labour standard-setting and enforcement were an important feature of mature, open democracies. Thus, moves in Ireland to develop a labour inspectorate system were in accordance with a concerted international movement on this topic.[51]

The manner in which governments introduce labour inspection regimes has not been extensively assessed. However, an interesting argument developed by Michael Piore (2005) is that two contrasting models – one called the 'Latin' model and the other, the 'Anglo-Saxon' model – have emerged in the past century from national endeavours to build labour inspection systems.

A characteristic of the Anglo-Saxon system is that the enforcement of labour regulation is spread over a number of agencies: in countries such as the UK and the USA, enforcement of labour standards such as health and safety, minimum wages and anti-discrimination is carried out by different public bodies that have only tenuous links with each other. Another feature is that the system is strongly complaint-based: the work of the labour inspectorate mostly involves responding to complaints from employees alleging violations of employment rights. A third feature of the system is that the emphasis is on seeking out violations of relatively straightforward regulations and then either threatening to impose, or actually imposing, the appropriate sanction/penalty to ensure compliance.

The Latin model of labour inspection, according to Piore (2005), operates in a contrasting manner. For a start, the system of labour regulation is more integrated and unified in a labour code and not divided into specialised parts. In addition, the labour code is normally enforced by a single agency, which allows for a more co-ordinated and holistic approach to labour inspection. When visiting an organisation, a labour inspectorate can invoke any labour regulation. Another distinctive aspect of the Latin model is the high level of discretion enjoyed by labour inspectors when enforcing standards. Piore suggests that they act as 'street-level bureaucrats', a term first coined in the 1960s to describe public officials who enjoy considerable autonomy when carrying out work tasks – policemen, teachers, social workers, for example. These workers require discretion and autonomy, as they work in complex situations that are not conducive to the application of prescriptive rules. They often have to make decisions that package together multiple objectives in a highly

---

[51]   Ireland ratified the ILO's Labour Inspection Convention in June 1951.

contingent manner. Labour inspectors in the Latin system have considerable autonomy to decide whether to enforce the law strictly when an organisation is found to have violated employment regulations (Piore & Schrank, 2007). For example, if an inspector discovered that an organisation was violating employment standards, but also was in financial difficulties, s/he might choose not to prosecute and, instead, to devise an alternative compliance plan that set down goals and targets for the organisation to come into line with employment regulations over a period of time. Thus, in the Latin system, labour inspectors are more concerned with promoting labour market order, which involves encouraging organisations to develop strategies that will allow them to comply with labour market regulations on a sustainable basis, rather than with enforcing employment legislation.

6.3   THE IRISH SYSTEM OF LABOUR INSPECTION

The Irish system of labour inspection is organised more like the Anglo-Saxon than the Latin model. The Labour Inspectorate in Ireland is one of six public bodies that have responsibilities to uphold employment rights. As a result, the Irish situation displays the institutional fragmentation characteristic of labour market regulation regimes in other Anglo-Saxon countries. The unplanned evolution of the labour inspectorate has not improved the co-ordination of the labour standard-setting machinery. The landmark move towards a national labour inspectorate occurred with the adoption of the Industrial Relations Act 1946, which consolidated labour inspection activity at the national level within the then Ministry for Industry & Commerce. The main remit of this service was to carry out an inspection, after a complaint of a violation of an employment right. It also was given the responsibility of enforcing Employment Regulation Orders, a standard-setting instrument to establish minimum pay and conditions in vulnerable sectors. However, in 1955, it was decided to separate the labour inspection and the enforcement of health and safety regulation, even though ILO guidance was to integrate the two functions.

Apart from this, the system of labour inspectorate established in 1946 changed little until the early 1970s. During this decade, however, the functions of the inspectorate expanded rapidly, due to new employment statutes assigning it additional responsibilities.[52]

---

[52]   The Inspectorate was assigned additional duties under the Industrial Relations Act 1969, the Employment Agency Act 1971, the Holidays (Employee) Act 1973 and the Protection of Young Persons Act (Employment) 1977. The 1980s was a quiet decade for the passing of employment law but things started to move again in the 1990s. The following Acts added further responsibilities to the Inspectorate: Worker

From the start of the 1970s until the end of the 1990s, the Labour Inspectorate section operated with a staff complement of 10 officials, most of whom were employed on junior civil service grades. For the most part, the activities of the inspectorate did not figure prominently in the industrial relations system, and the demand for the service was not high. Other parts of the industrial relations machinery, such as the Labour Court, had a much higher profile. The activities of the inspectors mostly involved responding to complaints of breaches of employment law. Their powers included the right to enter premises, demand sight of records, take copies of records, interview relevant people and initiate prosecutions. One view (Teague, 2005) was that inspectors were highly deferential to employers at the time and avoided prosecutions, whenever possible. When prosecutions were being considered, inspectors usually visited the employer several times both to acquire evidence and to leave the employer in no doubt as to what was unfolding. They also wrote formally to the employer at least three times, explaining the violations that had been detected and the nature of the imminent prosecution. During the 1970s and 1980s, the labour inspection function remained within the government ministry currently known as the Department of Employment, Trade & Enterprise. However, the service was re-organised and became known as the Employment Rights Compliance Service, divided into:

- An **Information Unit**, which dealt with all initial inquiries.
- An **Inspection Unit**, which carried out inspections.
- A **Legal Services Unit**, which prepares cases for prosecution.

Since 2000, important developments have occurred in relation to the Labour Inspectorate. The number of inspectors increased, from 10 to 17, to cope with the envisaged increase in the workload, due to the introduction of the National Minimum Wage Act 2000, which gave the Inspectorate the responsibility for its proper implementation. An additional four posts were created in 2003, bringing the allocation to 21. Yet this increase in numbers was not sufficient to allow the unit to deal adequately with the huge increase in the number of referrals to the employment rights bodies. This is not surprising, as the inspectorate, backed up by 7 administrative support staff, has a potential client base of 1.9 million employees and 100,000 employers. Government recognised the pressures on the system and, as a result, introduced a major organisational change plan to make the service more efficient. This plan had a number of dimensions.

Protection (Regular Part-Time Employees) Act 1991, Payment of Wages Act 1991, Terms of Employment (Information) Act 1996, Organisation of Working Time Act 1997.

A new telephone system was introduced so that the information unit could operate like a call centre, which would allow it to respond more effectively to inquiries. Callers to the information unit now are given a wide range of supporting information and told how to formalise complaints.

Another change was the introduction of a new case management system known as *Reconcile*.[53] This system, which is web-based, allows inspectors access to relevant information and files relating to a case, whether they are in the office or in the field.

A further change was the updating of inspection procedures. These changes placed a greater importance on the principle of 'rectification'. Where breaches of legislation are found, inspectors first try to put these violations right, without starting a prosecution. For example, if an employer is found to be not paying an employee the wage to which they are entitled, then the employer is given the opportunity to correct the situation by paying the arrears in full and will not be prosecuted if the back-dated payment is made. If rectification does not occur, then the inspectorate normally collects all relevant material, including records and starts a prosecution case.

TABLE 6.1: INSPECTION STATISTICS, 2002-2006

Year	Inspections/Visits	Prosecutions/Initiated	Arrears Recovered
2002	8,323	25	N/A
2003	7,168	20	€226,000
2004	5,160	14	€486,000
2005	5,719	25	€469,300
2006	15,670	12	€1,400,000

Table 6.1 outlines some basic statistics relating to labour inspections and shows the heavy rectification orientation of the service. It shows that labour inspectors carry out thousands of visits/inspections each year, but only a tiny fraction of these lead to prosecutions. In 2006, there were more than 15,000 inspections, but only 12 prosecutions were initiated. This figure shows that the Labour Inspectorate is not interested primarily in initiating prosecutions; it seems to regard its task as identifying infringements to labour standards and rectifying the situation by ensuring that employers put right the situation. In 2005, the 15,000+ labour inspection visits resulted in the recovery of €1.4 million, which averages out at under €90 per visit.

---

[53]   *Reconcile* is an acronym for Remotely Connected Online Communication for Labour Inspection & Enforcement.

6.4   THE LABOUR INSPECTORATE IN PRACTICE

Over the years, the Labour Inspectorate has become a key aspect of the industrial relations system but, in carrying out its activities, the Inspectorate faces a number of problems. One problem is that different avenues of redress are set out by different pieces of employment rights legislation. For example, some legislation enables employees to take a case to the Rights Commissioners, the Labour Court or the Employment Appeals Tribunal. Legal advice suggests that, in these situations, the role of the Labour Inspectorate is simply to ascertain whether the employer has kept proper records relating to wages and employment contracts. The Inspectorate can prosecute on this breach but other breaches must be handled by the Rights Commissioners. In other words, the Inspectorate is unable to enforce the substance of the legislation, which puts considerable constraints on its role. This is one example of the adverse consequences of the fragmentation of labour enforcement institutions in Anglo-Saxon countries.

A second problem is the confusingly different roles given to employment rights bodies by individual pieces of employment legislation – for example, the Payment of Wages Act restricts the role of the Inspectorate to ensuring that employers issue payslips; other complaints under the Act are addressed by the Rights Commissioners. As a result, it is conceivable that separate public agencies may be addressing the same alleged infringement of employment standards, causing unnecessary duplication in the enforcement process. A further problem is that, as employment legislation gets more specialised and complex, the activities of the labour inspectorate become more difficult. In particular, inspectors find it more difficult to prepare cases for prosecution that require quite a high level of legal competence. The situation is made worse because the inspectorate has limited access to in-house legal expertise.

Other problems relate to the organisation of the Employment Rights Compliance Service itself. There is a high level of staff turnover, which is unfortunate, as on-the-job experience is at a premium when carrying out inspections. Question marks exist about whether the training received by inspectors is comprehensive enough. Inspectors face a series of avoidable difficulties when carrying out their functions. Considerable legal ambiguity exists about what is the appropriate format of records that should be held by employers. One view is that this uncertainty could be resolved by the introduction of standard *pro forma* documentation (authors' interview with DETE officials). Another problem is that the burden of non-compliance proof in prosecutions rests on inspectors, which can add significantly to their workload. A further hindrance is that inspectors have a lack of access to domestic premises that are also places of work. Yet another problem is what is called the 'phoenix syndrome': the situation where a company closes down while being pursued for non-compliance with labour standards, but continues trading by creating another company under a different name. Many of these problems could be addressed by greater clarity in employment legislation.

TABLE 6.2: PENALTIES FOR VIOLATING LABOUR LEGISLATION

Legislation	Offence	Maximum Fines	
		Once-off / First Offence	Each Continuing Offence
Industrial Relations Acts 1946-2004	Failure to pay minimum rate	€952.30	€253.95
	Failure to keep records	€634.87	
	Refusal to produce records	€1,269.84	
	Obstruction		
	Failure to comply with lawful requirement of Inspector		
	Non-compliance with Labour Court Order		
Protection of Young Persons (Employment) Act 1996	All offences under the Act	€1,904.61	€317.43
Organisation of Working Time Act 1997	All offences under the Act	€1,904.61 (IR£1,500)	€634.85
National Minimum Wage Act 2000	All offences under the Act	€1,904.61 €12,697.38 – conviction on indictment	€253.95 €1,269.74 – conviction on indictment
Payment of Wages Act 1991	All offences under the Act	€1,269.74	
Protection of Employment Act 1997 (as amended by European Communities Protection of Employment Regulations 2000)	All offences under the Act	€1,904.61	
Employment Agency Act 1971	All offences under the Act	€2,000	€1,000

The penalties that employers face when they are found to be in breach of employment legislation are set out in **Table 6.2**. These range from a minimum of €634, to a maximum of €1,904. In theory, an employer can be fined for each individual violation of an employment standard per employee. Thus, if a firm with 20 employees was prosecuted successfully for breaching both the Organisation of Working Time Act and the National Minimum Wage Act, it would be fined €20,680.[54] At first glance, this seems a hefty enough penalty, but there is a rub. A successful prosecution is dependent on the employer having kept full records for employees. Where the firm has kept no records, it can only be fined €3,808.[55] Thus, the penalty system actually creates an incentive for employers not to keep records: the employer who keeps records is fined considerably more than the employer who does not. A cost/benefit analysis of this penalty system probably would conclude that rogue employers face no effective deterrent for not complying with labour standards.

6.5 REFORMING THE EMPLOYMENT RIGHTS REGIME: IMPLICATIONS FOR THE LABOUR INSPECTORATE

Considerable efforts have been made recently to reform the system of employment rights compliance. The reform agenda seeks to address two issues:

- Improving the co-ordination between the different employment rights agencies.
- Streamlining and consolidating the many stand-alone pieces of employment legislation that have been passed over the years.

The first reform initiative was the Review Group on the Functions of Employment Rights Bodies. The remit of this Group was 'to review the role and relationships of the Employment Rights Bodies, so as to recommend options to enhance the coherence and user-friendliness of the employment rights adjudication and enforcement systems'. After extensive consultation with a wide range of interested parties, the review proposed a range of changes, focusing on procedural matters, including:

- Improving the delivery of the employment rights service.
- Making the procedure simpler to pursue a case of alleged infringement of employment rights.
- Making the service more user-friendly, by creating a single point of contact.

---

[54] The fine is calculated as: [€1,904+(€634x19)] + [€1,904+(€254x19)] = €20,680.

[55] The fine is calculated as €1,904 x 2 – the fine for lack of records under both Acts.

- Consolidating the existing body of employment legislation to eliminate inconsistencies and overlaps
- Widening the repertoire of services offered to the public, such as delivering a more comprehensive mediation system.

Although these recommendations do not appear overly-radical, they did not win the full support of the various stakeholders of the employment rights and dispute resolution regime in the country. It is unclear why some were unhappy with the recommendations, as most of the objections to the review's recommendations were made behind closed doors. In response to representations of concern, the Department of Enterprise, Trade & Employment set up an internal review, which resulted in some of the Review Group's recommendations being set aside and the setting-up of an Employment Rights Compliance Group, whose remit was to create a set of specific proposals on institutional changes to ensure more effective enforcement and compliance with employment standards.

The Rights Compliance Group, which consisted of civil servants and the social partners, first established a set of principles that should underpin the reorganisation of the employment rights compliance system, which suggested that the system must:

- Be effective in promoting high levels of compliance with employment rights legislation.
- Be fair.
- Be simple to understand and use.
- Ensure that a person seeking to use the service must know where to go for information about the vindication of rights.
- Strive to ensure that waiting periods for the service are short, and that problems are resolved speedily.
- Allow those involved in an employment rights case to retain ownership of the problem, while, at the same time, facilitating confidence that the problem will be resolved.
- Serve the 'public interest' aspects of legislation adequately.
- Provide good value for money.

Several important proposed organisational reforms were put forward by the group. Perhaps the most significant was the idea of a new nine-level compliance model, described below:

- **Level 1:** Education and awareness are the main activities carried out at this level. These activities include advertising campaigns, education modules and seminars targeted at groups such as employers, migrant workers, students, etc.

- **Level 2:** Provision of information by the Employment Rights Information Unit is the focus of this level. The main activity involves operating a telephone service that provides information and guidance to the public on employment rights and how to pursue an employment rights case or make a complaint about an alleged breach of an employment right.

- **Level 3:** Complaints relating to the Protection of Young Persons Act and failure to keep records is the focus of this level. The recommendation of the group was that these offences should carry penalties to signal to employers that breaches will not be tolerated.

- **Level 4:** Complaints other than those relating to the Protection of Young Persons Act and failure to keep records are dealt with at this level. It also introduces a new procedure, whereby aggrieved employees are given the option of seeking redress *via* the Rights Commissioners rather than relying on the services of the Labour Inspectorate to take the case on their behalf to the law courts, which is currently the situation.

- **Level 5:** Complaints (other than those relating to the Protection of Young People and failure to keep records) that will be handled by the Labour Inspectorate are the concern of this level. In these cases, the Labour Inspectorate will take the lead role in pursuing the case, rather than the aggrieved employee, and will take cases to the Rights Commissioner rather than to the law courts, which is the current practice. If the Labour Inspectorate fails to find any breach of employment law, then the case is considered to be at an end.

- **Level 6:** This level establishes that the first hearing relating to cases that emerge from level 4 or Level 5 will be conducted by the Rights Commissioners.

- **Level 7:** Appeals to decisions made by the Rights Commissioners at Level 6 will be addressed at this level. Appeals will be adjudicated by the Labour Court or the Employment Appeals Tribunal, whichever is appropriate.

- **Level 8:** This level introduces a simplified procedure that allows the complainant to use a law court to obtain a court order when the employer has not honoured the award made by a Rights Commissioner, Employment Appeals Tribunal or Labour Court.

- **Level 9:** This level makes provision for an appeal to the High Court, mainly on a point of law. It is to ensure that full procedural justice is built into the compliance model.

While there was considerable agreement within the group on much of the new compliance model, there were also areas of disagreement. There was not full agreement on the enforcement of some employment legislation: employer organisations favoured the retention of the current system of civil courts making judgements on criminal transgressions, while trade unions favoured the approach proposed in the model, where redress is obtained through the employment rights bodies by the employee or the Labour Inspectorate. No consensus could be reached on a proposal that labour inspectors should have the ability to issue on-the-spot fines. There was also no agreement on a trade union proposal to take the Labour Inspectorate out of the Department of Enterprise, Trade & Employment and create a new stand-alone agency. Discussions were continuing on these, and other matters, when negotiations on a new social partnership deal, subsequently called *Towards 2016*, focused heavily on employment rights enforcement. These negotiations eclipsed the deliberations of the Employment Rights Compliance Group and the agreements that were reached in *Towards 2016* will have a big impact on labour inspection for some time to come.

6.6   *TOWARDS 2016* & EMPLOYMENT STANDARD-SETTING

An important part of *Towards 2016* was the creation of a new Office of the Director for Employment Rights within the Department of Enterprise, Trade & Employment.[56] The establishment of this Office expands significantly the existing Labour Inspectorate and increase the effectiveness of labour standard-setting activity in Ireland. *Towards 2016* did not prescribe a detailed compliance strategy for the new Office. Instead, the social partners were given a central role in developing the work programme of the new Office. Ongoing public discussions are envisaged between the social partners, officials of the Office and a new Advisory Board, to ensure that the compliance system is comprehensive, effective and responsive. A budget of €750,000 has been earmarked to develop educational and promotional activities associated with the enforcement and compliance of labour standards.

Towards 2016 considerably strengthens the labour standards enforcement and compliance regime. On the one hand, the staff of the Labour Inspectorate will increase from 31 to 90 by the end of

---

[56]   As this book went to print, the proposed Office of the Director for Employment Rights was constituted formally as the National Employment Rights Authority (NERA). This chapter reflects the proposed operation of the organisation as known at the time of writing. For updated information on NERA, see http://www.employmentrights.ie.

2007, and the back-up administrative, accounting and legal support services will also be expanded by 23 staff. In addition, five new Rights Commissioners will be appointed. On the other hand, the system of penalties and redress will be toughened up. A summary conviction for a breach of employment rights in the District Court could lead to a €5,000 fine, and even a custodial sentence, if appropriate. Penalties of up €250,000 could be levied on indictment for such things as non-maintenance of statutory employment records and transgressions under the Protection of Young Persons Act 1996. With regard to cases brought before Rights Commissioners, the Employment Appeals Tribunal and the Labour Court, *Towards 2016* specifies that a proper redress system should exist so that employees who win cases receive just and equitable rewards.

The procedures and practices set out in *Towards 2016* to obtain compliance with employment standards more or less follow those devised by the Employment Rights Compliance Group reviewed above. In addition to this new model of compliance, *Towards 2016* stipulates that there should be a more systematic approach to the monitoring of labour market trends, particularly in relation to changing patterns of employment, earnings and labour standards.

Another new arrangement created was the Redundancy Panel, a three-member panel that can be established on request, either by the representatives of employees in an organisation or by the employer, in certain situations of collective redundancies, involving the planned replacement of existing staff with other existing, or replacement, staff on materially reduced terms and conditions of employment. After hearing submissions from employees and employers, the Panel can make a request to the Minister of Enterprise, Trade & Employment to ask the Labour Court to get involved in the case.

A further new initiative set out in *Towards 2016* related to supporting employment standards through public procurement. In particular, a tighter set of procedures was agreed to ensure that public authorities could monitor more effectively how firms that have secured government contracts are complying with employment legislation and standards.

In addition, *Towards 2016* contains other new measures relating to the enforcement and compliance of labour standards and thus it stands apart from the other seven national social agreements in the manner in which it addresses so comprehensively and directly the matter of employment rights and their enforcement. The highly-controversial Irish Ferries industrial dispute of 2005 is the main reason why there was so much focus on employment standard-setting. *Towards 2016* certainly places the matter at the centre of industrial relations in the country.

6.6.1   Labour standard-setting under the new compliance model

The new compliance model can be interpreted as an effort at improving the 'supply chain' that connects the different institutional parts of the employment rights regime. The five principles of effective supply chain management are connectivity, collaboration, synchronisation, leverage and scalability. Each principle seems to have been addressed, at least to some extent, by the new compliance model, although this is unlikely to have been done intentionally. Thus, the model sets out to improve the **connectivity** between the various employment rights bodies by introducing procedural reforms that improve co-ordination between these bodies. On the matter of **collaboration**, *Towards 2016* states that 'the parties are agreed on the need for greater co-ordination between organisations concerned with employment rights compliance'. Joint action, for example, is envisaged between the Labour Inspectorate and the Department of Social & Family Affairs to investigate breaches of employment legislation. The new compliance model places considerable emphasis on improving the **synchronisation** of the different services to eliminate unnecessary overlaps between different bodies and to develop more concerted and focused efforts to uphold employment rights: thus, for example, explicit efforts are being made to dovetail the activities of the Rights Commissioners and the Labour Inspectorate. The new model also assumes a **leverage** process emerging, whereby greater liaison and co-ordination between the different agencies is likely to release additional activities to make the enforcement of labour standards more effective. Finally, a more integrated employment rights compliance regime is likely to secure **scalability**, as the collective impact of the various bodies will be greater than the sum of the individual parts.

Thus the new compliance model envisages the Labour Inspectorate increasingly being nested in a series of complementary relationships with other employment rights bodies. Dovetailing better with other agencies, it is anticipated, will enhance the capabilities and effectiveness of the new Office of Director for Employment Rights. At this stage, it is too early to say whether these organisational reforms will produce the sought-after dynamic effects. The gap between an organisational plan and organisational outcomes can sometimes be large, due to a multitude of factors. Inertia within organisations can reduce internal willingness to embrace change fully. Organisations can become overly-defensive about established mandates and ways of working and thus do not exploit the full opportunities that are created to work with other bodies. It would be naïve to think that the existing employment rights bodies are free of such traits. Implementing the new compliance mechanisms will be a challenge.

6.6.2   The new compliance system and the Latin model

A feature of the changes introduced by *Towards 2016* is that these focus largely on administrative, operational and technical matters. The traditional approach to labour law enforcement and compliance remains more or less intact: the emphasis is still very much on seeking out deviant employers and then rectifying the situation without issuing a penalty. Government and the social partners appear keen that this approach is maintained. Employer organisations have consistently voiced the view that organisations that do not comply with legally-based labour standards should face sanctions. Employers adopt this stance, in part because they realise that firms breaching the law are gaining an unfair advantage on good employers who comply with the law. However, they also take this position, as they realise that, in a complaints-based regulatory system, a public agency is mostly concerned with taking a case against an organisation in breach of a labour standard. It tends not to ask questions about the type of corporate strategies the organisation intends following to ensure compliance with the law in the future. In a complaints-based system, the deviant organisation is punished without any serious scrutiny of its internal human resource management architecture. Employers find this regulatory regime acceptable, as it more or less keeps the autonomy of the enterprise intact. Trade unions also seem happy with the traditional penalty-based approach, mainly because it is a visible and clear-cut form of punishment for the violation of labour standards.

Is there a case for not only altering the administrative system of the employment rights regime, but also changing the underlying system? According to Piore (2005), the approach taken to labour inspection by countries such as France and Spain, and more or less across Latin America, is superior to the Anglo-Saxon system. As outlined earlier, labour inspectors in the Latin system have considerable discretion in implementing a unified Labour Code. When implementing the Labour Code, inspectors tend only to enforce penalties when the violations involved are wilful and deliberate. Inspectors more often work with the enterprise in developing a compliance plan that ensures that specified labour standards are adhered to over time. The intention is to encourage firms to develop corporate practices and strategies that allow them to comply with standards, rather than bringing regulatory obligations down to the productivity levels characteristic of non-compliant firms. Thus, inspectors work as much as advisors and consultants to firms on business upgrading as public regulators of employment rights. Piore (2005) suggests that inspectors are able to perform both roles, as they have wide experience of different organisations and thus are in a position to disseminate best practice on how to comply with employment regulations.

On paper, the Latin model is attractive, because it is designed to ensure that firms comply with labour standards by upgrading business practices: compliance with labour regulations thus is more sustainable. In the context of Latin America, this approach appears to be eminently sensible, as over-rigid implementation of labour regulations might drive enterprises out of business with the consequence of disrupting the economic development process. However, despite the attractiveness of the Latin model, it is questionable whether it is suitable to the Irish case. Otto Kahn-Freund (1974), one of the founders of modern labour law, consistently warned that attempts to transplant an approach to labour law from one country to another probably would end in failure. This is because labour law is rooted in the social and institutional practices of a particular country, and thus is not easily transferred to a different national system. In this context, the Latin model may not be appropriate to Ireland, as it would require root-and-branch change to the Irish system of labour inspection. It would involve inspectors adopting an entirely new method of working, with which they have little experience and, probably, little empathy. The social partners also would baulk at changing the traditional enforcement method, thus depriving labour inspectors of their much-needed support. Thus, despite its appeal, at least on paper, the Latin model is simply too out of tune with the Irish system of labour inspection.

6.6.3   Avoiding the labour migration-social dumping trap

At the same time, some reservations can be expressed about the current direction of public policy towards labour enforcement in Ireland. One of the main reasons why the enforcement of labour standards figured so prominently in *Towards 2016* was the highly-controversial Irish Ferries industrial dispute. This dispute put the issue of companies displacing Irish workers with migrant workers at the centre of Irish employment relations. The strengthening of the enforcement and compliance of labour standards in *Towards 2016* was a response to that dispute. One danger with this development is that labour standard-setting becomes too dominated by the perceived social dumping effects of foreign workers arriving in Ireland: labour migration becomes synonymous with social dumping in the minds of many. However, the evidence to support this connection is weak. Nonetheless, this matter is worth looking at in further detail.

Social dumping arising from labour migration may manifest itself through job displacement and downward pressure on wages. The argument is that, if migrants have the same levels of skills and experience as indigenous workers in a particular sector, and if the demand for labour in that sector is stable, then job displacement could occur, as employers have an incentive to lay-off existing workers and to recruit migrants at a lower rate of pay. Thus, Irish workers lose jobs, and wage levels fall.

There have been few convincing empirical studies, either in Ireland or elsewhere, that have assessed the impact of migration on labour market outcomes. Studies investigating the matter in Austria, France, Germany and the UK reach the same conclusion: that migration does not adversely impact on the domestic workforce and that job displacement is considered to be low (Commander *et al.*, 2006). Another investigation into the impact of migration on wage levels found that it had a small, negative effect on the pay of domestic workers of between -0.3 to -0.8%. These findings are more or less in line with the extensive literature on the subject in the USA (Borjas, 2003). This suggests that migration has had little or no job displacement effect, but tends to depress the wage levels of unskilled workers.

These empirical studies are not in line with public opinion in Ireland on the matter. The popular view is that high levels of labour migration cause job losses amongst domestic workers, undermine working conditions and rights, and increase social tensions. The truth is that it is difficult to assess from official figures whether job displacement is happening. Thus, in 2005, there was a reduction of 19,400 Irish workers in the manufacturing sector, yet the number of non-Irish nationals employed in the sector increased by 10,900. Similarly, in the hotel and retailing sectors, the employment of Irish nationals decreased by 1,000, but employment by non-nationals increased by 5,200.

It seems clear that, without the participation of non-nationals in the hotel and retailing sectors, the strong recent output performance of these sectors would have slowed down, as there would have been 4,200 fewer jobs. Thus, non-Irish workers contributed positively to growth in these sectors. The case of manufacturing is less clear-cut, for the significant growth in jobs held by non-nationals was in the context of employment falling in the sector by 10,900. On the surface, it appears that some form of labour displacement was occurring, with non-nationals being recruited to jobs previously held by Irish workers. Although this scenario cannot be ruled out fully, it may well be that non-Irish nationals were taking jobs that Irish employees were reluctant to accept. It is simply hard to draw a definite conclusion. Moreover, even if there was some degree of labour displacement, this does not necessarily mean that a form of wage dumping was taking place, as most manufacturing jobs are governed by going rates of pay. Furthermore, even if non-nationals increased their share of jobs in the sector relative to Irish workers, is this a problem in the context of overall strong Irish employment growth?

Thus the issues of job displacement and wage dumping are as complex as they are contentious. Fears and anxieties fuelled by these accounts have been exacerbated by the high-profile Irish Ferries dispute. However, the increased incidence of non-compliance with labour standards should not be attributed to the entry of international workers into the Irish labour market. Rather, it is due to more structural economic processes that have emerged in developed countries (Manning & Goos, 2003). Almost everywhere, advanced economies are experiencing a radical change in labour demand dynamics, which involves rising relative demand for well-paid and low-paid work and falling relative demand for 'middling' jobs that can be replaced easily by technology. Much of the growth in low-paid jobs has manifested itself in urban labour markets (Farris & Reich, 2005). In many cities, small firms, and other new forms of business organisations, in a variety of industries, ranging from construction, supermarkets, restaurants, and janitorial services, are creating jobs that are effectively beyond the reach of employment legislation. These new forms of employment are a big source of Ireland's problems relating to labour standards enforcement. There is a migrant worker dimension to this problem, as it is increasingly international workers who take these precarious jobs. However, it is not labour migration that is the source of the problem. Instead, it is the process of economic development itself.

6.6.4 Labour standards and socially-responsible labour market behaviour

Thus, it is important not to frame the enforcement and compliance of labour standards around the matter of labour migration and social dumping; this is far too narrow a focus. Adverse labour market developments are the result of a multitude of complex economic forces that pose considerable challenges for labour standard enforcement strategies (Deakin, 2004). What is missing from the Irish discussion is any systematic debate on whether the traditional complaints-based approach is sufficient to deliver widespread compliance with labour standards in today's labour market. One of the first tasks of the new Employment Rights Office must be to assess the appropriateness to the Irish situation of pro-active labour standards compliance strategies that are being invented elsewhere. A fast-growing literature is emerging on these new strategies (Davies & Rideout, 2000). Much of the focus of this research is on how public agencies can use standard-setting activity to promote socially-responsible labour market behaviour.

One strand of this literature focuses on the creation of mechanisms within economic sectors designed to promote the adoption of industry-based employment standards or to monitor corporate behaviour to ensure that egregious employment practices are not being pursued (Estlund, 2005). These sector-level standard-setting arrangements invariably involve the representatives of employers and employees in creating codes of conduct that establish the boundaries between good and bad employment practices. These arrangements also exercise peer pressure on firms within the relevant industry to adhere to good employment practices. In more theoretical terms, these sector-level standard-setting initiatives address what is known as the 'reputation commons' problem. Within a particular industry, firms, collectively, may wish to maintain a positive reputation. However, individual firms may seek to 'free ride' and thus adopt practices that deviate from the collectively-agreed good employment practice code. In the short-term, the free-riding firm might benefit, as it does not have to incur the extra costs involved in complying with higher employment standards but, in the medium-term, the collective reputation of the sector is damaged: this is known as the 'tragedy of the commons' – self-seeking individual behaviour harms the collective interest (Ostrom, 1980). Sector-based standard-setting initiatives are an attempt to manage the 'reputation commons', by encouraging individual enterprises to act in a matter consistent with the reputation of the sector as a whole.

Another strand of this literature examines labour standard-setting activity within business networks (Locke *et al.*, 2006). Increasingly, the boundaries between individual firms are blurring, as they strive to enhance competitive performance. Stronger relationships and linkages between enterprises result in the success of an individual firm being dependent more directly on the corporate infrastructure in which it is located. Heightened commercial interdependency has resulted in those participating in networks developing a range of programmes to ensure high levels of quality, flexibility and responsiveness between firms that make up the business network. For the most part, these programmes aim at co-ordinating the commercial activities of the participating enterprises, but these same co-ordinating procedures increasingly are being used to establish standards inside the network with regard to worker welfare. The shift in focus has not been altogether altruistic. Some large firms, which are usually the lead organisation in the business network, have recognised that their market reputation could be damaged by a sub-contractor in the network not treating its workforce properly.

Thus, for example, many leading sports clothing firms, such as Nike, Adidas and Reebok, have introduced far-reaching programmes and procedures to ensure that their sub-contactors are not violating core labour standards. These companies are only too aware that scandals relating to health and safety or child labour could trigger a highly-damaging consumer boycott. However, using the supply chain to set labour standards is not restricted to large multinationals ensuring that their sub-contractors in developing countries manage their workforce in a decent and proper manner. It is spilling over into other commercial settings. For example, in many countries in Europe, arrangements are being built into large construction projects to ensure that all the companies involved comply with established employment rights. Some big companies, as part of their new drive towards corporate social responsibility, are putting in place procedures to monitor and audit employment relations regimes in supplier companies. These various initiatives essentially are seeking to diffuse worker welfare initiatives vertically through the supply chain.

A third strand of the literature involves new initiatives by public agencies, which vary in character and purpose. Some involve the development of a specialised institution dedicated to addressing one aspect of labour standard-setting. One example of such an institution is the Low Pay Commission, established by the UK Labour Government in 1999 (Metcalf, 2006). This body is charged with proposing levels and increases to the minimum wage. To do this, the Commission carries out extensive research and analysis of Government statistics, as well as surveying firms directly. In addition, it conducts extensive consultations with trade unions and employers' organisations, as well as with individual enterprises. The purpose of these activities is to develop a comprehensive evidence-based assessment of the impact of the minimum wage, so that the Commission is better placed to make recommendations on the extent to which it should be increased and how compliance with it could be improved.

Other initiatives that have been launched seek to develop more strategic approaches to labour standard-setting. For example, in 2005, the Canadian Government established a review that was charged with modernising Federal labour standards (Canadian Government, 2005). In addition to making recommendations with regard to updating employment legislation and re-organising administrative practices, the review team argued that a more focused approach should be developed to labour compliance and enforcement. In particular, it recommended that, rather than seeking to improve overall compliance with workplace standards, a more targeted approach should be adopted that aims to give more effective protection to the most vulnerable workers. It suggested that focusing on economic vulnerability would require a move away from the complaints-based model of enforcement to a more pro-active approach that would involve working with firms in vulnerable sectors, and with other public agencies, to ensure that a comprehensive safety-net existed for the least well-off in the labour market. Labour inspectors would not be looking out simply for infringements of laws, but would also be working with firms to prevent infringements taking place. These preventative activities involve inspectors working with employers and employees in setting goals and targets with regard to complying with labour market standards and then helping them to be met. Thus, inspectors deal with elaborating, implementing and evaluating organisational compliance plans and getting involved in campaigns promoting labour standards. Their role is as much to do with advice, as with enforcement.

Thus, there has been an emergence of new thinking about how to implement labour standards more effectively (Lobel, 2004). Behind this new thinking is dissatisfaction with standard approaches to the enforcement of labour standards. Conventional approaches to enforcement suffer from not enough inspectors, not enough penalties and not enough deterrence. In Ireland, it is questionable whether the traditional enforcement approach of the Labour Inspectorate has raised the costs of non-compliance high enough to outweigh the immediate gains of non-compliance. Most enforcement actions secure only the back wages owed to employees: as a result, employers risk very little by underpaying employees, even if they are detected – which is unlikely. The new, emerging compliance strategies suggest that, even if countries have a comprehensive and all-encompassing system of labour regulation, there may be an enforcement gap. The traditional approaches used to ensure compliance may not be effective enough and, as a result, may need to be supported by a wide variety of experiments on new forms of enforcement.

This new thinking on labour standard-setting has resulted in distinctly hybrid models of enforcement and compliance emerging in many countries. The architecture of these hybrid systems is country-specific but, invariably, it houses a variety of initiatives to improve compliance with labour standards. Some of these involve working with firms to develop internal human resource management systems that will ensure that they are in compliance with labour standards. Others involve labour inspectors working with groups of firms in particular sectors to establish systems of 'monitored self-regulation'. These systems invariably involve firms and labour inspectors establishing a code of conduct on labour standards, and then creating a monitoring mechanism to ensure compliance. Still further examples involve creating procedures that are designed to gather credible information relevant to compliance with labour standards. Thus, there seems to be a flurry of activity around new forms of enforcement and compliance of labour market standards. The worry is that, despite the expansion and some reorganisation of the Labour Inspectorate in Ireland, strategic thinking and activity on developing innovative compliance initiatives is lagging behind other countries.

6.7   THE LRC & THE NEW COMPLIANCE REGIME

The new compliance and enforcement regime for labour standards set out in *Towards 2016* is likely to impinge on the activities of the LRC in a number of ways. First, as a result of the changes that are being introduced, not only will the Rights Commissioners increase in number but they are likely also to play an even more prominent role in the enforcement of labour standards in the future. This will place a number of demands on the LRC, which administers and, to some extent, manages the Rights Commissioner Service. The LRC will have to ensure that Commissioners have access to comprehensive and ongoing training, so that they have the skills and knowledge to carry out their duties. It will also have to ensure that the support services provided for the Rights Commissioners are comprehensive and function well. Greater effort will be needed perhaps to make employees aware of the role of the Rights Commissioners. Well-designed awareness campaigns targeted at vulnerable employees in low risk sectors are probably needed the most. Overall, the LRC needs to examine its internal structure to ensure that it can support the growing role of the Rights Commissioners.

The lack of co-ordination and collaborative activity among the employment rights bodies has been a major theme in the recent discussions. The changes being introduced will attempt to address this. More joint initiatives between agencies are likely to be encouraged. Attempts at getting more collaborative activity will fall short, unless individual agencies make a concerted effort to play a full role in such initiatives. This places an onus on the LRC to assess what joint efforts with other agencies are feasible and desirable, so that it can help improve compliance with labour standards. There is little doubt that the new Office of the Director for Employment Rights[57] will step up awareness and educational activity on employment rights and compliance – it has a budget of €750,000 to do this.

The LRC should be considering ways it can contribute purposefully to this effort, by promoting its codes of conduct among firms or by giving them advice on the type of people management systems that might be required to ensure that they are in compliance with the law. The new enforcement regime, in other words, will require the LRC to take the matter of joined-up, inter-agency collaboration more seriously than ever before. Moreover, this joined-up activity need not involve only other employment rights bodies, but should also include employers, trade unions, and even NGOs. Alliance-building is likely to become an important activity in promoting compliance with labour standards and the LRC will need to consider how it will engage positively with this development.

The recent large-scale public policy activity on labour standards enforcement and compliance is just another piece of evidence in support of the growth in rights-based employment relations activity: more and more workers are prepared to vindicate employment rights. Part of this activity is the result of the growth of legislation in employment relations matters, and part of it is due to the emergence of economic sectors that trade unions find it difficult to organise. The emergence of rights-based employment relations activity has the knock-on effect of increasing awareness that, behind those

---

[57]   NERA – see footnote 57.

employees who are prepared to make claims, there are many more that do nothing about infringements of employment standards and suffer in silence. This gives momentum to the demand for more effective enforcement strategies. The LRC has to consider whether it is positioned properly to address the challenges that arise from rights-based employment relations.

For example, one of the consequences of the growth of rights-based employment relations will be increased demand for new non-legal approaches for the prevention and resolution of disputes. In response to this demand, the LRC may have to develop even further its preventative and advisory activity. For example, it might have to develop initiatives, such as drafting a model informal conflict management system that organisations could use to develop fair, impartial, efficient and appropriate processes to resolve issues at the lowest level, and at the earliest stage, so that these do not end up at one of the employment rights bodies. It might have to develop more pro-active policies such as working with particular public sector organisations to develop flagship examples of informal conflict management processes, from which other organisations can learn. The matter of the LRC training mediators in organisations, so that they can play an active role in in-house conflict management processes, will have to be seriously considered. Developing best practice guidelines for organisations on the use of external consultants as a third party in solving disputes is another matter that needs close attention. In other words, the emergence of rights-based employment relations agencies is generating a new dispute resolution agenda on which the Commission needs to take decisive and encompassing action.

6.8   CONCLUSION

For a long time, labour inspection was considered a peripheral, less than glamorous, part of industrial relations systems, but now it is in fashion in many countries around the globe. Labour rights compliance is gaining prominence, because of the decline of trade unions and collective bargaining activity on the one hand, and the rise in economic vulnerability on the other. Worker protection is very much back on the agenda. Without effective systems of labour inspection, the concern is that many workers may be deprived of their rights.

Developments in Ireland are in line with the international trend. In recent years, considerable efforts have been made to upgrade and strengthen the existing system of labour inspection. This chapter expressed concern that the changes to the Labour Inspectorate risk being too closely associated with the ongoing national debate about labour migration and social dumping. At the same time, it also suggested that the reforms being implemented will improve the effectiveness of the Labour Inspectorate.

The steps being taken to modernise the Labour Inspectorate are likely to bring at least five benefits to the system:

- More effective connections with other employment rights bodies, which should reduce the institutional overlaps and duplications that are currently in the system.

- A larger pool of labour inspectors, which should substantially increase the profile of what they do.

- A more active role for labour inspectors, as the constraints that limited their role in the past are likely to be removed.

- The creation of a more appropriate overall structure for labour inspections.

- A more professional Labour Inspectorate: the newly-established Office of the Director for Employment Rights is likely to lead to the introduction of more effective training programmes for inspectors and more effective management tools for the assessment and processing of cases.

And a more professional Labour Inspectorate will have a spillover effect on other employment rights bodies. In particular, it will require these bodies to ensure that their activities strongly complement the work of the new inspectorate. The LRC will not be exempt from this challenge.

These benefits are considerable and are likely to enhance the credibility of the Labour Inspectorate. At the same time, this chapter raised concern about the apparent lack of debate on the functioning of the Labour Inspectorate. In particular, there appears to have been little debate about whether the Labour Inspectorate should move beyond the complaints-based model and develop more pro-active, preventative activities to achieve better voluntary compliance with labour standards. It was suggested that other countries seem to be doing more on this matter than Ireland. Experimental initiatives on compliance and enforcement appear to have been launched elsewhere in recent times. Ireland can learn a lot from these initiatives, but no attempt should be made to transplant any measure from elsewhere, before it is customised to Irish traditions and practices. The main point is that modernising labour inspection is not simply about developing new structures and procedures, but also upgrading what inspectors do.

7

CREATING THE SAFE WORKPLACE: THE ROLE OF THE HEALTH & SAFETY AUTHORITY

7.1 INTRODUCTION

Healthy and safe workplaces are seen as a cornerstone of a civilised society. Equally, there is a consensus on the need for legislation and regulations, backed up with a public agency to enforce health and safety rules. Without a well-designed governance system, workplace health and safety standards might be sub-optimal. In economic sectors where competition is high and profit margins are low, some businesses, invariably a minority, may attempt to cut costs by not complying fully with health and safety standards, thereby putting their employees at risk. In the absence of a dedicated public agency, the threat posed by a range of chemical substances, and even working practices, may not be understood fully. Moreover, as economies and societies evolve, so the meaning of healthy and safe workplaces also changes and, without a public agency establishing norms about acceptable and unacceptable practices, a gap might emerge between employee expectations and organisational practice on health and safety matters. Thus, a public agency is required to oversee the diffusion of high-quality health and safety regimes within organisations.

This chapter examines the role of the Health & Safety Authority (HSA) in securing health and safety at work in Ireland:

- **Section 7.2** outlines the remit of the HSA and sets out data on the incidence of health and safety accidents at work, as well as prosecutions related to violations of health and safety legislation.

- **Section 7.3** explains the internal organisation of the HSA and the span of activities it carries out.

- **Sections 7.4** and **7.5** examine the inspection activities of the HSA, and recent innovations in this area.

- **Section 7.6** evaluates the move towards more preventative initiatives by the HSA and explains what this shift has meant for policy.

- **Section 7.7** assesses the lessons that the work of the HSA holds for the LRC.
- The Conclusion brings together in **section 7.8** the arguments of the chapter.

7.2   HEALTH & SAFETY AT WORK IN IRELAND

The Health & Safety Authority was established in 1989 and is responsible for the administration and enforcement of health and safety at work. It is a public agency, accountable to the Minister of State for Enterprise, Trade & Employment. In carrying out its responsibilities, the HSA undertakes a range of activities including:

- Promoting good standards of health and safety at work.
- Inspecting all places of work and monitoring compliance with health and safety laws.
- Investigating serious accidents, causes of ill-health and complaints.
- Carrying out and sponsoring research on health and safety at work.
- Publishing codes of practice, guidance and information.
- Providing an information service during office hours.
- Developing new laws and standards on health and safety at work.

In developing these activities, the HSA consults widely with employer and employee organizations, as well as with relevant experts. The headquarters of the Authority is in Dublin, but it also has offices in Athlone, Cork, Galway, Limerick, Sligo and Waterford.

An 11-member board is responsible for the development and implementation of the HSA's programmes and policies. The board is a tripartite body, consisting of three representatives from employer organisations and trade unions, as well as four independent members appointed by the Minister for State for Enterprise, Trade & Employment. The deliberations of the Board are supported by a number of advisory committees.[58] These committees bring together experts with specialised knowledge to examine particular health and safety issues, developing policy proposals based on up-to-date

---

[58]   In 2005, the advisory committees included the Construction Advisory Committee; the Farm Safety Partnership Advisory Committee; the Dangerous Substances Advisory Committee; the Regional Advisory Committees (Southern, North West, South East and Western); the Legislation & Guidance Sub-committee; the Audit & Finance Sub-committee; and the Strategic Review & Implementation Committee.

information and evidence. For example, during 2005, the Legislation & Guidance Sub-committee was involved in activities associated with the implementation of the Safety, Health & Welfare at Work Act 2005, including the completion of various guides to the Act and a range of regulations associated with its implementation. In many ways, these advisory committees are the engine room for policy development within the HSA.

The incidence of health and safety accidents and illnesses at work in Ireland is not out-of-line with other comparable countries, yet there is no room for complacency, as the number of fatalities and injuries remains significant. **Table 7.1** outlines the number of fatalities by economic sector in the period 2002-2007. It shows that, although 67 people lost their lives at work in 2007, the overall trend was downards. This decline was most marked in the construction sector: traditionally, the sector has been the source of most fatalities and injuries at work in Ireland and, indeed, in other countries.

TABLE 7.1: FATAL INCIDENTS BY ECONOMIC SECTOR, 2002-2007

	Economic Sector	2002	2003	2004	2005	2006	2007
A	Agriculture, hunting and forestry	14	20	13	18	18	11
B	Fishing	3	0	3	2	2	12
C	Mining and quarrying	3	1	0	6	2	2
D	Manufacturing	7	7	3	7	4	4
E	Electricity/gas/water	1	2	0	0	0	0
F	Construction	21	20	16	23	13	18
G	Wholesale/retail trade; repair of goods	1	4	4	8	3	1
H	Hotels and restaurants	0	2	0	0	0	0
I	Transport, storage and communication	7	9	6	5	4	9
J	Financial intermediation	0	0	1	0	0	0
K	Real estate, renting, business	0	0	0	1	2	2
L	Public admininstration/Defence	3	1	0	2	1	4
M	Education	0	0	1	0	0	0
N	Health/social work	0	0	1	0	1	0
O	Other community, social and personal services	1	4	2	2	1	4
Total		**61**	**68**	**50**	**74**	**51**	**67**

Source: http://www.hsa.ie/eng/Statistics/Fatal_Injury/.

Most fatal accidents at work are due to people being crushed or trapped by an object or machinery, falling from a height or being struck by a falling, moving or flying object. The rate of fatalities in the worst-performing economic sectors averages about 15 per 100,000 workers.

Table 7.2 sets out the number of non-fatal accidents reported to the HSA between 2002 and 2005. The biggest source of non-fatal accidents at work is manual handling, constituting 32% of the total in 2005. Falls, slips and trips, as well as injuries arising from material breakages, are also significant sources of non-fatal injuries. A worrying statistic is that 6% of non-fatal accidents arise from shocks, frights and violence from others. Sprains and strains made up 41% of the reported injuries; bruising, grazes and bites represented 17%; fractures 13% and open wounds 12%.

FIGURE 7.2: NON-FATAL INCIDENTS REPORTED TO THE HSA, 2002-2005

Economic Sector		2002	2003	2004	2005
A+B	Agriculture, forestry, fishing	1,900	1,500	1,970	1,900
C+D+E	Other production industries	5,500	5,500	3,370	4,500
F	Construction	4,500	5,300	5,820	5,700
G	Wholesale and retail	3,200	2,700	1,960	2,300
H	Hotels and restaurants	1,500	1,100	690	1,800
I	Transport, storage and communication	1,800	1,300	2,110	1,000
J+K	Financial and other services	1,800	600	770	600
L	Public administration/defense	1,400	1,300	1,300	1,900
M	Education		500	410	600
N	Health		1,900	2,830	2,700
O	Other Services	1,400	400	620	1,000
Total		**26,400**	**21,900**	**21,840**	**24,000**

Source: http://www.hsa.ie/eng/Statistics/Non-Fatal_Injury/.

7.3   THE ORGANISATION OF THE HSA

Internally, the HSA is divided into three main sections: workplace compliance and advice, prevention services and corporate services.

The Workplace Compliance & Advice section both enforces legislation and gives expert advice to employers and employees. It is divided into two main divisions: field operations and chemical safety.

The Operations division carries out a range of functions, including inspecting workplaces to ensure compliance with the law, investigating workplace accidents and providing information and guidance to economic sectors not covered by the HSA's Chemical Safety Division.

The Chemical Safety Division enforces all legislation relating to chemicals, and provides advice and information on accidents and emergencies relating to chemicals, particularly exposure to hazardous substances. It is divided into four specialised units:

- **The Hazardous Substances Assessment Unit**, which acts as the competent authority in Ireland for EU Directives on chemicals, which involves enforcing chemical-related Directives, conducting risk assessments of new and existing chemicals and participating in the development of EU chemical strategy.

- **The Occupational Hygiene Unit**, which enforces the legislation relating to exposure to chemical agents in the workplace and any related legislation. This activity involves carrying out laboratory analysis of asbestos samples taken during inspections and assessing the quality of removal work involving hazardous substances.

- **The Process Industries Unit**, which is the competent authority for the EU Seveso Directive, on environmental management, and is the national authority for the Chemical Weapons Convention, to which Ireland is a signatory. Carrying out these functions mostly involves doing inspections of workplaces and giving information and advice.

- **The ADR & Petrol Stations Unit**, which enforces legislation associated with the carriage of dangerous goods by road. It also certifies dangerous goods vehicle drivers, as well as providing certification to training providers and courses. In conjunction with local authorities, the Unit also enforces legislation in relation to the licensing of power stations. It has other ancillary functions relating to the provision of dangerous goods safety advisors and the planning and monitoring of a national programme of road checks.

The Prevention Services section is made up of three programmes:

- **Public Relations/Customer Service/Enterprise Support:** The Public Relations Unit co-ordinates the HSA's media and event activities. It organises conferences and seminars, manages the production and distribution of the HSA's publications, and co-ordinates thematic campaigns and promotional activities aimed at improving the health and safety performance of high-risk sectors. The Enterprise & Education Support/Customer Care Unit has a number of functions. First, it forms alliances with other public and private bodies to disseminate information and guidance on health and safety issues, particularly to small and medium-sized enterprises. It also develops a range of information packages, designed to increase the awareness of workplace health and safety representatives. And, it has a range of other functions, such as acting as the national contact point for the European Agency for Safety & Health at Work and the International Occupational Safety & Health Information Centre.

- **The Occupational Health Unit**, which carries out two main activities: one is to conduct inspection and enforcement duties on health-related matters; the other is to provide support and information to other sections inside the HSA in relation to the health of people at work. Included in this activity is the sensitive issue of bullying at work.

- **The Legal Services Unit**, which provides internal legal advice to the HSA and liaises with the State legal system on the conduct of prosecutions and the development of new health and safety legislation. It is considered to be the national expert unit on the legislative process relating to health and safety matters.

The Corporate Services Unit looks after the internal administration of the HSA, including finance, human resource and information technology matters. It also provides support for the Board and the various advisory committees in developing the HSA's strategic policies.

7.4   THE HSA & WORKPLACE INSPECTIONS

A key function of the HSA is to enforce legislation on occupational health, safety and welfare. Inspections of workplaces are used to ensure that organisations are complying with the law. If a HSA inspector concludes that an organisation is in violation of health and safety legislation, s/he may:

- Issue an Improvement Direction, under which an employer is required to develop an Improvement Plan that addresses the matters that the inspector considers may involve health or safety risks to other people (not only employees).

- Issue an Improvement Notice, stating that an employer has broken a provision of an Act or Regulation.

- Issue a Prohibition Notice, in relation to an activity that the inspector considers a risk to the health and safety of persons at work. This might require an immediate cessation of work.

- In certain cases, recommend the initiation of prosecutions.

- Give directions or instructions.

The HSA carries out a large number of inspections each year, although the number varies from year to year. For example in 2001, 14,929 inspections were conducted, but this number dropped to 10,704 in 2003, and increased to 13,552 in 2005. **Table 7.3** outlines the number of inspections by economic sector and inspection type in 2005. It shows that the vast majority of inspections were initiated by the HSA inspectorate: over 80% of inspections are for compliance; 11% followed on from complaints; and 8% related to accident reports. It also shows that the four economic sectors most inspected were construction, manufacturing, wholesale and retail trade and agriculture. Almost half of all inspections were in the construction industry.

TABLE 7.3: HSA INSPECTIONS BY ECONOMIC SECTOR & INSPECTION TYPE, 2006

Economic sector		Inspection type			
		Inspected for compliance	Investigate complaint	Investigate accident	Total inspections
A	Agriculture, hunting and forestry	1,408	17	32	1,457
B	Fishing	7	1	3	10
C	Mining and quarrying	384	53	57	478
D	Manufacturing	2,126	78	242	2,446
E	Electricity/gas/water	53	0	14	67
F	Construction	6,514	627	565	7,616
G	Wholesale/retail trade; repair of motor vehicles, personal and household goods	994	46	69	1,109
H	Hotels/restaurants	42	8	13	63
I	Transport, storage, communications	972	36	82	1,092
J	Financial intermediation	19	4	2	25
K	Real estate, renting, business	240	27	19	267
L	Public administration/defence	197	23	26	246
M	Education	47	7	8	62
N	Health/social work	97	23	17	237
O	Other community, social and personal services	149	12	25	186
Total		**13,250**	**938**	**1,177**	**15,365**

Table 7.4 sets out details of the enforcement actions that were taken as a result of inspections. It shows that, on average, 42% of inspections resulted in some form of enforcement action, although there is considerable variation between sectors. It is interesting to note that education, health/social work and parts of the public sector had amongst the highest enforcement/inspection ratios. The table also shows that written advice was by far the most frequent action taken by inspectors: written advice outweighed both prohibition notices and improvement notices by more than a factor of 10. If written advice is left aside, enforcement action was taken on 7% of inspections. Overall, the level of enforcement action was highest in mining and quarrying, education and agriculture. Unsurprisingly, most of the Prohibition Notices – 393 out of 493 – were in the construction sector. Most of the Improvement Notices were issued in the manufacturing and construction sectors – 131 and 181 respectively.

Table 7.5 provides information on prosecutions that arise from the work of the HSA. Prosecutions can be heard either summarily or on indictment – the table includes both types of cases. It shows that only a small number of enforcement actions lead to prosecutions. There was an increase in the number of prosecutions in the late 1990s and early 2000s, but this has tailed off in recent years; current levels of prosecutions are more or less the same as the numbers in the early to mid-1990s. The HSA has enjoyed a high level of success with convictions: only a tiny number of cases are dismissed each year. Relatively small fines are imposed in successful prosecution cases that are heard summarily; much larger fines are imposed in successful cases that are heard on indictment. Thus, for example, in 2005, fines totalling €31,588 were imposed in the 16 successful summary cases, whereas the figure was €431,338 for the successful indictment cases.

Table 7.5 provides information on prosecutions that arise from the work of the HSA. Prosecutions can be heard either summarily or on indictment – the table includes both types of cases. It shows that only a small number of enforcement actions lead to prosecutions. There was an increase in the number of prosecutions in the late 1990s and early 2000s, but this has tailed off in recent years; current levels of prosecutions are more or less the same as the numbers in the early to mid-1990s. The HSA has enjoyed a high level of success with convictions: only a tiny number of cases are dismissed each year. Relatively small fines are imposed in successful prosecution cases that are heard summarily; much larger fines are imposed in successful cases that are heard on indictment. Thus, for example, in 2005, fines totalling €31,588 were imposed in the 16 successful summary cases, whereas the figure was €431,338 for the successful indictment cases.

TABLE 7.4: HSA INSPECTIONS BY ECONOMIC SECTOR & ENFORCEMENT ACTION, 2006

Economic sector		Number of enforcement actions					
		Number of Inspections	Prohibition Notices	Improve-ment Notices	Improve-ment Directions	Written advice	% visits where action taken
A	Agriculture, hunting and forestry	1,457	82	141	0	327	38
B	Fishing	10	0	5	0	12	100
C	Mining and quarrying	478	19	25	0	181	81
D	Manufacturing	2,444	45	313	0	1,735	86
E	Electricity/gas/water	67	1	4	0	91	100
F	Construction	7,616	693	272	0	2,840	50
G	Wholesale/ retail trade; repair of motor vehicles, personal and household goods	1,108	8	114	0	836	86
H	Hotels/ restaurants	63	1	2	0	98	100
I	Transport, storage, communications	1,092	5	55	0	563	57
J	Financial intermediation	25	0	2	0	91	100
K	Real estate, renting, business	4,267	6	23	0	244	6
L	Public administration/ defence	246	1	16	0	175	78
M	Education	62	0	1	0	53	87
N	Health/social work	237	0	27	0	131	67
O	Other community, social and personal services	186	2	20	0	173	100
	Total	**15,365**	**864**	**1,019**	**0**	**4,663**	**43**

TABLE 7.5: OUTCOMES OF HSA PROSECUTIONS, 1993-2005

Year	Total	Successful(%)	Fines (€)
1993	30	87	11,925*
1994	37	78	31,035*
1995	24	96	13,440*
1996	35	77	19,600*
1997	39	77	26,500*
1998	55	89	45,675*
1999	63	89	80,240*
2000	64	86	115,673
2001	92	93	469,409
2002	91	90	160,958
2003	76	91	697,500
2004	41	91	1,331,636
2005	40	85	463,338

Note: * in Irish punts.

The figures in the **Tables 7.3** to **7.5** show that the HSA is not interested primarily in using inspections to take formal legal proceedings against organisations: inspectors are more interested in getting organisations to follow comprehensive health and safety policies. In the vast majority of cases, inspectors issue written advice, setting out guidance on how organisations can put right defects to health and safety regimes.

Although considered an indispensable part of its activity, the HSA recognises that there are limits to the role of inspections in the enforcement of health and safety legislation. This is simply because only 7% to 9% of workplaces are actually inspected each year or, to put it the other way round, roughly 93% of workplaces are inspection-free. Thus, the HSA is eager to develop smarter enforcement activity, so that it is more effective at protecting the health and safety of employees at work within the constraints of the budget established for its activities.

7.5   REDESIGNING INSPECTION ACTIVITY

In recent years, the HSA has been trying to move beyond the traditional model of inspection. This has involved developing innovative approaches to promoting health and safety at the workplace and designing new forms of inspections. Through widening its repertoire of enforcement activities, the HSA is seeking to raise compliance with health and safety legislation across the economy. Some of these innovative programmes are explained below.

7.5.1 The Construction Safety Partnership initiative

Construction has long been seen as a high-risk industry for health and safety accidents. Thus, it was considered appropriate to develop a pro-active initiative to improve worker safety on construction sites, and to reduce the high level of injuries and fatalities in the industry. Part of this targeted initiative involved continuing with traditional workplace inspection, but it also included other actions to increase awareness and behaviour on health and safety matters. Perhaps the most significant of these actions was the Construction Safety Partnership (CSP), which was established in 1999, and involved all the major stakeholders with an interest in promoting health and safety in the industry.[59] This partnership published a plan in 2000 (HSA, 2000) setting out a series of measures to upgrade health and safety in the construction industry, under four headings:

- Safety consultation.
- Safety training.
- Safety management systems.
- Actions by the HSA.

A host of initiatives resulted from the plan. A safety representative pilot project, involving a number of construction sites, was set up to develop best consultation practices between managers and employee representatives on safety, which would then be promoted more widely in the industry. This project was established to advance the Partnership's recommendation that safety representatives should be made mandatory on construction sites where more than 20 people are employed. The plan also resulted in increased safety training for construction workers, most of which was delivered by FÁS. One example was the Safe Pass programme, which delivered basic safety training to most workers in the construction industry. Another initiative was an innovative North/South collaborative project on safety management systems that required participating companies to adopt international, national and CSP guidelines and recommendations relating to health and safety. On the back of the CSP initiatives, the HSA committed 18 inspectors to work full-time in the construction industry, which contributed 10 extra inspection years to the sector.

---

[59] The members of the Construction Safety Partnership included the Department of Finance; ICTU; the Department of Enterprise, Trade & Employment; the Institute of Engineers of Ireland (IEI); the Health & Safety Authority (HSA); the Department of Environment & Local Government; the Construction Industry Federation (CIF); FÁS; and the Royal Institute of Architects of Ireland (RIAI).

The CSP produced another plan for 2003-2005, which identified further areas for concerted action (HSA, 2003). One was pre-construction/design/and procurement: the CSP's proposition was that adequate time-scales, as well as careful planning at the pre-construction stage, would improve the safety performance of construction sites significantly. To this end, the CSP established a variety of initiatives to improve the pre-construction stage of projects. These included developing new procedures so that health and safety matters were built into the pricing of projects; creating a register of competent project supervisors, both at the design and construction stage; and introducing best practice health and safety guidelines for organisations working on publicly- and privately-funded construction projects. The objective was to make pre-commencement improvements to the planning, design and procurement stage of construction projects in order to upgrade health and safety on sites.

Another aspect of the plan focused on strengthening industry-wide compliance with approved safety management systems. This included introducing a requirement to specify in invitations to tender the approved safety management systems that would be used by the company if awarded the contract; developing a register of consultants to ensure that only those with the proper qualifications and experience would be selected to perform this role; and maximising the use of the industry's Joint Safety Council checklist on all projects. The plan also set out a range of schemes to strengthen health and safety training in the industry and to increase promotion and awareness of the need for safety on construction sites. This 2003-2005 plan was also considered successful and a new plan has just been ratified for the period 2006-2009: the focus of this programme is on improving the management of health and safety risks in the industry (HSA, 2006).

Overall, the Construction Safety Partnership initiative can be considered successful in meeting the goals that it has set itself since its formation in 1999:

- The support of senior managers has been secured for the continuous improvement of health and safety performance on construction sites.

- Understanding has increased about the need for comprehensive health and safety policies and practices to be an integral part of the corporate governance of construction projects.

- Additional procedures have been introduced to improve the management of health and safety in the sector.

- Awareness and competence on health and safety matters has improved among construction workers.

- Shared understandings have been fostered amongst the participating stakeholders involved in the partnership, about the scale of the health and safety problem in the construction sector and what needs to be done to improve performance.

- More generally, the partnership has created a new institutional mechanism that goes beyond inspections to improve health and safety in the sector.

7.5.2 Developing new approaches to inspection

Nearly every public authority responsible for maintaining healthy and safe workplaces is considering the question of whether there are smarter ways to realise compliance with statutory standards, other than through spot inspections (Eymard-Duvernay, 2005). A large academic literature has emerged on this matter, much of which suggests that traditional forms of workplace inspections, which frequently are concerned with the top-down enforcement of detailed rules, may not be effective, as even a zealous inspection policy would result in only a tiny fraction of the total number of organisations being visited each year (Estlund, 2005). Moreover, command-and-control inspection strategies are seen as potentially counter-productive, as they might encourage firms to develop evasion tactics and might promote a general culture of resistance to complying with health and safety rules. As a result, enforcement becomes a source of confrontation between the regulatory authority and organisations: firms become less willing to co-operate and share information with the authority about how best to secure compliance with health and safety regulations. Health and safety at work is vulnerable to this bureaucratic model of inspection, since a public agency may be tempted to try and cover all contingencies by developing a mass of detailed rules (Lobel, 2006). In this situation, rules become too complex and prescriptive, which may encourage uncertainty among firms about whether they are in full compliance with the law. It may also make policing regulations by public agencies more difficult.

Almost everywhere, there have been attempts to develop health and safety enforcement procedures to avoid this problem of over-regulation. These attempts take a variety of institutional forms but most are based, to some extent, on the principle of conditional deregulation. In essence, conditional deregulation is about employers facing a light regulatory regime, if they choose to work with employees to ensure compliance with health and safety regulations. In other words, if organisations agree to comply with a minimum set of standards, uphold the statutory rights of employees and give employees a voice in the development of health and safety standards, then they will face few, if any, regulations, inspections or penalties. These arrangements normally contain the following features:

- A committee is established consisting of employee representatives and managers to develop the health and safety regime of the organisation and to monitor its effectiveness on an ongoing basis. Employees usually must approve all features of the health and safety regime.

- Managers and employees receive extensive education and training to develop their health and safety expertise.
- Managers and employers make credible commitments to each other about developing a safe workplace. Employees have the authority to develop health and safety recommendations and managers do their best to adopt these.
- Emergency plans are drawn up in the event of an accident, and a thorough investigation is conducted after an accident.
- Full written records are kept of the health and safety regime.

This system potentially brings benefits to all involved parties:

- Regulatory authorities benefit, as they spend less time inspecting workplaces that intend to comply with the law; as a result, they have more time to target rogue employers, who are violating regulations.
- Employers benefit, as they have the opportunity to customise the heath and safety regime to their particular circumstances.
- Employees benefit, as they have a greater voice in the design and operation of the health and safety regime.

Thus, the regulatory system becomes flexible and responsive, while, at the same time, the costs and contentiousness associated with inspection are reduced. In addition, the norms of government regulation are internalised within the workplace on a voluntary basis. It is a system that appears to be suitable to a business environment characterised by increased volatility and greater organisational heterogeneity.

The HSA has been influenced by this line of thinking. One interesting initiative it has developed is the Voluntary Protection Programme (VPP), modelled on a scheme pioneered by the Occupational Safety & Health Authority in the United States. The VPP, as operated by the HSA, certifies workplaces with exemplary health and safety management systems and records. Recognised organisations are also promoted as model workplaces. To qualify for VPP, organisations must have a health and safety system that meets rigorous performance standards. In addition, all relevant HSA standards must be met. The HSA conducts a rigorous on-site review process, before approving organisations as Star or Merit participants. The attraction of this certification to organisations is that it exempts them from routine inspections. The advantage for the HSA is that resources are released to address more high-risk health and safety cases. Thus, it is an initiative that attempts to involve organisations in more dynamic, beyond-inspection initiatives to improve health and safety standards.

This initiative still amounts to a small part of the overall activity of the HSA. Moreover, there is a view within the HSA that the initiative is fairly cumbersome to operate, as quite a lot of time has to go into making sure that applicant organisations meet the performance criteria of the programme. Nevertheless, the principle behind the programme remains influential in policy-making circles. For example, the Safety, Health & Welfare at Work Act 2005 made provision for the creation of joint safety and health agreements by the social partners in particular industries and sectors. These agreements are designed to put in place beyond-inspection procedures to police and supervise the implementation of relevant health and safety legislation. In particular, the agreements play a leading role in setting the health and safety agenda for specific economic sectors, thus increasing the sense of ownership of initiatives amongst the stakeholders. Finally, the agreements allow the HSA to engage more intensively with employers and employees to improve awareness and understanding of health and safety.

Although considerable efforts are being made to develop innovative methods to promote compliance with health and safety legislation, it must be emphasised that traditional inspections continue to be an important part of the armoury of the HSA. Moreover, there are ongoing efforts to improve the operation of the inspection system. For example, the Safety, Health & Welfare at Work Act 2005 introduced on-the-spot fines, so that inspectors could impose an immediate penalty for a breach of health and safety legislation. However, overall, the general thrust of the HSA's policy direction is to place less emphasis on the top-down enforcement of regulations, and to do more enabling work that involves orchestrating a wide range of activities, designed not only to respond to health and safety incidents, but also to prevent them happening in the first place. Prevention is a term that figures prominently and frequently in the language of the HSA.

7.6   THE HSA & THE PREVENTION OF WORKPLACE ACCIDENTS

Preventing workplace accidents and illnesses has been a long-standing theme of the HSA. It has produced codes of conduct and guidelines on a comprehensive range of health and safety matters, which give information on the threat posed by particular substances and practices and the policies that organisations need to introduce to comply with legislation. It has organised a range of publicity campaigns to increase awareness about health and safety dangers at work. Links have been made with schools and higher level educational institutions to integrate health and safety education into the curriculum, and to develop formal training and educational courses aimed at improving the competencies of health and safety managers and representatives. These activities are ongoing and the HSA seeks to continuously improve their impact. In recent years, it has decided to place more importance on this preventive side of its work.

This commitment to preventative initiatives is reflected in *A Strategy for the Prevention of Workplace Accidents, Injuries & Illnesses*, the HSA's strategy for 2004-2006 (HSA, 2004), which states that the aim of a comprehensive prevention strategy is to highlight the importance of high-quality health and safety procedures and practices in the workplace. Developing a range of preventative activities to raise the profile of health and safety is calculated to change organisational behaviour in relation to workplace health and safety. In addition, a prevention strategy is considered more likely to reach a wider audience and to stimulate greater awareness of health and safety matters. To a large extent, the new prevention strategy is the result of an assessment of the HSA's internal surveys on attitudes to health and safety management. These surveys were found that only a small number of organisations were either wilfully non-compliant or consciously compliant and that the vast majority of organisations were either broadly compliant or non-compliant due to a lack of awareness and information. A programme of prevention activities was considered the most appropriate way of raising the health and safety capabilities of the underperforming middle group.

Prevention is not always an easy concept to define, or give meaning to, in the context of employment relations issues but the HSA regards it simply as 'taking action now that will stop something happening in the future'. A preventative strategy is seen as having the following key mutually re-inforcing elements:

- Anticipating and managing emerging issues and trends.
- Developing close links with the HSA's client-base to obtain a better understanding of their health and safety behaviour.
- Developing innovative initiatives that meet the health and safety needs of particular industries and sectors.
- Establishing strategic alliances with organisations and other public sector bodies to upgrade health and safety practices on particular issues.
- Constructing a more effective regime of evaluation and monitoring to assess the impact of the HSA's policies and programmes.

To put this preventative strategy into action, the HSA must develop a more evidence-based approach to policy-making, establishing clear and measurable performance targets and putting in place an integrated system of evaluation and monitoring. It is useful to examine these three issues in greater detail.

The HSA believes that emerging business and labour market trends may lead to a variety of new health and safety threats, the scale and nature of which is presently unknown. For example, there is considerable uncertainty about the long-term health effects of repeated use of wireless technology. In addition, the growing numbers of women workers in the labour force are expected to create fresh health and safety challenges, as they have a different tolerance to hazardous exposure than men. Yet another issue is that the integrity of health and safety regimes in some organisations may be compromised by the intensification of outsourcing business functions and the greater use of temporary and part-time workers: do firms have proper control of potentially toxic substances that may be used by sub-contractors?

The HSA is committed to using an evidence-based approach to address such emerging health and safety issues and, indeed, many already existing threats and risks (Pfeffer & Sutton, 2006). There are a number of aspects to this approach:

- The collation and analysis of international and national statistics.

- The statistical profiling of customers, which involves examining a wide variety of factors such as economic sector, firm size, age of plant, age and gender composition of the workforce, and the associated level of health and safety risk for the organisation.

- Organising the data that is kept internally on the health and safety histories of particular firms, inspector visits and recorded complaints.

- Periodic surveys on the health and safety behaviour of particular profiled organisations and economic sectors to identify their general needs and attitudes.

Thus, for the HSA, an evidence-based approach is about marshalling all the appropriate relevant data available, in order to diagnose emerging problems and devise appropriate courses of remedial action. Tracking the behaviour of organisations in relation to established health and safety risks is another goal. The HSA is also devising what it terms 'smart intelligence' activities, which aim to define and map customer profiles, track their behaviour and needs, and identify how they set health and safety policies. These activities are seen as allowing the HSA to make interventions that are more sensitive to trends in particular sectors, the working patterns of specific organisations and the strategic posture of employees and employers to health and safety matters. To foster this evidence-based approach to its work, in 2005, the HSA introduced a new information system that organises data in a more transparent and systematic manner. This system is being used to identify emerging threats, assess their likely impact on a workforce, devise appropriate solutions to the identified challenges and design a series of metrics to evaluate the effectiveness of the developed strategy.

Through developing evidence-based policy-making, the HSA is seeking to move from a responsive, to an anticipatory, approach to health and safety matters. This approach involves the following sequence of activities:

- *What* – identify relevant sources of information.
- *How* – determine how access to sources can be achieved and whether external collaboration is appropriate.
- *Frequency* – determine who and how frequently to access sources.
- *Evaluate and act* – determine implications (if any) and the next steps to manage challenges.
- *Develop customer model* – the information required to enhance customer profile.
- *Review model* – review periodically to ensure that information is being identified and managed.

This evidence-based approach involves the HSA in surveying all possible information channels, to develop profiles about the severity of health and safety threats in industries and organisations. These profiles then are used to identify and put into order those problems that the HSA believes need priority attention. After this, the task is to investigate all possible means of addressing the identified problems, including examining the probable consequences of employing each of the possible means. Finally, the task is to choose a repertoire of policies that are most able to address the identified health and safety problems.

The HSA recognised that it cannot implement this approach to health and safety matters on its own and that it requires strategic alliances with other organisations. Accordingly, strategic alliances have been developed with a variety of employer and trade union organisations, as well as with public bodies, such as the Department of Health & Children.

The purpose of these alliances varies: some are used to diffuse information on health and safety to as wide an audience as possible; others take the form of open-ended projects between the HSA and individual organisations on health and safety-related issues. Thus, for example, there is a strategic alliance between the ESB and the HSA, which has given rise to a number of projects relating to stress at work and sickness and absenteeism policy. These project-based strategic alliances have a number of interesting features: each project contains explicit goals and timeframes for particular tasks, while projects also spell out the anticipated mutual benefits for the various participants. Thus, the strategic alliances have a practical, well-defined purpose, which commands the full support of the participating organisations.

A number of further initiatives have been introduced to advance the prevention programme. In 2005, a new workplace contact system was introduced, which the public can use either to make a complaint about poor health and safety cover at the workplace or to obtain information and advice on health and safety matters. Within the space of a year, the unit received 17,567 calls; of these, 15,343 were requests for information and publications and 2,124 were complaints about workplace safety. A package of initiatives was introduced to upgrade health and safety regimes in the small business sector, including tailored training programmes for owner-managers; a mentoring scheme, whereby small businesses with high-grade health and safety systems give practical guidance to other small businesses; and an intensive information and awareness campaign. Educational and training activities are being stepped up, to improve the competence of those with responsibility for introducing and maintaining health and safety systems in organisations. The HSA also intends to devise flagship models of best practice health and safety management. The public sector is seen as playing the lead role in highlighting how state-of-the-art processes can be developed to create safe workplaces, in a manner that yields productive benefits for organisations and individuals.

The HSA recognises that it needs to adopt an iterative approach to many of its preventative interventions. This involves refining programmes and schemes on a continuous basis, to take account of the experience gained from implementing initiatives and wider unanticipated developments. Consider the matter of bullying. The HSA published its first code of conduct and guidelines on the matter in the early 2000s. However, following a report by the Expert Advisory Group on Workplace Bullying (HSA, 2005a) the HSA decided to update this document. The revised code was published at the end of 2005, and puts greater emphasis on resolving incidents of bullying through the use of informal procedures inside organisations and professional mediation services (HSA, 2005b). In the wake of the publication of the new code, the Minister for Labour Affairs argued that it should be extended to cover all public sector employees, as the first code was only applicable in the private sector. Thus, through an ongoing process of consultation and deliberation, HSA policy on the prevention and resolution of bullying at work has been reformulated to make it a more effective and comprehensive policy instrument. This commitment to iterative policy-making reduces the possibility of the HSA getting too tied to established ways of doing things, which can be a source of organisational inertia.

7.7   LESSONS FOR THE LRC

The activities of the HSA potentially hold lessons for the LRC, even though its remit is quite different. One is the increased emphasis placed on smarter forms of inspections, which mostly involve developing more targeted interventions and encouraging inspectors to take a broader approach to their work, so that they give advice and guidance to organisations about health and safety matters rather than simply enforcing legislation. The LRC could learn from this activity.

There appears scope for the LRC to develop more targeted initiatives, designed to improve dispute resolution in a particular business sector or on particular dispute resolution activities. Moreover, the LRC perhaps could do more to encourage different parts of the organisation to adopt a broader interpretation of their activities. For example, when dealing with a dispute, conciliation officers should seek not only to get a settlement that is satisfactory to all parties but should also encourage the organisation to reflect on its practices, so that improvements can be made that make it less likely that such a problem will emerge in the future. No doubt, many conciliation officers already do this informally, but there may be a case for developing a more formal organisational approach to enlarging the role of established job functions.

A strong theme that emerges from the chapter is that the HSA now sees preventative activity as the 'name of the game' in terms of securing healthy and safe workplaces. At one level, the LRC has little to learn from this approach. For years, the Commission has been keenly aware of the importance of activities aimed at dispute resolution prevention and, indeed, mainly through its Advisory Services, has developed invaluable services. Moreover, as the recent launch of the Workplace Mediation Service shows, it is eager to develop new ways of preventing disputes. At another level, however, it may be worthwhile for the LRC to reflect on the HSA's decision to put prevention at the centre-stage of its strategy and to assess whether it should do likewise. On a more pragmatic level, it may be worthwhile for the LRC to examine some of the HSA's initiatives to assess whether these hold lessons for its work. For example, does the strategic alliance model that the HSA is developing hold any lessons for the LRC in terms of developing formal links with firms to provide a range of specified services? Could the LRC mimic the HSA and work with certain public sector organisations to develop flagship, state-of-the-art dispute resolution provision, in an effort to influence the behaviour of other organisations, both in the public and private sectors? Could it learn from the HSA's decision to strengthen its educational and training provision on health and safety and develop a programme aimed at increasing the competence of employers and employee representatives in resolving workplace disputes?

The chapter highlighted the strong emphasis the HSA places on collecting and codifying information and using this data to guide decision-making. This evidence-based policy-making is a simple idea: it means finding the best evidence that you can, interrogating these facts and acting upon this analysis, even though it might challenge established ways of doing things and traditional assumptions or ideas about how to address particular matters. Five principles underscore evidence-based policy-making:

- Building an organisational culture that faces hard facts.
- Senior managers must be committed to 'fact-based' decision-making, which means being committed to getting the best evidence and using it to guide actions.
- Avoid basing decisions on untested, but strongly-held, beliefs, what you have done in the past or on uncritical 'benchmarking' of experiments from other countries.
- Encourage experimentation and learning, but in a manner that allows for monitoring and evaluation.
- Look for the risks and drawbacks in policy proposals.

Evidence-based policy-making generates a number of benefits:

- New knowledge and insights are generated from inside, and outside, the organisation.
- Working assumptions and skills within the organisation are upgraded.
- Strategic interventions become more targeted and nuanced.
- Credible performance metrics are easier to set.

Chapter 2 on the activities and work of the LRC shows that it seeks to use the best evidence available to guide its actions, but it might benefit from elevating this to a key strategic objective. This would allow a more formal evidence-based approach to be adopted inside the organisation: action plans that guide interventions could be formulated using the five principles set out above. In an economic environment where the sources of disputes appear to be multiplying, and their nature appears more complex, the LRC must improve its services continually, so that they are in line with the needs of employers and employees: evidence-based policy-making facilitates this approach.

7.8   CONCLUSION

The main thrust of the work of the HSA is to co-ordinate internal, or self-regulatory, health and safety procedures and policies with external legislation and regulations. There are two prongs to this work by the HSA:

- One is smart inspection, which involves the HSA in targeting its limited inspection resources on economic sectors and particular organisations that the data shows are most likely to experience workplace accidents and illnesses or are less likely to comply with legislation; it also involves inspectors both rigorously enforcing the law and giving advice and guidance to organisations on how to best upgrade health and safety standards.
- The other is a series of preventative measures that amount to a regime of mandated self-regulation.

There are several dimensions to this latter activity:

- One is the mobilisation of all relevant stakeholders on particular health and safety topics, to establish a shared understanding on how to develop organisational procedures that ensure compliance with the law in the absence of inspection.
- Another is to establish best practice examples of organisational health and safety regimes, through a variety of schemes, and then make a concerted effort to publicise the merits of such procedures through awareness and campaigning initiatives.
- Yet a further aspect is through continuous educational and monitoring work, to ensure that the expertise exists inside organisations to address health and safety issues and that the HSA has knowledge of the strengths and weaknesses of particular heath and safety strategies.

Placing such an emphasis on prevention has meant that the organisation has had to introduce important changes to its organisational structure. The HSA is now more committed than ever before to evidence-based management, and to the use of performance metrics to assess the extent to which programmes have been successful. Some of these changes have been introduced recently, so it is too early to say whether they have been successful. But the indications are that the HSA is committed to being as innovative as possible in its endeavours to secure safe and healthy workplaces in Ireland.

8

THE CANADIAN APPROACH TO DISPUTE RESOLUTION – MAINSTREAMING ADR

8.1 INTRODUCTION

This chapter is concerned with examining the Canadian approach to dispute resolution and avoidance. In particular, it explores how a number of federal public dispute resolution agencies have sought to mainstream 'ADR' practices and principles within their existing programme of activities and services:

- **Section 8.2** provides an overview of the main characteristics of the Canadian employment relations system.

- The next sections examine in more detail the role and activities of four federal agencies that have a dispute resolution function: the Public Service Labour Relations Board (**section 8.3**); the Federal Mediation & Conciliation Service (**section 8.4**); the Labour Standards & Workplace Equity Directorate (**section 8.5**); and the Canadian Human Rights Commission (**section 8.6**).

- **Section 8.7** examines a number of governmental policy initiatives that have been introduced to promote the usage of ADR within the federal system.

- **Section 8.8** considers the key lessons for the Labour Relations Commission from the Canadian approach to dispute resolution and avoidance.

- The Conclusion brings together in **section 8.9** the arguments of the chapter.

8.2   THE CANADIAN EMPLOYMENT RELATIONS REGIME: AN OVERVIEW

Canada is a federal state and, under its Constitution, jurisdiction for employment relations is assigned exclusively either to the federal government or to the 10 provincial governments (Gunderson *et al.*, 2002). At the federal level, therefore, which is the focus of this study, there is a body of legislation and an associated set of public institutions that regulate employment relations in the public service – the federal public and parliamentary services – and a separate set of legislative and institutional arrangements for the governance of employment relations in the private industries and Crown (State) corporations that fall within the ambit of federal jurisdiction (see below). Conversely, each of the provincial governments have separate labour relations acts and associated institutional arrangements for those private and public sector employees that fall within their constitutional jurisdiction (Gunderson, 2002; Gunderson *et al.*, 2002).[60] Thus, for example, the province of Ontario has its own set of provincial labour laws, as well as a provincial-level Ministry of Labour, a public dispute resolution agency, a Labour Board and a Labour Court. Interestingly, however, both the federal and provincial labour relations legislation share common characteristics, in that they all:

- Establish Labour (relations) Boards that certify the exclusive bargaining agent for units of employees within a workplace.
- Set a minimum term for, and subject matter to be contained in, collective agreements.
- Establish procedures for legal strikes and lockouts.
- Establish ways of resolving disputes in relation to negotiation of collective agreements (mediation and conciliation).
- Establish ways of resolving rights disputes, based on the interpretation and application of collective agreements, through grievance and adjudication procedures.
- Define unfair labour practices.
- Establish Labour (Relations) Boards, which have a quasi-judicial status in relation to deciding on alleged violations of statutes.

---

[60] While virtually all of the provinces have separate labour relations acts for private and public sector employees, some provinces also have separate acts for the para-public, or quasi-public, sector, which includes employees in health care and education. Also, some provinces have specialised labour relations legislation that applies to particular occupations or industries, such as construction, the police and the fire services.

In a comparative context, Canada has a relatively moderate rate of unionisation, with a workforce density of 29.7% in mid-2006. Additionally, approximately 2.2% of employees, who are not union members, are covered by collective agreements, negotiated by certified bargaining agents. This figure of 29.7% actually represents a slight decline, as the comparative figure for the same period in 2005 was 30%. Interestingly, union membership actually rose by 62,000 to 4.1 million members in this period, but, because the overall rate of employment increase was much higher, density continued to fall, albeit marginally. Within this overall picture, however, there is a stark contrast between the public and private sectors: the public sector remains highly-unionised, at 71.4% in 2006, which represents a slight increase over the previous year; in marked contrast, union density in the private sector continues to decline sharply and, in mid-2006, accounted for only 17% of the private sector workforce.

In relation to collective bargaining, the Canadian system, at both the federal and provincial levels, is premised on the North American system of labour relations boards certifying trade unions as the bargaining agent for a particular group of workers – the bargaining unit (Gunderson *et al.*, 2002).[61] Thus the Canada Industrial Relations Board, an independent, representational, quasi-judicial tribunal is the body that is responsible for the certification of bargaining agents within those industries that fall under federal jurisdiction.[62] In the federal public and parliamentary services, the Public Services Labour Relations Board undertakes this role. This approach is replicated at the provincial level, for example, by the Quebec Labour Board and the Ontario Labour Board.

Certification is based on the evidence of majority representation. Critically, a certified bargaining agent (union) has exclusive rights to bargain on behalf of the respective bargaining unit. This certification process also imposes an obligation on the employer to engage in collective bargaining. Under this system, negotiated collective agreements are fixed-term, legally binding contracts that set out the terms and conditions of employment and related matters. Within this process, the parties have a duty to bargain in good faith, and strikes (union-initiated) and lockouts (employer-initiated) are both illegal during the term of the collective agreement. Although bargaining timetables vary from union to union, the average life span of a collective agreement in the federal jurisdiction is approximately three years. Consequently, the number of collective agreements due for

---

[61] A bargaining unit is generally a single workplace, considered appropriate for collective bargaining, in that there is a commonality of interests.

[62] The Canada Industrial Relations Board's jurisdiction extends to private sector employees in the territories of Nunavat, the Yukon and the Northwest Territories.

renewal is an important consideration for public dispute resolution agencies, as it is an indicator of the potential for industrial disputes.

In common with other advanced industrial economies, the period since the 1980s has been characterised by a marked, and general, downward trend in overt industrial conflict within Canada (Akyeampong, 2006; see **Table 8.1**).

TABLE 8.1: CANADA: STRIKES, LOCKOUTS & PERSON-DAYS NOT WORKED, 1980-2005

Year	Total	Workers involved '000	Person-days not worked '000	Days lost per 1,000 employees
1980	1,028	452	9,130	949
1981	1,049	342	8,850	896
1982	679	464	5,702	603
1983	645	330	4,441	469
1984	716	187	3,883	399
1985	829	164	3,126	316
1986	748	486	7,151	693
1987	668	582	3,810	358
1988	548	207	4,901	448
1989	627	445	3,701	331
1990	579	271	5,079	451
1991	463	254	2,516	230
1992	404	152	2,110	195
1993	381	102	1,517	141
1994	374	81	1,607	146
1995	328	149	1,583	141
1996	330	276	3,269	291
1997	284	258	3,608	318
1998	381	244	2,444	210
1999	413	160	2,443	204
2000	379	144	1,657	134
2001	381	221	2,199	174
2002	294	168	3,003	233
2003	266	81	1,736	131
2004	298	260	3,225	239
2005	293	429	4,107	301

Sources: Human Resources & Social Development Canada, Workplace Information Directorate; Statistics Canada, *Labour Force Survey*, cited in Akyeampong (2006).

For example, official work stoppages, initiated either by unions (strikes) or by employers (lockouts), fell from an annual average of 754 in the 1980s, to 394 in the 1990s, and just 319 in the current decade. The time-loss ratio also reveals an overall declining trend, from an annual average of 541 workdays lost per 1,000 employees in the 1980s, to 233 in the 1990s, to 203 in the 2000s.

Interestingly, the general improvements recorded in strike and lockout statistics has stalled somewhat in recent years. For example, the number of person-days lost through strikes and lockouts almost doubled from 1.7 million in 2003 to approximately 3.2 million in 2004, and rose again in 2005 to 4.1 million. Moreover, in this period, unions initiated about 84% of the total number of work stoppages, with the rest being started by employers. Similarly, the number of days lost per 1,000 employees more than doubled from 131 to 301 between 2003 and 2005. This substantial rise, in part, is explained by a number of long-drawn-out stoppages, involving relatively large unions. This trend is evident in the public and private areas under federal jurisdiction; while they accounted for only 6% of all strikes and lockouts between 2003 and 2005, they also recorded the largest share of days lost (33%) (see **Table 8.2**), largely due to a number of relatively long strikes, involving some large bargaining units in the telecommunications and broadcasting sectors.

TABLE 8.2: CANADA: STRIKES, LOCKOUTS & PERSON-DAYS NOT WORKED, BY JURISDICTION, 2003-2005

	Strikes & Lockouts		Days not Worked	
	'000	%	'000	%
Canada	**743**	**100**	**9,068**	**100**
Newfoundland & Labrador	22	3.0	523	5.8
Prince Edward Island	0	0	1	0
Nova Scotia	10	1.4	80	0.9
New Brunswick	19	2.6	177	2.0
Quebec	336	45.2	2,684	29.6
Ontario	230	31.0	1,385	14.3
Manitoba	20	2.7	47	0.5
Saskatchewan	19	2.6	104	1.1
Alberta	8	1.1	113	1.2
British Columbia	38	5.1	1,007	11.1
Total Provincial	**702**	**94.5**	**6.121**	**67.5**
Total federal	**41**	**5.5**	**2,947**	**32.5**

Sources: Human Resources & Social Development Canada, Workplace Information Directorate; Statistics Canada, *Labour Force Survey*, cited in Akyeampong (2006). Recent analysis of this data suggests that, at this time, it is not possible to determine whether the recent surge in days/time lost is due to a general change in the labour relations environment or to a confluence of workplace-specific factors (Akyeampong, 2006). Certainly, the key federal level public dispute agencies examined in this chapter did not consider that there has been a deterioration in labour management relations within their jurisdiction in recent years. Maintaining labour market stability, however, is a key public policy goal of the federal government, given the potential impact that industrial unrest can exert on the economy and the delivery of public services. In this context, these labour market 'signals' serve both to re-affirm the continued importance of public dispute resolution agencies and also to highlight the need for such bodies to continue to invest in enhancing their capacity for dispute resolution and prevention.

Having provided a brief overview of the Canadian employment relations system, the remaining sections of this chapter examine in more detail the role and activities of four federal level public dispute resolution agencies:

- The Public Service Labour Relations Board.
- The Federal Mediation & Conciliation Service.
- The Labour Standards & Workplace Equity Directorate.
- The Canadian Human Rights Commission.

8.3   THE PUBLIC SERVICE LABOUR RELATIONS BOARD

8.3.1   Mandate and jurisdiction

This section examines the development and use of mediation by the Public Service Labour Relations Board (PSLRB),[63] which is an independent, quasi-judicial, statutory tribunal responsible for administering the collective-bargaining and grievance adjudication systems within the federal public and parliamentary services.[64] The jurisdiction of the Board incorporates approximately 220,000

---

[63] The PSLRB is commonly referred to, in its organisational literature, as 'The Board'.

[64] This statutory role is derived from the Public Service Labour Relations Act and the Parliamentary Employment & Staff Relations Act. Under an agreement with the Yukon Provincial Government, the PSLRB administers the collective-bargaining and grievance adjudication systems under the Yukon Education Labour Relations Act and the Yukon Public Service Labour Relations Act.

employees and it operates within a highly-unionised environment, with a union density of between 65% and 70%. The Public Service Labour Relations Act 2005 (PSLRA) formally established this body in 2005 and, in so doing, it replaced the pre-existing Public Service Staff Relations Board.[65] Under the new legislation, the Board's mandate is to provide three main services:

- **Adjudication:** The Board hears labour relations applications, complaints and grievances referred to adjudication.

- **Mediation:** The Board provides mediation and conflict resolution services to assist parties to reach collective agreements, to manage their relations under collective agreements and to resolve complaints and grievances without recourse to a formal hearing.

- **Compensation analysis and research:** The Board monitors the compensation of employees in the public and private sectors, in occupations similar to those in the federal public service, by conducting compensation surveys and by compiling, analysing and publishing the aggregate results.

In practice, this mandate represents an encompassing agenda and reflects the fact that, in an employment relations context, the Board is somewhat of a hybrid body, in that it undertakes functions that, at provincial level, would be carried out by a number of separate agencies.[66] First, it is effectively the 'Labour Board' for the Federal Public Service, in that it is responsible for the certification process, whereby an employee organisation is recognised by the PSLRB as the bargaining agent for a group of employees in their relations with the employer. Certification is granted for a specific bargaining unit, which generally corresponds to a group of positions within the employer's classification system.[67] At present, there are 30 certified bargaining agents within the federal public and parliamentary services, although,

---

[65] This section describes activities that predate April 2005 and so the generic term, 'the Board', is used to refer both to the Public Service Staff Relations Board, which ceased to exist on 1 April 2005 and to the body that replaced it, namely the Public Service Labour Relations Board.

[66] An indication of this encompassing mandate is given by the fact that proceedings before the Board include grievance adjudication, arbitration, conciliation through Public Interest Commissions, mediation, applications for certification, revocation of certification, displacement, complaints of unfair labour practices, essential service agreements, determination of successor rights and enforcement of obligations of employer and employee organisations.

[67] Examples of certified bargaining units within the federal public service include the Programme Administrators, which encapsulates secretaries, clerical officers and programme officers; the Correctional Officers; the Lawyers Group; and the Foreign Services Officers. As in the private sector, 'commonality of interests' is an important factor in the certification of bargaining agents.

in practice, the majority of the PSLRB's work involves interactions with approximately 17 of these, due to the fact that a number of them are quite small bodies. The PSLRB is also responsible for all the other attendant issues associated with this certification process, such as enforcement of obligations on employer and employee organisations. Second, its adjudicative role in terms of grievance and rights redress ensures that it is the equivalent of the 'Labour Court' for federal public service employees. Finally, third-party intervention in the collective-bargaining process, in terms of providing arbitration or conciliation services, is normally the responsibility of an agency operating under the aegis of the Ministry of Labour at either the provincial or federal level.[68] In relation to regulating collective bargaining within the federal public and parliamentary service, however, this responsibility has been assigned to the PSLRB.

While the Board clearly has an encompassing agenda, the primary focus of this section is on the role it performs in relation to dispute resolution. Under the relevant enabling legislation,[69] the Board has responsibility for resolving disputes both between federal employees and their employer, and between parliamentary employees and their employer, on all matters pertaining to:

- Unionisation.
- Collective bargaining of conditions of employment.
- Requests for interpretation of collective agreements.
- Unfair labour practice complaints.
- Grievances filed by federal public and parliamentary service employees.[70]

8.3.2   Mediation and dispute resolution

Within the PSLRB, a dedicated Dispute Resolution Services (DRS) team is responsible for offering impartial, third-party assistance to the parties (employers and employees), in resolving disputes through the

---

[68]   In Ontario, for example, the Ministry of Labour has responsibility for promoting a stable and constructive labour relations climate and, within this department, a dedicated division, Labour Management Service, provides neutral, third-party assistance to trade unions and employers, through collective agreement conciliation and mediation, the appointment of arbitrators and the provision of collective bargaining information.

[69]   The Public Service Labour Relations Act governs staff relations in the federal public service. The Parliamentary Employment & Staff Relations Act governs staff relations in the Library of the Parliament, the House of Commons and the Senate. The Board is the administrative tribunal charged with administering both of these Acts.

[70]   The PSLRB also is the administrative tribunal charged with ruling on complaints against reprisals that occur as a result of federal employees exercising their rights relating to workplace health and safety, under Part II of the Canada Labour Code.

provision of professional mediation, conciliation, examination, investigation and training services.

In 1999, the Board introduced a pilot mediation initiative, the catalyst for which was an emerging consensus within the Board concerning the limitations of the formal statutory grievance adjudication process as a mechanism for resolving workplace grievances. Although the existing approach was effective, it was recognised that, in many instances, the specific issue described in a grievance was indicative of a much more pervasive problem, related to the nature of employer-union relationships, which could not be adequately addressed using the formal, and somewhat legalistic process, of grievance adjudication. There also was concern about a growing backlog of cases, and the decision to explore the potential of a mediation option was encouraged further by the increased usage of ADR in the commercial and family courts.

Following extensive discussions with employers and trade unions, the Board initiated a 12-month pilot project, in which mediation was established as the default option for all grievances and complaints that were referred to the Board for adjudication, unless one of the parties informed the Board in writing that it did not wish to engage in this process. If mediation was refused, or if the process failed to resolve a grievance, the case then was referred to adjudication for a formal hearing.

Rather than recruiting mediators from the private sector to provide this service, the Board provided extensive training to members of the Board and the Board's staff mediators. Additional training was also provided on an ongoing basis, during the pilot period of the project. The only condition on the use of Board members as mediators was that, if a grievance dispute was not resolved through mediation, a different Board member would hear and determine the matter on its merits at a subsequent adjudication. Training workshops on mediation were organised for representatives from the employers and the bargaining agents.

Within this mediation process, the PSLRB mediator functioned as an impartial third-party, whose role was to facilitate constructive dialogue between the conflicting parties, with a view to assisting them in crafting their own mutually-acceptable resolution to the conflict. During the initial 12-month pilot period, over 500 files were processed through mediation and, significantly, it was found that the involvement of the mediator had resulted in a successful outcome in approximately 85% of cases. This positive assessment was validated, moreover, by an independent external evaluation carried out in 2001, which concluded that the pilot mediation project had achieved a high degree of credibility and satisfaction with the large majority of participants, who considered it to be a fair and constructive approach to dispute resolution (Zweibel et al., 2001). As a result of this evaluation, the positive feedback from employers and unions, and the rate of success achieved by the project, the Board decided to mainstream mediation as a permanent and integral part of its approach to resolving disputes in the federal public service. The central role of mediation in dispute resolution was re-inforced subsequently by the PSLRA, which establishes mediation on a statutory footing as one of the key services to be provided by the PSLRB.[71]

Under the regulatory framework afforded to the Board by the PSLRA, employers and bargaining agents now have access to mediation in three areas:

- **Mediation,** following a referral to **adjudication** (default option for grievances or complaints referred to the Board).

- **Preventative mediation**, where parties to a conflict may request the intervention of the mediation team, even where a file has not been officially referred to adjudication.

- **Mediation**, as part of **collective bargaining**, which is briefly discussed below.

The PSLRA provides the regulatory framework for collective bargaining in the federal public service and, under this legislation, two methods are available for resolving collective-bargaining disputes: binding arbitration and the referral of a dispute to conciliation.[72] The bargaining agent is free to choose the method of dispute resolution for each respective bargaining unit and it must select one or the other, prior to giving notice to bargain.[73]

Regardless of the method of dispute resolution chosen, in the course of their negotiations, the parties may reach an impasse, at which point either party can request the services of a mediator from the PSLRB's Dispute Resolution Service. Equally, at any time, the Chair of the PSLRB may appoint a mediator to confer with the parties and to endeavour to assist them in settling the dispute, if requested to do so or on his/her own volition. This positioning of mediation within the collective bargaining process is an important development, as the parties are aware that, if they fail to resolve their differences,

---

[71] Section 13 of the PSLRA states: 'The Board's mandate is to provide adjudication, mediation services, compensation analysis and research services in accordance with this Act'.

[72] The conciliation method gives employees the right to strike, under certain prescribed conditions, and is often referred to as the 'conciliation/strike route'.

[73] The exception to this is that the PSLRA establishes binding arbitration as the only method available for parliamentary employees and, therefore, there is no right to strike. According to the PSLRB, the trend is for professional groups to choose arbitration, in part because this involves making comparisons with similar occupations in the private sector, while the 'blue-collar' trade groups and office workers tend to choose the conciliation/strike route as traditionally they have more industrial relations clout or muscle within the system.

they will have to engage in mediation. In this manner, mediation is not an alternative to existing processes but, rather, is integrated formally within the established collective-bargaining procedures. Indeed, in practice, the PSLRB's labour officers contend that that there is not a strong demarcation between conciliation and mediation, as in both instances the focus of the third-party agent is to resolve disputes and also, if possible, to repair and improve relationships. Critically, the PSLRB adopts a relatively pro-active approach to the mediation process, as it is clearly designed to focus the parties' attention on achieving a credible and creative settlement. In this regard, the approach to mediation resonates with the concept of interest-based bargaining, in that not only is there a strong emphasis on focusing on the issues and generating a solution, but it also aims to provide a platform for improved labour-management relations.

The time-bound nature of collective agreements in the Canadian context re-inforces the PSLRB's emphasis on assisting the parties to reach a solution, as both the employers and the bargaining agents know that, if they fail to resolve the dispute in mediation, depending on the 'route' they have chosen, either they will have a decision imposed through arbitration or, potentially, if the collective agreement expires, they will face the prospect of potential industrial conflict, in the form of a strike or lock-out. Significantly, professional practitioners within the PSLRB are of the view that institutionalising mediation formally within the collective-bargaining process has improved the effectiveness of the dispute resolution services and also is beginning to inform and shape, in an incremental manner, the quality of the employment relations within the federal public service. Critically, the parties can avail of the mediation services of the Board at any time during their collective negotiations. Confidentiality remains a key aspect of the mediation process, and information garnered by the mediator during a formal session remains confidential and is not used to inform subsequent stages of the dispute resolution process. In the opinion of the Board, this has been critical in building the legitimacy of the process from the perspective of both the employers and the trade unions.

If the involvement of a mediator does not result in an agreed settlement, and where the selected route is 'conciliation', a Public Interest Commission (PIC) may be appointed by the Minister, on foot of a recommendation by the Chair of the PSLRB. The mandate of the PIC is to listen to the parties and to try to assist them resolving their differences. However, if no agreement is reached, the PIC will issue a report with recommendations for settlement of the dispute to the Chair of the PSLRB, within 30 days of its appointment.[74] In the event

---

[74] A PIC may be composed of one person, or a panel of three, and all members of a PIC are selected from a panel, jointly agreed by the parties.

that the PIC does not bring about a settlement, the bargaining agent in question has the option of taking strike action, provided it meets the conditions for such action prescribed by the Act.

Arbitration boards, where that is the chosen method of dispute resolution, are established in the same manner as the PICs.[75] In most cases, the parties will have reached agreement, in part assisted by the intervention of a mediator, on a substantial number of provisions before arbitration is requested and, therefore, the role of the Arbitration Board is to rule on the remaining matters.[76] In conducting its proceedings and in rendering its award, the Arbitration Board is required to consider a number of factors, including conditions of employment in similar occupations outside the public service, the state of the economy, the need to maintain appropriate relationships between classification levels in the public service, and the government's fiscal circumstances. An Arbitration Board award is binding on the parties and usually forms a supplement to the collective agreement. As noted above, mediation can be availed of at any stage of the dispute resolution process. Consequently, with the consent of the parties, the adjudicator can halt the arbitration process and seek to mediate an agreement with the parties, without prejudice to the parties coming back before him/her for an arbitration ruling, if the mediation approach is unsuccessful.

In late 2000, the Dispute Resolution Service was assigned the task of designing and delivering a customised joint management/labour national training programme on 'interest-based negotiation and mediation'. The programme was not aimed at training 'practitioners' – that is bargaining agents, labour officers, etc. – to become mediators but, rather, on building their understanding of what mediation entails, how it differs from traditional approaches and the potential benefits of using it. Significantly, the focus of this highly-interactive programme went beyond a discussion of dispute resolution techniques *per se*, as it was designed to encourage managers and unions to begin to explore the dynamics of their current relationships, with a view to putting in place a foundation for the development of a more collaborative, joint problem-solving approach to the resolution of workplace issues and grievances. In this regard, the training programme clearly correlated with the underlying thinking that drove the development of the pilot mediation project. In delivering this

---

[75] The main difference is that they are established by the Chair of the PSLRB at the request of either party.

[76] Interestingly, there is scope under the legislation for the Chair of the Board not to appoint an Arbitration Board immediately, if it is apparent that the parties have not engaged fully with the PSLRB mediation service in seeking to resolve the dispute or, at least, in streamlining the issues under dispute. In such instances, the parties are redirected back to the mediation service for further discussions, before an Arbitration Board is appointed eventually.

programme, the Dispute Resolution Service embarked on what it described as a 'cross-country training blitz', and this extensive activity was further supported by the development of a video/CD-ROM, *Best Interests: An Introduction to Grievance Mediation* (PSSRB, 2002). By early 2006, approximately 2,000 individuals had participated in the training programme; the feedback from both employers and unions has been positive, and demand for this training remains high. From the outset, this initiative was supported by the Treasury Board,[77] a major federal public service employer, and the two main trade unions: the Public Service Alliance of Canada and the Professional Institute of the Public Service of Canada. This commitment has been a key factor in the success of the training programme.

Interestingly, there is also a dispute resolution/prevention dimension to the work of the Compensation & Analysis Service, which was established with the enactment of the PSLRA in 2005. Under this legislation, the Board was mandated to monitor the compensation of employees in the public and private sectors, in occupations similar to those in the federal public service, by conducting compensation surveys and compiling, analysing and publishing aggregate results.[78] Through this compensation analysis and research service, the Board aims to contribute to the promotion of more harmonious labour-management relations, by providing the parties to collective bargaining with impartial, accurate and timely information to inform and support their compensation negotiations.[79] This information is used also to assist the deliberations of the Arbitration Boards and PICs in seeking to resolve collective-bargaining disputes.

In positioning mediation specifically at the very centre of its approach to dispute resolution, the PSLRB has sought to achieve a number of interrelated objectives:

- To improve labour relations between bargaining agents and employers.
- To facilitate the parties taking greater ownership of the process of finding a solution to workplace disputes.
- To reduce the number of cases going to formal adjudication, by its nature a lengthier, costly and more 'adversarial' process.
- To develop the dispute resolution skills of the participants.

---

[77] The Treasury Board is equivalent to the Department of Finance in Ireland, in that it is seen as the employer in terms of the federal public and parliamentary services.

[78] Under the Act, the Chair can also direct the Board to carry out other market-based research relevant to compensation.

[79] The PSLRB indicated that, prior to undertaking this role, there often would be protracted discussions between employers and unions over 'wage data' and appropriate comparators, even before the formal process of collective bargaining had begun.

These objectives clearly indicate that the development and evolution of the Board's mediation programme goes beyond a narrow focus on improving the mechanics of dispute resolution to incorporate a more comprehensive agenda, premised on encouraging the employers and unions to shift from an adversarial, to a problem-solving, style of bargaining. This emphasis on encouraging more collaborative relationships clearly has influenced the design and character of the Board's mediation service. In particular, as **Table 8.3** suggests, the mediation service provided draws on the discourse and techniques associated with interest-based bargaining and joint problem-solving. Within the mediation session, for example, there is a strong emphasis on the mediator assisting the parties to define the issues in a dispute more clearly and to try and find acceptable and creative solutions. Similarly, it also accentuates the transformative, or future-focused, dimension of mediation, whereby the process of the parties engaging constructively to potentially craft an agreed solution can provide a basis for repairing and/or improving their future relationship, premised on a co-operative problem-solving approach to workplace issues.

TABLE 8.3: THE MEDIATOR'S ROLE

Encourage the sharing of information.	Identify and narrow the issues.
Help the parties to understand each others' views.	Promote constructive dialogue.
Shift the focus from the past to the future.	Shift the focus from one of blame to a creative exchange between the parties.
Encourage flexibility and creativity.	Help the parties to evaluate alternatives realistically.

In the last five years, the PSLRB has conducted approximately 2,000 mediations and, significantly, the parties have assisted in crafting durable and creative solutions in approximately 85% of the cases that went to mediation. The delays in reaching a satisfactory outcome have also been reduced, as a result of the increased usage of mediation. Additionally, the Board estimates that the use of mediation in the resolution of both individual and collective grievances and complaints also has reduced the financial and emotional costs normally associated with the more formal, and legalistic, process of adjudication.

In terms of the development of more robust collaborative relationships between management and unions, the Board maintains that this process is still in the early stages and that it will take time to build the necessary levels of trust, although, even at this juncture, there are tangible signs of progress. The Board recognises that it will take a considerable investment by all of the stakeholders to achieve a sustainable transformation in the quality of employment relations within the federal public service, as it has been characterised traditionally by a rather confrontational, and adversarial, approach to collective bargaining. As such, the emphasis within the 2005 legislation on developing a more collaborative employment relations culture is a relatively new departure within the federal public service.[80] At one level, both employers and trade unions have demonstrated their willingness to explore alternative non-traditional mechanisms, not only in resolving workplace conflict but also in improving industrial relations in general. At the same time, also they can resort quite easily to more traditional, and confrontational, bargaining postures and positions, depending on the issue in hand.

Importantly, the work of the PSLRB provides a platform for developing more co-operative management-employee interactions and it clearly accords with the general thrust of government policy, as enshrined within the PSLRA. Under this Act, for example, departments and agencies must establish joint labour-management committees, as a potential mechanism for improving relations, although the legislation is fairly non-prescriptive as to how these structures should operate. Indeed, it is recognised generally that the success of the Board's mediation programme was one of the primary catalysts behind the Treasury Board's decision to require, as part of this legislation, that all departments and agencies establish informal conflict management systems as part of the new public service modernisation programme.[81] Significantly, the Board, and its professional staff, who have been the main protagonists in advocating the potential of mediation and ADR in general, remain committed to using innovative approaches to resolving disputes. In particular, the Board highlights that actively supporting the development of more harmonious relationships between public service employers and employees has the potential to improve the capacity of the federal public service to serve the public interest and to provide a value for money service.

---

[80] This new approach to employment relations was influenced by a review carried out in 2001 (ACLM, 2001), which the interviewees from the Board indicated was the first time since 1967 that this issue had been formally reviewed at federal government level.

[81] Interestingly, a number of these federal bodies have sought additional information on the Board's mediation activity, with a view to seeing whether they could adopt a similar approach within their organisations.

8.4   THE FEDERAL MEDIATION & CONCILIATION SERVICE

At the federal level, the Labour Program, which is part of the Department for Human Resources & Social Development Canada (HRSDC), and is headed by a Minister of Labour, is responsible for industrial relations, occupational health and safety and labour standards and workplace equity. Within the Labour Program, the Federal Mediation & Conciliation Service (FMCS) has responsibility for providing dispute resolution and dispute prevention assistance to the trade unions and employers, under the jurisdiction of the Canada Labour Code, and for advising the Minister of Labour on industrial relations matters.

The FMCS derives its authority from the Canada Labour Code (Part 1), which governs industrial relations in all federally-regulated private sector industries, including international and interprovincial rail; road and air transportation; shipping and longshoring operations; telecommunications; broadcasting; banking; federal Crown corporations, such as Canada Post; nuclear power; grain handling; and uranium mining. Approximately 1.1 million private sector[82] employees fall within the ambit of federal labour legislation, although they represent only 8.5% of the total Canadian labour force. The nature of these industries, however, in that they comprise the key elements of the nation's infrastructure, ensures that they are of major strategic importance to the effective functioning of the economy. For example, given the sheer size of Canada, the transportation sector (rail, road, air and marine) is of pivotal importance to the economy. These factors ensure that the strategic importance of the FMCS's role securing labour market stability is much more important than the number of employees that fall within its jurisdiction might suggest at first. Union density among federal jurisdiction employees is approximately 32%, considerably higher than for the private sector in Canada (17%). The figure for federal employees, moreover, has remained fairly static over the last two or three years, while the unionisation rate varies dramatically between federally-regulated industries, from 70% in the transportation sectors, down to just 1% in the banking industry. Finally, around 1,500 collective agreements are negotiated by bargaining agents under the Canada Labour Code and, in any given year, approximately 500 to 600 are subject to renewal.

In seeking to fulfil its statutory remit, the FMCS has developed gradually a fairly comprehensive set of conflict management services and initiatives, designed to help foster more harmonious and co-operative labour-management relations throughout Canada.

---

[82]   This includes employees of federal Crown corporations.

Importantly, in seeking both to improve and to modernise its dispute resolution/prevention services, and also as part of an attempt to broaden the scope of its activities so that they are not so closely tied to the collective-bargaining cycle, since the mid-1990s, the FMCS has been prepared to engage in a significant degree of policy experimentation and innovation. In particular, it has been to the fore in adopting and customising some of the principles and practices associated with ADR into the operational activities it delivers to unions and employers. Consequently, the FMCS's integrated conflict management system now encapsulates five key strands of activity:

- **Dispute resolution**: The provision of conciliation and mediation assistance to parties engaged in collective bargaining.

- **Dispute prevention**: An extensive range of preventative mediation and grievance mediation services, aimed at resolving differences and improving union management relations during the closed period of a collective agreement.

- **The Labour-Management Partnerships programme**: This provides seed funding for innovative projects, designed to improve relations between labour and management.

- **Administration** of Ministerial appointments of grievance arbitrators, unjust dismissal adjudicators and wage recovery referees, under the Canada Labour Code.

- **Research and analysis** to aid in the development and implementation of industrial relations policy.

Given the focus of this book, the remainder of this section will concentrate on examining the first three of these activities:

- Dispute resolution.
- Dispute prevention.
- The Labour Management Partnerships programme.

8.4.1   Collective bargaining dispute resolution – Conciliation and mediation services

The procedures governing the collective-bargaining process in the federal jurisdiction, including dispute resolution through conciliation and mediation, are laid down by Part 1 of the Canada Labour Code. The FMCS's role, as mandated by the Code, is to intervene in situations where the parties have reached an impasse in their collective-bargaining negotiations, with a view to assisting them to reach an agreed settlement. Collective agreements in Canada are time-bound, legal instruments and, as such, the FMCS's interventions generally are linked to disputes that emerge in the negotiations between the employer and the certified bargaining agents around the renewal of a collective agreement. Indeed, as indicated earlier, both strikes and lockouts are illegal during the term of a collective agreement.[83]

During the negotiations for a collective agreement, if the parties reach an impasse, or if they fail to 'engage', either the bargaining agent or the employer can file a 'notice of dispute' with the Minister of Labour. The Minister has a number of options once this happens but, in the vast majority of cases, will appoint a conciliation officer, who will assist the parties pro-actively to try and reach a mutually acceptable agreement. The FMCS team of professional conciliators are highly-skilled and experienced industrial relations practitioners. Significantly, as is the norm in Canadian industrial relations, these conciliators are openly recruited from the HR and trade union community and, as such, their high level of competency is premised on years of practical experience. A time limit of 60 days normally is set for the conciliation process, although this can be extended by mutual agreement. If conciliation fails to secure an agreement, the parties do not acquire the right to engage in industrial action until 21 days after the conciliation process has been completed and a number of other legal requirements have been met. Additionally, in order to prevent the outbreak of industrial strife, mediation will be generally made available to the parties at this stage. While mediation appointments are generally made once formal conciliation procedures under the Canada Labour Code have been completed, the Minister of Labour can appoint a mediator, at any time, at the request of either party or on his/her own initiative. The initiation of mediation does not influence the acquisition of the right to strike or lockout. In almost all cases, mediators are officers of the FMCS, although 'external' mediators are used in a minority of cases.

The manner in which the FMCS's conciliation and mediation services are provided ensures that they are an integral part of the formal collective-bargaining negotiations process between employers and bargaining agents. Indeed, it is interesting to note that 48% of clients surveyed indicated that they had availed of both mediation and conciliation services in a formal dispute resolution context (HRSDC, 2002). In both instances, while the emphasis is on assisting the parties to reach an agreement, the conciliator and/or mediator plays a relatively pro-active, and, at times, interventionist role in the process. As in the case of the PSLRB, this activity has strong parallels with interest-based bargaining, in that the 'FMCS' official is trying to get the parties to focus on the issues and to craft an appropriate solution to these. In fact, as part of its ongoing policy

---

[83]   However, disputes also can emerge in relation to the negotiation of the first collective agreement.

experimentation, the FMCS recently has established an interest-based conflict resolution unit. The sequencing of conciliation and mediation also influences the atmosphere of interaction. In particular, the fact that mediation represents, in most cases, the last 'official' chance to reach an agreed solution assists in focusing attention on settling the issue(s) in question, and the mediator will draw on various techniques to reinforce this context. Equally, in appropriate circumstances, the mediator also will attempt to exploit the future-focused, or transformative, potential of mediation, with a view to improving or enhancing future relations between the parties.

Critically, through its conciliation and mediation assistance, the FMCS enjoys an extremely strong reputation among the key stakeholders for resolving labour disputes without work stoppages. Indeed, in the period 2005/2006, the success rate ('disputes handled to finality without a work stoppage') reached an all-time high of 97%.[84] Additionally, the number of labour disputes requiring intervention from the FMCS has decreased significantly in the past two years, reaching an all-time low of 269 for a 12-month period between March 2005 and March 2006. In order to put this into perspective, the average figure over the previous 25 years was 325 *per annum*. Interestingly, despite this 'success rate', and the overall low number of disputes requiring FMCS intervention, the number of days lost due to industrial conflict increased between March 2005 and 2006: this apparent anomaly is the product of a trend identified in the first section of this chapter – the occurrence within the federal area of a small number of protracted disputes involving large bargaining units, and therefore large numbers of workers. Indeed, during 2005/2006, there were a number of high-profile, protracted disputes, involving telecommunications workers, broadcasting employees, air traffic controllers and railway workers. Given the strategic importance of these types of industries, the FMCS clearly recognises the necessity of minimising overt industrial unrest and, as such, even in the context of the falling numbers of disputes, from a public policy perspective, the saliency of the FMCS's dispute resolution and, indeed, dispute prevention activity remains strong.

8.4.2   Dispute prevention: Preventive mediation and grievance mediation

In recent years, the FMCS has invested considerably in developing its capacity to provide a high-quality, and effective, range of dispute prevention services, designed to resolve differences and to improve the quality of union-management relations during the term of a collective agreement. In developing such services, the FMCS has

---

[84]   This data was obtained from a briefing paper supplied by FMCS officials interviewed by the authors.

drawn strongly on ADR principles and practices and has sought purposely to integrate these approaches, where appropriate, into its activities, in order to enhance the quality of the service it provides to employers and unions.

The FMCS now offers unions and employers a comprehensive preventive mediation programme, which aims to help parties build and maintain constructive working relationships. Within this programme, a variety of services are offered, customised to meet the needs of particular workplaces (see **Table 8.4**). The union and employer must however jointly request these services. Delivering this range of services is dependent on a team of highly-skilled and experienced mediators and, as already indicated, the FMCS has made a concerted effort to strengthen its 'dispute prevention' capacity through the provision of training (in part, funded by federal initiatives) and open recruitment.

TABLE 8.4: THE PREVENTIVE MEDIATION PROGRAMME

Service	Objective
Negotiation skill workshop	This workshop provides employers and unions with an opportunity for joint training and informal discussions on the process of negotiation, in general, and the use of interest-based negotiation concepts, in particular.
Committee effectiveness workshop	This workshop provides training in a range of skills and competencies to assist unions and management in establishing and/or revitalising joint committees within their workplace.
Joint problem-solving workshop	This workshop is designed for parties who wish to explore alternative ways of working together, in respect of a broad range of regular workplace issues. Although similar to interest-based negotiations, this workshop does not focus on collective bargaining
Facilitation	The FMCS provides a mediator, who acts as a facilitator for joint processes – for example, those seeking to resolve a major workplace issue.
Relationship by Objectives programme	This programme seeks to enable employers and unions to redesign a relationship that has become ineffective or dysfunctional. In particular, guided by a team of mediators, they will seek to reach agreement about the problems and identify a variety of solutions.
Grievance resolution workshop	This workshop offers the parties an opportunity to analyse their grievance process jointly, with a view to developing, if required, an agreed set of actions to improve it.

The FMCS also has established a grievance mediation service, to provide unions and management with an informal and low-cost alternative to arbitration. Under this initiative, employers and unions have an opportunity to meet and attempt to resolve grievances and other underlying issues, with the assistance of an experienced officer from the FMCS. Embarking on this route is not dependent on the waiving of any employment rights. If the parties fail to resolve the issue in question, they retain the right to proceed to formal grievance arbitration.

8.4.3 The Labour Management Partnerships Programme

In 1991, the FMCS launched its Labour Management Partnerships Programme (LMPP). This innovative policy development, which is still in operation, is designed to encourage more effective labour management relations in the workplace or at sector/national levels, by providing funding assistance that supports efforts by unions and management to explore jointly new ways of working and the potential of working together to address shared problems. Between 1997 and 2004, approximately $13.8 million was allocated to projects under the LMPP. In particular, the LMPP offers financial support, on a cost-shared basis, to employers and unions for three types of joint projects:

- **Workplace projects:** These are joint management-labour 'pilot projects', designed to promote productive, fairer, more accessible workplaces and improved union-management relations and understanding. Typical activities include workshops and specialised training for unions, management and employees on topics, such as occupational health and safety, joint working and absenteeism.

- **Conference projects:** This strand includes symposiums, fora and seminars on key labour-management issues.

- **Research projects:** This incorporates a range of research activities, such as focus groups, surveys and round table workshops to assist the parties in improving their relationships.

In 2004, a comprehensive evaluation of the LMPP in the period 1997-2002 was undertaken by the HRSDC.[85] Importantly, this evaluation report highlighted that the LMPP had generated a number of positive impacts over the period of review. First, the participant survey indicated that LMPP projects were considered to have produced substantial (60%) or some (34%) benefits on the quality of labour-management relations. In addition, the vast majority of the case studies indicated key outcomes, such as improved levels of trust,

---

[85] See HRSDC (2004). This evaluation was based on statistical and qualitative data drawn from three sources: a survey of 200 LMPP participants; 21 case studies of LMPP (18% of the projects funded in this period) and 16 key-informant interviews with senior trade union and business leaders, academics and senior policy officials.

enhanced communications and reductions in long-standing difficult relationships. Second, this report highlighted that the LMPP projects had contributed to positive outcomes, such as improved productivity, enhanced employee performance, reductions in absenteeism and increased employee participation in decision-making. Finally, the LMPP was credited with assisting the prevention and/or resolution of ongoing and imminent labour disputes and, indeed, 77% of the survey respondents indicated that such projects had benefited the settlement of disputes. Additionally, the case studies also revealed similar outcomes, in terms of the contribution of LMPP projects to dispute prevention and the reduction in the number of official grievances.

This evaluation also identified specific areas for improvement in order to improve the impact of this programme. In particular, the report highlighted the need to:

- Reach more workplaces and, in particular, to encourage participation by more SMEs.
- Increase the dissemination of the knowledge and lessons learned.
- Enhance the longer-term sustainability of project results.

Importantly, the FMCS has embraced these recommendations pro-actively – for example, the capacity to sustain the results of the project is now one of the criteria used to evaluate proposals for LMPP funding. The positive outcomes generated by the LMPP clearly demonstrate the potential for public policy to achieve tangible improvements in organisational performance and the employment relations environment, through the provision of targeted support, designed to encourage management and unions to explore new ways of working together. The FMCS's emphasis on promoting the establishment and maintenance of constructive labour-management relations through initiatives, such as the LMPP, is premised in part on encouraging the parties to adopt a deliberative problem-solving approach to workplace issues. In this context, interestingly, the boundary between dispute resolution and dispute avoidance becomes more blurred.

Indeed, the LMPP clearly recognises the potential of ADR to contribute to improvements in the quality of union-management relations. In 2004/05, it supported an ADR project, designed to promote the use of non-traditional approaches to resolving workplace grievances in SMEs. The catalyst for this ADR project was the joint recognition by the International Union of Operating Engineers (IUOE) and a Halifax-based employer, Our Neighbourhood Living Society, of the problems associated with the approach of resolving grievances through a traditional arbitration process. In particular, the traditional approach to arbitration hearings was becoming increasingly associated with soaring costs and time delays and, moreover, was failing to address more substantial underlying issues, such as the quality of employment relations within organisations. Indeed, the problems associated with traditional arbitration, in the opinion of both the employers and the unions, were having a negative impact on the labour-management environment within workplaces.

In seeking to develop a mutually-acceptable, legitimate and cost-effective alternative process, suitable for SMEs and unions, both parties consulted Karen Sasko, Director of the Canadian Joint Grievance Panel Inc. Sasko established this body in 1998, to provide a cost-efficient, and alternative, dispute resolution procedure to traditional grievance arbitration for both unions and employers.[86] The IUOE and Our Neighbourhood Living Society then secured funding from the LMPP for an ADR project that had three specific goals:

- To implement a new labour management standard for dispute resolution in SMEs, in particular.

- To provide a forum, in which employers and unions could begin to gain ownership of the resolution of their labour disputes, without third-party intervention.

- To increase awareness about how the Joint Grievance Panel Process works and the potential benefits of using this particular form of redress.

Aside from the provision of funding, the association with the LMPP was considered important, in terms of giving the project a public policy *imprimatur*, which conferred on it a degree of credibility and legitimacy in the eyes of both employers and unions. The funding was used specifically to support Sasko in developing, in consultation with the unions and employers, a user-friendly manual and associated two-day training programme on a Joint Grievance Panel Process for SMEs. Critically, the training programme that was put in place was a highly-interactive process, as the aim of the project was not merely to inform participants about the workings and benefits of this alternative approach to resolving disputes, but also to begin to encourage them to work together in a more co-operative and problem-solving manner. **Table 8.5** outlines the main characteristics of the Joint Grievance Panel Process that was promoted through this particular ADR project.

---

[86] The organisation was incorporated formally to protect the integrity of the joint grievance panel process, and it is recognised for this purpose by the Canada Labour Relations Board, the Ontario Labour Board and the British Columbia Labour Board.

TABLE 8.5: THE CANADIAN JOINT GRIEVANCE PANEL PROCESS: AN OVERVIEW

Schedule 1	Schedule 2
The panel is comprised of four members: two union representatives and two employer representatives, not associated with the local union or employer who has the grievance.	An arbitrator is selected from an agreed list.
No arbitrator is used, as the panel provides the decision in an executive session.	Two panelists are used: one employer and one union. As in **Schedule 1**, neither should have any direct association with the grievance in question.
No lawyers or case law are permitted.	If the grievance proceeds to **Schedule 2**, as a result of deadlock in **Schedule 1**, the panel cannot include individuals who participated in **Schedule 1**.
Labour representatives present their case to the panel with the grievor present, as well as the union steward and other necessary witnesses.	
Employer representatives present their case, with the supervisors and other witnesses present.	No lawyers or case law are permitted.
Typical grievances include discipline issues, job postings, work assignments and absenteeism.	Labour and employer representatives present their case before the arbitrator and the two panelists.
The decisions rendered are final and binding, but not precedent-setting.	A one-page decision is issued by the arbitrator, and provided to the parties within 48 hours of the hearing.
Each grievance is heard, and a decision reached, based on its own merit.	Examples of grievances heard include deadlocked cases from **Schedule 1**, disciplinary grievances, contract language interpretation and any issue that does not require a precedent-setting decision.
All decisions are rendered on the day of the hearing, and parties are informed within 48 hours. If the cases are deadlocked, the case may proceed to Schedule 2 of the JGPP or to a traditional arbitration board.	There is no deadlock in this instance, as the arbitrator can make a final decision.

The parties to this project have identified a number of potential benefits associated with the usage of this particular ADR process to address workplace grievances. First, it provides an expedited and effective process for parties to resolve their grievances. Although the number of grievances heard during the course of a one-day hearing depends on the complexity of the cases, on average, between four and eight grievances can be resolved in one hearing under Schedule 1 (see **Figure 8.5**); under Schedule 2, this figure drops to between two and three cases resolved per day. This outcome contrasts sharply with the experience of the traditional arbitration approach, where single-case hearings last for two to three days on average. Second, this process provides for a final, and binding, decision. Decisions, however, are non-precedent setting, which is important in terms of both parties' willingness to engage with it. Equally, this also facilitates the panelists in being more open-minded about how they approach issues. Third, this approach is premised on experienced practitioners making decisions jointly, without the involvement of either third-party bodies or lawyers and, as such, they 'own' the process and its associated outcomes. The speed of the process, combined with the fact that lawyers are not involved, also contributes to considerable cost efficiencies, with estimated financial savings of between 35% and 40%, as a result of using this approach, compared to traditional arbitration. Finally, the Joint Grievance Panel Process is designed to complement the existing, and agreed, mechanisms for resolving workplace grievances. The fact that this process did not represent a threat to the practices and procedures established by collective agreements was an important factor in the unions' willingness, in particular, to embrace this ADR innovation.

The roll-out of this training program has enhanced unions' and employers' awareness of this non-traditional approach to resolving grievances and the demand for the services of the Canadian Joint Grievance Panel has risen as a result. Interestingly, however, the Director of this body also contends that, as a result of participating in the training workshop, the unions and employers are displaying a greater willingness to work together in intervening and resolving potential problems, early and close to the point of origin, before they become formalised grievances. This project, therefore, has encouraged a degree of innovation and experimentation in relation to internal conflict management, and also has contributed to an enhancement of the dispute resolution/prevention skills of many of those who participated in it.

8.4.4 The FMCS: An overview

This section has described how the FMCS, in seeking to fulfil its statutory mandate, has developed gradually a high-quality, and flexible, conflict management system. The FMCS continues to enjoy a high level of credibility and legitimacy amongst its key client groupings – politicians, unions and employers – and, in client surveys, it continues to score highly, particularly with regard to the levels of satisfaction with the quality of the services provided. As is the case with other public dispute resolution agencies, developing and delivering a quality service is heavily dependent on the skill and experience of its staff, and the FMCS benefits from having a strong cadre of officials, with deep experience of the industrial relations environment and also considerable skill in the use of both traditional, and alternative, dispute resolution/prevention approaches. The policy of recruiting experienced practitioners appears to be an important factor in sustaining this high level of organisational competency. The FMCS also has been willing to use the principles and practices associated with ADR to assist in improving and modernising its services and to broaden the scope of its operational remit. Importantly, new initiatives have been designed and implemented in a manner that builds on the prevailing legal and institutional context, in order both to improve the current system for dispute resolution/prevention and to enhance the quality of employment relations in general. Therefore, there is no sense that ADR is associated with any attempt to circumvent collective agreements or statutory-based employment rights. In seeking to encourage a shift from adversarial to more co-operative problem-solving employment relations, the boundary between formal dispute resolution and dispute avoidance activity also has become increasingly blurred. Finally, the FMCS remains committed to ongoing policy experimentation and innovation. As part of this, the FMCS recognises the importance of developing initiatives and services that can assist employers and unions in enhancing their in-house capacity to craft innovative and sustainable solutions to workplace problems.

8.5   THE LABOUR STANDARDS & WORKPLACE EQUITY DIRECTORATE: MEDIATION & THE UNJUST DISMISSAL PROCESS

8.5.1   The unjust dismissal process

Within the federal-level Labour Program, the Labour Standards & Workplace Equity Directorate's activities are concerned with establishing and protecting employees' rights to fair and equitable conditions of employment. The operations of this Directorate are intended to promote and enforce compliance with the provisions of Part III of the Canada Labour Code, the Fair Wages & Hours of Labour Act, and the Employment Equity Act. This section of the chapter considers the 'alternative dispute resolution' initiative that has been developed as an integral part of the Labour Standards Directorate's process for addressing alleged cases of unjust dismissal. First, however, it is necessary to describe the overall process for dealing with unfair dismissal cases (see **Figure 8.1**).

In accordance with federal employment law, an employee working for a federally-regulated industry, who feels that they have been unjustly dismissed from their employment, has the right under Section 240 of Part III of the Canadian Labour Code to file a complaint of unjust dismissal with the Labour Standards Directorate. Under sub-section 241(2) of the Canadian Labour Code, a Labour Program Inspector[87] is mandated to endeavour to assist the parties to the complaint to reach a mutually-agreed settlement. Consequently, the statutory role afforded to the Labour Program Inspector with

---

[87]   In some documentation, these officials are referred to as 'Labour Assistant Officers'.

regard to unfair dismissal cases is one of dispute resolution. This contrasts with the regulatory role these same officials perform in relation to other divisions of the Canada Labour Code – for example, statutory holiday pay or payment of wages – where they have a regulatory role in terms of both encouraging compliance and/or ensuring enforcement of the appropriate employment legislation.[88]

FIGURE 8.1: DISPUTE RESOLUTION: THE UNJUST DISMISSAL PROCESS (PART III OF THE CANADA LABOUR CODE)

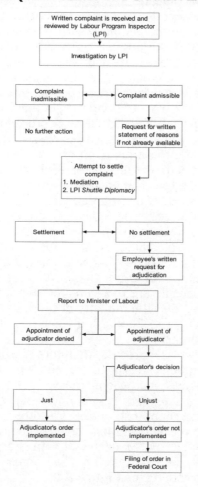

---

[88] In recent years, there has been an increased emphasis on working pro-actively with employers to upgrade their HR practices and encouraging compliance with federal employment law.

There are three stages to the unjust dismissal process currently operated by the Labour Standards Directorate (see **Figure 8.1**). On receiving a filed complaint for alleged unfair dismissal, a Labour Program Inspector first will determine its admissibility. If the complaint meets the necessary criteria, the Inspector will contact the parties – employer and employee – directly and offer them the voluntary option of engaging in mediation in seeking to resolve their respective dispute.

If the option to mediate is declined by either party, the Labour Program Inspector will initiate a process of 'investigative shuttle diplomacy', in an attempt to broker a resolution to the dispute, without proceeding to formal adjudication. This involves separate negotiations with each of the parties, using mail, telephone and in-person interviews. A central element of this process is an 'informal investigation', in which the employer will be asked both about its HR practices and the case in question. In particular, through appropriate questioning, the Inspector aims to bring to light any evident failings in relation to the grievance and disciplinary procedures that were followed and to highlight any apparent weaknesses in the employer's case; as, in adjudication, the onus is on the employer to show that the dismissal was justified. The Inspector also will engage with the complainant on this matter. The Inspector then will propose what s/he considers to be a viable and appropriate offer and will actively encourage the parties to settle, including undertaking, if necessary, further bilateral negotiations with both sides. This form of 'investigative shuttle diplomacy' is the more established, and traditional, approach for resolving unfair dismissal disputes without resorting to adjudication and, even though it takes a lot longer to achieve a settlement, people are more comfortable with this process, as evidenced by the fact that the majority of cases still are resolved in this manner. For example in 2005/2006, 65% of all referrals were resolved using this approach.

Within the unfair dismissal process, therefore, parties are provided with two separate options designed to resolve their dispute – mediation or investigative shuttle diplomacy. If, however, it is not possible to achieve an agreed resolution using either of these approaches, the complainant can make a written request to the Minister of Labour for the appointment of an adjudicator to make a ruling on the complaint of unfair dismissal.[89] In the period between 2001 and 2006, on average, a quarter of all unfair dismissal cases were referred to adjudication (see **Figure 8.2**).

---

[89]   Under the Code, it is the Minister who has the authority to decide whether to appoint an adjudicator.

FIGURE 8.2: ADJUDICATED CASES AS A % OF ALL UNFAIR DISMISSAL CASES, 2001/02-2005/06

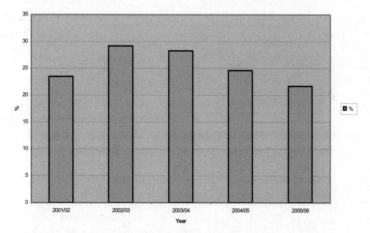

If an adjudicator is appointed, a hearing is scheduled, at which both sides have an opportunity to present evidence on the case. Adjudicators are drawn from the legal community – practising lawyers or judges – and, although the Federal Government employs them, they have an arms-length relationship with the Labour Standards Inspectorate. The procedures used at adjudication hearings are less formal than those in a civil court – for example, the rules of evidence are relaxed, to ensure that all evidence is available to the adjudicator. Equally, however, adjudication hearings still are relatively formal, and quasi-legalistic in character, compared both to the earlier stages of the unfair dismissal process and to the more general industrial relations-style conciliation. During a hearing, parties are free to call on witnesses and, if they wish, they can be represented by a lawyer; however, it is the adjudicator who leads the process and effectively controls all inputs. After hearing and considering all the relevant evidence, the adjudicator will make a decision on the fairness of the dismissal, which is binding on both parties. If the adjudicator finds the dismissal was unjust, s/he has the power to determine the remedy entitlement and, in such instances, the employer may be ordered to:

- Re-instate the employee with, or without, compensation for lost wages.

- Pay compensation for lost wages without reinstating the employee.

- Do anything that is equitable in order to remedy any consequences of the dismissal – for example, clear an employee's record of any reference to the dismissal, pay legal costs, etc.

The decision of an adjudicator is final and it cannot be appealed in court.[90] Interestingly, the adjudicator can order re-instatement, which is something a civil court cannot mandate, in instances where a civil remedy is sought in relation to an unfair dismissal case.[91] As is evident from **Figure 8.3**, re-instatement occurs in only a small minority of adjudicated cases.

FIGURE 8.3: RE-INSTATEMENT AS A % OF ALL ADJUDICATED UNFAIR DISMISSAL CASES, 2001/02-2005-/06

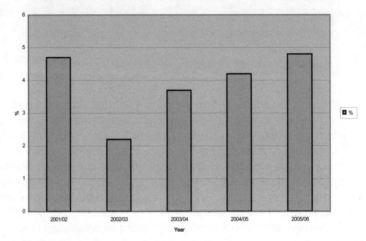

8.5.2   Mediating unjust dismissals

As indicated earlier, the role of the Labour Program Inspector in relation to unfair dismissal cases is to seek to achieve a resolution and it is under this legislative authority that the Labour Program has established an alternative dispute resolution option in the form of a Mediation Service. This initiative began in 1999, when the Labour Program, with financial assistance from Justice Canada's Dispute Resolution Fund, implemented a pilot ADR scheme for dealing with unjust dismissal cases, in the provinces of Ontario and Alberta. The

---

90   It may be the subject of an application for review by the Federal Court of Canada, under certain limited circumstances.

91   Adjudicators and the courts have concurrent jurisdiction in this area and, although it seldom happens, it is possible for an employee to file a civil action against the employer, while the Labour Standards Directorate investigates the unjust dismissal. Equally, an individual may decide to pursue their claim only through the civil courts.

impetus was the growing concern about both the rising administrative costs associated with adjudication referrals and the increasing delays in processing cases through the system. In particular, it was recognised that although the established method of 'investigative shuttle diplomacy' was capable of resolving disputes, it was neither timely nor necessarily cost-effective. Indeed, one characteristic of this dispute resolution mechanism was that numerous complaints, after relatively lengthy negotiations, were settled on the 'steps of the courts', just prior to the adjudication session, but after the appointment of an Adjudicator and the scheduling of a hearing. Thus, not only did the parties have to undergo a fairly lengthy process before reaching a settlement, but the Labour Standards Directorate also incurred unnecessary administrative and financial costs.

In this context, the objective of the pilot ADR project was to develop a more effective, and cost-efficient, mechanism for the resolution of unjust dismissal complaints, by establishing a mediation option within the formal dispute resolution process. In order to ensure it had sufficient capacity to deliver such a service, the Labour Program sourced customised mediation training for virtually all of its Labour Program Inspectors from the FMCS. In addition, a number of suitable Inspectors were identified and provided with additional third-level external mediation training, creating 'a cadre of mediation experts' within the Directorate.

The initial pilot ran for a year, after which the Labour Program undertook an evaluation of its impact. Significantly, this evaluation demonstrated that mediation had enabled the parties to participate in resolving complaints in a more flexible, informal and collaborative manner, compared to the traditional rights-based approach that, traditionally, had characterised unjust dismissal cases. From an administrative perspective, this evaluation also highlighted the capacity of mediation to function as a more efficient, and less costly, dispute resolution mechanism. On the basis that this mediation experiment had achieved the two objectives of reducing costs and improving the quality of service, the Labour Program decided to mainstream it, by rolling it out in every province, through the provision of mediation training for all Labour Program Inspectors. As indicated earlier, all parties are now offered mediation as the first option, once a claim has been deemed admissible. In accordance with the Labour Standards Directorate's commitment to meeting the needs of the Canadian workers and workplaces and offering the most comprehensive process available, field officers continue to receive, on top of their initial mediation training, between three and five days training per year in ADR methods, thus ensuring that they continue to keep apace with the latest developments in this evolving discipline.

A Labour Program Inspector, with specialised training and experience in leading mediation, conducts the unjust dismissal mediation process. Within a mediation session, the mediator will structure the discussions, organise information, assist the parties in articulating their concerns and identify opportunities for agreement. In particular, the mediator will draw on a range of techniques and approaches to create a positive environment that encourages the parties to engage in open and honest dialogue, examine their positions, achieve understanding, explore creative solutions and potentially develop a joint resolution. Although a mediator may point out opportunities for agreement, and assist in the framing and writing of any potential settlement, the parameters and content of such a settlement are determined by the parties. This contrasts with inspector-led negotiations ('investigative shuttle diplomacy'), where the official takes the lead in seeking to create a possible resolution. Although the mediator is an active participant in the process, their status is that of a neutral third-party. As such, s/he is precluded from making a judgement as to the relative merits of an unfair dismissal case being processed. Equally, the mediator's role is to assist the parties in reaching an agreement, rather than actually pushing for a resolution. This contrasts with 'shuttle diplomacy', where the official in question will encourage the parties actively to reach a settlement, in a manner akin to a conciliator in collective-bargaining-style negotiations.

Confidentiality is an important dynamic underpinning the effectiveness of the mediation process, as it is considered to foster a more open, and honest, dialogue between the parties. Everyone present at a mediation session must sign a confidentiality agreement and, if the end result is that a complaint continues to proceed to adjudication, no documentation obtained during mediation can be forwarded to the adjudicator. In addition to the actual parties to the dispute, other participants (for example, a friend, spouse or legal counsel) may attend a mediation session in a supportive capacity; however, as the primary focus is on encouraging an open discussion between the two parties, these 'additional attendees' are requested to limit their participation in the actual process.

If, in the context of the mediation, the parties signify their willingness to resolve the dispute, they will seek to write, with the assistance of the mediator if required, a mutually-agreed settlement document. If this process is successful, both parties will sign the settlement document, which, although confidential, has the status of a legal document. In a small number of cases, having had initial discussions with an assigned mediator, the parties may settle their dispute without a formal mediation session being convened. Additionally, in some cases, the parties may fail to reach a settlement in the context of the mediation process, but the case is subsequently withdrawn and, as such, from the Directorate's perspective, it is closed. In the overall number of unfair dismissal cases considered to be settled (that is, closed) through the use of the ADR mediation option, the Labour Program includes both of these instances. If a dispute is not resolved through mediation, the complainant retains the right to make a written request to the Minister of Labour to appoint an adjudicator to rule on the unjust dismissal complaint. While the Labour Standards Directorate actively promotes the benefits of mediation, it is important to recognise that participation in this process remains wholly voluntary and the mediation of an unfair dismissal case can proceed only if both parties agree. Additionally, in certain circumstances, mediation is not considered by the Directorate to be appropriate, in particular when one of the parties has an addiction or other impairment of cognitive reasoning. Similarly, mediation is not offered in situations of abuse or violence.

Although ADR mediation contrasts with a rights-based approach to unfair dismissals, this does not represent in any way a weakening of an individual's principles or their statutory employment rights, as the process is purely voluntary. More specifically, experience highlights that the majority of such cases are highly subjective in character, with the catalyst often being a misunderstanding. Similarly, it is also evident that, in many cases, the employers did not have in place progressive grievance and disciplinary procedures. This provides an amenable context for mediation, which has the capacity both to accommodate grey areas in disputes and to focus on underlying tensions. Consequently, the emphasis within a case can be shifted from a debate about who is right and who is wrong towards a focus on improving understanding, enhancing current practices and gaining a mutually-agreed resolution.

8.5.3 The Mediation Service: Operational outcomes

Since 2001, the ADR mediation option has been mainstreamed into the formal process for handling unjust dismissals. As part of this process, the Labour Standards Directorate and its field officers have had to work pro-actively with clients and representative groups to foster a greater understanding of the mediation process and, in particular, to address any concerns and also to highlight the potential benefits. Interestingly, the Directorate is of the view that there is now a greater awareness of mediation, which in part reflects a broader societal interest in experimenting with new ways of resolving disputes. Since 2001, the number of cases progressed through mediation has ranged from 123 to a high of 208, with an average figure of 175 for the period between 2001 and 2006 (see **Table 8.6**). It is important to recognise that the highest percentage of total cases progressed though this dispute resolution mechanism in any one year period was just 15.1%, with the average figure being 13.4%.

TABLE 8.6: UNFAIR DISMISSAL CASES, 2001/02-2005/06

Year	Total Unfair Dismissal Cases	ADR Mediation Cases	ADR Mediation Cases as % of all UD Cases
2001/02	1,283	123	10.4
2002/03	1,414	208	14.7
2003/04	1,415	195	13.8
2004/05	1,257	190	15.1
2005/06	1,250	160	12.8

However, as is evident from **Table 8.7**, the traditional approach of a Labour Program Inspector engaging in separate negotiations with the parties remains the dominant dispute resolution method in relation to unjust dismissal cases. Thus, while the development of the mediation option has been an important and innovative initiative, still only a minority of cases are progressed through this avenue of redress. More specifically, it demonstrates that the mediation option was designed to complement, rather than replace, existing dispute resolution mechanisms and, as such, its impact has been to enhance the flexibility of the dispute resolution service.

TABLE 8.7: UNFAIR DISMISSAL CASES SETTLED WITHOUT REFERRAL TO ADJUDICATION, 2001/02-2005/06

Year	Total No. Settled	Settled by Labour Program Inspector		Settled by ADR Mediation	
		No.	% of all settled	No.	% of all settled
2001/02	953	856	89.8	97	10.2
2002/03	1,012	859	84.9	153	15.1
2003/04	1,005	860	85.6	145	14.4
2004/05	893	134	85	134	15
2005/06	923	809	87.6	114	12.4

A recurring theme in all the chapters to date has been the importance of providing conflict management services that are both relevant and effective. The Mediation Service's capacity to achieve a relatively high settlement rate of between 71% and 79% in the period under consideration clearly demonstrates both its relevance and effectiveness (see **Table 8.8**).[92]

---

[92]   As indicated earlier, settled cases include cases that produced a settlement document; cases that were settled following initial contacts but before a formal

TABLE 8.8: ADR MEDIATION OPERATIONAL OUTCOMES, 2001/02-2005/06

Year	ADR Mediation Cases	Settled at Mediation	Settled before Mediation	Not Settled but Withdrawn	Adjudication Requested	% Settled
2001/02	123	86	9	2	26	79
2002/03	208	127	9	17	55	74
2003/04	195	117	14	14	50	74.4
2004/05	190	118	6	10	50	73.6
2005/06	160	87	8	19	46	71

It is also a highly efficient service, as it takes considerably fewer days to settle a case – from the day it is filed to the case being officially closed – using this method, compared to the more traditional method of 'investigative shuttle diplomacy' (see **Figure 8.4**). The Mediation Service's clear capacity to provide an effective, fair and efficient service re-affirms that its role since its introduction has been to enhance the overall quality of the dispute resolution service provided by the Directorate in relation to the processing of unjust dismissal cases.

FIGURE 8.4: TIME TAKEN TO COMPLETE AN UNFAIR DISMISSAL CASE, 2001/02-2003/04

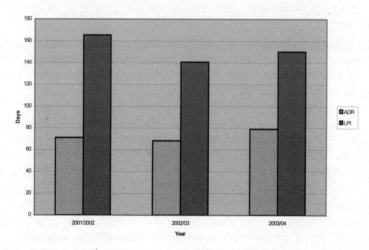

mediation session was undertaken; and cases where there was no settlement document, but the case was subsequently withdrawn.

8.5.4   The benefits of mediation

The initial evaluation of the pilot project, in conjunction with the practitioner's assessment of how the process has functioned subsequently, suggests that there is a range of potential benefits associated with the use of mediation, including:

- **Time-efficient:** As indicated earlier, processing a claim through mediation is considerably quicker than the Labour Program Inspector-led negotiations. At present, a mediation session takes place within eight to 12 weeks of a complaint being filed and, on average, it is possible for a mediator to achieve a resolution within two to four hours of a session commencing. In stark contrast, the average time from the date the complaint is received to the date of decision from the adjudicator is some 60.5 weeks. This efficiency is clearly beneficial for all stakeholders – claimants, respondents, representative groups and officials.

- **Ownership and empowerment:** Mediation provides an opportunity for empowerment, in that the parties to a dispute have the capacity to create their own 'customised' resolution to a dispute. Thus, they can control the outcome of their dispute, rather than having a decision imposed on them by a third party, through adjudication.

- **Sustainability:** This sense of ownership, allied to the fact that mediation has a greater capacity to get to the 'root cause' of a dispute, creates a context in which the agreed settlement is likely to have a more lasting impact.

- **Future-focused:** Mediation has the capacity to encourage future co-operation between the parties to a dispute, which is particularly important in small rural communities or when re-instatement is sought.

- **Closure:** Mediation has demonstrated its ability to bring closure to long-standing disputes, in which there is often a high level of personal emotional investment. Interestingly, there is also anecdotal evidence to suggest that claimants, who have decisions issued in their favour, are not always pleased with the content and, therefore, a sense of grievance can linger.

- **Voice:** Mediation is premised on both parties expressing themselves and communicating their views. Engaging in this process, therefore, does not represent a weakening of an individual's statutory rights or principles, as affording 'voice' to participants is a central dynamic of the mediation session. Additionally, the option to engage in mediation remains voluntary and does not preclude a complainant from seeking to have a case adjudicated.

- **Win-Win:** A successful resolution to mediation is dependent on reaching an agreement that is mutually acceptable to both parties and, as such, it has the potential to create a win-win situation, in contrast to a formal adjudication, which will result inevitably in a winner and loser.

- **Cost-efficient:** Mediation provides the parties with an informal, and low-cost, alternative to the more lengthy, and legalistic, adjudication process. It also generates administrative savings for the Labour Program, in terms of servicing the unfair dismissals process.

Interestingly, in one province (Ontario), the Labour Standards Directorate is currently piloting the use of voluntary ADR mediation in certain divisions of the Canadian Labour Code, where the Labour Program Investigator normally would be engaged in enforcement-style activity. This is a somewhat controversial initiative, given that it is seeking to introduce ADR into a context where there are clearly-defined, enforceable legislative rights that cannot be signed or negotiated away. In recognition of this statutory context, the initiative has been used primarily in relation to wage disputes. Although the pilot is still running, and no formal evaluation has been conducted as yet, one informed practitioner suggested that it was unlikely that it would be mainstreamed, given the somewhat controversial nature of the initiative.

Although this last point highlights that there can clearly be limits to the applicability of ADR in certain rights-based contexts, overall, the development of the mediation option as an alternative to a traditional rights-based approach to addressing unjust dismissal cases has been an innovative development that has clearly delivered benefits for all the stakeholders, namely the central administration, the officials, the claimants and respondents. Importantly, the development and mainstreaming of this ADR approach to unfair dismissals works, because it is incorporated into the established procedures with a view to enhancing and improving the quality of the dispute resolution service provided by this public agency. In particular, this ensures that using mediation to resolve such disputes is not associated in any way with a weakening of statutory-based employment rights.

8.6   THE CANADIAN HUMAN RIGHTS COMMISSION: DEVELOPING ADR WITH A PUBLIC INTEREST[93]

The Canadian Human Rights Commission (CHRC) is empowered by the Canadian Human Rights Act to investigate and try to resolve/settle complaints of discrimination in employment and in the provision of services, goods and accommodation that fall within the federal jurisdiction. Under this Act, discrimination is prohibited on the following grounds: race, national or ethnic origin, age, sex, sexual orientation, marital status, family status, disability and conviction for which a pardon has been granted. The Commission is also responsible under the Employment Equity Act for ensuring that federally-regulated employers provide equal employment to the four designated groups: women, Aboriginal peoples, people with disabilities and members of visible minorities. Finally, the Commission also is mandated to develop and conduct information and discrimination prevention programmes.

This section of the chapter is concerned primarily with the CHRC's activities in relation to dealing with complaints of discrimination against federally-regulated employers, unions and services providers. In particular, this section focuses on how the Commission has remodelled its dispute resolution process to incorporate a range of ADR services as part of an overall strategy, designed to reconfigure the strategic identity of the organisation towards an increased emphasis on problem-solving, prevention and knowledge development in the area of human rights.

8.6.1   Strategic change: Towards a new problem-solving ethos

Under the overall direction of the Chief Commissioner, the CHRC is organised into four branches (see **Figure 8.5**):[94]

- **A Dispute Resolution Branch**, which integrates all services related to processing a complaint into one functional unit.

- **A Discrimination Prevention Branch**, which provides a comprehensive service, focused on developing a more positive, and productive, relationship with employers, while providing strategic advice and support.

---

[93]   In addition to interviews with senior officials, official reports and briefing reports provided by interviewees, this case study also draws on information and analysis provided on the CHRC's website, http://www.chrc.ccdp.ca.

[94]   The staff is divided between the CHRC's headquarters in the federal capital of Ottawa and six regional offices.

- **A Knowledge Centre**, which emphasises policy development, legal advice, statistical analysis and knowledge, to enhance the level of understanding of human rights within Canadian society.

- **A Strategic Initiatives Branch**, which responds to emerging issues and seeks to combat broader problems of a systemic nature.

Within this organisation structure, the Commissioners, an eight-member body appointed by the Governor in Council,[95] play a pivotal role, as they issue decisions both on whether to deal with cases and also on the disposition of cases put before them (see **Figure 8.6**).

FIGURE 8.5: CANADIAN HUMAN RIGHTS COMMISSION: ORGANISATION CHART

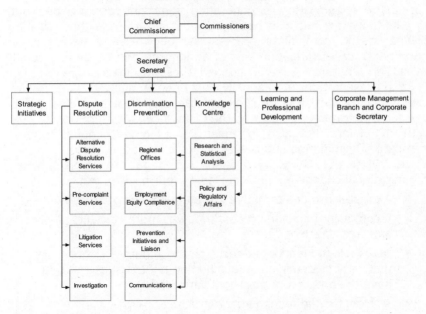

In instances where a case cannot be resolved, or where there is an important public interest dimension, the Commission can refer complaints to the Canadian Human Rights Tribunal, a separate quasi-judicial, statutory body, which can undertake further inquiry into

---

95   In Canada, the Governor in Council is the Governor General, acting on the advice of the federal cabinet. In addition to the Chief Commissioner, members of the Commission may be appointed on either a full, or part-time, basis.

whether the case contravenes the Canadian Human Rights Act.[96] In such instances, the Tribunal convenes a public hearing and renders a decision, substantiating or dismissing the complaint. If the CHRC participates in the Tribunal's hearings, it is on the basis of representing a position it considers to be in the public interest. If a complaint is substantiated, the Tribunal has powers to issue an appropriate remedy.[97]

Beginning in 2002, the Commission instigated a major change management process, designed to improve its services and to strengthen its capacity to undertake all aspects of its mandate.[98] The catalyst for this transformative program was well-documented problems associated with the traditional manner in which the Commission addressed and processed complaints. In particular, the CHRC's complaints process was considered to be too slow and cumbersome, resulting in lengthy delays and an increasing backlog of cases. The system also was generating significant cost overruns, due in part to delays but also because of the central role that litigation played in the complaints process. Although clearly necessary in appropriate cases, litigation was often lengthy and costly and could, by its very nature, create a context that was inaccessible without legal representation. Additionally, experience showed that it was clearly not the best tool in all circumstances. These problems clearly exerted a detrimental impact on the CHRC's capacity, not only to deal with complaints, but also to undertake its broader public interest mandate of eliminating and preventing discrimination.

In 2002, the CHRC developed and began to implement an organisational change agenda centred on four basic principles:

- A greater use of alternative dispute resolution methods.

- A complaint handling process that was more efficient, timely and cost-effective.

- New tools to identify and focus on those human rights cases that raise systemic or serious human rights issues and that have the greatest human rights impact.

- A strengthened management structure.

---

[96] The CHRC is the only body that can refer a case to the Canadian Human Rights Tribunal.

[97] Remedies can include cessation of a discriminatory practice; adoption of a special programme; introduction of new policies and procedures; financial compensation for lost earnings; expenses; legal fees, a written apology; and a financial award to cover personal feelings.

[98] An internal briefing paper, *Innovation Change Management: An Alternative to Legislation*, provides a comprehensive overview of the CHRC's strategic change initiative (see http://www.chrc.ccdp.ca/about). This case study draws on the analysis provided by the document.

The overall goal of this new strategic agenda was to eliminate the backlog of cases, by putting in place processes that emphasised early intervention to resolve disputes before they became complaints and allowed ADR, in particular, mediation, at all stages of the complaint process. Additionally, it was recognised that there was a need to focus more resources on new areas, such as discrimination prevention, knowledge research and regulatory initiatives.

The first stage of this major change project involved intensive consultation with key stakeholder groups and the general public. This consultative exercise re-affirmed the problems caused by the lengthy delays in processing claims and it was clear that the public wanted a Human Rights Commission that had the organisational capacity both to process claims more efficiently and also to focus more effectively on addressing systemic discrimination and preventative activities. This consultative exercise also revealed concerns from certain employers and service providers that the CHRC, at times, appeared to be complainant-friendly in its operational focus.

At the same time, the CHRC also undertook, again in consultation with key stakeholders, an intensive re-evaluation of its enabling legislation, in order to explore more fully the potential advantages afforded to it by this legislative framework. This self-analysis not only re-affirmed its statutory role of representing the public interest within the human rights framework, but also highlighted the potential latitude afforded to the CHRC by the legislation to change how it dealt with human rights issues. This analysis confirmed that it was consistent with the promulgation of human rights that mechanisms for redress be available in as many places, and as quickly as possible, and that, in appropriate cases, it may be sufficient for the parties to a human rights dispute to participate co-operatively in informal or formal internal workplace dispute resolution systems, for example.

Following from this consultative and analytical stage, the CHRC implemented a series of organisational and policy changes, designed to improve its performance as a public institution with a legislative-based human rights mandate. Critically, a central element of this new approach was the positioning of alternative dispute resolution mechanisms at the very heart of its dispute resolution process. Having introduced a mediation service in 1999, and having offered a form of mandatory conciliation since 1977, the CHRC now sought to provide a more comprehensive and integrated range of alternative mechanisms of redress. In essence, this was achieved gradually over the period 2002-2005, through the development of a dispute resolution model that built on existing services, through the adoption of new initiatives and an element of reconfiguring established approaches. Recognising the need to enhance its organisational capacity substantially in relation to ADR, the Commission combined an extensive training programme with the open recruitment of highly-experienced, professional mediators.[99] The design and implementation of this new dispute resolution model was informed by ongoing consultation with the relevant stakeholders.

In seeking to ensure that this emerging ADR model both was of a high quality and accorded with their public interest mandate, in 2003 the Commission established an ADR Advisory Council, comprised of eminent jurists. This body provides advice to the Chief Commissioner on alternative dispute resolution, as it relates to human rights and public interest issues, and it has played an important role in clarifying the CHRC's principles and improving its ADR processes. Thus, in 2003, the CHRC established the Alternative Dispute Resolution Service to provide a comprehensive mediation and conciliation service to clients. As part of its work, this unit also has initiated an awareness programme for employers, service providers, unions and advocacy groups, designed to foster a better understanding of the ADR model and encourage its usage.

In addition to remodelling its dispute resolution process, the CHRC also introduced changes to its litigation strategy and invested additional resources in other areas, such as prevention and policy development. This major restructuring of the organisation was completed in 2005 and it is considered to have equipped the Commission with a broader set of tools required to execute its mandate under the Canadian Human Rights Act.

Significantly, this transformative programme also reconfigured the CHRC's strategic identity, as it now fulfils its role of representing the public interest within the human rights framework, through an increased focus on problem-solving and dispute prevention, as opposed to litigation and sanctioning.

8.6.2   A remodelled dispute resolution process

The dedicated Dispute Resolution Branch comprises four interrelated sections: the Alternative Dispute Resolution Services; Pre-Complaint Services; Investigations; and Litigation (see **Figure 8.5**). Through the integration of all of the services related to processing a complaint, this branch now provides a comprehensive one-stop approach to dealing with complaints. **Figure 8.6** provides a diagrammatic overview of the CHRC's integrated dispute resolution process.

---

[99]   For example, the CHRC recruited a leading human rights lawyer as the head of the ADR unit, who is also the most senior mediator in the organisation. Interestingly, the CHRC recognised that, to recruit the right people, it had to pay the 'market rate', which was above the public service pay levels at the time for such positions.

**FIGURE 8.6: CANADIAN HUMAN RIGHTS COMMISSION:
DISPUTE RESOLUTION PROCESS**

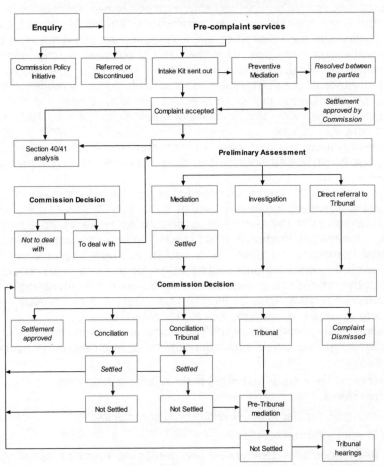

8.6.3   Pre-complaint services

Given the problems associated with the growing backlog of cases, as part of its focus on improving its case management approach, the Commission has introduced a number of changes to its Pre-Complaint Services Division, which deals with the initial inquiries from the public concerning potential instances of discrimination. This set of services is managed by interdisciplinary teams, who 'triage' potential complaints from the outset, with a view to determining the most appropriate course of action for that specific inquiry. This approach ensures that considerable professional experience and knowledge is brought to bear on individual cases from the initial point of inquiry and, as such, it reinforces the new emphasis within the conflict management system on early, and swift, intervention. Initial inquiries at this stage are screened to ascertain whether the matters raised fall within the jurisdiction and mandate of the Commission. Where this is not the case, individuals are referred to an organisation that may be able to address their concerns and, from the CHRC's perspective, the matter is discontinued. Similarly, it is possible at this stage to refer an issue to another branch of the Commission for a possible policy initiative, or for action by the Discrimination Prevention Branch. If the matter is considered to fall within the mandate and jurisdiction of the CHRC, an experienced official initiates discussions with the complainant/'inquirer', and also the potential respondent, at which stage, if it is considered appropriate, they will be offered preventative mediation.

Preventative (pre-complaint) mediation, which was introduced in 2005, is a voluntary process provided by the ADR Services Branch that aims to assist the parties to a dispute to arrive at an agreed solution, which can be implemented quickly, in order to addresses the potential complainant's main concerns. In addition to the process being offered to complainants, potential respondents can also request preventative mediation, provided they have signed a Memorandum of Understanding with the CHRC.[100] This mechanism focuses on providing a rapid resolution, so as to avoid a particular dispute escalating and becoming an official complaint. From the CHRC's perspective, preventative mediation offers a number of particular advantages:

- It provides a quick and rapid mechanism for resolving problems.
- It avoids problems becoming official complaints.
- It is an informal process.
- Respondents, in general, are less defensive, which increases the likelihood of achieving resolution.
- It is consistent with the Public Service Management Act's emphasis on the use of informal conflict management systems.

Although the Commission places a strong emphasis on the early, and quick, resolution of problems, preventative mediation is only offered in appropriate cases. It is not offered if any of the following circumstances prevail:

- It is a highly complex case.
- The case raises legal issues that require clarification by the Court or Canadian Human Rights Tribunal.

---

[100] In the latter instance, the respondent must secure the complainant's consent.

- The case is one of a series of disputes.
- The case has a history of unsuccessful dispute resolution.

If the preventative mediation option is declined, or the process does not yield an agreement, the case is returned to the relevant intake team and filed as an official complaint.

This emphasis on providing a more comprehensive pre-complaints service, in which there is a strong emphasis on screening all inquiries, has resulted in important time-savings for the CHRC, in terms of pro-actively preventing complaints from being filed and also in relation to any subsequent investigations of the substantive issues raised in complaints. It is also indicative of the changes in the organisation's mindset, as previously discussions between officials and potential complainants would have focused on the administrative practicalities of filing a complaint and explaining the process. Now, however, such discussions are more solutions-focused, in that they will seek to examine the issue and provide expert advice as to the most appropriate approach to resolving the particular issue.

A critical step at this stage, in terms of the overall case management, involves the assigned Intake Officer, drawing on the advice of other members of the team, analysing or screening the filed complaint to see whether it raises issues under Sections 40[101] and 41 (see **Table 8.9**) of the Canadian Human Rights Act. It if does, a Section 40/41 Analysis is submitted to the Members of the Commission, for a decision on whether to deal with the case. This emphasis on screening reflects the CHRC's re-evaluation of the enabling legislation and, in particular, its use of section 41(1)(a) in appropriate cases to refer human rights complaints back to the place of origin, where there is an internal grievance procedure in place to address human rights issues. This strategic decision to encourage organisations actively to explore all internal options for resolving disputes, before seeking third-party assistance, has been re-inforced by the emphasis within the Public Service Management Act 2005 (see below) on federal agencies and departments developing their own informal conflict management systems. The Discrimination Prevention Program, moreover, complements this activity, as it works with federally-regulated organisations to prevent discrimination and to develop in-house strategies to resolve human rights complaints effectively and efficiently.

---

[101] Section 40 indicates that the Commission shall not pursue a complaint, where the alleged discrimination complaint is based purely on statistical evidence that purports to show that members of one or more of the designated groups are under-represented in the federally-regulated employer's workforce.

TABLE 8.9: SECTION 41 OF THE CANADIAN HUMAN RIGHTS COMMISSION ACT

41. (1) Subject to section 40, the Commission shall deal with any complaint filed with it, unless in the respect of that complaint, it appears to the Commission that:

(a) The alleged victim of the discriminatory practice to which the complaint relates ought to exhaust grievance or review procedures otherwise reasonably available;

(b) The complaint is one that could be more appropriately dealt with, initially or completely, according to procedures provided for under an Act of Parliament other than this Act;

(c) The complaint is beyond the jurisdiction of the Commission;

(d) The complaint is trivial, frivolous, vexatious or made in bad faith; or

(e) The complaint is based on acts or omissions, the last of which occurred more than one year ago.

When a filed complaint does not raise issues under section 40/41, or if the members of the Commission decide to deal with it after reviewing the analysis, the next step for officials is to carry out a Preliminary Analysis. This process, first piloted in 2005, reflects the Commission's emphasis on identifying the most appropriate way to resolve the parties' particular concerns, quickly and informally. This process involves a human rights specialist engaging in a frank and open discussion with the parties, in order to assist them to clarify and narrow the issues, identify agreed facts, and establish, if possible, some realistic expectations regarding the case, including the most appropriate next steps in the process. This quick, but informed, preliminary assessment can generate a number of potential outcomes, including:

- The complaint is settled.
- The parties agree to participate in mediation.
- The complaint is referred to a more appropriate grievance or review procedure.
- A report is prepared to guide and speed up an investigation (expedited investigation).
- The complaint is withdrawn.
- A report is submitted to the Commission, recommending the disposition of the complaint.
- The parties decide that the issues raised in the complaint could be addressed effectively by a policy study, by the Commission's work in discrimination prevention, or through another type of public interest initiative.

- In certain cases, where complex issues are involved, such as the interpretation of a statute, the matter can bypass the investigation stage entirely and proceed to a tribunal.

8.6.4 Mainstreaming and expanding mediation

One of the possible outcomes of the Preliminary Assessment is that the parties agree to engage in mediation and, as indicated earlier, an ADR Services Branch has been established to provide a comprehensive mediation and conciliation service to clients. As already highlighted, potential complainants and respondents have an opportunity to engage in preventive mediation before a complaint is formally filed, and a defining feature of the Commission's ADR framework is that mediation is available at any stage of the complaint process, up to the commencement of hearings before the Canadian Human Rights Tribunal (see **Table 8.10**).

TABLE 8.10: CANADIAN HUMAN RIGHTS COMMISSION: MEDIATION OPTIONS

Preventative mediation	Offered after an initial inquiry, but before a complaint is officially filed.
Pre-investigative mediation	Offered after the preliminary assessment stage, but before an investigation is initiated.
Mediation – during investigation	An investigation that has begun is halted to give the parties an option to mediate a settlement.
Mediation – pre-Tribunal hearing	During the preparation for a formal Tribunal hearing, the parties may be offered the option of engaging in pre-hearing mediation. This is administered by the Tribunal, rather than the CHRC.

Having first been introduced in 1999, mediation is now a central element of the Commission's ADR architecture, and this approach seeks to assist parties in resolving their problems without recourse to a more confrontational adjudicative process, in which solutions are imposed on the parties. Mediation within the Commission is designed to be more facilitative than evaluative, in that the emphasis is on assisting the parties to a dispute to develop a customised solution that meets their needs and interests, as opposed to an overt focus on apportioning blame or the relative merits of the case. Although the ADR Services Branch pro-actively champions the use of its services, mediation remains a voluntary and confidential process and participating in it is without prejudice to any further steps the parties may take. For example, if either party refuses to engage in mediation after the initial preliminary assessment, the case moves directly to the investigative stage.

As in other mediation initiatives, in both Canada and in other jurisdictions, the role of the mediator is pivotal to the success of the process, which is why the CHRC has invested considerable time and resources in building its internal capacity to provide a high-quality service. If the parties agree to engage in mediation, the assigned mediator meets with them to discuss the ground rules for mediation, explain how the process will work and agree the necessary practical arrangements.[102] Critically, while remaining impartial – in terms of evaluating who is right and who is wrong – the mediator is duty-bound to bring the 'public interest' to the attention of the parties; this involves indicating clearly what is considered appropriate from a human rights perspective. In this regard, the mediator provides information on the Canadian Human Rights Act, Commission Policy and legal precedents. In particular, all resolutions reached during mediation must be consistent with the Commission's fundamental goal of eliminating and preventing discrimination. Consequently, where a complaint, for example, alleges that a discriminatory policy may also affect others, the mediator will ensure that the agreed settlement includes measures to correct this, through changes in the policy and/or the development of new procedures or practices. Therefore, while remaining neutral in terms of favouring either the complainant or respondent, the mediator will intervene actively in the 'public interest'. This interventionist dimension is a significant aspect of the Commission's approach to mediation and is indicative of how it has sought to customise and tailor a particular dispute resolution mechanism to meet its organisational mandate and strategic goals.

One of the perceived advantages of mediation is that it affords the parties the opportunity to craft innovative solutions that meet their own particular needs and interests, as well as the public interest. Mediated settlements reached within the Commission have included a broad range of solutions, including:

- Apologies.
- The provision of training.
- Financial compensation.
- Re-instatement in a position.
- Charitable donations.
- Payment of lost wages.
- The development of new polices and procedures.

---

[102] In mediation, the parties may meet together, or separately, with the mediator during discussions. In some instances, where a meeting is impractical, the mediation may be carried out by telephone.

Importantly, the nature and content of these types of mediated settlements accords with the aims of the Canadian Human Rights Act, which seeks not necessarily to punish people but rather to resolve human rights problems and to prevent them from happening again.

If the mediation process produces an agreed settlement, it must be approved formally by the Commission, which is responsible for reviewing all ADR settlements, from the perspectives of fairness and the public interest. Once approved, the settlement has the status of a legal document that can be enforced, if required, through the courts. Significantly, since 2003, the CHRC monitors all approved settlements that emanate from either mediation or conciliation, in order to ensure that the agreed remedies are being implemented. Of the ADR settlements approved between 2003 and 2005, and subsequently monitored, 589 have been deemed closed, 374 remain active and five have required some form of enforcement activity. However, if the mediation process does not yield a resolution, the case proceeds to the next stage of the dispute resolution process, namely investigation.[103] The continued expansion and promotion of mediation demonstrates that, from the Commission's perspective, this alternative form of redress is delivering for all of the stakeholders – the Commission, respondents, claimants and the public.

8.6.5 Investigation

A complaint may be forwarded to the Investigation Unit, either directly after a preliminary assessment or following the failure to achieve an agreed settlement at pre-investigative mediation. An investigation involves the gathering of evidence on the case through an examination of relevant documents and witness interviews, and the preparation of an Investigator's Report in which the findings are presented and analysed and a recommendation is made to the Commission as to the most appropriate course of action in relation to the complaint. The Investigator's Report is disclosed to the parties, who have an opportunity to make submissions on it to the Commission.

To improve this process, cases are now assigned to grounds-based multi-disciplinary teams comprised of investigators, legal experts and policy advisors, drawn from both the Dispute Resolution Branch and the Knowledge Centre. A senior-level case review committee provides additional support to these teams. While the actual investigations continue to be carried out by individual investigators, the relevant specialised team provides ongoing expert advice and guidance and reviews the Investigation Report before it is submitted to the Commission. As each team specialises in a particular area of

---

[103] In such circumstances, the parties may agree to submit a joint statement of facts to the investigation unit in order to speed up that process – expedited investigation.

discrimination (one of the protected grounds), it has a greater capacity for dealing with particular complaints, resulting in more thorough and expeditious investigations or other more appropriate and creative solutions. As already indicated, it is possible for an investigation to be halted to allow the parties to engage in mediation. Similarly, as each team reviews all of the complaints relating to its area of expertise, it is ideally positioned to be able to identify trends or emerging issues, and this information is used to inform the CHRC's work in relation to policy development, research work and prevention activities.

A new streamlined investigation report format has also been developed that includes a legal and analytical framework and an enhanced emphasis on the public interest perspective. The objective of this new format is to guide the investigator towards a greater focus on the issues that are relevant to the complaint. This new format, allied to the fact that the reports now emerge from a team-based process, also has brought a greater level of consistency to the investigative reports.

Once cases have proceeded through the investigation stage, it is the responsibility of the Commission to decide, drawing on the Investigation Report, the disposition of the complaints before them, resulting in one of the following outcomes:

- Referral of a complaint to conciliation.
- Referral of complaint to the Canadian Human Rights Tribunal for further inquiry.
- Dismissal of a complaint, when the Commission determines that further inquiry by a Tribunal is not warranted.

8.6.6   Conciliation: The second strand of ADR

In addition to mediation, the ADR Services Branch also provides conciliation, which is the second strand of the Commission's alternative dispute resolution framework. In effect, the Commission has the authority to refer complaints for mandatory conciliation, at any point after the filing of a complaint and before a Tribunal hearing begins, though it is used primarily post-investigation. First introduced in 1977, the Commission's approach to conciliation did not change until the introduction of mediation in 1999. This proved to be a catalyst for a re-evaluation of its traditional conciliation model and, as part of the overall change programme, a new enhanced conciliation model has now been put in place, incorporating two streams: conciliation with referral (introduced in 2003) and conciliation with assessment (introduced in 2005). The objectives of this new Conciliation model are two-fold:

- To give the Commissioners more options for dealing with complaints.

- To encourage the parties to settle rather than go to the Tribunal for adjudication.

Although influenced by mediation, this revamped conciliation model also built on many of the existing elements of conciliation that operated within the Commission and, while it is the second strand of the Commission's ADR services, it differs from mediation in that:

- It is a mandatory process that does not require the consent of the parties.
- In most cases, it occurs after an investigation.
- While remaining neutral, the conciliator has a more directive role in seeking to guide parties towards an agreed settlement.
- It is a more evaluative process, in that the conciliators, unlike mediators, can give direct feedback on the strengths and weaknesses of arguments, opinions and proposals,
- The conciliator will use official documents (the investigation report and/or assessment report) to influence the negotiations with the parties.

In 2003, the CHRC initiated conciliation with referral, which involves the Commission deciding to refer a case to the Tribunal, but also appointing a conciliator giving the parties 60 days to try and settle the case. If conciliation does not result in a settlement, the case is referred directly to the Tribunal. The advantages of this approach is that it is much quicker, given both the time limits on conciliation and the fact that the case is not reviewed again by the Commissioners. Additionally, this process encourages settlement, as the parties know that, if they do not settle, the case will move swiftly to adjudication.

In 2005, a second stream was adopted in the form of Conciliation with assessment, where the Commission appoints a conciliator and set a time limit of up to four months to reach an agreed resolution. This process begins with a human rights expert preparing an assessment of the complaint, based on a new comprehensive investigation report, submissions from the parties and the assessor's interactions with them. This assessment report includes the summary of the facts, the legal issues raised and reference to applicable case law, and an assessment of the likely outcome at a Tribunal, including any remedies. When the conciliation process begins, the conciliator will use the assessment report to guide the negotiations and, in particular, s/he will seek to focus discussions on the merits of the case and to explore the viable options for settlement that are reasonable, in light of the evidence at hand. While taking a more directive role in terms of guiding the negotiations and offering advice to the parties, the conciliator remains impartial and is there to represent the public interest. The conciliator also has the authority to terminate the process if the parties do not follow the rules (for example, minimum standards of participation),[104] if there is any question about a party's capacity to participate, if a party's decision is the product of fear or coercion, or if the process is taking too long.

The advantage of this process is that the assessment gives the parties additional information to assist them in considering their options and, in this regard, is seen as potentially encouraging them to settle. Equally, if the conciliation does not result in a settlement, the Commission can draw on both the assessment report and a conciliator's report in making a decision whether the case should go to the Tribunal. The conciliator's report will include a description of the process, including how parties participated, and any other information that could assist the members of the Commission in reaching an informed decision. Although the conciliation process is confidential, the parties can agree, even if a complaint is not settled, to a statement of facts, in order to save time at a later stage in the dispute resolution process.

As with mediation, in assisting the parties to frame a potential settlement document, the conciliator must ensure that it addresses fully the public interest.

Experience to date suggests that the remedies included in conciliation-based settlement documents are the same as those highlighted earlier in relation to mediation, in that they combine monetary and non-monetary outcomes and also, where appropriate, commitments to change policies and/or introduce new procedures. Again, any such settlements have to be approved by the Commission and all approved settlements are monitored to ensure that the agreed elements are being fully implemented.

8.6.7   A focused, high-impact litigation strategy

As part of its strategic change programme, the CHRC also has adopted a new focused litigation strategy, in which the organisation now determines, on a case-by-case basis, the scope and nature of its participation, after assessing a number of factors, including whether the case raises broad policy issues, relates to major policy concerns or raises new points of law. This new approach enables the Commission to continue to support the parties at pre-Tribunal mediation, while concentrating vigorously on pursuing at the Tribunal public interest cases with a broad and far-reaching human rights and legal impact. Prior to this, the CHRC counsel, though not required by statute, would have participated fully in all Tribunal hearings, an approach that not only consumed a significant proportion of the

---

[104] The minimum standards of participation include participating in an initial conversation with the conciliator on the process, and either making an offer or responding to an offer.

organisation's resources but also drew criticism from some respondents who thought that the CHRC was too closely aligned with the complainant's interests.

As already indicated, if a case is not settled by the CHRC, or if it considers the case to have important public interest considerations, the Commission can refer it to the Canadian Human Rights Tribunal for adjudication (see also **Figure 8.6**). Interestingly since 1997, the Tribunal has offered, in appropriate cases, a pre-hearing mediation option. While the CHRC participates in this process, it is as a representative of the public interest position only, and the process is managed and administered by the Tribunal, rather than by the Commission. Interestingly, an external evaluation of the Tribunal's mediation programme concluded that complainants, respondents and CHRC counsel all considered this pre-hearing mediation option to be a positive service that offers a valuable settlement opportunity (Zweibel & MacFarlane, 2001). Indeed of the 98 complaints completed at the Tribunal stage in 2005, 72 (73.5%) were resolved by Tribunal-sponsored mediation.

The second element of this new strategy involves the CHRC counsel in targeting litigation resources on what is considered, from a public interest perspective, to be high-impact cases. In operational terms, this more selective approach meant that, in 2005, for example, the litigation team participated in 13 of the 24 cases that continued to a Tribunal hearing. From the CHRC's perspective, this more targeted strategy has been validated by the advancement of human rights in a series of high-impact cases, including cases before the Supreme Court, since 2002. Additionally, this new approach also has facilitated a broader deployment of the organisation's legal resources – for example, legal experts now engage with cases at an earlier stage of the complaints process and are also directly involved in preventative projects.

8.6.8   Discrimination prevention and knowledge development

It is important to note that an integral feature of the new approach to dispute resolution is that it has been designed to support and complement activities being undertaken by other branches of the organisation, particularly in relation to prevention and knowledge development. The Discrimination Prevention Branch operates a Discrimination Prevention Programme, in which it works with employers to prevent discrimination and to develop strategies to resolve complaints effectively and early. As part of this programme, for example, a federal employer can sign a Memorandum of Understanding, through which it commits to working formally with the Commission on human rights issues. The CHRC assists such organisations in determining problematic areas or issues affecting human rights in the workplace, and helps them to develop the tools needed to combat sources of discrimination and to put in place appropriate approaches and effective internal redress mechanisms. Recently, moreover, the CHRC has established an Employer Advisory Committee, comprised of representatives from MOU signatories, to provide insights into the impact and effectiveness of the CHRC's practices and initiatives. The Discrimination Prevention Branch clearly is supporting and complementing the Dispute Resolutions Unit's emphasis on 'encouraging' parties to engage fully with internal dispute resolution mechanisms to address their problems, close to the point of origin and without direct third-party involvement. Similarly, the information and knowledge that is gathered from more focused screening and case load analysis is being captured and used by the Commission to support capacity-building within the Knowledge Centre, particularly in relation to policy development and the design of research initiatives. The development of both multi-disciplinary teams and specialised investigative teams has facilitated this increased exploitation of the practical and expert knowledge associated with dispute resolution.

8.6.9   Outcomes and benefits

The development since 2002 of a comprehensive dispute resolution process, premised on early intervention and the provision of ADR services, has improved substantially the efficiency and effectiveness of the CHRC's case management system. As is evident from **Figure 8.7**, the ability of the Commission, since 2003, to close more cases than it has accepted has resulted in its chronic backlog of cases, which was a considerable constraint on its organisational effectiveness, being virtually eliminated.

FIGURE 8.7: CASES IN & CASES OUT, 2002-2005:
ELIMINATING THE BACKLOG

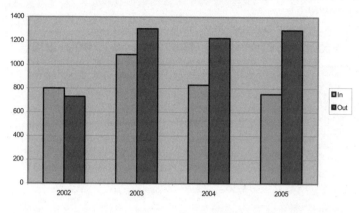

The increased efficiency of the Commission's remodelled approach to dispute resolution is also demonstrated by the fact that its active caseload fell by 47% between 2002 and September 2006 (see **Figure 8.8**).

FIGURE 8.8: ACTIVE CASES IN INVENTORY, 2002-2006[105]

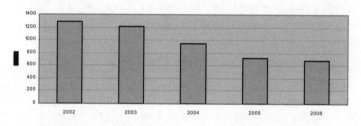

Improved efficiency has also resulted in a decline in the average age of cases, from just over 25 to 9.5 months, between 2002 and 2006 (see **Figure 8.9**). This is indicative of the increased speed with which cases now move through the dispute resolution system and, given the public's concern about the lengthy delays in processing cases, this improvement is an important outcome for the CHRC. The number of cases that are two years or older has also declined from 27% to 5% of the active caseload. Although the complexity of some cases, particularly those that involve systemic issues, ensures that there will

---

[105] The 2006 figure is for the end of September 2006.

always be a number of live 'older cases', the Commission has striven to ensure that this now represents only a small proportion of its active caseload.

FIGURE 8.9: AVERAGE AGE OF CASES, 2002-2006

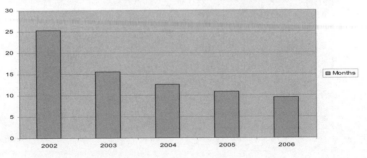

As Table **8.11** suggests, the CHRC's increased capacity to render final decisions is premised on it having at its disposal an integrated set of mechanisms for addressing cases of alleged discrimination. Moreover, this perspective is re-inforced, if one considers how cases were dealt with by the CHRC in 2005, for example.

TABLE 8.11: FINAL DECISIONS BY TYPE, 2002-2005

Method	2002	2003	2004	2005
Section 40/41 Analysis	46	213	340	428
Dismissed	317	395	406	392
Settled	301	499	369	352
Referred to Tribunal	70	195	109	119
Total no. of cases	**729**	**1,302**	**1,244**	**1,291**

In 2005, 428 (33%) of the total figures for decision were premised on not dealing with a complaint pursuant to section 40/41 of the CHR Act. The 10-fold increase in the number of such cases over 2002 highlights how focused screening, based on a re-evaluation of the enabling legislation, has contributed to the Commission's capacity to manage its case load. The fact that, in 353 of these cases, the complainants were asked to pursue other redress mechanisms first demonstrates the CHRC putting into practice the policy of encouraging parties to seek to solve problems, close to the point of origin, prior to engaging with a third party.[106] Consequently, during the course of 2005, the Commission dealt with 863 complaints, in terms of making a decision to dismiss a complaint, approve a settlement or refer the matter to a Tribunal.[107] Interestingly, there were 392 dismissed cases, representing approximately 45% of all the cases dealt with (863 cases). These dismissals generally occurred at the stage where cases had been submitted to the Members of the Commission for decision following an investigation.[108] Settlements, primarily as a result of mediation or conciliation, accounted for 41% of all cases dealt with in 2005.[109] Finally, 14% of the 863 cases were referred to the Tribunal, which compares to a figure of 12% for the previous year. Despite this slight increase, it is evident that recourse to adjudication is clearly a minority option in relation to dealing with claims of alleged discrimination at the federal level in Canada. Having previously been characterised as slow and cumbersome in processing cases, with attendant problems of lengthy delays and a chronic backlog of cases, by reconfiguring its approach to dealing with complaints of discrimination, the CHRC has considerably improved its organisational efficiency and effectiveness.

Aside from improvements in efficiency and effectiveness, the CHRC contends that putting a comprehensive package of ADR services at the very centre of its dispute resolution model has also improved the quality of the service provided. In particular, as with other examples of mediation explored in this book,[110] the CHRC argues that resolving disputes through mediation or conciliation has the capacity to generate a number of potential benefits for stakeholders: in particular, it is quick and effective; it is solutions-focused; there is a greater sense of ownership; the outcomes are more likely to be implemented without resistance; it can yield more innovative and customised

---

[106] In the remaining 75, such decisions were comprised of cases that were out of time, out of jurisdiction, trivial, frivolous or vexatious.

[107] This figure is the total number of decisions (1,291) minus the 428 decisions not to deal with a complaint pursuant to section 40/41. It is important to note that the latter are actually part of the official active caseload, as this analysis occurs after a complaint has been filed with the Commission.

[108] Cases can be dismissed for a number of reasons, such as lack of sufficient evidence or merit or because the respondent has taken appropriate action to remedy the situation. This latter point re-affirms that the aim of the Commission is to eliminate and prevent discrimination, as opposed to necessarily seeking punishment for infringement of the law.

[109] In a very small number of cases, the parties actually settled the matter on their own.

[110] See, for example, the description of the Labour Standards Directorate's Mediation Service, the LRC's Workplace Mediation Service or the chapter on the Equality Tribunal.

solutions; it is informal and less stressful; it provides for win-win situations; and it can repair or improve relationships.[111]

Additionally, the increased use of alternative dispute resolution and prevention measures has reduced the workload in case management, allowing for a shift in resources to other areas of the CHRC's mandate, such as research, policy development and discrimination prevention. By working pro-actively with stakeholders, the CHRC is helping both to increase human rights awareness and to strengthen internal redress mechanisms across the federal system, so that employees and others can have access to human rights protection through processes that are close both in time and proximity.

8.6.10 Defining features

Through a sustained process of organisational and strategic change, the CHRC has developed a flexible, integrated and dynamic dispute resolution and prevention process. At one level, this 'model' appears quite complex and highly-formalised. Nonetheless, through a combination of early intervention, innovative approaches, and an emphasis on ensuring that cases are channelled towards the most appropriate form of redress, the CHRC has reduced delays, contained legal costs and delivered an improved service for all its stakeholders. The adoption of multi-disciplinary and cross-functional teams – for example, the 'triage' teams that assess the 'most appropriate approach' for initial complaints – enables the CHRC to exploit more fully the collective knowledge and professional expertise that resides within the organisation to address disputes in a customised manner. It is also important that the different stages of the process are linked, so that, while disputes may not be settled by a particular intervention, at least it should inform the next stage of the dispute resolution process.

Critically, alternative dispute resolution is at the very heart of the CHRC's remodelled approach to complaints of alleged discrimination. An interesting aspect of this is that mediation is available at any stage of the dispute resolution process, as it is recognised that the point at which parties are willing to engage in open and respectful discussions may, and does, differ. The flexible range of mediation options, in conjunction with the new approach to conciliation, ensures that the CHRC provides multiple opportunities for settlement, without recourse to quasi-judicial tribunal hearings.

The CHRC also has designed its approach to ADR to ensure that its public interest mandate remains paramount. Interestingly, this has resulted in adopting a relatively 'interventionist' mode of ADR, in that:

---

[111] The benefits associated with mediation or conciliation have been discussed in more detail in other sections of this chapter and elsewhere in this book.

- Mediators/conciliators will intervene pro-actively in the process to ensure that the public interest is maintained, including, where necessary, ensuring that all agreed settlements address issues that have wider public implications.
- All 'ADR' settlements have to be approved by the Commission.
- All settlements are monitored to ensure that all elements of the agreed settlement are implemented in full.

The strategic change undertaken by the CHRC is also premised on increased investment in dispute prevention and knowledge development and, as already indicated, the new approach to dispute resolution seeks to support and complement these other areas of activity. Thus, while the CHRC's mandate remains focused on eliminating and preventing discrimination, it seeks actively to achieve this goal through a problem-solving focus that incorporates dispute resolution, dispute prevention and knowledge development.

8.7 FEDERAL GOVERNMENT: SUPPORTING THE DEVELOPMENT OF ADR

All of the federal organisations described in this chapter have attempted pro-actively to enhance and improve their capacity for dispute resolution and avoidance through the increased use of ADR approaches. While, in part, this was driven by the desire of internal actors to improve their pre-existing approaches, it is also evident that these types of innovative initiatives have also benefited from the supportive environment for ADR created by a number of federal government policy initiatives. This section of the chapter provides an overview of two such policy initiatives:

- The Dispute Resolution Fund.
- The Informal Conflict Management System under the PSLRA.

Between 1998 and 2002, the Dispute Resolution Services (DRS) team at the Department of Justice managed the disbursement of $6.9 million in funding for innovative Dispute Resolution 'seed projects' within federal departments and agencies. The objectives of this Dispute Resolution Fund were four-fold:

- To assist funded organisations in reducing the costs and time spent in managing disputes.
- To improve parties' satisfaction with the outcomes of dispute resolution.
- To foster further internal dispute resolution initiatives within federal organisations.

- To use the funded projects to encourage other organisations to adopt similar initiatives.

While the Department of Justice recognises that it needs to build a more rigorous evaluation framework into the funding process, in order to generate better quantitative data on the impact of the funded projects, even the limited data that it has collected provides an important snapshot of the potential impact on cost-savings within various government organisations. In particular, seven of the 51 Dispute Resolution Fund projects have provided the DRS team with firm data that identifies over $6.8 million in cost-savings, directly related to these funded projects. The DRS team expects that the innovative dispute resolution systems that have been put in place under this Fund will continue to reap considerable cost-savings for years to come. **Table 8.12** provides a summary of two such examples.

TABLE 8.12: EXAMPLES OF QUANTIFIED COST-SAVINGS ASSOCIATED WITH DISPUTE RESOLUTION FUND PROJECTS

Canadian Food Inspection Agency (CFIA)	Correctional Services Canada (CSC)
CFIA received $208,500 from the Dispute Resolution Fund to create a settlement team that resolved 53 litigation cases under the supervision of CFIA's Dispute Resolution Services. As a result, CFIA has estimated conservatively that, over the period 1 January 1999 to 31 March 2003, it realised savings in direct litigation costs of $2.5 million.	The CSC received $356,000 from the Dispute Resolution Fund. The CSC has reported that direct service delivery projects produced cost-savings of approximately $1,145,000 over a one-year period. This figure is based on the resolution of 230 conflicts through mediation.

In addition to these examples of 'hard data' cost-savings, participants also have highlighted a number of positive 'soft data' developments, particularly in relation to 'access to justice' issues and outcomes. Although the DRS team recognises that considerable hard cost-savings data and soft qualitative data have been lost as a result of poor evaluation practices, the overall conclusion is that the Dispute Resolution Fund has made an important contribution to the development of innovative and alternative dispute resolution approaches within the federal public service.

Significantly, the Federal Government's emphasis on encouraging the increased usage of ADR, through the Dispute Resolution Fund and other policy initiatives, such as the Inter-Departmental Shared Mediators Programme, was effectively institutionalised within the PSLRA, under which all federal departments and agencies were mandated to establish by mid-2005 their own in-house informal conflict management system (ICMS). This statutory requirement to develop ICMS reflected the government's emphasis on strengthening organisational capacity and effectiveness, in part through the introduction of new approaches for the prevention and resolution of workplace disputes. It also highlights the government's concern with developing more effective labour management relations, which have the capacity to minimise workplace conflict that could potentially disrupt the delivery of government policies and programmes. Central to this is the emphasis on resolving problems as close to the source as possible. Equally, this initiative was viewed as having the potential to contribute to a more harmonious, and respectful, working environment for employees. As highlighted earlier, the development of this initiative by the Treasury Board was heavily influenced by the PSLRB's positive experience of using mediation to resolve grievances and disputes. This is evident in the fact that the ICMS model is premised on the incorporation of alternative dispute resolution methods into the existing rights-based structures, to form a multi-option conflict management system. Importantly, the aim of the ICMS is not to replace, but to supplement, existing dispute resolution mechanisms.

In seeking to assist federal organisations in developing their own tailored ICMS, the Treasury Board formulated a formal policy directive that outlines 10 key principles, which should inform and shape this process (see **Table 8.13**).

One of the federal agencies that has taken the lead in developing an ICMS model is the CHRC. Within this organisation, a steering committee, comprised of management, employees and union representatives, was established to develop an ICMS. Drawing on their own experience of ADR methods and a formal, intensive, two-day workshop, this group developed an ICMS model comprised of three principal components:

- **Prevention:** This is to be achieved through enhanced internal communications and the provision of training in conflict management and diversity issues.

- **Self-directed resolution:** This strand of the model focused on building internal competencies through focused discussion, consultation and conflict coaching.

- **Third-party resolution:** Finally, the new ICMS model would use internal and external practitioners to provide facilitation, mediation and conflict conferencing services.

TABLE 8.13: ICMS: THE KEY PRINCIPLES

Consultation	The ICMS must be developed in consultation with the key stakeholders, including bargaining agents, senior managers, HR advisors and legal services.
Voluntary	The use of the system at any stage of conflict is strictly voluntary.
Flexible	The process must be available at all stages of a conflict, and users must have the option of switching between ICMS and formal processes at any time.
Accessible	Employees must be made fully aware of the ICMS and how it works.
Accompaniment/ representation	Employees may be accompanied to ADR processes such as mediation by a person of their choosing, including their bargaining agent representative.
Confidential	Confidentiality is an integral part of this ICMS.
Impartial and neutral	The individuals providing conflict management systems must be neutral and impartial, and cannot be directly linked to the parties to the dispute.
No retaliation	No employee shall be subject to retaliation, or reprisal, as a result of using the ICMS in accordance with the directive.
Respect for collective bargaining and statutory and workplace rights	Outcomes from the process must comply with workplace rights, legislation and provisions of negotiated agreements, also accord with organisational objectives.
Senior ICMS Officer	A senior ICMS official must be designated in each organisation.

Interestingly, the Director of the CHRC's ADR Services unit has been designated as the Senior ICMS officer and, thus, brings extensive professional and practical knowledge of ADR to bear on the ongoing evolution of this model. This example also illustrates that, within the formal policy directive, there is scope for organisations to tailor the ICMS to their own particular needs. Through this particular policy initiative, the federal government has signalled clearly its commitment to the mainstreaming of alternative and innovative approaches to the resolution of workplace disputes. Moreover, this clear policy stance has strengthened the activities of the various organisations discussed in this chapter in relation to diffusing new approaches to conflict management.

8.8   THE CANADIAN EXPERIENCE: LESSONS FOR THE LABOUR RELATIONS COMMISSION

This chapter has explored how a number of federal agencies in Canada have sought to improve their capacity for conflict management, through the development of a range of dispute prevention and resolution services, in which there has been an increased emphasis on the use of 'alternative' avenues of redress. This section of the chapter explores some of the key lessons for the Labour Relations Commission from the Canadian experience.

Although all of the organisations discussed in this chapter are strong advocates of the potential benefits of ADR in dealing with both individual and collective disputes, it is important to highlight that they have designed and implemented these new initiatives in a manner that supports and/or complements the established approaches to dispute resolution provided by such agencies. In this regard, the policy dialogue around the use of ADR has focused on how it can assist in enhancing organisational capacity for dispute resolution and avoidance, rather than on replacing more traditional and established approaches. For example, while the Labour Standards Directorate considers the mediation of unfair dismissals to be an important policy innovation, this approach caters only for approximately 14% of all such cases. Importantly, therefore, the increased use of ADR, both by public dispute resolution agencies and also internally by federally-regulated agencies and departments, has evolved in a manner in which it is not perceived as a threat to, or weakening of, collective bargaining processes, established grievance and disciplinary procedures or statutory-based employment rights. Instead, the introduction of new, or expanded, ADR approaches is viewed as contributing to the development of a more flexible, and integrated, conflict management system. In seeking to develop such a suite of services, however, there appears to be merit for the LRC in exploring how to build in a stronger sequential or procedural dimension, including perhaps agreed time limits, to the dispute resolution process, so that parties are fully aware of the various stages through which a dispute can travel and also of the outcomes of failing to resolve an issue at a given stage.

In part, the catalyst for seeking to develop new initiatives or approaches in the Canadian organisations reviewed were problems with the existing system – for example, spiralling costs and lengthy delays in processing cases. However, in some instances, these initiatives were driven by recognition of the need to ensure that the public dispute resolution/prevention services provided reflected ongoing economic, social and labour market changes. The FMCS's recent policy initiatives are clearly premised on the need to ensure that the integrated set of services it provides are relevant to the changing employment relations landscape and are capable of connecting with the dynamics of workplace change.

The examples discussed in this chapter highlight the importance of engaging in a degree of policy experimentation and evaluation, before any new initiatives are mainstreamed. Similarly, while agencies like the FMCS, the CHRC and the PSLRB have increased their portfolio of services, they have done so on an incremental basis, gradually introducing new, or reconfiguring existing, services. This approach enabled the organisations to explore the appropriateness of new approaches in specific contexts and also ensured that the design of mainstream initiatives was informed by practical experience. Introducing new services, or expanding existing services, constitutes an important commitment in terms of financial and human resources and also has implications for overall service delivery. Consequently, the LRC needs to create space and to provide resources for a degree of policy experimentation and evaluation, particularly in relation to the design and delivery of new initiatives and projects. Experimentation also afforded the FMCS and the PSLRB the scope to customise ADR-style approaches to the specific needs of the organisation. It would be important that, in seeking to adopt any new and innovative initiatives, the LRC would tailor them in accordance with its organisational objectives and the employment relations landscape in which it operates.

In the Canadian context, innovations in ADR also have been encouraged by a broader societal interest in the potential of alternative mechanisms for resolving disputes, with the legal arena being at the forefront in encouraging the greater use of mediation, for example.[112] Certainly, the policy initiatives described in this chapter have benefited from the fact that there are active formal, and informal, 'communities of practice' that function as ongoing sources of training and advice on good practice in relation to ADR and conflict management in general. This suggests that the LRC would benefit from exploring the potential of establishing stronger linkages with other practitioners, both in the public and private sector, in order to facilitate the exchange of information and good practice in relation to ADR approaches.

The LRC operates in an increasingly rights-based employment relations context, similar to the Canadian organisations reviewed. As highlighted earlier, in Canada, mediation has been introduced to address cases where individuals consider that their employment

---

[112] A number of the mediators in the CHRC came from a legal community and, in Canada, there has been increased recourse to court-mandated mediation in commercial disputes, for example. A further indication of societal interest in exploring new ways to solve disputes/problems is the fact that secondary school pupils are now learning about negotiation and mediation as part of the formal curriculum.

rights or human rights have been infringed, without any sense that this represents a dilution of their statutory rights. Ensuring that ADR approaches are confidential and voluntary in character, and that engaging in them is without prejudice to any further steps the parties may take, appears to be of particular importance in achieving this outcome. In the case of the CHRC, which developed a remodelled approach to dispute resolution, it has re-inforced its public interest mandate as the body with responsibility for eliminating and preventing discrimination.

This example also highlights the importance of a public body having a clear strategic identity, as this provides a supportive framework for its work, including, in the case of the CHRC, undertaking a major transformative programme that incorporated significant internal reorganisation and an increased reliance on multi-disciplinary specialised teams to deliver dispute resolution services. Additionally, while the CHRC operates within the context of enabling legislation, the changes it has undertaken demonstrates how public bodies can shape the mandate that is afforded to them. As the LRC case study indicated, the Commission has adopted a pro-active and relatively expansive approach to its statutory mandate and, in the process, has forged a strong and clear strategic organisational identity. In the context of a rapidly-changing employment relations landscape, maintaining this identity may necessitate exploring in the medium- to long-term the potential benefits to be achieved from changing its internal functional structure. More immediately, while the LRC is committed to increasing its usage of cross-divisional teams, the CHRC example suggests that this team-based approach must be institutionalised more formally within the Commission's conflict management system. For example, initiatives such as the Working Together projects may have potential for establishing a small number of multi-disciplinary teams, which could become specialists in providing a comprehensive conflict-management service within key sectors of the public service. The development of a more formalised, and institutionalised, team-based approach could also be the basis for building into the LRC's conciliation activity a more strategic, and longer-term, focus that, as noted in the case study, is a long-term objective of the Conciliation Division.

Retaining the credibility of key stakeholder groups is also important in introducing new dispute resolution services and, consequently, a feature of the Canadian examples was the degree of consultation with employer bodies, trade unions and identity-based representative groups in the planning of new initiatives. Additionally, however, it is evident that bodies such as the PSLRB, CHRC and the FMCS have had to undertake a highly pro-active role in terms of advocacy campaigns, designed to build awareness of the potential benefits of their ADR services. Therefore, there is a degree to which the relevant public body has to generate a 'demand' for any new service. Such advocacy activity can also be important in building better linkages with sectors of the economy that traditionally may not have engaged significantly with public dispute resolution agencies, such as the SME sector. In recent years, the LRC has developed a more enhanced communications strategy; continuing to develop this will provide an important institutional support to new projects and initiatives, particularly those focused on specific target groups – for example, the SME sector.

All of the agencies in this chapter also have had to invest considerably in order to ensure they have sufficient capacity to deliver an increased range of services, in particular those that fall within the ADR framework. This has involved extensive training of staff, and a number of agencies have benefited from federal programmes focused on ADR training. Agencies also have actively recruited individuals with considerable experience in areas such as mediation, in order to ensure they have the sufficient organisational capacity to deliver such services. This is not a new development, however, as it is the established norm for both federal and provincial-level public dispute resolution agencies to recruit experienced negotiators from both the ranks of employers and trade unions to work as conciliators, for example. The LRC case study clearly highlighted that providing a flexible, high-quality service is dependent ultimately on the experience and skill of its staff. Maintaining this capacity into the future in an ever-changing environment may necessitate not only ongoing investment in professional development, but also exploring the issue of open recruitment.

In aiming to develop a more comprehensive conflict management system, it is evident that a number of the organisations examined also have focused increased attention on preventative initiatives. Additionally, where problems have emerged, there is now a strong emphasis on early, and swift, intervention to prevent problems festering and positions hardening. This approach has been re-inforced by a strong focus on encouraging federally-regulated organisations to develop, and enhance, their in-house capacity for resolving disputes. An integral part of the work of agencies, such as the PSLRB and the FMCS, is focused on improving client organisations' in-house dispute resolution practices and procedures, so that they have the capacity to address problems close to the point of origin, without recourse to a third party. Indeed, the CHRC has used its enabling legislation to develop a strong policy position, in which, if there are appropriate internal avenues of redress in place, the parties must exhaust these first before engaging with the CHRC formally. This raises the issue of the LRC exploring, in consultation with the social partners, the possibility of putting in place arrangements, for appropriate cases, under which the parties would have to demonstrate more clearly that they have sought genuinely to resolve the issue at a lower level before engaging with the Commission.

Critically, the organisations discussed in this chapter have benefited directly, and indirectly, from a supportive public policy context. As outlined earlier, a number of federal initiatives – the Dispute Resolution Fund; the Inter-Departmental Mediators Program and the Partnership Fund – have provided additional resources that organisations have used either to build their own capacity in ADR or to fund specific ADR-related projects aimed at client bodies. More specifically, this governmental support for ADR has been institutionalised within the PSLRA, under which all government departments and agencies are mandated to develop their own in-house informal conflict management system (ICMS) to complement, and support, established grievance and disciplinary procedures. This policy context has provided a supportive institutional environment for experimenting with new forms of dispute resolution – for example, the mediation programme initiated by the PSLRB now supports the development of ICMS in various government departments. It is also evident that a key objective of this increased public policy focus is not merely to enhance organisational conflict management systems *per se*, but also to contribute to overall improvements in management-employee interactions. As noted earlier, this was a key factor underpinning the development of the PSLRB's mediation programme, which inspired this ICMS policy initiative. Similarly, the key objective of the FMCS's activities is on encouraging the adoption of best practice in relation to industrial relations procedures and arrangements, in order to improve the quality of management-union/employee interactions. The prioritisation of this broader goal of improving the quality of employment relations has been an important catalyst for the work of the individual Canadian public dispute resolution agencies and has afforded them an opportunity to undertake a more expansive approach to their mandate. At one level, this confirms the approach undertaken by LRC, in that the Commission has a broad mandate, focused on improving the quality of employment relations within Ireland. Similarly, the LRC has invested increased resources into dispute prevention activities and also has established the building of individual organisations' in-house capacity for dispute resolution as one of its key strategic goals. In seeking to achieve its strategic goals, however, there is clearly a need to operate within the wider public policy context and, in particular, to enhance the level of collaboration with other State agencies concerned with workplace and workforce development. In the Canadian context, the government has sought to 'hardwire' ICMS in government organisations, through a legislative mandate. In the Irish context, it may be possible for the LRC to explore the potential of using existing sectoral and local partnership arrangements within the public service to examine the scope for developing an ICMS that would complement established arrangements. In this regard, it is interesting to note that there are some examples in the private sector, where existing partnership arrangements have provided the basis for the development of new arrangements for handling individual grievances and/or progressing collective-bargaining-related disputes.[113]

8.9   CONCLUSION

This chapter has explored in some detail how a number of federal public dispute resolution agencies in Canada have engaged pro-actively in policy experimentation and innovation, with a view to enhancing their capacity for dispute resolution and avoidance. Importantly, the adoption of ADR principles and practices was an integral feature of these policy initiatives, with the result that ADR effectively has been mainstreamed within the public dispute resolution architecture. Government policy, moreover, has provided direct, and indirect, support for such activity, culminating in the institutionalisation of internal, informal conflict management systems within the federal public service. Critically, the public policy debate around ADR in Canada has focused on its potential both to enhance dispute resolution/prevention capacity and also to contribute to the development of more co-operative union-management relations. Indeed, rather than seeking to replace, or undermine, collective agreements or statutory employment rights, the Canadian public dispute resolution bodies have focused on integrating ADR approaches and practices into the prevailing legal and institutional context. In this context, the process of mainstreaming ADR approaches not only has complemented existing established procedures, but also has contributed to the emergence of a more flexible, and dynamic, system of conflict management across the public system. The nature of these improvements, moreover, has provided a stronger platform for the development and promotion of a more co-operative and problem-solving style of union-management relationships in the federal areas, although it is recognised that this policy objective is still very much in an embryonic stage of development.

---

[113] A major private sector company, which has well-established partnership arrangements, has introduced mediation and an ombudsman, as part of agreed procedures for dealing with disputes that arise in relation to collective bargaining, which are designed to reduce the reliance on third-party involvement.

9

ACAS & THE UK SYSTEM OF DISPUTE RESOLUTION

9.1 INTRODUCTION

The main public agency in Britain responsible for preventing and resolving employment disputes is the Arbitration, Conciliation & Advisory Service (Acas). It was established in 1974, initially under the title, Conciliation & Arbitration Service, mostly to help improve collective-bargaining processes by providing conciliation and mediation services. The creation of the service was a direct outcome of the highly-influential Donovan Commission, which sought to improve the operation of the mainly voluntarist system of British industrial relations. The organisation was renamed Acas in 1976 and it very quickly acquired a high public profile, due to its role in trying to resolve the large-scale collective industrial relations disputes that were occurring regularly in Britain at the time. Thus Acas very quickly developed the image of being part-and-parcel of the collective-bargaining system and, indeed, the architects of the system regarded this function as its core role (Towers & Brown, 2000).

In this chapter, we examine how Acas has attempted to modernise not only its activities, but also its identity, so that it is seen not simply as a trouble-shooter for collective disputes. Among staff at Acas, there is increasing recognition that important labour market and industrial relations changes require the organisation to interact with firms on a broader range of activities and in new ways. As a result, a number of initiatives, and some internal re-organisation, has taken place in recent times, the purpose of which is to establish Acas as the main public agency for the promotion of high-quality employment relations in Britain, rather than as the agency for resolving employment disputes. Before these developments are reviewed, it is best to outline the core services that Acas has provided over the years (**section 9.2**).

9.2   ACAS SERVICES

Acas is governed by a Council, made up of representatives from business, trade unions and independents. The Council is responsible for determining the strategic direction, policies and priorities of Acas, and for ensuring that its statutory duties are carried out effectively. The organisation employs over 900 people and has offices throughout England, Scotland and Wales.

Acas offers a number of statutory services free of charge. The first is **conciliation**, which is provided for both collective and individual disputes. Collective conciliation is offered normally when collective negotiations between employers and unions get into difficulties. Individual conciliation is provided after an employee lodges an application with the employment tribunal service. The purpose of individual conciliation is to try and obtain a settlement before a tribunal hearing. Over the past decade, Acas has been able to settle three-quarters of the individual disputes it has addressed. The second service is **mediation** for both collective and individual disputes. A fairly narrow definition is adopted for collective mediation; it usually refers to making recommendations on how to resolve an employment dispute, after consulting with the parties involved. Individual mediation is used to settle potential disputes about employment rights. A third service is **arbitration**, which is provided also for collective disputes and individual disputes, although the latter only came on stream in 2001. Collective arbitration normally takes the form of 'final offer' arbitration, which involves an arbitrator choosing between the final claims of employers and employees. However, the numbers of collective arbitration cases are small, which suggests that both employers and unions are reluctant to use the service. Individual arbitration was introduced in 2001, largely in response to a Government aim of increasing the use of ADR procedures and to reduce the numbers of tribunal cases. A fourth function of Acas is to offer a range of **advisory services**, including a telephone helpline, which people can ring to obtain information and guidance about employment rights and what procedures to follow, should they feel that their rights have been infringed. Training is used extensively to increase awareness of good organisational dispute resolution procedures and dispute resolution capabilities within organisations. Acas also provides advice to organisations on how to resolve particular disputes and to increase their problem-solving capacity.

9.3   THE CHANGING INDUSTRIAL RELATIONS ENVIRONMENT

Much has changed in British industrial relations since Acas was set up in the 1970s. Some aspects of this change have been distinctive, the policy towards trade union of successive Thatcher governments, for example, but other elements closely resemble unfolding developments in Ireland. Both islands appear to have shared three similar experiences:

- A significant decline in collective disputes.
- A decline in trade union density.
- The growing influence of labour law in the governance of the employment relationship.

In Britain, collective disputes have declined from 761 in 1987, to 92 in 2005, the lowest number ever recorded in British industrial relations history. **Figure 9.1** sets out the number of days lost due to employment disputes and the number of workers involved in disputes between 1991 and 2005. Although the trend across the period is erratic, both figures are at historical low points. There are now fewer collective industrial relations disputes, involving fewer workers, and having the least impact on the economy, than ever before.

FIGURE 9.1: UK: DAYS LOST & WORKERS INVOLVED IN INDUSTRIAL DISPUTES, 1991-2006

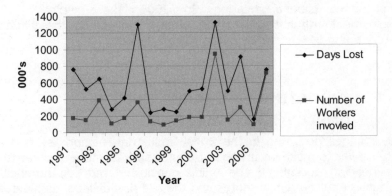

A decline in trade union density is another parallel development across the two countries. In autumn 2004, the rate of union membership (union density) among all workers in the UK was 26%, a fall of 0.6% compared with 2003. Union density among employees is higher, at 28.8%, although this is on a downward trend too. Some of the characteristics of union density are worth spelling out:

- Density rates are slightly higher for women than for men, and higher among older employees.
- More than one-third of those aged 35 and over are union members, compared with one-quarter of those aged 25 to 34.
- Full-time employees are more likely to be trade union members; 31.5%, compared with 21.1% of part-timers.
- There are large differences in union density among employees in the various parts of the UK: the highest (39.3%) was in Northern Ireland, compared with the lowest (22.8%) in the South East.

A third common feature is the growing influence of labour law in the governance of the employment relationship. For example, when first established in the mid-1970s, employment tribunals were asked to adjudicate in less than 10 jurisdictions. One estimate now puts the number of jurisdictions at 80 (Acas, 2005a). Like Ireland, the increase in the volume (and complexity) of labour law, alongside the decline in trade union density, has led to the emergence of a rights-based dimension to employment relations. This development, in conjunction with a range of other factors, has fragmented the 'voluntarist' system of British industrial relations. In turn, this has had an impact on the work of Acas. In particular, as with the LRC, the demand for Acas services to settle collective disputes between employers and trade unions has declined, whereas the number of individual employment dispute cases has increased. In Britain, a useful measure of this trend is the number of applications for an employment tribunal hearing. In 2005, there were 115,042 employment tribunal cases, the second highest in the system's history and a 61% increase over the past decade.

9.4   ADJUSTING TO CHANGE IN NEW EMPLOYMENT TIMES

The changes occurring in the British industrial relations system are very similar to those occurring in Ireland: both countries appear to be experiencing declining trade union density, a reduced number of collective employment disputes and the rise of individual employment rights. Inside Acas, discussions started to take place about whether the organisation's external image of helping to solve collective employment disputes – which was not the case in reality – might limit its ability to work effectively in the new industrial relations situation. A decrease in its budget from Government, which required it to make 100 staff redundant, made these discussions far from academic. Very quickly, a consensus emerged that internal changes needed to be made to expand, and reshape, its portfolio of activities. To signal that a process of internal renewal was underway, in 201, the Acas Council inserted the term 'working life' into the organisation's mission statement: the full statement now reads:

"... to improve organisations and working life through better employment relations'.

The focus on improving working life resulted from the findings of a number of surveys of modern workplaces in Britain. One survey found that recorded employee dissatisfaction was very high in many British organisations. Another found that a high level of supervision exists in British workplaces, relative to other European countries. A further finding was the high level of absenteeism in many organisations. Other factors, such as conflicts generated by public sector change management programmes, were also cited as influencing the decision to insert 'working life' into the mission statement of the organisation (Edwards, 2007).

The new mission statement was important, as it signalled a more targeted, and strategic, approach to the provision of dispute resolution services. One important organisational change that resulted was the creation of a new Strategy Unit, as part of a Knowledge Directorate for Research & Evaluation. This Unit's remit is to enhance Acas's voice in public debates on employment relations matters; improve its policy analysis and corporate planning capability; and strengthen its contribution to, and influence on, policy thinking and development.

Another important change was the identification of six themes to constitute the core work of the organisation in forthcoming years:

- Workplace effectiveness and productivity.
- Enterprise and SMEs.
- Individuals and working lives.
- Equality and diversity.
- Public service reform and change management.
- Regionalisation.

This new targeted approach resulted in the creation of theme groups inside the organisation. Theme groups create an informal matrix structure inside the organisation, as they bring together people not only from different functional parts of the organisation, but also from the 'field' and headquarters. The theme groups sit on top of established programmes and operations, with the intention of creating new cross-cutting initiatives. The theme groups have a number of inter-related objectives:

- To develop Acas' thinking and activities in the identified priority themes.

- To capture and use the unrivalled knowledge in Acas about employment relations.

- To develop a speedy, and effective, response to major public policy initiatives on employment relations.

- To strengthen the external 'voice' of Acas on employment relations.

The theme groups, which normally consist of five to six members, operate in a formal manner. Each theme group is not only chaired by a Board member, but also reports to the Board. A member of the Strategy Unit services each group by preparing background papers, reports of meetings and briefs for chairs.

9.5   COLLECTIVE INDUSTRIAL RELATIONS

Providing conciliation to help solve collective employment disputes is a long-standing and core activity of Acas (Dix & Oxenbridge, 2004). It is what the organisation is best known for and it is probably what it does best. **Figure 9.2** outlines the trend in demand for collective conciliation since the organisation was established in 1974. It shows that the biggest demand for the service was in the 1970s, when the level of industrial unrest was running at a high level. Demand for the services fell off dramatically in the 1980s, when legislative changes to industrial relations and trade unions introduced by the then Conservative Government started to bite. However, the trend since the late 1980s, has remained more or less constant, oscillating between 1,200 and 1,400 requests each year. This is still a fairly big number and suggests that, although there have been significant changes to the labour market, Acas still requires the capacity to help solve collective employment disputes.

Most of the collective disputes addressed by Acas concern matters related to pay. Also, the organisation deals with a sizeable number of disputes relating to trade union recognition; Acas involvement in this area has increased since the Employment Act 1999 introduced new procedures to resolve trade union recognition disputes.

FIGURE 9.2: REQUESTS FOR COLLECTIVE CONCILIATION, 1974-2004

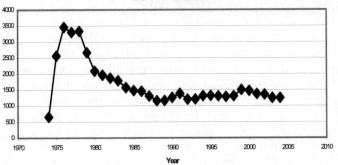

The new procedures assign Acas three roles in the resolution of recognition claims:

- Acas conciliators provide advice to employers on voluntary and statutory recognition procedures.
- Acas plays the role of verifier in recognition ballots - it ensures that ballots are conducted properly.
- Acas offers a conciliation service when disputes or disagreements arise over union access to the workplace and what bargaining units are covered in a new recognition agreement.

Whereas employers normally ask Acas for implications on the statutory recognition procedures, and the consequences of not complying with them, unions mostly want Acas to provide independent verification of employer-led ballots. Overall, pay and recognition now represents the lion's share of collective conciliation cases. In over 80% of cases, the conciliation provided leads to a successful settlement of the dispute.

9.6 ACAS & EMPLOYMENT TRIBUNALS

Employment Tribunals were set up over 30 years ago by the Donovan Commission, as a complement to the system of collective bargaining, to deal mostly with disputes concerning individual workplace rights. Because of its statutory duty to provide conciliation for individual employment disputes, Acas automatically gets involved in nearly all types of applications to the Tribunal. For example, during the year 2004/2005, Acas conciliated in 86,816 actual or potential applications to employment tribunals; it is estimated that only 23% of these ended at an employment tribunal.

This work has acquired greater significance over the years. At the end of the 1970s, the number of tribunals averaged about 40,000 annually, but now the number consistently reaches about 100,000. Acas believes that it has managed to deal relatively successfully with the rise in the number of cases. In its first 20 years, for example, the organisation resolved two-thirds of applications to employment tribunals but, during the past decade, the success rate has increased to about three-quarters of all cases. Acas has sought continuously to improve its activities related to employment tribunals. For example, in 2003, it installed a new computerised system, which allows for more in-depth information about relevant cases to be passed more quickly to the employment tribunal service.

However, in 2001, the government commenced a process to modernise the employment tribunal service. Several factors lay behind this decision:

- One was the three-fold increase in employment tribunal applications during the 1990s.

- Another was the increasing juridification, and complexity, of tribunal proceedings, which were the opposite of the initial motivations for setting up the service.

- A further concern was the rising costs of operating the tribunal system, which stood at £69.7 million in 2004/5.

The result of this process was the Employment Act 2002, which introduced a number of reforms to employment tribunals and to the dispute resolution system, more generally. The key reforms of the Act oblige employers to introduce either a three-step, or a modified two-step (which can be used in a restricted number of dismissal cases), statutory disciplinary and dismissal procedure.

The three-step version involves:

- Informing the employee of what the employer intends to do.
- Meeting with the employee.
- Dealing with the employee's appeal.

The modified procedure involves:

- Writing to the employee about their dismissal.
- Giving them the right to an appeal.

These procedures apply where the employer intends to take disciplinary action (for example, suspension on reduced pay, or without pay, or demotion) in relation to the employee's capability and/or conduct. They also apply to dismissals involving:

- Capability dismissal.

- Conduct dismissals.
- Individual redundancy dismissals.
- Non-renewal of fixed-term contracts.
- Retirement dismissals, in circumstances where the employee could claim unfair dismissal.

Where retirement is by mutual consent, there is no requirement to follow the new procedures. In addition, the procedures do not apply when employers give warnings or suspend an employee on full pay. Employers, of course, have the option of developing their own internal dispute and disciplinary procedures, provided these at least match the provisions of the Act. Employees are obliged to use internal dispute resolution procedures, before they can file an employment tribunal application: failure to do so will result in the application not being accepted. On the other hand, employers who fail to introduce and operate the statutory procedures, or their equivalent, will be liable to higher penalties should they lose an employment relations tribunal.

These new regulations impinge on the work of Acas. Until the Employment Act 2002, Acas had a duty to conciliate any time between the filing of a tribunal application and an actual hearing. Because the new legislation seeks to encourage parties to settle at a early stage of a dispute, the Act sets down a seven-week period for Acas conciliation on claims such as breach of contract, unlawful pay deductions and redundancy, while the period for unfair dismissals cases is 13 weeks. Disputes relating to discrimination and equal pay are excluded from the new fixed conciliation periods. A degree of flexibility was introduced by the Act, as Acas was given permission to continue conciliation for a further two weeks after the end of a fixed period, if it considered that the parties were close to a settlement.

These arrangements have been in place since 2004 and initial experiences have raised a wide range of concerns. One major worry is that, rather than promoting the settlement of disputes quickly, the new procedures have weakened procedural justice for employees.

Acas is uneasy with the new arrangements. First, it sees itself as being asked to deliver a much more intensive conciliation service in the context of reduced resources: for example, the organisation will suffer a 16% reduction in its budget in 2007/08. In addition, the organisation is of the view that placing fixed periods for conciliation is far from best practice, as settling an employment dispute takes time; it considers the seven-week period far too short to offer meaningful conciliation. Acas has responded to this new regime by introducing a differential conciliation service, which will lead to priority being given to open, rather than fixed, period cases. In addition, Acas considers that the regime places even more emphasis on developing dispute prevention rather than resolution activities. In particular, it sees the need for more widespread use of alternative dispute resolution procedures at the workplace. However, the organisation argues that a considerable amount of training and guidance is required to ensure that ADR procedures are diffused properly inside organisations, although it is ready to provide this service.

9.7   THE ACAS TELEPHONE HELPLINE

Acas runs a telephone helpline to provide those who have an employment grievance or are involved in an employment dispute with information on employment law, employment rights, best HRM practices or available options to obtain further advice on how to resolve a problem. The service deals with about 800,000 callers each year. Acas carries out regular surveys to obtain information on who uses the service and their views on the service they receive. The latest survey suggests that employers and employees (or their representatives) use the service in more or less equal numbers (Acas, 2005b). In terms of the characteristics of the callers, 70% were female. Approximately 40% of callers were aged between 35-49, 25% aged 50-59, and 20% aged 25-34. Overall, the ethnicity of the callers reflected that of the wider population, with 94% of the callers classifying themselves as 'white'.

Although the helpline received calls from all industries, a disproportionate number came from the construction, retail, hotel and restaurant sectors. About 67% of the callers were from the small firm sector, while only 6% were from workplaces with more than 500 employees. The majority of calls came from employees, and 70% worked in small firms, which is much higher than the broader distribution of employees by workplace: about 30% of those in employment work in small firms. Around 54% of callers came from the private sector, while 25% came from the public sector. About one-third of callers worked in organisations that had a HR specialist or department. The vast majority of callers used the helpline more than once, with repeat users making on average three calls. Employees were more than three times more likely to call than employers.

Table 9.1 sets out the subjects dealt with by the helpline. It shows that pay-related issues were the most frequent subject and that employees were most likely to call about redundancy and holiday pay, whereas employers were more likely to call about notice periods and sickness leave. Moreover, employers were more likely to raise multiple issues than employees.

TABLE 9.1: SUBJECTS COVERED BY THE ACAS
TELEPHONE HELPLINE

Employees		Employers	
Redundancy/redundancy pay	26%	Sick pay/absence	30%
Holiday entitlement/pay	25%	Notice period/pay	30%
Notice period/pay	22%	Holiday entitlement/pay	28%
Grievance procedures	20%	Redundancy/redundancy pay	28%
Dismissal	16%	Dismissal	27%

Acas's customer survey indicates a high degree of satisfaction with the service. The vast majority of respondents stated that the information they received was easily understood and very useful. Nearly all respondents stated that the staff operating the helpline gave enough time to discuss the query in full, and dealt with the inquiry in a sympathetic, and professional, manner. Over half of employers calling the helpline stated the advice and guidance they received prompted them to change, or update, workplace policies or procedures. The survey also found that three out of five employees, who considered making a claim to the Employment Tribunal before ringing the helpline, decided not to after receiving advice. Thus, the evidence from this positive feedback is that the helpline is highly valued by both employers and employees.

9.8 WORKPLACE EFFECTIVENESS & PRODUCTIVITY

9.8.1 The Acas model workplace

The new emphasis on preventative dispute resolution activity led to the design of the Acas model workplace. The purpose of this model is to encourage organisations to adopt employment relations practices that allow them to improve performance, through creating a better working environment. The core principles promulgated by the model are set out in **Table 9.2** below. The thrust of the model is that a good working environment depends first on the creation of formal procedures that allows issues such as grievances and disputes to be dealt with quickly and fairly and, second, on the proper functioning of systems of consultation, communication and health and safety.

A number of activities have developed as a result of the adoption of the model workplace. First, contact has opened up with a number of Regional Development Agencies (RDAs), which are charged with promoting business activities in particular areas. As a result of this liaison, the promotion of good employment relations has been written into the economic development plans for certain regions. In addition, some RDAs have included Acas speakers in workshops and conferences on economic development and have sponsored Acas-organised events on topics, such as the relationship between good employment relations and productivity.

TABLE 9.2: THE ACAS MODEL WORKPLACE

Formal procedures for dealing with disciplinary matters, grievances and disputes that managers and employees know about and use fairly.

Ambitions, goals and plans that employees know about and understand.

Managers who genuinely listen to and consider employees' views, so everyone is actively involved in making important decisions.

A **pay and reward system** that is clear, fair and consistent.

A **safe and healthy place to work**.

People to feel valued, so they can talk confidently about their work and learn from both successes and mistakes.

Another dimension to this activity is conducting employment relations audits in organisations. Referred to as 'health checks' by Acas staff, these audits involve assessing the employment relations practices of an organisation against the Acas model workplace. Invariably, these audits identify problem areas that need correction by the organisation. In 2004/05, Acas carried out 400 of these visits. Acas also works with organisations on in-depth workplace projects. For the most part, this involves working with managers, employees and representatives to establish partnerships. For example, Acas may help employees and managers to carry out a diagnostic review of the organisation to assess the type of enterprise partnership arrangement that best suits the organisation. In other cases, workplace projects may involve helping organisations to develop effective policies and practices across the spectrum of employment relations matters.

Yet a further dimension to Acas's employment relations activity has been lobbying government to introduce public policies likely to improve the management of the employment relationship. Thus, for example, Acas made a submission to government in the wake of the *Accounting for People Task Force Report*, arguing that effective human capital management was an essential component of corporate governance and that companies should include a transparent and meaningful section on the topic in annual reports. It also suggested that Acas staff could provide support and training to companies on how to report accurately on human capital developments. In other submissions, Acas argued that it could play a positive role not only in developing a national support framework for the promotion of family-friendly employment policies, but also in achieving a greater harmonisation of activities relating to human rights and equality. Thus, the purpose of its lobbying activities was not only to highlight the importance of high-quality employment relations, but also to ensure that Acas played a central role in the delivery of that goal.

9.9   EQUALITY & DIVERSITY

Internal research conducted by Acas suggests that, although women represent about half of the workforce, they account for only a third of applicants in the areas of unfair dismissal, breach of contract, and wages protection, but 70% of cases in the area of discrimination (Fox, 2005a). The research also argued that there is no good reason for the lower level of claims from women outside the area of discrimination: evidence suggests that they are as aware of their employment rights as men; and that there is no discernible difference between males and females in experiencing other problems at work or in job separations. Why men are more likely than women to seek vindication of employment rights is unclear. However, factors such as men being more likely than women to work in a unionised setting, and women being more likely than men to express higher levels of job satisfaction and be 'loyal' employees, are probably a large part of the explanation.

Another trend uncovered by Acas is that men and women usually behave differently, once they have made an employment tribunal application. In particular, women are more likely than men to have their cases resolved by Acas conciliation, prior to a tribunal hearing; the difference is particularly striking in unfair dismissal cases. A further gender difference is that women are less likely than men to have their case dismissed, or disposed of at an early hearing. Overall, it would appear that women are less likely to use formal/legalistic routes to enforce rights, even though they are as likely as men to face problems at work, and far more so in the area of discrimination.

Establishing that a gender dimension existed to employment grievances encouraged Acas to develop a suite of initiatives on the theme of equality and diversity. A feature of this activity is hands-on advice and training for organisations on how to write and operate a diversity policy. For example, Acas worked with the Metropolitan Housing Partnership to improve its diversity programme. This involved Acas staff in delivering 50 diversity training workshops to increase staff awareness of relevant legislation, of what constitutes discrimination, existing company diversity policies and effective procedures to prevent and resolve cases. The workshops not only increased internal company awareness, but also led to a more integrated approach to the implementation of the diversity policy. Another example is the assistance that Acas staff provided to the

Pensions Trust on introducing a state-of-the-art diversity policy: Acas staff advised the Pensions Trust on a diversity and equality programme that fully complied with relevant legislation, provided training to line managers on best practice diversity and equality practices, and monitored progress in implementing the policy.

Other more preventative initiatives have also been launched. For example, Acas set up a confidential telephone advice service, called Equality Direct, in partnership with the three equality commissions that exist in Britain. It is specially designed for small businesses, and provides help on managing issues such as disability, race, sex, age and other equality issues. A variety of initiatives have been set up with the Greater London Council (GLC) on diversity; some relate to creating a monitoring and evaluation system to assess progress made in improving equality for the workforce and involves creating benchmarking standards to assess moves towards greater equality. Another initiative involves working with the GLC to introduce a diversity compliance procedure, as part of its procurement policy.

9.10 ENTERPRISE & SMEs

9.10.1 The Acas pilot scheme for small firms

At the turn of 2000, the British Government established two important taskforces to examine matters relating to labour market regulation. One was the Better Regulations Taskforce, which was given the remit to develop strategies to reduce regulatory burdens on business. Part of its activity involved reviewing procedures used to enforce employment regulations, to assess whether these could be streamlined and made more effective. At the same time, another taskforce was established to assess the operation of the Employment Tribunal system. Independently of each other, both taskforces recommended that small firms needed to receive more free employment law advice and have access to mediation to help them resolve employment disputes. These targeted programmes were considered necessary, as it was found that the majority of applications to Employment Tribunals involved small firms.

Acas was assigned the responsibility of implementing these recommendations, which resulted in the introduction of a pilot programme covering mediation, appeals and employment law visits for small and medium-sized companies (Fox, 2005b). The pilot programme was restricted to two geographical areas: Yorkshire/Humberside and London, and a budget of £100,000 was allocated to the initiative, which was to run for one year.

Each part of the programme was designed differently. The mediation part provided third-party mediation, both facilitative mediation and directive, for disputing parties in SMEs. Whereas facilitative mediation is a service that aims to help disputing parties to identify issues and options for resolving differences, directive mediation is about the mediator making formal recommendations about how to settle a dispute. Facilitative mediation was carried out by internal staff, while external directive facilitation was carried out by members of the Acas panel of independent mediators.

The appeals part of the programme involved members of the Acas panel of independent persons hearing an appeal against an employer's decision at the final stage of an internal discipline or grievance procedure. A formal set of terms and conditions were written for appeal hearings, and all parties to a dispute had to agree to these in advance of the proceedings. The terms and conditions obliged the parties to set out the issues in dispute in writing before the appeals hearing, to agree to abide by the stipulated hearing process, and to accept the recommendations made by the mediator.

The employment law advisory visits were the third part of the programme and involved Acas staff visiting small firms to give information on employment legislation and to promote employment practices that would ensure that the organisation was in compliance with the law. An extensive training programme was developed for Acas staff involved in the initiative, so that they could deliver a high-quality service.

An intensive programme of promotion and publicity was used to generate interest in the initiative: advertisements were placed in a wide range of professional and trade journals; articles were written for numerous newspapers; information leaflets were produced and circulated through a number of outlets, such as Citizen Advice Bureaux; and Acas helplines in London and Leeds were asked to identify potential clients for the pilot programme. Despite this significant publicity campaign, the take-up for the scheme was relatively low. Only 26 mediations were completed, consisting of 9 appeals/directive mediations and 17 facilitative mediations. Altogether, 109 employment law visits were made, 18 of which resulted in mediation. An additional 25 enterprises were given advice by telephone.

9.11 EMPLOYMENT LAW VISITS

An evaluation scheme was built into the employment law visit project to assess its impact. The evaluation involved interviewing participating employers and employees at the start, middle and end of the project, to assess the impact of the visits. In total, 107 visits were carried out; 71 in Yorkshire/Humberside and 38 in London. **Table 9.3** gives the break-down of issues addressed by the visits.

TABLE 9.3: TOPICS COVERED BY ACAS EMPLOYMENT LAW VISITS

Issue or type of help	% of total
Contract terms and conditions	49
Problems with individual employees	31
Review of discipline and grievance procedures	29
Implementing a discipline/grievance procedure	25
Sickness/absence	28
Redundancy/dismissal	21
Employment law advice	21
Performance	21
Other	14

The table shows that many of the employers taking up the employment law visits wanted help or advice with multiple issues. At the beginning of the process, employers were interviewed about their expectations of the programme; the vast majority said that they wanted help with developing or implementing employment procedures, and advice about employment regulations. At a second interview, three-quarters of the employers who wanted help with a specific problem said that the advice they received was highly valuable, as it ensured that they avoided an Employment Tribunal. The majority of those who sought advice about developing or implementing procedures stated that the advice they received was easy to understand. About 60% of those wanting advice, by this stage, had implemented the advice they had received. Employers also stated that the employment law visits led to improvements in the employment relationship, although employers who sought help with individual disputes reported greater improvements than those who needed general advice.

Overall, 96% of employers expressed high satisfaction with the assistance they received from the employment law visits. Roughly 68% considered that the Acas advisor provided all the help needed; only 4% felt that the advisor provided no help. Employers who sought help to solve a particular problem were more appreciative of the help than other employers.

9.12 MEDIATION

The mediation activity that took place addressed a range of disputes, including those between employer/employee, manager/supervisor and supervisor/employee. The disputes concerned a wide range of employment relations matters, including equal treatment, pay entitlements, bullying, and sickness benefits. Most of the mediations involved disputes that were going through the employer's internal grievance or disciplinary machinery. Poor impersonal relations were an element to most of the disputes, which tends to be the norm.

Acas staff conducted interviews with employers and employees to determine the impact of mediation, in terms of repairing and improving the employment relationship. The most significant result from this assessment was that, in the vast majority of cases, mediation had a positive impact. In some cases, not only did mediation help to settle deep-seated disputes, it did so in a manner that improved organisational performance. Only in two cases did the mediation lead to a severance package and the employee leaving the firm. In the other cases, the mediation process led to apologies, new supervisory arrangements, and re-interpretation of employment contracts and terms and conditions. Most agreements normally covered explanations and apologies, commitments about behaviour, and changes to working practices and procedures.

Despite these positive outcomes, participants in the mediation cases had mixed views on the process. On the positive side, the parties identified a number of benefits. Perhaps the most important was the role of the skilled external mediator. Both employers and employees communicated that it was the mediator who ensured a successful outcome, in most cases. Another benefit was that the introduction of mediation caused the parties involved to adopt a more conciliatory approach to each other, thereby creating a better climate for the resolution of the dispute. A third strength was that the mediation process gave all the parties to the dispute the opportunity to tell their side of the story, and to hear the other party's story, for the first time. This full exchange of views allowed the dispute to be recast in a manner more amenable to a settlement. A fourth benefit was the ability of the mediator to unpack the dispute into stand-alone issues that made composing an agreement easier.

However, not everything went smoothly with the mediations. In some instances, the parties in a dispute expressed a preference for an investigation, which would have involved external parties uncovering and analysing evidence and then reaching a view about the nature and cause of the dispute. Some participants only reluctantly agreed to mediation, once they found out that an investigation was not possible. Even though these participants found mediation to be helpful in the end, they remained of the opinion that an investigation would have been the best course of action. A further relatively-negative comment was that the mediation process was seen as a trying experience. Some found the engagement with the other parties to the dispute difficult; others found the meetings long and stressful; and a number of parties felt mediation created a situation in which they could not exercise full control or completely pursue their interests.

Thus, the mediation scheme had both strengths and weaknesses but, overall, it received a positive endorsement from the participants. On balance, employers seemed more satisfied with mediation than employees. Employees would have preferred investigation and adjudication, rather than mediation. Employers regarded the process as useful, in terms of resolving particular problems and creating new procedures for the better handling of disputes in the future. Interestingly, although employers and employees said positive things about the scheme, both were equivocal about whether they would use the process in the future. Reservations related to the need for careful planning of the process, the need to establish full buy-in into the process and to make the process less onerous in terms of time commitments. These comments raised doubts about whether Acas would be able to translate the pilot scheme successfully into a permanent ongoing process. The chief lesson that appeared to be learned by Acas from the pilot scheme was that it tied up considerable resources, without yielding significant long-term benefits. As a result, the organisation is of the view that a new way has to be found to improve the quality of dispute resolution in the small firms sector.

9.13 PUBLIC SERVICES REFORM & CHANGE MANAGEMENT

9.13.1 Acas in the NHS

When modernising its vision and activities, Acas identified the issue of change management in the public sector as an important area of work. This area was prioritised, due to the political importance attached to reforming the provision and delivery of public service in the UK. Large-scale organisational change of this type was seen as creating considerable tension and conflict in the workplace, which may warrant an Acas intervention. In addition to this strategic thinking, Acas was receiving an unprecedentedly high level of requests from National Health Service (NHS) Trusts, due to merger activity triggering widespread organisational restructuring.

As a first step to developing a comprehensive suite of support services to advance public sector modernisation, Acas decided to review the workplace projects in which it was involved with NHS Trusts (Stuart & Martinez Lucio, 2005). These projects involved Acas staff running facilitation workshops on improving workplace relationships and managing organisational change, advising on implementing new employment practices and procedures, and assisting with specific employment grievances. This evaluation was timely, as it allowed an assessment to be made of Acas's role in helping to address problems arising from *Agenda for Change*, the most far-reaching reform to pay determination ever undertaken in the British public sector.

Acas developed workplace projects, as a result of requests it received from NHS Trusts. In most cases, the need for assistance arose from Trusts merging activities, which resulted in the creation of new organisational units. These mergers led to a whole host of people-management issues, such as harmonising workplace terms and conditions, rewriting employment contracts and establishing orderly manager-employee relations in a new organisational setting that combined sites with sharply-contrasting employment relations histories. External assistance was required from Acas because of the inability of established bodies to handle the employment relations implications of organisational change, joint negotiation, or joint consultation bodies in particular, to address properly the issues thrown up by the merger process.

Thus, part of Acas' assistance was to strengthen manager-employee interactions, to improve organisational effectiveness in a manner that commanded support from both sides. This led to workshops on the principles of workplace partnerships and advice on organisational changes to implement this form of working. Both managers and trade unions were happy to involve Acas staff in developing new employment relations arrangements and resolving particular disputes, while they particularly valued the contribution of Acas' staff in facilitating joint workshops. The role of Acas' staff in these events was considered worthwhile for a number of reasons:

- They provided information on how other organisations addressed problems similar to those experienced by participating managers and employees.
- They presented best practice examples of employment relations procedures, from which workshop participants could learn.
- They managed workshops skilfully, so that managers and employees spoke openly about problems and started to develop shared understandings about organisational advances.
- They ensured that, when discussing conflict matters, participants focused on issues of interest and on how to create arrangements that were sustainable in the longer term.
- They encouraged both managers and employees to adopt new standards of behaviour and expectations when interacting with each other.

Overall, the role of Acas in organising workshops to help improve employment relations in the NHS was supported by all parties. However, the workshops did not run completely smoothly. One problem was that the high turnover in NHS HR staff meant that Acas people had to renew relationships frequently. As a result, developing a consistent and continuous programme of work proved difficult. Another problem was that early workshops were considered more effective than later sessions. This was because the first workshops addressed directly the issues and problems that were identified by participants, while subsequent sessions involved the more tedious work of developing the nuts and bolts of agreements. A related difficulty was that some middle managers were reluctant to attend later sessions, as they considered the problems solved. However, this caused employees to question managers' commitment to the process. A final issue raised about the workshops was that all participants considered that the outcomes of the workshops could have been published more widely throughout the organisation.

Measuring the impact of Acas workshops is difficult to determine, due to a lack of objective, widely-shared indicators of performance. Nevertheless, participants of the various workshops considered the events to have positive impacts. The main benefit was improved relationships between management and union representatives. These changes, in turn, improved the effectiveness of the consultation machinery significantly. Employment relations also improved, due to better manager-union relations, as it became easier to implement some of the agreements emerging from the Acas process. Acas advisors suggested that a requirement to write action plans was a key factor ensuring the success of the workshops, which ensured that the workshops were not just 'talking shops'. Action plans typically involved writing-up new terms of reference for consultation arrangements, protocols for the conduct of meetings and agreements for new employment procedures.

9.14 PROMOTING ADR

Acas started a number of projects, which fall loosely under the umbrella term 'ADR', to strengthen its preventative mediation activities (Podro & Suff, 2005). Some of this work involves new training initiatives – for example, Acas has designed a Certificate of Mediation, which is being used by a number of large firms to train selected employees in a variety of ADR practices and procedures, so that they can address disputes and grievances immediately when they arise at the workplace. The Certificate in Mediation is externally-accredited by a nationally-recognised mediation institute; in addition, it is recognised by the CIPD and those who take the course gain concessionary points should they decide to take the CIPD's diploma course. Another interesting development in the area of training is the revamping of the Senior Advisory Training Programme. An important part of this change involves overhauling and updating the language used, when the organisation gets involved in employment disputes; this language uses terms closely associated with ADR.

Another aspect of ADR work involves linking up with other agencies to deliver new services – for example, recently Acas launched a pilot project with the Health & Safety Executive (HSE) on the issue of stress. This project involves holding workshops for 100 companies that have signed up for the project. Matters such as writing and implementing a stress policy, and handling employment stress-related disputes, will be covered in the workshops. The anticipation is that the workshops will allow the involved companies to introduce the HSE Stress Management Standards. The HSE, which has responsibility for stress at the workplace, was eager to link up with Acas, in light of its extensive knowledge and experience in developing advisory and preventative workshops on employment relations issues. Another initiative involves the delivery of interest-based bargaining support and advice for employers and unions in local government, in order to make the annual collective-bargaining round less confrontational. In addition, it provides advice and assistance for local authorities in complex cases of equal pay for work of equal value.

Yet a further dimension to Acas' work on ADR is working with government departments to introduce ADR-related schemes and lobbying government to do more on the matter. For example, it has helped the Department of Constitutional Affairs to establish an in-house mediation system, involving the creation of procedures that immediately come into effect when an employment dispute emerges. Acas is also involved in what is known as the 'two-tier workforce agreement', which is an ADR procedure to deal with employment disputes, when workplaces are transferred from the public to the private sectors, due to contracting out of services. This was seen as an important initiative, as it advances a non-legalistic approach to the settling of disputes. Acas is eager to see more ADR initiatives set up and is talking to government on the matter; although nothing concrete has emerged from these discussions, Acas officials are of the view that it will not be long before ADR principles are diffused into employment relations practices in the public sector.

9.15 THE FUTURE OF ACAS

Acas has launched a large number of innovative actions in recent years. Most of these initiatives seek to increase the organisation's dispute prevention activity. Acas is keen to be seen as a conflict management agency, rather than a dispute resolution body. Dispute resolution is essentially a fire-fighting operation, which involves putting out the flames of discontent, once an employment dispute has been ignited. Conflict management, on the other hand, involves a more integrated, pro-active approach to creating an environment inside organisations, in which employment disputes are less likely to emerge. It is also about installing procedures to address disputes quickly and fairly when they do arise; thus it merges dispute prevention and resolution.

In many ways, these activities have followed the classic routines adopted by organisations when trying to change their identity. First, a new mission statement is written to signal that the organisation is about to reform and develop a new purpose. Invariably, it is change in the external environment that lies behind the decision to reform. Then an internal discussion begins about new goals and a fresh vision for the organisation. From these discussions, shared understandings develop about the organisation's key tasks and its core activities. Without a purposive mission, a clear vision and agreed goals, internal conflict and resistance to change can emerge that undermines organisational effectiveness. The development of new, shared understandings impacts on the culture and structure of the organisation. New ways of working are developed, different norms and values emerge with regard to what is seen as successful, and unsuccessful, activity. Organisational leadership is seen as critical in the transition from an old, to a new, culture. The end result is a transformation in the role and identity of the organisation, which leads to it being interpreted in a new way.

Acas has embarked upon a process of organisational change similar to that mapped out above. It has still some way to go, before this organisational transformation is complete. As a result, it is premature to suggest whether this process will be successful. Nevertheless, a number of developments are worthy of comment. First, within Acas, there appears to be considerable agreement about the need for change: most staff are fully behind the idea of turning Acas into a conflict management organisation, and are eager and willing to develop new initiatives that will advance this goal. Thus, shared understandings have been forged around a new vision for the organisation, and new projects have been developed in an effort to realise this vision. While these are all positive developments, some of these initiatives, while broadly successful, appear not to have had the spillover effect hoped for by Acas.

Consider the small firms project. Although this initiative was broadly successful, it took considerable effort to obtain this outcome. Much work had to be done to get the necessary number of participants to make the project feasible. A lot of hands-on work by Acas advisors was required to ensure that the employment law visits and the mediation went well. Both employers and employees were not mentally tuned into the potential benefits of dispute resolution practices, such as mediation: it was as if the idea had arrived before its time. As a result, the inputs into the project probably outweighed the outputs. A similar scenario is unfolding with regard to the promotion of ADR in the public sector. Acas advisors have done highly-innovative work with some health trusts, but a question mark hangs over the extent to which the ADR practices promoted have filtered down into the organisation. Thus, the long term change that results from these Acas pilot initiatives is open to doubt.

Overall, Acas's quest to transform itself into a conflict management agency is not happening either quickly or smoothly. Most of the problems it is encountering have little to do with the calibre of Acas activities, but have more to do with the nature of the external environment. A whole raft of changes has taken place in labour markets and employment relations systems, which have created a new context for the management of disputes in the workplace. Acas is eager and willing to supply assistance to ensure that high-quality conflict management systems are used in the new context, but it seems that the demand for fresh approaches to workplace disputes is not particularly high. It is hard to explain definitively why this should be the case, but three factors appear to be at play:

- First, in workplaces where trade unions have a presence, the response to new employment times is usually to make pragmatic adjustments to established collective dispute resolution systems.

- Second, in workplaces where the principles of modern human resource management systems dominate, the emphasis is on building internal systems with little external assistance, particularly from Acas.

- Third, in recent years, there has been a huge growth in small firms, many of which do not have the HR expertise to develop advanced conflict management systems.

Together, these three factors are holding up the demand for new initiatives on conflict management; as a result, organisational renewal at Acas is still a work in progress.

APPENDIX: *CODE OF PRACTICE ON HANDLING WORKFORCE ISSUES: ADR PROCEDURE*[114]

Introduction

This paper sets out a procedure for resolving disputes arising from the application of the *Code of Practice on Handling Workforce Issues*. All the parties agree that the procedure should be a last resort and all will make their best efforts to resolve problems by agreement. We also support the Government criteria that ADR should be fast, efficient and cost-effective.

The need to exhaust local procedures

The parties must exhaust all normal local procedures, as required by paragraph 9 and paragraph 13 of the *Code*, before invoking the Alternative Dispute Resolution procedure (ADR) provided for in paragraph 14.

Who is responsible for resolving disputes?

The ADR procedure will be under the supervision of an independent person, appointed from an approved list supplied by ACAS. If the parties so agree, they may appoint two 'wing members' with an employer and trade union background to assist the independent person.

The dispute resolution process

Disputes will be resolved using the following three-stage procedure.

Stage 1: Initial reference to the independent person
The independent person will be invited to answer three questions:

(i)   Is this a dispute about the application of the *Code*? If the answer is 'No', the matter can proceed no further. If 'Yes', then the independent person will move to question (ii).

(ii) Have the parties exhausted local procedures? If the answer is 'No', then the parties will be invited to make further local efforts to resolve the dispute. If 'Yes', then the independent person will conduct an independent assessment, by answering question (iii) and giving reasons for the answer.

(iii) Do the terms and conditions of employment on offer to new employees comply with the *Code*? If the answer is 'Yes', then the matter is deemed to be concluded and the contractor can continue to offer the same package of conditions to new

---

[114] LACSAB (2004).

employees. If the answer is 'No', then the dispute will proceed to Stage 2.

Time limit: Twenty working days.

Stage 2: Discussions with a view to reaching an agreement on compliant terms and conditions
Stage 2 begins with the parties being invited to seek to resolve the matter through further discussions.

The independent person will make themselves available to the parties to facilitate the process. The parties also have the option of establishing other arrangements for mediation.

If the parties can reach an agreement consistent with the *Code*, then the matter is closed and the new package of conditions of employment will be applied both to new starters and to those employed during the dispute.

If no agreement can be reached within the allotted time, then the dispute will proceed to Stage 3.

Time limit: Ten working days, with the possibility that this might be extended by the agreement of the parties and with the consent of the independent person.

Stage 3: Final Reference to the Independent Person
The independent person invites the parties to make final submissions. If the independent person then believes it would be worthwhile, the parties may be given a short period of further discussion.

If there is no value in giving the parties more time or, if during any discussion the parties were unable to agree on how to bring the matter to a successful conclusion, then the independent person will proceed to a final, binding arbitration. Having heard the evidence and reached a conclusion, the independent person will impose a revised package of terms and conditions applicable to each of the affected employees.

Time limit: Ten working days.

10

DISPUTE RESOLUTION & EMPLOYMENT STANDARD-SETTING IN SWEDEN

10.1 INTRODUCTION

Sweden is a small, successful open economy, consisting of 4.2 million employees. About 70% of the workforce is in the private sector, with the remaining 30% in the public sector. The economy is highly organised, with over 80% of employees belonging to a trade union: a corresponding number of employers are affiliated to an employer's organisation. On the labour side, the three main organisations are the Swedish Trade Union Confederation (LO), the Confederation of Professional Employees (TCO) and the Swedish Federation of Professional Associations (SACO). On the employer side, the main organisation is the Confederation of Swedish Enterprise: it is made up of 37 industry-based employer associations, representing 54,000 Swedish enterprises with a total labour force of 1.6 million. In addition, the Swedish Agency for Government Employers and the Swedish Association of Local Authorities & Regions represent the interests of public sector employees.

This chapter examines features of the dispute resolution and employment standard-setting systems in Sweden:

- **Section 10.2** outlines some important landmarks in Swedish industrial relations history, as these have had a strong impact on the character of dispute resolution.

- **Section 10.3** shows how the dispute resolution system in the country is heavily embedded within collectivist industrial relations institutions and practices. It also highlights how these collective industrial relations institutions have undergone important changes during the past two decades.

- **Section 10.4** outlines the role and remit of the Mediation Office, created in 2001 to promote efficient, problem-free industrial relations in the country, while **section 10.5** considers the role of the Labour Court.

- After this assessment, the role of Equality Ombudsmen in creating and maintaining equal treatment standards in the labour market is outlined in **section 10.6**.

- **Section 10.7** examines the activities of the Work Environmental Agency, another aspect of the employment standard-setting regime.

- **Section 10.0** assesses the lessons that the Swedish system holds for Ireland.

- The Conclusion brings together in **section 10.9** the arguments of the chapter.

10.2 THE SWEDISH INDUSTRIAL RELATIONS SYSTEM: SOME LANDMARKS

The historical origins of Swedish industrial relations history have an important bearing on the current approach to employment dispute resolution in the country (Elvander & Holmlund, 1997). First, the emergence of organised labour at the turn of the 20th century was not met with a violent response by employers: the 'December Compromise' of 1906 is considered a landmark agreement, as the employers' organisation, SAF, recognised the right of employees to organise themselves in the absence of serious industrial conflict. In return, the LO recognised the right of employees to hire and fire workers freely and to exercise managerial control over enterprises. This agreement was exceptional, as the right of employees to organise in trade unions at that time was the source of large-scale conflict in many other countries. Thus, consensus and compromise were important initial conditions of the Swedish industrial relations system and have had a strong influence on employer and employee behaviour ever since.

Another important spillover from the December Compromise was that it averted the introduction of a battery of legislation to govern industrial relations activity. The only early piece of labour law was a 1906 Act establishing a National Conciliator's Office, which the social partners could call upon if negotiations were not going smoothly. Thus, voluntarism is a second important feature of the industrial relations system in Sweden: the internal affairs of trade unions or employer organisations are not regulated by the law, and both social partners are eager that this remain the case. The country has no legal mechanism that obliges the automatic extension of collective agreements, nor does it have a statutory minimum wage provision. The high level of trade union density and employer representation ensures that voluntarism is the core organising principle of the industrial relations system: non-union industrial relations are almost a non-issue in the country.

A third landmark in Swedish industrial relations history was the Collective Agreement Act 1928, which laid down that collective agreements are binding upon the contracting parties and the members they represent. The Act also stipulated that employers and employees cannot enter into agreements that conflict with an actual existing collective agreement. Further, the Act prohibited industrial action that was designed to change the contents of an agreement. The Act was important, as it signalled employer buy-in into the principle that collective agreements should be at the centre of the Swedish industrial relations system – a principle that remains today, as over 90% of employees are covered by collective agreements. Another notable event in 1928 was the setting up of a Labour Court, to settle disputes about the interpretation and implementation of collective agreements and employment law.

A fourth important landmark was the Saltsjobaden Agreement, signed in 1938 between the LO and SAF. This agreement is significant, because it represented the joint efforts of the social partners to keep the government out of industrial relations activity. During the first part of the 1930s, Sweden experienced widespread industrial unrest that prompted the government to bring forward a sweeping programme of employment legislation to regulate labour market behaviour. To stave off this programme, the social partners committed themselves in this agreement to binding rules, designed to promote orderly negotiating procedures in pursuit of collective agreements. In combination, these rules amounted to the introduction of a peace obligation into the negotiations of collective agreements: real constraints were placed on the use of industrial action to pursue collective bargaining demands.

Overall, the three established core features of the Swedish industrial relations system are collectivism, voluntarism and institutional procedures promoting compromise.

10.3 THE SYSTEM OF COLLECTIVE AGREEMENTS & CORPORATISM

From the mid-1950s until the late 1980s, these features manifested themselves in a highly-centralised system of collective agreements. It was these centralised agreements that led Sweden to be widely regarded as the Mecca of European-style, corporatist industrial relations during the early 1970s and 1980s (Katzenstein, 1985). A defining feature of these centralised agreements, sometimes called the Rehn-Meidner model, after the two economists who first designed them, was how they compressed the wage structure. Wage agreements not only ensured that pay was consistent with maintaining low inflation and high employment, but also that the gap between the top and bottom earners was relatively narrow. As a result, the central agreements were widely lauded, as being able to maintain internal cohesion, while at the same time advancing external competitiveness; equity and efficiency were combined in the one wage formation system (Calmfors & Forslund, 1991).

Despite its impressive record, the Swedish corporatist model of wage determination came under considerable pressure towards the end of the 1980s. Employers, in particular, became less and less committed to the system of centralised wage bargaining (Alexopoulos & Cohen, 2003). They wanted decentralised wage bargaining instead, as it would allow pay levels to be customised to the needs of particular economic sectors, and even organisations. Employer dissatisfaction with the system reached a head in February 1990, when SAF, the main employer organisation, withdrew from the centralised wage negotiations. This move effectively brought to an end the corporatist model of wage determination and changed the institutional context for pay-setting. Employers remained committed to the principle of collective agreements, but wanted these to be concluded at the sector level. Trade unions were deeply unhappy with this move and, as density levels remained high, the danger was that the country would descend into a period of significant industrial relations instability.

This point was not lost on the then Social Democratic government, which almost immediately set up a group of experts, known as the Rehenberg group, to support orderly wage-negotiation processes by providing economic and wage data. Mediators were also provided to assist wage negotiations experiencing difficulties. However, despite these efforts, the break-up of the centralised wage determination system led to increased industrial unrest. In 1995, for example, there were a large number of strikes and other forms of industrial disputes across a range of economic sectors. In response to this situation, the government invited the social partners to discuss creating a more orderly collective-bargaining procedure. These discussions led, in 1997, to the social partners signing the *Co-operation Agreement on Industrial Development & Pay Determination*, more commonly known as the Industry Agreement (Evlander, 2002).

The cornerstone of the Industry Agreement, which covers most of the manufacturing sector, was that collective bargaining should be conducted in a manner that promotes 'industrial development, profitability and competitiveness'. The main institutional innovation of the agreement was the creation of an Industrial Committee, consisting of leading trade union and employer representatives, to preside over a new collaborative procedure for collective bargaining.

Under this procedure, negotiations for a new collective agreement would start about three months before the existing agreement had come to an end. Because the long-established peace obligation prohibits industrial action during the lifetime of a collective agreement, this procedure made it very difficult for either employers or unions to use, or to threaten, industrial action as a bargaining tactic when negotiating a new agreement.

The procedure also stipulates that, if a new agreement has not been signed a month before the end of the existing collective agreement, then the Industrial Committee will appoint an independent chairperson to lead the negotiations so that an agreement can be secured in due time. These independent chairpersons can ask either party to elaborate on a particular bargaining issue they are putting forward to get a better understanding of its merits and to test the degree of support, or opposition, for the issue. The chairpersons can also put forward their own initiatives, in an effort to solve a particular impasse in the negotiations. An important role of the independent chairpersons is to ensure that the parties do not use delaying tactics to see out the existing collective agreement, so that the possibility of industrial action enters the negotiation process. Moreover, the role of the independent chairperson is not simply to get an agreement between the parties, but a settlement that has given due consideration to prevailing national economic and labour market circumstances.

The arrangements established by the Industrial Agreement apply to about 130 of the 580 collective agreements that exist in the country, covering about half of the country's employees. Moreover, the collective agreements covered by the Industrial Agreement are negotiated first, which tends to set the pattern for the other agreements that are negotiated subsequently. Thus, the Industry Agreement is an important aspect of the current wage-setting process and both trade unions and employers were happy to sign it. For their part, trade unions considered it as a way of maintaining the heavily-collectivist ethos of Swedish industrial relations. Employers, on the other hand, saw it as a way of locking trade unions into industrial relations stability, without re-entering corporatist wage bargaining (Sheldon & Thornthwaite, 1999).

The Industrial Agreement encouraged the introduction of similar arrangements for the public sector. As a result of an employer initiative, two new joint committees were set up in 1999 for public sector employees. One was established at the central level, more or less replicating the functions of the Industrial Committee of the Industrial Agreement. Thus, it obliges the parties to enter into negotiations about a new agreement before the existing one expires. It also provides for the appointment of an independent chairperson (mediator) should the negotiations get into difficulties; however, the initiating powers of independent chairpersons are not as extensive in the public sector as they are in the private sector. The other joint committee was given the power to appoint independent mediators to help resolve disputes about the implementation of central agreements at local level.

10.4 THE NEW MEDIATION OFFICE

Although the government prompted the social partners to discuss a new procedure to promote stable collective-bargaining negotiations, it did not play an active role in the discussions. However, it was quick to act in the wake of the Industrial Agreement to build on its provisions. In particular, the government established a Commission in 1997 to examine an enhanced role for public mediation in the pay-determination process. The report of this Commission, which was opposed by the trade unions, led in 2000 to the government abolishing the National Conciliator's Office, first set up in 1920, and establishing in its place a new National Mediation Office. The new Office was assigned three tasks (Eriksson, 2006):

- To mediate in industrial relations disputes.
- To promote an efficient wage-determination system.
- To manage the national wage statistics regime.

The Mediation Office can engage in either voluntary or compulsory mediation activity. Under voluntary mediation, the Office may appoint one or two mediators, normally at the request of the social partners, to assist negotiations on a new collective agreement. Both parties must accept the nominated mediator/s before they can be formally appointed. In cases of compulsory mediation, the Mediation Office can appoint a mediator without the agreement of the parties, if it decides that a risk of industrial conflict exits in collective-bargaining negotiations. The Mediation Office cannot use compulsory mediation in cases where trade unions and employers have committed themselves to the collaborative process set out in the Industrial Agreement.

The task of a mediator appointed by the Mediation Office is to try and obtain an agreement between the parties, consistent with prevailing national economic circumstances. The parties are obliged to attend any meetings called by the mediator; failure to attend results in a fine. Mediators must also try and persuade the parties to postpone or cancel any planned industrial action. If the parties do not agree to a request to postpone or cancel planned action, the mediator can ask the Mediation Office to order a postponement of the action for up to 14 days. This two-week period is considered a cooling-off time, in which intensive efforts should be made to reach a settlement to the employment conflict.

The other main task of the Mediation Office is to promote an efficient wage formation process, which is considered to be the conclusion of collective agreements that facilitate a low rate of inflation and a high rate of employment. To this end, the Mediation Office seeks the development of timetables for the bargaining process that will allow the conclusion of a new agreement before the existing contract period expires. It also holds regular workshops for the social partners to inform them of wage, employment and inflation trends in the hope that they will take these into account when formulating collective-bargaining demands. The Mediation Office is required to maintain a high-quality statistical service on wages, so that negotiations are conducted based on evidence and information.

The Mediation Office employs 12 people, most of whom work on the compilation of wage statistics. The Office does not employ full-time mediators: mediators are appointed to individual disputes from an in-house roster. Most of the people on the roster have served previously as negotiators with one or other of the social partners. In addition, the Office has six regional part-time mediators at its disposal, to deal with local disputes.

After initial opposition from trade unions, the Office has successfully integrated into Swedish industrial relations arrangements. In 2004, for example, a mediator was appointed to assist negotiations on new collective agreements on 24 occasions, an unusually high number, explained by the fact that it was the year for the tri-annual general bargaining negotiations. All the mediations dealt with wage disputes and were carried out on a voluntary basis: there was no need to invoke the compulsory mediation powers of the Mediation Office.

The Mediation Office has been involved in actual industrial disputes. For instance, in 2004, the biggest employment relations dispute in the country involved electrical contractors and the electricians' trade unions. About 1,800 electricians went on strike over pay rates and working time arrangements. After 13,000 working days had been lost, the Mediation Office received a request to appoint a mediator to help solve the dispute. The mediator launched a number of very well-thought-out initiatives, which played a central role in guiding the parties to a settlement.

Sweden's move from a highly-centralised system of wage determination over the last decade was difficult initially, but now has stabilised: both trade unions and employers have adjusted their behaviour to the new system. The system seems to be effective. **Figure 10.1** shows that there have been fewer than 20 strikes each year for the past decade. Like other industrialised countries, the country has experienced a marked decline in collective employment disputes. The transition from corporatism now appears complete, as none of the parties are actively seeking a return to the period of highly-centralised wage agreements. An important feature of this transition is that it has been achieved without undermining the collectivist foundations of Swedish industrial relations. There has been little 'individualisation' of employment relations in Sweden. Collective relations between trade unions and employers remain at the centre of the Swedish industrial relations systems, and considerable efforts are made to maintain these arrangements. For example, in some sectors, collective agreements are concluded that do not include any specified pay increase, so that employers have a degree of freedom to establish their own pay rates in response to the prevailing commercial situation. Thus, both employers and trade unions are willing to accept flexibility within the context of the collective agreement system (Ahlberg & Bruun, 2007).

FIGURE 10.1: SWEDEN: STRIKES, 1985–2005

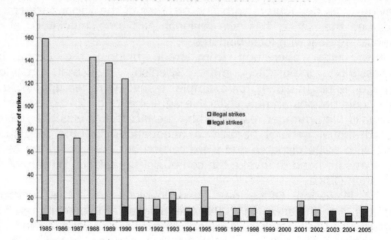

10.5 NEGOTIATIONS, DISPUTES & THE ROLE OF THE LABOUR COURT

The collectivist ethos of the Swedish industrial relations system is found in other aspects of its functioning. One of the legislative cornerstones of the Swedish industrial relations system is the Co-Determination Act 1976. A basic principle of this piece of employment legislation is that disputes between employers and employees should be settled by negotiation. The law distinguishes between three different types of negotiations with regard to employment disputes.

The first type is co-determination negotiations, which cover disputes relating to work supervision, the impact of business strategies on working conditions, and changes to employment conditions of individual employees. Employers are required to consult with unions, with regard to plans involving any substantial change. Should the parties fail to agree, the matter is referred to a higher relevant negotiating level. If an agreement is still not reached at this stage, then the employer has the final say. The whole thrust of the process is to provide employees with a voice on decisions that will effect their employment conditions.

A second set of negotiations relate to disputes concerning the interpretation, or application, of collective agreements or legislation. As a first step, the parties must try to resolve these disputes by negotiation. However, if these attempts fail, then the matter is usually resolved by the Labour Court.

Disputes relating to the creation of a collective agreement are the third area covered by collective agreements. As already seen, both employers and employees are bound by the agreements that their organisations negotiate on their behalf. They are not allowed to reach separate agreements that violate the central agreement. In addition, a peace clause operates during the lifetime of a collective agreement. The Co-Determination Act 1976 is fairly prescriptive about the situations in which industrial action is not permitted both in the public and private sectors. Other legislation puts restrictions on industrial action in the public sector.

The Swedish Labour Court is a special court set up to hear and rule on industrial relations disputes. Two conditions must be met before a dispute can be brought before the Labour Court:

- A case must be lodged by an employer or employee organisation.
- The case must relate to a dispute arising from either a collective agreement or the law on the right to participate in decision-making.

An individual employee, who is not a union member, who wishes to bring a case against his/her employer must do so at a county court. Unionised employees must get their union to bring their claim to the Labour Court. If the trade union is unwilling to bring a case on behalf of an individual worker, then the person can pursue the matter independently at a county court. Thus, most of the work of the Labour Court relates either to the operation of collective agreements or to employment grievances sponsored by the social partners.

Before a case can be referred to the Labour Court, the social partners must try to solve the dispute through negotiations at the local level. If these negotiations fail, then the matter is transferred up to the sector level, where trade unions and employer representatives try to find a settlement, sometimes with the use of arbitration. When hearing a case, the Court is usually made up of seven members, although only three members sit in some straightforward cases. When the seven-member Court sits, there are three neutral members and two members representing the interests of employers and employees respectively. Altogether, there are 25 members of the Court, but only the Chairman is employed full-time. The Court has its own administrative staff and employs junior court lawyers who help the Chairman manage the caseload and prepare judgements.

There is normally a pre-hearing before the Labour Court. Both parties are usually required to make a written submission to this session. At the pre-hearing, the representatives of the parties are investigated to ascertain what actually is being disputed. This is important, as it informs the parties what is required of them to substantiate their case. The attitudes of the parties involved in the case are assessed to test the possibilities of an amicable settlement. At the full hearing, the Labour Court applies standard court procedures. It is up to the parties themselves to present their case to the court. The representations of the parties are the deciding factors used by the Court to make a decision. Members of the Court play an active part in proceedings by asking questions of the parties and making observations. There are specific regulations about who is allowed to appear as a party in cases. If the case concerns the rights of an employee belonging to a trade union, or a company affiliated to an employer's organisation, the case must be brought to the court by the respective trade union or employers' organisation. Judgements of the Court are normally enforced in the same way as any other judgement of an ordinary court.

Hearings at the Labour Court are free of charge, although most of the time the losing party pays costs for the winning side. On average, it takes around six months from the time a case is lodged with the Court until a judgement is passed. The number of cases brought before the Court varies from year to year, but it normally amounts to between 400 and 450, of which a relatively high number are settled amicably at the pre-hearing stage. Normally, the Court makes about 150 to 160 judgements each year. For the most part, the Labour Court judgements are accepted by both parties. However, in the early 2000s, an employer brought a case under the European Convention for the Protection of Human Rights & Fundamental Freedoms, alleging that the Labour Court did not handle their case impartially, as there were too many social partner representatives relative to the number of lay members. However, the claim was not upheld under the European Convention and the Labour Court was exonerated.

Two aspects of this dispute resolution system stand out. One is the emphasis placed on the parties themselves to obtain a resolution to a dispute. Well-established arrangements are in place at the local and sector levels to address workplace disputes. Moreover, there is an accepted norm that these arrangements should be exhausted, before a case is referred to the Labour Court. Thus, the Labour Court in Sweden is truly a 'court of last resort', unlike its counterpart in Ireland, which sometimes is drawn into employment disputes too early. A telling statistic is that, while the Swedish Labour Court made around 140 rulings in 2005, the Irish Labour Court made about 680 rulings of one form or another. The other feature of the dispute resolution process is the virtual absence of any procedures to address individual employment relations grievances: employment relations disputes are more or less housed within a collective industrial relations framework. This is a major point of difference between countries such as Ireland, which are from the Anglo-Saxon industrial relations tradition, and thus give more recognition to the individual employee, and continental European industrial relations systems, which are founded more or less on the principles of corporatism and collectivism. Thus, the major drive in many Anglo-Saxon countries towards 'individualised' dispute resolution procedures is not even under consideration in Sweden, or indeed in other European countries. However, there are other features of the Swedish employment system, particularly in relations to employment rights, which are broadly similar to the Irish situation.

10.6 THE OMBUDSMAN, EQUALITY & EMPLOYMENT RIGHTS

Almost all advanced democracies have some type of Ombudsman's Office. These are usually public bodies that oversee certain aspects of government activity, or investigate complaints against the actions of government departments. The Ombudsman's Office first was invented in Sweden and this institution plays a role in upholding employment rights in the country. More specifically, Sweden has four Equality Ombudsmen – the Equal Opportunities Ombudsman, the Disability Ombudsman, the Ombudsman against Ethnic Discrimination and the Ombudsman against Discrimination on Grounds of Sexual Orientation. The activities of these Ombudsman Offices more or less correspond to the work of the Equality Authority in Ireland.

Thus, for example, the Equal Opportunities Ombudsman is responsible for supervising employer compliance with gender equality legislation. It is also required to investigate complaints of sex discrimination and harassment. In addition, the Ombudsman has to provide information, advice and support on gender equality matters. Probably the lion's share of the Ombudsman's time goes on ensuring that gender equality plans, which are compulsory for all firms with more than 10 employees, are implemented fully. A significant part of its action on this matter involves giving employers guidance on how to develop such plans. Another aspect of this work is collecting, and evaluating, a random sample of several hundred gender plans to see whether they comply with the law. If employers refuse to co-operate with the Ombudsman by not submitting gender plans, then they can be fined repeatedly until they comply. Employers are obliged to put right any defects identified in their gender plans by the Ombudsman. If an employer refuses to do so, then the matter can be referred to the Equal Opportunities Commission, a 13-person body, made up of eight ordinary members and five members representing trade unions and employers. This Commission may threaten the employer with a fine, if the employer does not come into compliance with the law. The fine can be re-imposed, until the employer makes the necessary changes to the gender plan.

The Equal Opportunities Ombudsman also has the responsibility to investigate claims of discrimination and harassment, on foot of a complaint made by an individual employee. The investigation normally is conducted by the legal staff of the Ombudsman Department. If an investigation finds that there is substance to the complaint, the Ombudsman is obliged first to seek voluntary solutions to the case, which mainly involves arranging settlement negotiations between the employer and the complainant. A settlement package normally involves making pay adjustments or providing damages to a complainant. If the matter cannot be settled through voluntary negotiations, then the Ombudsman can take the case to the Labour Court for jurisdiction.

The Ombudsman carries out a range of activities to promote gender equality. For example, it holds regular meetings with the Mediation Institute to encourage specific action on gender equality, when collective agreements are being negotiated. In addition, it convenes networks of trade union and employer representatives, who have the responsibility of promoting gender equality in the workplace, to launch concerted and focused action on the matter. The Equal Opportunities Ombudsman also works with the three other equality ombudsmen to develop joint action. It is hard to assess the effectiveness of this particular form of collaborative action. In some countries, mostly from the Anglo-Saxon tradition, there is a move towards having a single organisation to promote equality. The argument for a single agency is that a more integrated, and co-ordinated, approach is taken to the promotion of gender equality in the labour market. There is no move, however, towards amalgamating the various Ombudsman bodies in Sweden.

10.7 THE WORK ENVIRONMENT AGENCY

The principle of labour inspection is long-established in Sweden. The Act on Protection against Occupational Risk in Private Industry 1889 established a regional system of labour inspection. This system was complemented by the creation of the Occupational Health & Safety Board in 1949. In 2001, the Government decided to integrate the two systems and to establish the Work Environment Agency (WEA). The main objectives of the WEA are to reduce the risk of ill-health and accidents in the workplace and to promote a holistic approach to the improvement of the working environment. To this end, the WEA is charged with ensuring that organisations comply with work environment and working hours legislation. In addition, the WEA has the responsibility to respond to queries and complaints, provide advice and publish information that helps the creation of safe and healthy workplaces.

The WEA employs about 800 people: 300 of these are located at the head office in Solona, and the remainder at 10 local offices dispersed around the country. It is governed by a lay board, made up of the Director General, who operates as chairperson, six members selected on the basis of their expert knowledge in the area, and two trade union representatives. An important function of the Agency is to ensure that companies comply with employment standards established by EU and national law. The WEA also uses non-statutory regulations, which it is responsible for drawing up, to govern the working environment. Regulations, of which there are more than 200, normally do not carry legal liability, even though they oblige employers to take some action. They can cover all aspects of the work environment, apply to particular groups of employees (for example, women), or have particular purposes (for example, relate to specific industries, certain technical installations and materials, certain work processes or exposure to specific substances). Regulations can be very detailed and prescriptive, but they normally try to set minimal standards. Individual regulations are updated, when appropriate.

On the labour inspection front, over the past few years, the WEA increasingly has shifted away from enforcement inspections to investigating whether employers have the procedures and resources to comply with the requirements laid down in labour law. Particular attention is spent on verifying the quality of the internal monitoring arrangements with regard to employment standards. If the WEA finds that these are defective, then it can issue prohibition/improvement notices. These are not binding instructions but, if organisations fail to comply with the substance of the notice, the WEA can impose a fine for non-compliance. This shift from labour inspection to 'diagnostic monitoring' is of growing importance within the WEA. It is also becoming more sophisticated, as investigations are starting to focus on particular industries or business activity rather than stand-alone organisations.

Consider the investigation conducted by the WEA into the work environment of 112 call centres. The purpose of the investigation was to assess the extent to which the call centres were meeting their obligations to introduce systematic work environment management systems, as set out in a 2001 Regulation. It found that many organisations were failing to carry out regular and systematic assessments into the physical, psychological and organisational aspects of the work environment. The lack of proper assessments was seen as leading to a poor working environment in many of the call centres. In relation to the physical environment, the WEA found that many call centres had excessively narrow workstations, workstations at an incorrect height, incorrect work postures, display units placed too high for users and excessive glare from lamps. The report was also critical of lengthy work periods in front of a computer screen, limited work content and little work variation in physical and mental activities. The final report found a host of problems in the call centres, including inadequacies in relation to the physical work environment, as well as in relation to working time schedules. As a result of the report, about 86% of the workplaces inspected were required to make changes, which were far-reaching in some cases.

An interesting aspect of the report is that it not only recorded the deficiencies of deviant call centres, but also established best practice guidelines for the creation of a good work environment in call centres. These guidelines are based on actual practices found in the few call centres that did not receive any criticisms from the WEA. The guidelines include the following:

- Companies should work continuously to increase the amount of variation in work, both physically and mentally, through the development of richer work content.
- Employees working on the telephone and the computer should have a five- to 10-minute break after every one to two hours of work.
- Integrated and systematic assessments must be carried on the work environment on a regular basis.
- Management should use motivation and encouragement to promote good work results, and bonus systems should be used to support, encourage and stimulate.
- Regular and frequent meetings and discussions should be held between individuals and managers, both on an individual and group basis.
- Good career development opportunities should be provided for employees.

- Employees should have access to a comprehensive occupational health service in the workplace.

This investigation by WEA into call centres is significant, as it represents a subtle shift in the inspection process. Instead of seeing inspection as a narrow instrument of enforcement, a broader approach is adopted, grafting 'diagnostic monitoring' onto the process. Diagnostic monitoring involves a comprehensive review of representative organisations in a particular business activity to reveal internal variation in the characteristics, and dynamics, of work environments and to find out what makes for good, and bad, practice. A feature of the inspections is not simply to spot breaches of regulations and statutes, but to identify the reasons behind non-compliance. In addition, the diagnostic monitoring procedures attempt to establish a cross-company benchmarking process, whereby underperforming organisations can upgrade their practices by learning from the practices and procedures of good companies. Thus, diagnostic monitoring is about moving inspections away from top-down enforcement procedures to creating dynamics within companies, so that good practices undercut bad practices, rather than the other way round.

10.8 DRAWING LESSONS FROM SWEDEN

Collectivism and voluntarism are the two main features of the Swedish industrial relations system, connected together by a number of institutional procedures that promote consensus-making behaviour on the part of the social partners. These highly country-specific characteristics facilitate the creation of credible commitments between employers and trade unions, which ensure that the social partners gain an assurance about each other's behaviour. As a result, both employers and trade unions have a high level of confidence that each will use industrial relations procedures in a responsible manner. Thus, industrial relations procedures have a lot of integrity. Of course, employment disputes arise, and both employers and trade unions get disgruntled about particular developments, but they do not behave in a manner that could undermine the credibility of the entire system.

Clearly, this mutually-re-inforcing relationship between collectivism and voluntarism is due to a range of country-specific factors. As a result, it would be naïve to suggest a transfer of Swedish industrial relations procedures to Ireland. Nonetheless, some lessons of potential relevance to the Irish situation can be drawn from the Swedish experience.

One of the most distinguishing features of the Swedish system of dispute resolution is the onus placed on the social partners to make every effort to resolve conflicts themselves, independently of the public dispute resolution procedures. Both employer organisations and trade unions spend a lot of time, building up internal capacities to problem-solve and to settle disputes, including holding specialised training workshops, some of which are organised jointly. In addition, the social partners spend a lot of time in ensuring that the rules and procedures set up to resolve disputes, both inside organisations and at the sector level, are fully supported by all the relevant parties. These arrangements are reviewed frequently to assess their effectiveness and to evaluate whether they could be improved.

This practice of trade unions and employers solving disputes by themselves holds lessons for Ireland. It is now widely accepted that the Labour Relations Commission and the Labour Court get involved in too many employment relations disputes, too quickly. Not enough emphasis is placed on the social partners building their own autonomous arrangements to settle disputes. For example, when a disagreement arises about the implementation of a social partnership agreement, the LRC is drawn almost immediately into the dispute – and, frequently, the matter ends up at the Labour Court. This is a situation that needs the attention of the social partners. New procedures and practices have to be created that encourage the voluntary resolution of disputes, in the absence of the public machinery. More joint activities need to be launched between IBEC and ICTU, to build up the problem-solving and dispute-resolution capabilities of both organisations.

There are signs that this type of activity is starting to happen. A recent agreement between Oxigen Environmental Ltd and SIPTU is one example of innovative action in this area. This agreement covers a number of issues, but the most relevant part for the analysis here is a new five-point grievance and dispute resolution procedure, the first of which may end in the LRC or the Labour Court getting involved, the second of which (if chosen voluntarily) involves the appointment of two joint facilitators who will mediate on the issues in dispute. If this referral to the facilitators does not result in a solution, then the dispute will be referred to a Disputes Resolution Panel for binding arbitration. This binding leg of the procedure involves an agreed outside chairperson, as well as the two facilitators. Interestingly, if the final binding decision is made by a majority, the dissenting opinion will not be recorded. Developments like these are to be welcomed, as they show a more pro-active approach to the settlement of disputes by employers and trade unions, though to date this development remains the exception rather than the rule.

A second lesson that can be taken from the Swedish practice is the importance the Mediation Office attaches to holding workshops and seminars for negotiators of collective agreements, in order to help them to conclude efficient collective agreements that are in the interests of the parties and the country. The Labour Relations Commission should learn from this experience and hold specialised workshops, designed to improve features of the dispute resolution practices, both within companies and at national level. For example, it should be using the extensive in-house data it holds on referrals to identify what problems and issues arise most frequently. Then it should devise a seminar, perhaps in conjunction with IBEC and the trade unions, or with the IMI, that focuses on best practice policies on the particular issue that has given rise to so many grievances. It could also hold workshops on more generic, innovative dispute resolution practices, to equip human resource managers and trade union representatives with knowledge and expertise of the most up-to-date practices. An important issue for the staff of the Mediation Office is that they remain connected to the practising industrial relations community in the country and this should be the same for the activities of the LRC.

A third lesson from the Swedish experience that may have some import for the Irish situation is the move away from conciliation towards the wholehearted embracement of mediation. Between 1920 and 2000, the country had a National Conciliator's Office, but this was closed down after the establishment of the new Mediation Office. The move away from conciliation to mediation was motivated by a desire to have stronger, more purposeful forms of public interventions into employment disputes. Conciliation was considered to be too mild an approach to dispute resolution, which did little to challenge the entrenched positions of the various parties in a dispute. Mediation was considered a more directive form of dispute resolution, which would allow mediators to get to the essence of a dispute more quickly, by obliging the parties to justify their positions and being able to propose settlement paths to the conflict. This development in Sweden raises the question whether the LRC should focus more on mediation, rather than conciliation. It may be an answer to the 'narcotic' effect that appears to have emerged in recent years, which has resulted in some organisations becoming too dependent on the services of the conciliation team to conclude agreements with its workforce.

A fourth lesson that can be learned from Sweden is the manner in which the Work Environment Agency goes about promoting compliance with employment laws. This public agency increasingly interprets its role as not simply the search for deviant organisations not complying with employment laws and regulations. Rather it is adopting a new enforcement approach that involves periodically surveying a multitude of organisations in the same type of industry or business – call centres, construction sites, nursing homes or whatever – to assess the extent to which they comply with employment standards. The organisation regards its role as codifying how, and why, some organisations are more compliant with the law than others and to create the conditions whereby the practices of the most compliant firms are introduced to the least compliant organisations. Thus, the new regulatory approach is about challenging organisational habits and routines that result in non-compliance with legal statutes. It seeks to produce information on alternative ways of doing things that make compliance possible, even attractive. All in all, it is an approach that is as much about changing bad practice as it is about penalising it: a regulatory process is put in train so that the divergence in compliance performance is narrowed through a process of levelling up, not levelling down.

The enforcement and compliance strategy being pursued by the WEA is of most relevance to the activities of the newly-established Office of Director for Employment Rights, which is charged with monitoring adherence to labour market standards. However, the Labour Relations Commission could also learn from this strategy. In particular, it may be worth considering the idea of targeting a particular industry or business, which is the source of a relatively high number of referrals to the Rights Commissioners or the LRC, and then launching a series of activities to upgrade dispute resolution and employment relations. For example, the LRC could launch an assessment into why some companies in a particular industry are better able to adhere to relevant codes of LRC conduct than other companies. Such an assessment could result in a benchmarking process emerging, where the non-compliant companies can compare their practices with complying companies. The basic thrust is to develop activities that will highlight deficient employment relations and dispute resolution practices and to create the know-how and motivation among the deficient firms to adopt new practices. The ethos of such pro-active activity must be framed in terms of support and collaboration, if it is to succeed.

10.9 CONCLUSION

There is no one, universal, best way of settling employment disputes. Procedures and practices to keep employment disputes and grievances at a minimum must fit with the cultural and institutional traditions of a particular country. At the same time, these same practices and procedures require frequent reform and modernising to keep pace with economic and social changes. In this modernisation process, it is important to examine innovative developments in other countries to see whether these hold lessons for Ireland and whether they could be introduced into the prevailing system, if suitably amended.

The most significant features of the Swedish system are the onus placed on the social partners resolving disputes by themselves; the move away from conciliation to the extensive use of mediation in the industrial relations system; and the use of diagnostic monitoring in promoting compliance with employment standards. The institutional mechanisms used to realise these goals may not be applicable fully to the Irish case, but the goals themselves have relevance to the Irish situation. The task now is to investigate whether Ireland can learn from the best features of the Swedish industrial relations system, in a manner compatible with Irish industrial relations traditions.

11

CONCLUSIONS:
ORGANISATIONAL CAPABILITIES
& DISPUTE RESOLUTION:
KEY ISSUES GOING FORWARD

11.1 INTRODUCTION

This book has reviewed a number of dispute resolution and employment rights bodies that function as an integral part of the Irish state's relatively comprehensive, and effective, public dispute resolution architecture:

- The Labour Relations Commission (**Chapter 2**).
- The Labour Court (**Chapter 3**).
- The Equality Tribunal's Mediation Service (**Chapter 4**).
- The Employment Appeals Tribunal (**Chapter 5**).
- The Labour Inspectorate (**Chapter 6**).
- The Health & Safety Authority (**Chapter 7**).

The book also examined dispute resolution and avoidance systems in three other countries – Canada (**Chapter 8**), the United Kingdom (**Chapter 9**) and Sweden (**Chapter 10**). In particular, it has outlined what these respective bodies do, indicated the challenges they face, examined the innovative and practical strategies they are adopting, and considered the lessons they provide in relation to the public policy challenge of maintaining and building capacity in dispute resolution and standard-setting in the context of rapid economic, labour market and workplace change.

This research has amassed considerable information and insight into the strengths of different organisations, how they relate to the environment in which they operate, and how successful they have been in carrying out the tasks they were established to complete. It makes proposals that could assist these organisations in maintaining and building their capacity to deliver an effective public policy service.

Therefore, the aims of this final chapter are two-fold:

- First, it seeks to order and make coherent the diverse findings of the research, in terms of key issues that the dispute resolution and employment rights bodies should consider in developing their strategies going forward.

- Second, this chapter also seeks to explore the implications of this research for the work of the LRC; in particular, the organising theme of this discussion is whether the organisational capabilities of the LRC need to be reconfigured in light of the findings of this research. `

11.2 ORGANISATIONAL CAPABILITIES & THE LRC

Successful organisational performance arises when a corporate strategy is realised fully. To execute a corporate strategy, the organisation must have a detailed appreciation of its resources, and the ability to convert these into capabilities that permit it to advance its objectives fully. Organisational capabilities relate to this conversion process. If resources are transformed into highly co-ordinated bundles of capabilities, an organisation can be said to possess high-grade organisational capabilities. High-grade organisational capabilities are considered to confer a number of unique attributes on an organisation (Kay, 1993). One is inimitability, which refers to the extent to which the organisation possesses expertise and knowledge that other organisations find difficult to acquire or copy. Another is **durability**, which relates to the capacity to deliver a service to a consistently high standard over a period of time. A third attribute is **relevance**, which refers to the degree to which the activities of the organisation fit with the environment in which the organisation operates. A fourth property is **reputation**, which refers to the esteem in which the organisation is held in the environment in which it operates.

The extent to which these attributes emerge within an organisation depends on its architecture (Kogut, 1996). Organisational architecture is how the organisation is structured internally: it establishes the rules that govern how different parts of the organisation relate to each other, and shapes the relationships members of the organisation have with each other. The nature of the organisational architecture has a strong influence on the extent to which an organisation can assess developments in its environment, whether it has a close understanding of the knowledge-base of its internal resources, the degree of internal flexibility it has to adapt to changing situations, and its capacity to maintain close working relationships with other organisations.

Over the years, the LRC is widely considered to have possessed high-grade organisational capabilities. It enjoys a strong reputation among employers and trade unions for delivering services that help to resolve workplace conflict, particularly collective industrial disputes. Its programmes appear to be relevant, as the demand for them is high. The consensus is that, without the activities of the LRC, the level of recorded employment disputes would be higher. The organisation possesses a unique knowledge-base on the variety of dispute resolution practices and processes that can be employed to settle workplace conflict; no other organisation possesses a similar repository of dispute resolution expertise. Surveys of clients that have used the LRC show that the organisation delivers services to a consistently high standard. Thus, on all measures, the LRC has been a high-performing organisation.

However, as the business strategy literature stresses, organisational capabilities that are meaningful today can quickly become redundant in a fast-changing social and economic environment (Teece *et al.*, 1997). The core proposition of this book is that the industrial relations environment in which the LRC is operating has changed, altering not only the context in which workplace conflict arises, but also the approaches taken to resolve disputes. Thus, the core question is: to what extent does the new environment for preventing and resolving workplace disputes require the LRC to alter its core organisational capabilities?

Before that question is addressed directly, it may be useful to set out again briefly the types of influences that are driving change:

- **The changing composition of the labour market:** More women than ever before are working in Ireland, and the female share of the labour force is set to rise even further in the next decade. In addition, there has been a significant growth in the internationalisation of the labour market in recent years. About 10% of the labour force is made up of people who were not born in Ireland. These labour market trends require new people-management policies in the workplace, which, if not properly implemented, could lead to workplace conflicts and disputes. Thus, for example, with more women working, it is important that greater attention is paid to equal pay and equal treatment policies. Similarly, with more migrants working in Ireland, it is important that they receive all their legal employment entitlements and are treated with respect at work.

- **The decline of collective representation in the Irish economy:** Large numbers of employees are unorganised, do not belong to a trade union and are not covered by collective agreements. In this context, traditional collective-based grievance and disciplinary procedures for resolving employment-related disputes are not in place and, therefore, there is a need to consider what mechanisms for voice and/or grievance resolution operate in the non-unionised sector. Equally, for public dispute resolution agencies, that traditionally deal with unionised organisations, there is now the challenge of how they position themselves within an increasingly-diverse employment relations landscape.

- **The growth of non-union multinationals:** Ireland is an extremely open economy, a feature of which is the large number of multinational companies in the country. Many of these companies do not recognise trade unions. One argument is that these companies are operating state-of-the-art dispute resolution policies, focused on the individual; but, actually, little is known about the nature and extent of these arrangements. However, interesting questions arise about how the dispute resolution bodies relate to these non-union multinationals. For instance, can bodies like the LRC learn from the dispute resolution practices of these non-union multinationals?

- **The growth in employment legislation:** Employees now enjoy a wider range of employment rights than ever before. A more pervasive role for employment law weakens the traditional, voluntarist principles of Irish industrial relations, based on free collective-bargaining, and encourages employees to regard their participation in the labour market as legal subjects, rather than as part of a collective organisation, such as a trade union. In these circumstances, employees are more likely to use public dispute resolution bodies to vindicate their employment rights. Consequently, the public dispute resolution architecture must have the capacity to resolve both disputes of rights, as well as disputes of interest, in a fair, effective and expeditious manner.

- **The rise of small firms:** There are more than 60,000 small firms in Ireland, which employ large numbers of people in total. A feature of many small firms is that they do not have formalised, comprehensive, human resource management departments, largely because of a lack of resources. In the absence of expert knowledge, small firm owners may not be aware of the full range of employment legislation. Moreover, they may not be aware of the key policies and procedures that help to prevent and resolve disputes.

- **The push for public service modernisation:** Almost everywhere, governments are trying to improve the design and delivery of public services; the Irish government is no exception. Over the past 15 years, through the Strategic Management Initiative programme, the Irish government has been trying to modernise public services and, in the context of the new social partnership agreement, *Towards 2016*, the parties have agreed to an extensive programme of change. Large-scale organisational change of the kind being sought invariably generates workplace disagreements and disputes; the LRC's experience under the previous agreement, *Sustaining Progress*, was that resolving such disputes was a protracted and difficult process. This raises the question of the role that the public dispute resolution agencies should adopt in relation to the management of change in the public service.

- **The professionalisation of human resource management:** For many reasons, human resource managers are developing more sophisticated policies and practices. Recruitment and selection policies tend now to be better designed, as do human resource development plans. Similarly, new approaches are emerging in the management of workplace disputes. On the one hand, human resource managers seek to settle disputes closer to their point of origin and to use more comprehensive approaches to the management of disputes. On the other hand, they adopt a more clinical approach to workplace disputes, so that grievances are settled expeditiously. This greater professionalisation will impact on the work of the dispute resolution agencies. For example, human resource managers may become reluctant to use the agencies, as they consider this inevitably will lead to the dispute being drawn out.

These, and other, developments have changed the context in which the dispute resolution and employment rights bodies carry out their designated tasks. The new context is evident in the employment relations statistics. For example, on the one hand, the figures show that the number of strikes and other major collective industrial disputes is at an all-time low. On the other hand, there has been a substantial rise in the number of individual and small-scale workplace disputes handled by the dispute resolution bodies. The new context is encouraging debate about the activities of the dispute resolution and employment rights bodies. It is argued that the resolution of employment disputes is being framed in new ways, and that the dispute resolution bodies should be playing a leading role in the diffusion of these innovations (Teague, 2005). Another argument is that employment rights agencies must develop more sophisticated strategies, some of which should be non-legal in character, to increase compliance with employment standards. Thus, the new context, so the argument goes, requires different parts of the public policy regime responsible for enforcing labour standards and resolving disputes to re-think established activities.

To test the strength of this argument, this study assessed the extent to which dispute resolution and employment bodies are changing the procedures and practices used to resolve workplace compliance and enforce labour standards. Questions raised in the investigation included:

- Is adjustment to the new industrial environment happening everywhere?
- Are established ways of resolving disputes being made redundant as a result of the new industrial relations environment?
- What types of changes are occurring to the activities of the dispute resolution and employment rights bodies?
- Are these changes significant enough to ensure that dispute resolution continues to be carried out in a fair and efficient manner?
- Will the character of the dispute resolution bodies change radically, as a result of unfolding economic and social developments?
- Will there even be a need for public dispute resolution bodies in the future?

The lessons learned from the answers to these questions are set out below. Probably the best way to start reporting the findings is to answer the last question first.

11.3 RESOLVING DISPUTES: THE NEED FOR PUBLIC INSTITUTIONS

Workplace conflict happens and the resulting organisational and human costs can be hefty. On occasions, disputes can get so intense that the parties involved are unable to resolve the problem by themselves (Arrow *et al.*, 1995). Such a situation courts all sorts of problems: the imposition of a settlement by one party on another, resulting in a clear winner and loser emerging from the dispute; or the continuation of conflict, fuelled by embittered relations between the protagonists. Thus, although conflict at work is almost inevitable, dispute resolution that satisfies the interests and aspirations of all the participants is not. An important finding of this research is that the institutional design of the dispute resolution system, as well as the employment standard-setting regime, has an important bearing on its performance. Another related finding is that a dispute resolution system with a strong public dimension is more likely to contain a series of values, rules and procedures that facilitate fair, and speedy, settlements to grievances and conflicts.

Public institutions are an important part of a dispute resolution system for three reasons. First, public institutions help to establish the social norms that govern acceptable, and unacceptable, behaviour in the workplace. They carry out a number of functions to this end:

- Information systems are created, so that organisations and employees are aware of their legal rights and obligations.

- Advice is provided about the import of particular employment laws and what constitutes good people management policies.

- Advocacy is used to promote employment practices considered to be socially-responsible: thus, for example, equal opportunity agencies develop a range of activities to promote fair treatment in the workplace.

- Training is provided to ensure that organisations have the expertise to address workplace conflict, and related problems, effectively.

Thus, public institutions play an important role of developing the framework for appropriate dispute resolution and employment standard-setting behaviour.

Second, public institutions are required to establish quasi-judicial processes within the employment dispute resolution system. These processes play an important role: they give public authorities the power to bring together disputing parties involved in employment conflict, with a view to reaching a settlement. This 'convening power' is particularly useful in situations where relationships between the disputing parties have reached an impasse (Dorf, 2003). Thus, public agencies involved in dispute resolution can perform the role of honest broker in difficult negotiations that arise occasionally when employers and trade unions are trying to reach a collective agreement. Sometimes, employment legislation requires the public institutions to operate more legalistically and to make a decision whether particular employment relations practices are consistent with statutory or regulatory rules. Through this quasi-judicial role, public institutions can impose a penalty default on an organisation, which is not complying with employment standards or a collective agreement. A penalty default is the situation where a party (or parties) to a dispute faces sanctions that make them worse off than if they had complied with the original rule or deal: an organisation that is found not to be complying with the law is obliged not only to put right their improper practices, it is also likely to lose reputation, which could have all sorts of consequences. The presence of public institutions ensures that fairness is more likely to be built into the dispute resolution system.

Third, while the last two decades have witnessed a dramatic decline in overt industrial conflict within advanced industrial economies, high-profile and protracted disputes, particularly in key sectors, still retain the potential to exert a negative influence on the employment relations environment. Although a return to the high levels of industrial unrest of the 1970s and 1980s is highly unlikely, maintaining labour market stability remains a key public policy objective for all of the countries considered in this study. Intensified international competition also has focused attention on the potential advantages associated with improving the quality of employment relations, both in enhancing the delivery of public services and also in conferring a degree of competitive advantage. An effective, credible and fair system of dispute resolution and avoidance is a key ingredient in the development of a more collaborative, problem-solving culture of employee relations. Significantly, in Ireland and Canada, the public dispute resolution bodies have been to the fore in promoting the need for organisations to adopt good practice conflict management practices and procedures and also to develop more partnership-style relationships with employees and their representatives.

The continued relevance of public dispute resolution bodies is an important finding. In the USA, there has been an enormous growth in the use of company-level ADR procedures to settle workplace disputes (see Stone, 1999; Lipsky, Seeher & Finche, 2003; Dunlop & Zack, 1997). This emphasis on internalising the settlement of workplace conflict has raised concerns that ADR is being used as vehicle for weakening statutory-based employment rights and collective bargaining, as well as undermining the public dimension to employment-related dispute resolution. In part, these concerns reflect the fact that the design, and operation, of alternative dispute resolution systems in the private sector within the USA is becoming almost entirely employer-promulgated. It should be recognised, however, that a number of US federal and state dispute resolution agencies have also experimented with ADR programmes, with positive results.

Significantly, however, the evidence from some of the case study countries, Canada in particular, is that new dispute resolution practices can be introduced that do not confer unfair advantages on employers in the settlement of workplace disputes. Innovative and alternative approaches to the prevention and resolution of workplace disputes can be diffused in a manner that enhances and complements the role of public resolution bodies and established collective arrangements in the workplace. Modernising dispute resolution systems is not a euphemism for employer-promulgated ADR employment practices, but rather a basis for developing innovative and legitimate services and initiatives designed to enhance the public dispute resolution bodies' capacity to resolve and prevent disputes.

11.4 REFORMING DISPUTE RESOLUTION: THE INTERNATIONAL EXPERIENCE

The comparative case studies show that important changes have been occurring to all three national public dispute resolution systems. Moreover, the reform that has been taking place has been strongly incremental in character; there has been no attempt to re-organise the system root-and-branch.

In Canada, the government has taken the lead in developing a new strategy on dispute resolution. For example, it passed the Public Service Labour Relations Act in 2005, section 207 of which obliged government departments to establish an informal conflict management system. The purpose of this system is to introduce new approaches for the prevention and resolution of workplace disputes, in a way that builds upon established employment relations procedures, such as collective bargaining. As the chapter on Canada (**Chapter 8**) shows, this move by government strengthened other initiatives to diffuse new approaches to conflict management in the workplace. By taking the lead in the reform of employment dispute activities in the country, the government gave extra meaning and momentum to the modernisation of this important aspect of employment relations in the country.

A different reform strategy was adopted by Acas in Britain. At the centre of this strategy was an attempt to recast the organisational identity of Acas: rather than being seen as a troubleshooting body, used to settle major collective industrial relations disputes, the organisation wanted to be seen as the national public agency that guided the diffusion of state-of-the-art dispute resolution practices, both in the public and private sectors, and which formed authoritative views on what constituted best practice people-management practices. Although government has expressed interest in developing alternative dispute resolution procedures, it has not been a strong supporter of Acas in this regard. And, although Acas has set up interesting projects, it has found it difficult to forge meaningful and sustainable connections with private sector organisations, in particular with the SME sector, on dispute resolution matters. As the LRC case study demonstrated, however, connecting with the SME sector is a common challenge facing public dispute resolution agencies. Overall, Acas has not been fully successful in its efforts to refashion its identity, although the strategy is still ongoing.

The Swedish dispute resolution system remains strongly embedded in both collectivist and voluntarist employment relations institutions. Both employer organisations and trade unions remain committed to keeping government out of employment relations, and there is little evidence that organisations are showing interest in new ADR approaches to workplace conflict. Yet, what the collective organisations do in relation to dispute resolution has changed, gradually and incrementally, over a period of time. The changes have resulted in a move away from conciliation towards an active form of mediation. They have also led to new agreed procedures between unions and employers, which radically reduce the possibilities of industrial action during the negotiation of new collective agreements. Thus, the Swedish case is an example of a dispute resolution system being changed from within. The emphasis has not been on major transformative change, but on gradual reform, so that important changes can be introduced without jeopardising the underlying ethos and principles of the overall system.

The clear message from the international evidence is that there is no appetite anywhere for far-reaching change. Thus, the case studies suggest that incremental change is probably the most appropriate pathway for Ireland. The character of the dispute resolution and employment standard-setting regime in Ireland militates against a major transformational strategy, as many different institutions are responsible for preventing and resolving disputes and for enforcing labour standards. Although separate, there are numerous instances where these institutions have overlapping responsibilities. In this situation, it would be extremely difficult to get across-the-board buy-in for large-scale reform; some institutions would be fearful of losing competencies to other agencies, while other institutions might be reluctant to take on new roles that involve a departure from traditional work practices.

Similarly, there is limited support within the political system, or amongst the social partners, for a large-scale reform programme in this area. For example, while articulating the need for reform of certain aspects of the system, the social partners are fairly comfortable operating within the present institutional framework. Thus, the institutional configuration of the Irish dispute resolution system, and the attitude of the key stakeholders within the system, effectively rules out radical change. Gradual, incremental change is the only realistic reform path for the Irish situation. Like elsewhere, the emphasis must be on the re-organisation of specific programmes and the addition of new programmes within the present institutional framework. This suggests that the traditional programmes of the LRC are not redundant, but have to be 'recombined', so that their content is updated and they are delivered in a new way.

11.5 DOING IT THE IRISH WAY

An important finding from the comparative case studies is that it would be short-sighted for the Irish dispute resolution and employment rights bodies to reform their activities, simply by mimicking perceived best practices from elsewhere. There is no one, universal, best way to manage workplace conflict. Although dispute resolution bodies in different countries provide similar services, they do so in sharply-contrasting institutional and social settings. These distinctive national settings have a major impact on the character and the implementation of dispute resolution programmes. Moreover, they tend to connect different programmes together in unique ways. As a result, the success of a particular dispute resolution programme is closely tied to the institutional context in which it is being implemented, which may be lost if the programme is transferred mechanically to another country.

At the same time, the Irish dispute resolution and employment rights bodies must be aware of what is happening elsewhere. They must seek to improve their own performance by learning from other experiences. If another country is doing something new that appears successful, then this development must be assessed to see whether it is appropriate to the Irish context and to estimate what adjustments might be needed to allow it to enhance already-established programmes. The *motif* must be to learn from others in a manner that best fits the Irish context. There are signs of Irish agencies engaging in this form of learning-by-monitoring activity. For example, the Voluntary Protection Programme introduced by the Health & Safety Authority (HSA) is based largely on a scheme pioneered in the USA. The programmes used by the Labour Relations Agency (LRA) to promote interest-based bargaining also have their origins in the USA. However, overall, there is probably a need for the organisations to engage more in this type of learning, particularly in relation to devising new strategies to obtain more effective compliance with employment legislation and also in developing innovative approaches that complement and enhance established procedures for resolving both disputes of interest and disputes of rights. In this context, this book seeks to add to, and inform, this learning process.

From the case study evidence, it cannot be said that Ireland is out of step with international trends in relation to the reform of public policy regimes for dispute resolution and employment standard-setting. Like other countries, Ireland has been doing a lot to adapt this regime to the new industrial relations environment. The Equality Tribunal, for instance, was established with the remit to develop a mediation dimension to its activity, a practice that previously had not been used a great deal by the public dispute resolution agencies in Ireland, at least not formally. The three-fold increase in employment inspectors, alongside important reforms to their role, was significant and has not been paralleled anywhere else in Europe. The LRA and HSA, too, have busy introducing new schemes and have been examining the effectiveness of their established programmes. Thus, from the evidence of the case studies, Ireland is doing as much as other countries, if not more in some instances, to reform dispute resolution and employment standard-setting activity. Change is happening across a wide range of areas. The emerging pattern from these reforms has been to deepen further 'responsive regulation' and problem-solving within the Irish dispute resolution and employment rights bodies.

Responsive regulation seeks to integrate 'soft' and 'hard' regulatory policies within the one enforcement regime. Consider the Health & Safety Authority. At the same time as inspecting construction sites to ensure compliance with labour standards, the HSA is working with trade unions and employers to develop joint voluntary initiatives to improve health and safety in the industry. The underlying premise of responsive regulation is that command-and-control rules can no longer be enforced properly: in today's decentralised economy, an army of inspectors would be required to ensure compliance with statutory rules and government simply does not have the resources for this. Responsive regulation seeks to meet this challenge by making compliance and enforcement strategies simpler, and more flexible, for employers, trade unions and employees, while at the same time more effective.

A key trait of responsive regulation is the *delegation* of rule enforcement, but only in the context of a wider framework of escalating penalties and sanctions. The approach amounts to building a form of conditional self-regulation into enforcement strategies. In practice, this means that organisations are allowed to design their own methods of achieving the goals of statutory rules, provided these comply with publicly-established minimum conditions. Moreover, organisations are allowed to police themselves, provided the procedures used to self-monitor, and self-correct, are carefully designed, open to some form of credible validation process, and enjoy the confidence of those most directly affected by them. The external validation of internal procedures for complying with statutory rules is perhaps the most important aspect of responsive regulation. Conditional self-regulation reaches its maximum potential when organisations behave as 'good' employers. However, all employers are not good, and this is why the 'big gun' of penalties must be retained within the regulatory regime.

Thus, the ability of firms to design their own rules is set within a regulatory framework of escalating interventions: organisations are kept inside the bounds of public accountability and legal enforcement. If they fail to reach minimum national standards, they face sanctions and penalties. Responsive regulation has import for employment standard-setting in Ireland, as it combines voluntary and legal methods to settle workplace conflict.

Problem-solving is the second major theme in the overall employment relations strategy of government and the social partners and, as the case studies demonstrate, it is an integral feature of the public dispute resolution architecture in Ireland. A problem-solving approach to dispute resolution promotes a variety of institutional mechanisms and procedures, operating both inside, and outside, organisations, to address workplace conflict (Fisher, Ury & Patton 1991). There is a heavy bias towards solving disputes near to the point where they first arise. In addition, problem-solving encourages assessment of different settlement methods, to evaluate their effectiveness in carrying out the tasks they were set up to do. Part of this involves giving those who use public dispute resolution mechanisms the opportunity to evaluate their experience.

Yet a further aspect of the problem-solving approach challenges adversarial approaches to the settling of workplace conflicts. Many modern dispute resolution systems, particularly those in the Anglo-Saxon tradition, have been constructed on the assumption that interactions between employees and employers are competing and adversarial (Lewin & Peterson, 1988). An adversarial approach to the resolution of employment disputes normally follows this sequence:

- The setting of target points – what the parties would like to achieve.

- The setting of reservation points – the points below which the parties seek not to go.

- The ritual of offer and counter-offer that produces reciprocal concessions.

- The arrival at a compromise solution, at some point where the target and reservation points overlap for the two parties.

In a nutshell, a 'split the difference' ethos pervades the 'adversarial' approach to dispute resolution (Farber & Katz, 1979).

Of course, the adversarial approach can produce solutions to workplace conflict, but it can generate avoidable employment disputes also, as a 'them and us' mentality encourages both employers and employees to adopt unreasonable stances in the workplace or in negotiations about employment relations matters (Feuille & Hildebrand, 1995). Moreover, in an adversarial system, the possibility exists of the dispute resolution institutions being used by employers and employees to gain advantage in their respective bargaining strategies.

In contrast, a problem-solving approach adopts a different track. It frames dispute resolution as part of a wider, ongoing process of building co-operative relationships between employers and employees

(Cutcher-Gershenfeld, 2001). Thus, as much emphasis is placed on dispute prevention, as on dispute resolution. One consequence of this approach is to move dispute resolution institutions towards strategies that actively encourage employers and employees to adopt practices and procedures that promote fair, and efficient, methods of preventing workplace conflict (Mitchell & Banks, 1996).

A problem-solving approach carries a number of important implications for the design of dispute resolution and employment rights bodies. First, it is consistent with the notion of responsive regulation. Problem-solving encourages decentralised, non-legalistic ways of resolving disputes, but it also recognises the continuing importance of labour market regulation, in terms of setting frameworks and standards in the employment system. Voluntary and regulatory procedures are seen as complementary, rather than in collision with one another. Second, the problem-solving approach questions the neutrality principle that strongly influences the organisation, and practice, of dispute resolution agencies. According to the 'neutrality' principle, a dispute resolution agency must remain 'above' the employment relations system, so that it does not run the risk of being tarnished as 'pro-business' or 'pro-trade union'. However, the problem-solving approach encourages the dispute resolution agencies to adopt an active role in promoting practices that promote the fast, and fair, resolution of workplace disputes: the dispute resolution agencies are not neutral, as they are biased towards high-quality dispute resolution practices. Third, the problem-solving approach recognises the need for a plurality of dispute resolution procedures, both public and private, and inside and outside of the firm. A dispute resolution system that has a range of procedures to address grievances in the workplace is more likely to realise the principles of procedural and substantive justice (Budd & Colvin, 2005). Thus, the problem-solving approach endorses fully 'collective' employment relations institutions and the important role played by trade unions in the labour market. At the same time, the approach recognises fully the role of non-union workplaces in the modern Irish economy and is willing to work with these organisations to ensure that employees have access to proper procedures for the resolution of workplace conflict. In fact, given the relatively open-ended ethos of the problem-solving approach, it would welcome cross-organisation learning between union and non-union organisations on dispute resolution practices.

Thus, responsive regulation and problem-solving are emerging from the case studies as two of the key underlying themes behind much of the work of the dispute resolution and employment rights bodies in Ireland. It is not that these bodies have been consciously guided by these two principles when carrying out their activities; instead, they arrived at this form of policy-making through working out solutions, with the social partners, to the problems and challenges they face. The willingness of public agencies and the social partners to adopt a collaborative problem-solving approach to emerging, and, at times, complex, challenges they face is one of the embedded strengths of the public dispute resolution system in Ireland and, as such, it is important that this intangible asset continues to inform, and to shape, any future strategies for modernisation.

Quite pragmatically, many of the bodies reviewed in this book have recognised that established programmes and schemes need to be revised to keep pace with economic and social developments. However, this form of pragmatic action in the face of new challenges has had far-reaching consequences, as it has resulted in a new governance structure emerging for employment rights and dispute resolution. The first signs of this new governance structure can be detected both in the discussions about the need to change dispute resolution and employment rights to make them more user-friendly and in the behaviour of the related public bodies. There is growing recognition that these services have to be delivered in a more integrated manner. Most of the agencies appreciate that the labour market has been changing rapidly and, as a result, they display a willingness to adopt new programmes. However, while a new governance structure based on the principles of responsive regulation and problem-solving may be emerging, it cannot be considered to be working optimally. Further change is required by many agencies and below we focus on the adaptations that the LRC needs to consider so that its activities are more consistent with the new governance regime.

11.6 DISPUTE RESOLUTION & EMPLOYMENT STANDARD-SETTING AS A VALUE-CHAIN

Although Ireland now possesses a relatively effective, and comprehensive, public framework for dispute resolution and employment standard-setting, the somewhat *ad hoc* manner in which this system has evolved does pose challenges. For example, the role of these bodies can be confusing, as they have overlapping responsibilities. To the employee with an employment grievance, it is not always clear which is the appropriate agency to contact. One finding of this research is that the connections between the various dispute resolution and employment rights bodies are not particularly high. Agencies talk about the presence of informal, behind-the-scenes relationships, but no meaningful formal collaboration involving two or more of the bodies was found. Moreover, a great deal of wariness was found about working with other agencies. Bodies appeared more interested in protecting their turf, rather than initiating collaborative activity. This finding is consistent with a number of other reports that regard the dispute resolution and employment rights service as too fragmented and, like these reports, the current research considers that there needs to be more integration between the relevant bodies.

Some action has been taken on this matter, in the context of a formal review by the Department of Enterprise, Trade & Employment of the functions of the various employment rights bodies. A key focus of the ongoing work in this area has been on seeking to establish a common contact point for the various services, which would refer the person with an issue to the most relevant agency. Reform of this kind would improve the service but this study suggests that it may not be enough. In a sense, the dispute resolution and employment rights services should be considered more as a 'value-chain': different bodies should stop regarding themselves as more or less stand-alone entities delivering discrete services, but rather as part of an interconnected set of agencies, whose activities can be considered as delivering a joint product. Together, these bodies determine the overall calibre of the dispute resolution and employment rights system. Without the emergence of a value-chain mentality, relationships are unlikely to be developed between agencies that can lead to more concerted action on identified dispute resolution and employment rights problems.

Thus, a case exists for building more positive forms of collaboration between the agencies, but collaboration should not be developed for collaboration's sake. In relation to the LRC, it must consider whether there are any problems that it faces, which could be addressed more effectively by working with another organisation than by working alone. Some forms of collaboration are likely to be relatively small-scale: for instance, working with the Labour Court to assess whether the procedure through which cases are referred from the LRC to the Court could be improved. Other initiatives might be more ambitious: for example, the LRC might wish to follow the British and Canadian examples and work with the Employment Appeals Tribunals to establish a mediation option for employment dismissal cases. This collaboration, moreover, should not be limited to the area of dispute resolution *per se*: for example, the LRC, given its statutory mandate, should be actively exploring how it can build on the relationship it has already fostered with the National Centre for Partnership & Performance, given that both organisations are concerned with improving the quality and effectiveness of employment relations in Irish workplaces. However, any joint work with other agencies must be focused strongly on an identified problem, and a full understanding of the activities that are involved and the resources required to make the initiative a success. Collaboration can be beneficial, but it can also be time-consuming.

11.7 ETHICS & STANDARDS IN DISPUTE RESOLUTION

Earlier, it was pointed out that public agencies remain important to the functioning of the Irish system of dispute resolution. At the same time, there have been new, potentially significant, developments in dispute resolution outside the work of the public agencies, particularly the LRC. Although this trend cannot be quantified precisely, there appears to have been a noticeable growth in the use of consultants in addressing workplace conflict. Some of these consultants are being hired to help develop interest-based bargaining systems inside organisations. Others are being used as third-party mediators, or facilitators, to help resolve particular workplace conflict cases. This development raises interesting questions concerning the ethics and standards of these third parties to workplace dispute resolution systems (Menkel-Meadows, 1997). For example, if these people-management consultants operate in the absence of ethical guidelines, then doubts can be raised about their neutrality and about whether employees covered by such arrangements actually enjoy procedural justice.

In many parts of the USA, where the private use of third-party mediators to resolve employment disputes has grown enormously, there has been an attempt by the public authorities to establish codes of conduct to create minimal standards and ethics to which organisations and consultants should adhere, when seeking to resolve workplace conflict. These codes of conduct for workplace conflict resolution involving third parties address the key issues of procedural justice, neutrality, trust and standing. In developing these codes, public authorities in the USA seek to establish consistency and even-handedness. The LRC may not wish to develop such a code of conduct in Ireland, but it might need to consider developing a set of guidelines relating to acceptable, and unacceptable, workplace conflict management practices; its experience leaves the LRC well-placed to do so.

The greater use of consultants to help manage internal workplace conflict systems is interesting for other reasons. In the first part of this chapter, it was argued that, over the years, the LRC has enjoyed strong organisational capabilities in the areas of inimitability, durability, relevance, and reputation. To some extent, these capabilities came about, because the LRC was the monopoly provider of dispute resolution services. However, the growth in the use of private consultants to address different facets of workplace conflict makes the market of dispute resolution services more contestable. The degree of inimitability enjoyed by the LRC has been weakened, as some of the services it traditionally provided are being replicated by consultants. Moreover, if more and more companies start to devise conflict management systems premised on the use of private consultants, then sooner or later the relevance of the work of the LRC will be challenged. Thus, the growth in the private market for dispute resolution (fuelled both by public and private sector organisations) can be regarded as a strategic threat to the organisational activities of the LRC.

A third matter raised by the growing use of consultants in dispute resolution is training and certification. Many of those employed as dispute resolution consultants have considerable employment relations experience, either as human resource managers or trade union officials. Clearly, this experience should stand them in good stead, when working in a workplace conflict situation. However, whether experience alone is a sufficient credential to operate as a third-party neutral in a workplace situation is open to doubt. Surely, more formal training is required to equip private consultants to deliver workplace conflict management services adequately? This matter raises the awareness of best practice adequacy of training provision in Ireland in relation to employment dispute resolution. The case study on the Mediation Service of the Equality Tribunal (**Chapter 4**) highlighted how none of those involved in setting up the service had any formal training in the area of mediation and had to go outside Ireland to receive it. The LRC, therefore, as part of its efforts to strengthen and modernise its organisational capabilities, should be developing some initiative to promote best practice in employment dispute resolution through its key stakeholders training. Overall, however, the point is that the development of the private market for dispute resolution has created a series of challenges for the LRC.

11.8 STRUCTURE, CONDUCT & PERFORMANCE

The LRC has done much in recent years to improve the operation of its organisational architecture. A computerised case-management system has been introduced to administer parts of the organisation better, particularly the operation of the Rights Commissioners. The Conciliation Service has been re-organised to be pro-active and strategic in the delivery of its services. More regular formal training sessions have been introduced for the Rights Commissioners. New initiatives, such as the mediation service, have been launched. The organisation has become more closely involved in the smooth operation of the national social partnership agreements, through administering the 'ability-to-pay' procedure. Thus, through its actions, the LRC is eager to maintain a high-quality dispute resolution service and to keep pace with developments in the external institutional and market environment, but this study suggests that it may have to do even more, if it is to upgrade its organisational capabilities.

The internal organisational structure of the LRC has developed over the years. Traditionally, conciliation has been the core activity of the organisation, but other activities, such as the advisory service, have been added on to this core activity gradually. This expansion has allowed the organisation to deliver a more comprehensive range of services. In recent years, there has been an effort to obtain greater co-operation between the different parts of the organisation. For example, the conciliation service has established Working Together projects that involve members from the conciliation and advisory teams. Blurring the boundaries between conciliation and advisory functions is a very positive development, as it allows different dispute resolution techniques to be applied to a particular organisational problem. One argument that appears to have plausibility is that conciliation and advisory services should be integrated even further, so that teams containing a variety of dispute resolution skills are formed within the organisation. Developing cross-functional teams would allow an employment dispute to be addressed from a variety of perspectives. Thus, when an organisation contacts the LRC for help in solving a workplace dispute, it will not be able to use only the conciliation service; instead, it will have to buy into a package of dispute resolution services. In addition to conciliation, the organisation, for example, might obtain a diagnostic assessment of its employment relations systems, to identify areas that need improvement and would facilitate 'disputes' being channelled to the most appropriate dispute resolution mechanism. Integrated team-working, in other words, would allow the LRC to address more effectively problems, such as organisations becoming over-dependent on its activities. The move from functional units to cross-functional teams should be given serious consideration by the LRC.

Another matter that needs some consideration is the greater use of evidence-based management. Consider the matter of the growing number of individual and small-scale cases being handled by the Rights Commissioners: information on these cases perhaps could be used to obtain a better profile of the nature of the firms that are most frequently involved, the type of employees affected, and the common causes of conflict, and so on. This evidence would allow for a more informed discussion on the viability of a pro-active initiative to address this significant problem. The Canadian Human Rights Commission, for example, pro-actively uses information and knowledge garnered in the dispute resolution process to inform directly policy development, research activities and preventative initiatives. The thrust of evidence-based management is to organise information at the disposal of the organisation in a manner that allows for dispassionate decision-making.

An important finding that emerges from the comparative case-studies is that mediation is taking on a higher profile in employment dispute resolution systems. The LRC has developed a programme in this area recently, but this service only operates in response to a demand for mediation by an organisation. Other countries have taken a more pro-active approach to mediation, and the LRC might consider doing likewise. For example, it should consider whether the informal conflict management system (ICMS) being introduced into various parts of the Canadian public sector is a model appropriate to the Irish context. Under the ICMS, a range of processes, including coaching, negotiation, mediation and neutral evaluation, have been established to enable employees in a workplace to prevent and resolve conflict by themselves, or with the help of a neutral third-party. The system, which is endorsed by both management and trade unions, is not an alternative to existing processes, as it is integrated with established collective bargaining and grievance procedures. One possibility that the LRC should consider is piloting such a scheme in some parts of the public sector. An initiative of this kind would send a strong signal that the LRC is eager to develop within organisations fair, impartial and appropriate processes to resolve conflict at the lowest level and at the earliest stage. This could encourage trade unions and employers to do more to prevent disputes from arising wherever possible and, whenever they do arise, to facilitate their resolution informally. The LRC must do more to be seen as a leader in the diffusion of new dispute resolution processes. Interestingly, as the case studies highlight, bodies such as the Equality Tribunal in Ireland and the PSLRB and Labour Standards Directorate in Canada have sought to embed ADR within their dispute resolution processes by formally establishing 'mediation' as a default option.

At the same time, the LRC should not establish a variety of workplace experiments on conflict management on an *ad hoc* basis. If anything is to be learnt from the Acas case study, it is that the uncontrolled launching of pilot schemes can lead to a lot of work with little sustainable return. Before the LRC develops any kind of experimental project, it has to be carefully thought-out and meticulously planned. This should involve intensive consultation with the key stakeholders, and also an emphasis on policy experimentation and monitoring, before any new innovation is mainstreamed. Additionally, as the case studies demonstrate, once a new approach is adopted formally, there is a need for the sponsoring public agency to undertake a comprehensive advocacy campaign, designed to improve clients' understanding of the new approach and to promote the potential benefits of using it.

A final point is that it is the staff of the LRC who will have a key role in ensuring that the LRC possesses high-grade organisational capabilities. It is the staff of the organisation who deal with employers and employees on a daily basis, in an effort to prevent or resolve workplace conflict. The success of their action depends as much on their tacit skills – their ability to interact with people effectively, for example – as on implementing formal procedures. Solving disputes often requires them to combine discretion and formal rules in highly-customised ways. Thus, to be effective, LRC staff need to enjoy a fair degree of autonomy in the work they do. At the same time, the experience and knowledge of individual staff needs to be shared widely with other staff. Transferring knowledge inside organisations can be done formally or informally. The LRC must develop an internal organisational system that combines discretion on-the-job and knowledge-sharing. The evidence suggests that the LRC has such a system, but it needs to monitor this matter continuously and to consider ways in which present arrangements can be strengthened. For instance, the LRC should be recruiting on an open competition basis, rather than from the ranks of the Civil Service, so that it gains access to an even greater pool of talented individuals.

11.9 CONCLUSION

The LRC has a good reputation for helping to resolve disputes in a fair, and fast, manner. This reputation is well-deserved, as the LRC seeks continuously to modernise its internal organisational capabilities to keep pace with labour market developments. The changes taking place in Irish society, and in the Irish economy, some of which echo developments in other advanced economies, while others are country-specific, are substantial. These changes are generating a range of challenges to public dispute resolution and employment rights bodies in Ireland, and elsewhere. The dispute resolution and employment rights regime has responded to these challenges in an impressive manner. Interesting initiatives have been launched in the broad areas of responsive regulation and problem-solving, which have begun a process that will lead to a new governance regime emerging in Ireland, in relation to workplace conflict. However, more needs to be done, and the LRC must play a full role, if not a leading role, in ensuring that innovations continue to be made to the dispute resolution system. Suggestions as to how the LRC could improve its services further have been made, but it is up to the LRC itself to consider carefully what moves to make to ensure that its organisational capabilities make a strong contribution to the building of high-performing, high-quality organisations in modern Ireland.

BIBLIOGRAPHY

Acas (2005a). *Annual Report*, London: Acas.

Acas (2005b). *Acas Telephone Helpline: Findings from the 2005 Customer Survey*, Acas Research & Evaluation Section Research Papers 02/05, London: Acas.

ACLM – see Advisory Committee on Labour Management Relations in the Federal Public Service (Canada).

Advisory Committee on Labour Management Relations in the Federal Public Service (Canada) (2001). *Working Together in the Public Interest*, Ottawa: Treasury Board of Canada.

Ahlberg, K. & Bruun, N. (2007). 'Sweden: Transition through collective bargaining', in Blanke, T. & Rose, E. (eds.), *Collective Bargaining Wages in Comparative Perspective: Germany, France, the Netherlands, Sweden & the United Kingdom*, New York: Kluwer Publications.

Akyeampong, E.B. (2006). 'Increased work stoppages', *Perspectives on Labour & Income*, August, pp.5-20.

Alexopoulos, M. & Cohen, J. (2003). 'Centralised wage bargaining and structural change in Sweden', *European Review of Economic History*, Vol.7, No.3, pp.331-363.

Arrow, K., Mnookin, R., Ross, L., Tversky, A. & Wilson, R. (1995). *Barriers to Conflict Resolution*, New York: W.W. Norton & Co.

Ayres, I. & Brathwaite, J. (1992). *Responsive Regulation: Transcending the Deregulation Debate*, Oxford: Oxford University Press.

Barrett J. & O'Dowd, J. (2006). *Interest-Based Bargaining: A Users Guide*, Victoria, Canada: Trafford Press.

Borjas, G. (2003). 'The labour demand curve is downward-sloping: Re-examining the impact of immigration of the labour market', *Quarterly Journal of Economics*, Vol.118. No.4, pp.1335-1374.

Budd, J. & Colvin, A. (2005). *Balancing Efficiency, Equity & Voice in Workplace Resolution Procedures*, Working Paper 1050, Minnesota: Industrial Relations Centre, University of Minnesota.

Bush, R. & Folger, J. (1994). *The Promise of Mediation: Responding to Conflict through Empowerment & Recognition*, San Francisco: Jossey-Bass Publishers.

Calmfors, L. & Forslund, A. (1991). 'Real-wage determination and labour market policies: The Swedish experience', *The Economic Journal*, Vol.101, No.408, pp.1130-1148.

Canadian Government (2005). *Modernising Federal Labour Standards*, Consultation Paper, Ottawa: Government of Canada.

Commander, S., Heitmuller, A & Tyson, L. (2006). *Migrating Workers & Jobs: A Challenge to the European Social Model*, IZA Discussion Paper series, No.1993.

Cronin, M. (2004). *Industrial Relations & Human Resource Management Practice in Ireland: Analysis of 12 Years of the Labour Relations Commission Advisory Services Division Company Reviews*, Dublin: Government Publications.

Cutcher-Gershenfeld, J. (2001). 'In whose interest? A first look at national survey data on interest-based bargaining in labor relations', *Industrial Relations*, Vol.40, No.1, pp.3-20.

Cutcher-Gershenfeld, J. (2003). 'How process matters: A five-phase model for examining interest-based bargaining', in Kochan, T. & Lipsky, D. (2003), *Negotiations & Change from the Workplace to Society,* Ithaca, Cornell University Press.

D'Arcy, C. & Garavan, T. (2006). *Unfair Dismissal: Insights into the Employee's Experience of the Employment Appeals Tribunal,* paper to the Irish Academy of Management Annual Conference, University College Cork.

D'Art, D. & Turner, T. (2002). 'An attitudinal revolution in Irish industrial relations: The end of "them and us"' in D'Art, D. & Turner, T. (eds.), *Irish Employment Relations in the New Economy*, Dublin: Blackhall Publishing.

D'Art, D. & Turner, T. (2005). 'Union recognition and partnership at work: A new legitimacy for Irish trade unions?', *Industrial Relations Journal*, Vol.36, No.1, pp.121-139.

Davies P. & Rideout, R. (eds.) (2000). *Legal Regulation of the Employment Relation,* Amsterdam: Kluwer Law International.

Deakin, S. (2004). *Renewing Labour Market Institutions,* Geneva: International Labour Office.

Department of Enterprise, Trade & Employment (2004a). *Report of Review Group on Functions of the Employment Rights Bodies*, Vol.1, Dublin: Government Stationery Office.

Department of Enterprise, Trade & Employment (2004b). *Report of Review Group on Functions of the Employment Rights Bodies,* Vol.2: Submissions, Dublin: Government Stationery Office.

DETE – *see* Department of Enterprise, Trade & Employment.

Dex, S. & Smith, C. (2002). *The Nature & Pattern of Family-friendly Employment in Britain,* London: Joseph Rowntree Foundation.

Dix, G. & Oxenbridge, S. (2004). 'Coming to the table with Acas: From conflict to co-operation', *Employee Relations*, Vol.26, No.5, pp.510-530.

Dobbin, F. & Sutton, J.R. (1998). 'The strength of a weak state: The rights revolution and the rise of human resource management divisions', *American Journal of Sociology*, Vol.104, No.2, pp.441-476.

Dorf, M. (2003). 'Legal indeterminacy and institutional design', *New York Law Review*, Vol.78.

Dunlop, J. & Zack, A. (1997). *The Mediation & Arbitration of Employment Disputes,* San Francisco: Jossey-Bass Publishers.

Edwards, P. (1992). 'Industrial conflict: Themes and issues in recent research', *British Journal of Industrial Relations*, Vol.30, No.2, pp.361-404.

Edwards, P. (2007). *Justice in the Workplace: Why It Is Important & Why a New Public Policy Initiative Is Needed*, Provocation Paper, Series 2, No.3, London: Work Foundation.

Elvander, N. & Holmfund, B. (1997). *The Swedish Bargaining System in the Melting Pot: Institutions, Norms & Outcomes in the 1990s*, Stockholm: Arbetslivinstitutet.

Elvander, N. (2002). 'The new Swedish regime for collective bargaining and conflict resolution: A comparative perspective', *European Journal of Industrial Relations,* Vol.8, No.2, pp.197-216.

Employment Appeals Tribunal (2000-2005). *Employment Appeals Tribunal Annual Report* (various), Dublin: Employment Appeals Tribunal.

Equality Tribunal (2001-2006). *The Equality Tribunal Annual Report* (various), Dublin: Equality Tribunal.

Equality Tribunal (2002). *Developments in Alternative Dispute Resolution (ADR): The Equality Tribunal's Mediation Service Two Years On*, Dublin: Equality Tribunal.

Equality Tribunal (2002-2006). *Mediation Review* (various), Dublin: Equality Tribunal.

Eriksson, K. (2006). 'The Swedish experience in mediating collective labour disputes', Unpublished paper.

Estlund, C. (2005). 'Rebuilding the law of the workplace in an era of self-regulation', *Columbia Law Review*, Vol.125, No.2, pp.31-46.

Eymard-Duvernay, F. (2005). *Economie Politique de l'Entreprise*, Paris: Repères, La Découverte.

Fairris, D. & Reich, M. (2005). 'The impacts of living wage policies: Introduction to the Special Issue', *Industrial Relations*, vol.44, pp.1-13.

Farber, H. & Katz, H. (1979). 'Interest arbitration, outcomes and the incentive to bargain', *Industrial & Labor Relations Review*, Vol.33, pp.228-40.

Fernie, S. & Metcalf, D. (2004). 'The organisational ombuds: Implications for voice, conflict resolution and fairness at work', in Lewin, D. & Kaufman, B. (eds.), *Advances in Industrial & Labor Relations 13*, Toronto: Elsevier Canada, pp.97-138.

Feuille, P. & Hildebrand, R. (1995). 'Grievance procedures and dispute resolution', in Ferris, G., Rosen, S. & Barnum, D. (eds.), *Handbook of Human Resource Management*, Oxford: Blackwell.

Fisher, R., Ury, W. & Patton, B. (1991). *Getting to Yes,* 2nd ed., New York: Penguin Books.

Fitzgerald, J. (2005). 'When I get older, losing my hair, many years from now: Ireland – an ageing multicultural economy', in Malone, J. (ed.), *The New Ireland & Its Sacred Cows*, Dublin: Liffey Press.

Foley, K. (2005). 'Communication oils the wheels of change', *Labour Relations Review*, No.1.

Folger, R. & Cropanzino, R. (1998). *Organisational Justice & Human Resource Management*, London: Sage Publications.

Fox, M. (2005a). *Gender Differences in Enforcing Employment Rights*, Acas Research & Evaluation Section Research Papers 07/05, London: Acas.

Fox, M. (2005b). *Evaluation of the Acas Pilot of Mediation, Appeals & Employment Visit Services to Small Firms*, Acas Research & Evaluation Section Research Papers 05/05, London: Acas.

Government of Ireland (2003). *Sustaining Progress*, Dublin: Government Publications.

Government of Ireland (2007). *Towards 2016*, Dublin: Government Publications.

Gunderson, M. (2002). 'Collective bargaining and dispute resolution in the public sector', in Dunn, D. (ed.), *The Handbook of Canadian Public Administration*, Oxford: Oxford University Press.

Gunderson, M., Ponak, A. & Taras, D. (2002). *Union-Management Relations in Canada*, Toronto: Toronto University Press.

Gunnigle, P. (2000). 'Paradox in policy and practice: Trade unions and public policy in the Republic of Ireland', *IBAR*, Vol.21, No.2, pp.39-54.

Gunnigle, P., Heraty, N. & Morley, M. (2002). *Human Resource Management in Ireland,* Dublin: Gill & Macmillan.

Gunnigle, P., O'Sullivan, M. & Kinsella, M. (2001). *Organised Labour in the New Economy: Trade Unions & Public Policy in the Republic of Ireland*, paper to the Irish Academy of Management Conference, Derry.

Health & Safety Authority (2000). *Construction Safety Partnership Plan 2000-2002*, Dublin: Health & Safety Authority.

Health & Safety Authority (2003). *Construction Safety Partnership Plan 2003-2005*, Dublin: Health & Safety Authority.

Health & Safety Authority (2004). *A Strategy for the Prevention of Workplace Accidents, Injuries & Illnesses*, Dublin: Health & Safety Authority.

Health & Safety Authority (2005a). *Report of the Expert Advisory Group on Workplace Bullying*, Dublin: Health & Safety Authority.

Health & Safety Authority (2005b). *Code of Practice on Workplace Bullying*, Dublin: Health & Safety Authority.

Health & Safety Authority (2006). *Construction Safety Partnership Plan 2006-2009*, Dublin: Health & Safety Authority.

Hooker, H., Neathey, F., Caseborne, J. & Munro, M. (2007). *The Third Work-Life Balance Survey: Main Findings*, Employment Relations Research Series, No.58, London: Department of Trade & Industry.

HRSDC – see Human Resources & Social Development Canada.

HRSDC (2002). *Labour Program: Federal Mediation & Conciliation Service: HRSDC Client Satisfaction Research* (internal report to Human Resources Development Canada, Ottawa: Human Resources & Social Development Canada.

HSA – *see* Health & Safety Authority.

Human Resources & Social Development Canada (2004). *Summative Evaluation of the Labour Management Partnerships Program: A Summary of Statistical & Qualitative Research Results*, Ottawa: Human Resources & Social Development Canada.

Hyland, M. (2005). *Migrant Workers & Access to the Statutory Dispute Resolution Agencies*, Dublin: Labour Relations Commission.

Kahn-Freund, O. (1974). 'On uses and misuses of comparative law', *Modern Law Review*, Vol.37, No.1, pp.26-27.

Katzenstein, P. (1985). Small States in World Markets, Ithaca, NY: Cornell University Press.

Kay, J. (1993). *Foundations of Corporate Success*, Oxford: Oxford University Press.

Kelly, E. & Dobbin F. (1999). 'Civil rights law at work: Sex discrimination and the rise of maternity policies', *American Journal of Sociology*, Vol.105, No.2, pp.455-92.

Kochan, T. & Lipsky, D.B. (eds.) (2003). *Negotiations & Change from the Workplace to Society,* Ithaca: Cornell University Press.

Kochan, T. (2005). *Restoring the American Dream: A Working Families' Agenda for America*, Cambridge, MA: MIT Press.

Kochan, T., Lautsch, B. & Bendersky, C. (2000). 'An evaluation of the Massachusetts Commission against Discrimination's alternative dispute resolution program', *Harvard Negotiation Law Review*, Vol.5 (Spring), pp. 233-78.

Kogut, B. (1996). 'What firms do? Co-ordination, identity and learning', *Organisational Science*, Vol.7, No.5, pp.502- 523.

Kruse, B. (2002). Research evidence on the prevalence and effects of employee ownership', *Journal of Employee Ownership & Finance*, Vol.14, No.4, pp.65-90.

Labour Court (2000-2006). *The Labour Court Annual Report* (various), Dublin: Government Publications.

Labour Relations Commission (1992). *Code of Practice on Dispute Procedures, including Procedures in Essential Services*, Dublin: Government Stationery Office.

Labour Relations Commission (1993). *Code of Practice on Duties & Responsibilities of Employee Representatives & the Protection and Facilities to be Afforded them by their Employer*, Dublin: Government Stationery Office.

Labour Relations Commission (1997–2006). *Labour Relations Commission Annual Report* (various), Dublin: Government Publications.

Labour Relations Commission (1998a). *Code of Practice on Sunday Working in the Retail Trade*, Dublin: Government Stationery Office.

Labour Relations Commission (1998b). *Code of Practice on Compensatory Rest Periods*, Dublin: Government Stationery Office.

Labour Relations Commission (2000). *Code of Practice on Grievance and Disciplinary Procedures*, Dublin: Government Stationery Office.

Labour Relations Commission (2002a). *Code of Practice detailing Procedures for Addressing Bullying in the Workplace*, Dublin: Government Stationery Office.

Labour Relations Commission (2002b). *Code of Practice on Voluntary Dispute Resolution*, Dublin: Government Stationery Office.

Labour Relations Commission (2004a). *Code of Practice on Victimisation*, Dublin: Government Stationery Office.

Labour Relations Commission (2004b). *Enhanced Code of Practice on Voluntary Dispute Resolution*, Dublin: Government Stationery Office.

Labour Relations Commission (2005a). *A Quality Shift in Employment Relations: Statement of Strategy 2005-2007*, Dublin: Government Stationery Office.

Labour Relations Commission (2005b). *Migrant Workers & Access to the Statutory Dispute Resolution Agencies,* Dublin: Government Stationery Office.

Labour Relations Commission (2005c). *Report on 'Sustaining Progress'*, Dublin: Government Stationery Office.

Labour Relations Commission (2006). *Code of Practice on Access to Part-Time Work*, Dublin: Government Stationery Office.

Labour Relations Commission (2007). *Code of Practice for Protecting Persons Employed in other People's Homes*, Dublin: Government Stationery Office.

Labour Relations Commission, Advisory Services Division (2004). *Effectiveness of Codes of Practice Survey*, Dublin: Government Stationery Office.

LACSAB – *see* Local Authority Conditions of Service Advisory Board.

Lane P. & Ruane, F. (2006). *Globalisation & the Irish Economy*, IIIS Occasional Paper, Dublin: Trinity College.

Lewin, D. & Peterson, R. (1988). *The Modern Grievance Procedure in the United States,* New York: Quorum Books.

Lewin, D. (1987). 'Dispute resolution in the non-union firm: A theoretical and empirical analysis', *Journal of Conflict Resolution,* Vol.31, No.3, pp.465-502.

Lewin, D. (2001). 'IR and HR perspectives on workplace conflict: What can each learn from the other?', *Human Resource Management Review*, Vol.11, No.4, pp.453-485.

Lipsky, D., Seeher, R. & Finche, R.D. (2003). *Emerging Systems for Managing Workplace Conflict: Lessons from American Organisations for Managers & Dispute Resolution Professionals*, San Francisco: Jossey Bass.

Lobel, O. (2004). *The Renew Deal: The Fall of Regulation & the Rise of Governance in Contemporary Legal Thought*, San Diego Legal Studies Paper no. 07-27, San Diego: University of San Diego Law School.

Lobel, O. (2006). 'Beyond experimentation: The case of health and safety administrative governance in the United States', in de Burca, G. & Scott, J. (eds.), *New Governance & Constitutionalism in Europe & the USA*, Oxford: Hart Publishing.

Local Authority Conditions of Service Advisory Board (2004). Code of Practice on Handling Workplace Issues: ADR Procedures, London: Local Authority Conditions of Service Advisory Board.

Locke, R., Quin, F, & Brause, A. (2006). *Does Monitoring Improve Labour Standards?: Lessons from NIKE*, MIT Sloan Research Paper No.4612-06, Cambridge, MA: MIT.

LRC – *see* Labour Relations Commission.

Manning, A & Goos, M (2003). *Lousy & Lovely Jobs: The Rising Polarisation of Work in Britain,* Centre for Economic Performance Working Paper, London: London School of Economics.

McCartney, J. & Teague, P. (2004). 'The use of workplace innovations in Ireland: A review of the evidence', *Personnel Review*, Vol.33, No.1, pp.8-42.

McGill, A. (2005). 'The Labour Relations Commission users' satisfaction survey', *LRC Review*, No.5.

Menkel-Meadow, C. (1997). 'When dispute resolution begets disputes of its own: Conflicts among dispute professionals', *UCLA Law Review*, No.1851.

Metcalf, D. (2005). 'British unions: Resurgence or perdition? An economic approach', in Fernie, S. & Metcalf, D. (eds.), *Trade Unions: Resurgence or Decline?*, London: Routledge.

Metcalf, D. (2006). *The Impact of the British National Minimum on Pay & Employment*, Centre Economic Performance Working Paper, No. 1481c, London: London School of Economics.

Mitchell, C. & Banks, M. (1996). *Handbook of Conflict Resolution: The Analytical Problem-solving Approach,* London and New York: Pinter.

Mulvey, K. (2005). 'An bóthar romhainn – The road ahead: The role of the Labour Relations Commission and the future of third party intervention', paper to the 5th Annual Irish Universities Association HR Conference, National University Galway.

Mulvey, K. (2006). 'The regulation of work and labour standards: "Is there a race to the bottom?"', *The Countess Markievicz Memorial Lecture*, National University of Ireland, Galway, 29 June.

O'Byrne, B. (2005). *Is the Equality Tribunal Providing a Satisfactory Mediation Service to its Customers?*, unpublished Master's Thesis, University College Dublin.

O'Donnell, R. & Teague, P. (2001). *Partnership at Work in Ireland: An Evaluation of Progress under Partnership 2000*, Dublin: Government Publications.

O'Donnell, R. & Thomas, D. (1998). 'Social partnership and policy-making', in Healy, S. & Reynolds, B. (eds,), *Social Policy in Ireland,* Dublin: Oak Tree Press.

Ostrom, E. (1980). *Governing the Commons: The Evolution of Institutions for Collective Action*, New York: Cambridge University Press.

Partnership 2000 (1996) Dublin: Government Stationery Office.

Peterson, R. (1992). 'The union and the non-union grievance system', in Lewin, D. et al. (eds.), *Research Frontiers in Industrial Relations & Human Resources*, East Lansing: Michigan State University Press.

Pfeffer, J. & Sutton, R. (2006). *Hard Facts, Dangerous Half Truths & Total Nonsense; Profiting from Evidence-Based Management*, Boston: Harvard University Press.

Piore, M. & Safford, S. (2005). *Changing Regimes of Workplace Governance: The Shifting Axes of Social Mobilization & the Challenge to Industrial Relations Theory*, mimeograph, Cambridge, MA: Dept of Economics, MIT.

Piore, M. & Schrank, A. (2007). *Norms, Regulations & Labour Standards in Central America*, CEPAL - Serie Estudios y Perspectivas No.77, Mexico City: CEPAL.

Piore, M. (2005). *Looking for Flexible Workplace Regulation in Latin American & the United States*, prepared for presentation at 'Labour Standards Application: A Compared Perspective', Buenos Aries, Argentina, 28-30 November.

Podro, S. & Suff, R. (2005). *Making More of Alternative Dispute Resolution*, ACAS Policy Discussion Papers No.1, London: Acas.

PSSRB – see Public Services Staff Relations Board.

Public Services Staff Relations Board (2002). *Best Interests: An Introduction to Grievance Mediation*, DVD, Ontario: Public Services Staff Relations Board.

Roche, W. & Geary, J. (2001). 'Collaborative production and the Irish boom: Work organisation, partnership and direct involvement', in *Economic & Social Review*, Vol.31, No.1, pp.1-36.

Roche, W. (1997). 'Industrialisation and the development of industrial relations', in Murphy, T. & Roche, W. (eds.), *Irish Industrial Relations in Practice,* Dublin: Oak Tree Press.

Rousseau, D. (2004). 'Psychological contracts in the workplace', *Academy of Management Executive*, Vol.18, No.1, pp.67-72.

Saunders R. & Dutil, P. (2005). *New Approaches in Achieving Compliance with Statutory Employment Standards*, Vulnerable Workers Series No.6, Toronto: Institute of Public Administration, Canada.

Sheldon, P. & Thornthwaite, L. (1999). 'Swedish engineering employers: The search for industrial peace in the absence of centralised collective bargaining', *Industrial Relations Journal*, Vol.30, pp.514–532.

Slicter, S., Healy, J. & Livernash, E. (1960). *The Impact of Collective Bargaining on Management*, Washington, D.C.: The Brookings Institution.

Stone, K. (1999). 'Employment arbitration under the Federal Arbitration Act', in Eaton, A.E. & Keefe, J.H. (eds.), *Employment Dispute Resolution & Worker Rights in the Changing Workplace,* Madison, WI: Industrial Relations Research Association.

Stuart, M. & Martinez Lucio, M. (2005). *Acas in the NHS: Helping Improve Employment Relations in response to 'Agenda for Change'*, Acas Research & Evaluation Section Research Papers 06/05, London: Acas.

Supiot, A. (1999). 'The transformation of the workplace and the future of labour law in Europe: A multi-disciplinary perspective', *International Labour Review*, Vol.138, No.1, pp.31-46.

Susskind, L., McKearnan, S. & Thomas-Larmer, J. (1999). *The Consensus Building Handbook*, Thousand Oaks, CA: Sage Publications.

Sustaining Progress: Social Partnership Agreement 2003-2005 (2003), Dublin: Government Stationery Office.

Taoiseach – see Department of the Taoiseach.

Teague, P. & Donaghey, J. (2004). 'The Irish experiment in social partnership', in Katz, H., Lee, W. & Lee, J. (eds.), *The New Structure of Labor Relations*, Cornell: ILR Press.

Teague, P. (1999). *Economic Citizenship in the New Europe*, London: Routledge.

Teague, P. (2005). *Towards Flexible Workplace Governance: Employment Rights, Dispute Resolution & Social Partnership in the Irish Republic*, Dublin: Policy Studies Institute, Trinity College.

Teece, D. & Pisano, G. et al. (1997). 'Dynamic capabilities and strategic management', *Strategic Management*, Vol.18, No.7, pp.509-533.

Thomas, D. (2002). *The Irish Social Partnership 1987-2000: An Evolving Economic & Social Governance*, unpublished PhD thesis, University of Newcastle.

Towards 2016: Ten-Year Framework Social Partnership 2006-2016 (2006), Dublin: Government Stationery Office.

Towers, B. & Brown, W. (2000). *Employment Relations in Britain: 25 years of the Advisory, Conciliation & Arbitration Service*, London: Blackwell.

Trevelyan, G. (2006). 'Workplace mediation – A perspective from the ACAS experience', *Labour Relations Review*, No.6.

Wallace, J., Gunnigle, P. & McMahon, G. (2004). *Industrial Relations in Ireland*, Dublin: Gill & Macmillan.

Walton, R. (1987). *Managing Conflict: Interpersonal Dialogue & Third Party Roles*, Reading, Mass.: Addison-Wesley.

Walton, R., Cutcher-Gershenfeld, J. & McKersie, R. (1994). *Strategic Negotiations: A Theory of Change in Labor-Management Negotiations*, Boston: Harvard Business School Press (reprinted by ILR Press, Ithaca, 2000).

Zweibel, E. & Macfarlane, J. (2001). *Systemic Change & Private Closure in Human Rights Mediation: An Evaluation of the Mediation Program at the Canadian Human Rights Tribunal*, Ottawa: Government Stationery Office.

Zweibel, E., Macfarlane, J. & Manwaring, J. (2001). *Negotiating Solutions to Workplace Conflict: An Evaluation of the Public Service Staff Relations Board Pilot Grievance Mediation Project*, Ottawa: Government Stationery Office.

FURTHER READING

Blancero, D. (1995). 'Non-union grievance systems: Systems characteristics and fairness perceptions', *Academy of Management Best Papers Proceedings*, pp.84-88.

Bordogna, L. & Primo Cella, G. (2002). 'Decline or transformation? Change in industrial conflict and its challenges', *Transfer*, Vol.4, pp.585-602.

Boxall, P. & Purcell, J. (2003). *Strategy & Human Resource Management*, Basingstoke: Palgrave Macmillan.

Canadian Human Rights Commission (2005). *Annual Report*, Ottawa: Government Stationery Office.

Carnevale, P. & Pruitt, D. (1992). 'Negotiation and mediation', *Annual Review of Psychology,* Vol.43, pp.521-82.

Colvin, A. (2003). 'Institutional pressures, human resource management and the rise of non-union dispute resolution procedures', *Industrial & Labor Relations Review*, Vol.56, No.3, pp.375-92.

Conference Board of Canada (2005). *Industrial Relations Outlook – Pulling Together, Pulling Apart*, Ottawa: Conference Board of Canada.

Conference Board of Canada (2006). *Industrial Relations Outlook – Shifting Ground, Shifting Attitudes*, Ottawa: Conference Board of Canada.

Costantino, C. & Merchant, C.S. (1996). *Designing Conflict Management Systems: A Guide to Creating Productive & Healthy Organizations*, San Francisco: Jossey-Bass Publishers, Inc.

Cutcher-Gershenfeld, J. (1994). 'Bargaining over how to bargain: Addressing the limitations of interest-based bargaining in labor negotiations', *Negotiations Journal*, Vol.10, No.4, pp.323-35.

Delaney, J. (1996). 'Workplace co-operation: Current problems, new approaches', *Journal of Labor Research*, Vol.17, No.1 (Winter), pp.45-61.

Dundon, T. & Rollinson, D. (2004). *Employment Relations in Non-Union Firms*, London: Routledge.

Dunlop, J. (1984). *Dispute Resolution: Negotiations & Consensus-building*, Dover, MA: Auburn House Publishing.

Eaton, A. & Keefe, J. (eds.) (1999). *Employment Dispute Resolution & Worker Rights in the Changing Workplace*, Illinois: Industrial Relations Research Association.

Edelmann, L. (1990). Legal environments and organisational governance: The expansion of due process in the American workplace, *American Journal of Sociology*, Vol.95, No.2, pp.1401-40.

Federal Mediation & Conciliation Service (2003). *Alternative Dispute Resolution Project: The Canadian Joint Grievance Panel*, Ottawa: Federal Mediation & Conciliation Service.

Feuille P. & Chachere, D. (1995). 'Looking fair or being fair: Remedial voice procedures in non-union workplaces', *Journal of Management*, Vol.21, No.1, pp.27-43.

Feuille, P. (1992). 'Why does grievance mediation resolve grievances?', *Negotiation Journal*, Vol.8, No.2, pp.131-45.

Fleming, S. (2003). 'Further challenges lie ahead on the route to public service modernisation', *LRC Review*, Issue No.2.

Kalev, A., Dobbin, F. & Kelly, E. (2006). 'Best practices or best guesses? Diversity management and the remediation of inequality', *American Sociological Review*, Vol.71, No.1, pp.589-917.

Labour Relations Commission (2002). *Strategy Framework 2002-2004*, Dublin: Government Publications.

McCormack, J. & Lanyon, S. (1997). 'Alternative dispute resolution in labour relations: A tale of two provinces', in J. Macfarlane (ed.), *Rethinking Disputes: The Mediation Alternative*, Toronto: Montgomery Publications.

Metcalf, D. (2005). 'British unions: Resurgence or perdition? An economic approach', in Fernie, S. & Metcalf, D. (eds.), *Trade Unions: Resurgence or Decline?*, Routledge: London.

National Centre for Partnership Performance (2002). *Achieving High Performance: Partnership Works –The International Evidence*, Dublin: National Centre for Partnership Performance.

National Centre for Partnership Performance (2003). *Information & Consultation: Case Study Review of Current Practice*, Dublin: National Centre for Partnership Performance.

National Centre for Partnership Performance (2005). *Working to our Advantage: A National Workplace Strategy*, Dublin: National Centre for Partnership Performance.

Osterman, P., Kochan, T., Locke, R. & Piore, M. (2001). *Working in America: A Blueprint for the New Labour Market*, Cambridge, MA: MIT Press.

Rowe, M. (1997). 'Dispute resolution in the non-union environment', in Gleason, S. (ed.), Frontiers in *Dispute Resolution in Labor Relations & Human Resources*, East Lansing: Michigan State University Press.

Schelling, T. (1960). *The Strategy of Conflict*, Cambridge, MA: Harvard University Press.

Society of Professionals in Dispute Resolution (SPIDR) (1998). *Guidelines for Voluntary Mediation Programs Instituted by Agencies Charged with Enforcing Workplace Rights*, Washington, D.C.: Society of Professionals in Dispute Resolution.

Stone, K.V.W. (2001). 'The new psychological contract: Implications of the changing workplace for labor and employment law', *UCLA Law Review*, Vol.48, pp.519-661.

Susskind, L. & Cruikshank, J. (1987). *Breaking the Impasse: Consensual Approaches to Resolving Public Disputes*, New York: Basic Books.

Ury, W., Brett, J.M. & Goldberg, S. (1998). *Getting Disputes Resolved: Designing Systems to Cut the Costs of Conflict*, San Francisco: Jossey-Bass.

Walton, R. & McKersie, R. (1965). *A Behavioural Theory of Labor Negotiations: An Analysis of a Social Interaction System*, New York: McGraw-Hill.

INDEX